No Pardons to Ask, nor Apologies to Make

No Pardons to Ask, nor Apologies to Make

The Journal of William Henry King, Gray's 28th Louisiana Infantry Regiment

Edited by
Gary D. Joiner, Marilyn S. Joiner,
and Clifton D. Cardin

Voices of the Civil War
Peter S. Carmichael, Series Editor

The University of Tennessee Press / Knoxville

To all the soldiers of the Civil War, both South and North, whose voices remain unheard.

Cloth: 1st printing, 2006.
Paper: 1st printing, 2025.

The Voices of the Civil War series makes available a variety of primary source materials that illuminate issues on the battlefield, the home front, and the western front, as well as other aspects of this historic era. The series contextualizes the personal accounts within the framework of the latest scholarship and expands established knowledge by offering new perspectives, new materials, and new voices.

Library of Congress Cataloging-in-Publication Data

King, William Henry, 1828–1903.
No pardons to ask, nor apologies to make : the journal of William Henry King, Gray's 28th Louisiana Infantry Regiment / edited by Gary D. Joiner, Marilyn S. Joiner, and Clifton D. Cardin.—1st ed.
p. cm. — (Voices of the Civil War)

Includes bibliographical references and index.

ISBN 978-1-57233-461-8 (hardcover)
ISBN 979-8-89527-083-7 (paperback)

1. King, William Henry, 1828–1903—Diaries.
2. Confederate States of America. Army. Louisiana Infantry Regiment, 28th.
3. Soldiers—Louisiana—Diaries.
4. Louisiana—History—Civil War, 1861–1865—Personal narratives.
5. United States—History—Civil War, 1861–1865—Personal narratives, Confederate.
6. Louisiana—History—Civil War, 1861–1865—Regimental histories.
7. United States—History—Civil War, 1861–1865—Regimental histories.

I. Joiner, Gary D.
II. Joiner, Marilyn S.
III. Cardin, Clifton D. (Clifton Dale), 1957–
IV. Title.
V. Voices of the Civil War series

E565.528th .K56 2006

973.7'463'092—dc22 2005020451

By close inspection of the deeds of others we may discover the strand upon which they have wrecked, and by steering to a different point of the compass, may avoid a like catastrophe. Justice should ever be our polar star, and if we strike upon reefs in the way though we may go down we will feel our consciences acquitted. Is it so with those who seek unjust aims! The answer is easy.

William Henry King, 1879

Contents

Illustrations

Figures

Maps

Foreword

After learning that some Texas officers were carrying out a profitable, although highly illegal, trade with Union authorities in 1864, Confederate infantryman William Henry King drew comfort in knowing that the men who served under these seditious officers were becoming a mutinous rank and file. "Hoozah for them!" King wrote in his diary. "That this is a 'rich man's war, & a poor man's fight,' needs no further proof." King's declaration of class warfare was not a rare emotional outburst. Throughout the war, the Louisianan soldier complained to his diary about a wide range of injustices that he blamed for the Confederacy's declining war effort. King's protests are remarkable for their insight into how dissent against the Confederacy could flourish alongside expressions of patriotism. Criticism of the cause did not signify King's rejection of Southern independence. He might have been disgusted with Confederate politicians, Richmond's policies, and his own officers, but his anger and frustration never led to alienation, never turned him against his comrades, and never transformed him into a Unionist. King's harsh condemnations actually reveal his clear-eyed understanding of the stakes of war. He recognized that his slave society would be lost if the South capitulated to the North, and he criticized those in power because he feared that the politicians and generals might sabotage an independence movement that he considered the South's best hope.

King's diary brilliantly conveys the complex, fluid, and often contradictory make-up of Confederate loyalties. Historians have fiercely debated the role of class conflict as a cause of defeat. One group of scholars has argued that lower-class protest imploded the Southern nation. William A. Blair, in *Virginia's Private War,* was one of the first scholars to successfully challenge this perspective by showing how political dissent could flourish without simultaneously destroying loyalty to nation. Although Blair's study focused on the Old Dominion, King's journal supports Blair's findings that call for a more nuanced reading of social protest in the Confederacy.

King's diary also helps us understand how private feelings of honor shaped highly public and political feelings about the Confederacy. As Bertram Wyatt-Brown has brilliantly explained in *Southern Honor,* white Southerners possessed a heightened sense of self-worth because of the institution of slavery. The enslavement of African Americans intensified white fears of being subordinate to another human being of any color. Dependence and servility, even in their most subtle expressions, created internal feelings of shame that denied a man reputation and the self-respect of others. King was like many white Southerners who were relentlessly driven to command others. He simply refused to consent to anyone serving as his master in the army. The military regime, however, demanded deference and discipline, which King bitterly resisted until the end. His frustration at serving under soldiers whom he considered inferior frequently led to entertaining diatribes in his diary. On one occasion, when kept on guard duty for an extra fifteen minutes, King flew into a rage and demanded justice from the officer of the day. The officer determined that while King had indeed been kept at his post too long, those in charge of the post had simply miscalculated the time; they were not negligent in their duties. This did not placate King, who complained to his diary: "Why did he [the officer of the day] not bring us face to face, & act upon the testimony of both parties? Was he afraid a different decision might be forced upon him?" King concluded that "a private has a dim prospect of redressing his wrongs when they come from an officer." Similar passages fill *No Pardons to Ask, nor Apologies to Make.* Few published diaries from a private better capture the turmoil that could reverberate between officers and the rank and file.

King's anger arose from a belief in independent manhood that energized his political beliefs, causing him to rail against any form of authority, whether it took the form of military, government, or class control. King's caustic and highly critical observations make his journal invaluable, for he does not resemble the typical soldier who served in either the Army of Tennessee or the Army of Northern Virginia. Soldiers in both of these armies typically welcomed centralized authority as a necessary means to prosecute the war. King, however, never transformed himself into a Confederate nationalist. Maybe his hostility toward centralized authority was exceptional, or maybe his important journal indicates that Southern soldiers in the Trans-Mississippi constructed a unique expression of Confederate identity.

Peter S. Carmichael
University of North Carolina at Greensboro

Acknowledgments

The editors gratefully acknowledge the assistance of several individuals who provided critical information. The late Phyllis Strayhan Farris, a native of Bossier Parish and a relative of William Henry King, answered many early questions posed by Clifton Cardin. Mrs. Ferris initiated contact with Mrs. Shirley Hampton, William Henry King's great-granddaughter. Mrs. Hampton offered details about her family's history and allowed the editors access to her information. Without her, King's story would have remained a great mystery. Nita Cole, social historian and former archivist of the Bossier Parish History Center, provided supporting information on Bossier Parish and regional history. Eric J. Brock, social historian and author, was instrumental in identifying locations and personalities within Shreveport that were mentioned in the diary. He permitted the use of photographs from his extensive collection. Two superb genealogical researchers, John Andrew Prime and Joe Slattery, assisted in identifying some of the people King mentioned and acted as sounding boards during the research phase of this project. Rebeccah Shackleford, while a student at Louisiana State University in Shreveport, initiated the arduous task of transcribing the diary. Finally, Dr. Thomas A. Pressly, a physician who could easily be a historian, helped to identify the numerous maladies mentioned in the diary as well as the physicians who treated them.

Gary D. Joiner
Marilyn S. Joiner
Clifton D. Cardin

Editors' Note

The editors have made every effort to retain William Henry King's composition, grammar, punctuation, and style. Parenthetical marks are original to the manuscript, while the editors' insertions are in brackets. Passages that were underlined by King have been italicized here. Similarly, where monetary amounts were expressed, we have used the conventional decimal-point format (as in $5.00), whereas King typically elevated the figures for cents and underlined them.

Some of the opening pages of the transcript were torn and, in several instances, corners of pages were missing. Certain words and passages were also illegible. All of these places have been noted in brackets. The material included in Appendix 2, which King referred to as "Extras," also retain the character and formatting of the author. These final pages were often in poor condition, with several pages only surviving as torn or stained fragments.

Introduction

In December 1860 South Carolina seceded from the United States of America, declaring itself to be a "separate and independent state." Within months other states followed, including Louisiana, which seceded on January 26, 1861. In March these states allied together as the Confederate States of America, with Jefferson Davis as provisional president. They adopted a constitution very similar to the United States Constitution but with a stronger focus on the autonomy of the individual states. A month later, the first shots of the Civil War were fired at Fort Sumter, South Carolina, by troops under the direction of Louisiana-born Gen. P. G. T. Beauregard. Within a year, on April 28, 1862, New Orleans surrendered in response to a demand by Union Adm. David Farragut, and Gen. Benjamin Butler's troops occupied New Orleans. The war had arrived in Louisiana.

Into this turbulent picture came William Henry King, who on April 30, 1862, took the oath of allegiance to the Confederate States of America. Concurrently, he took the oath as a soldier of the State of Louisiana (militia). King spent five days preparing to march to Monroe in northeastern Louisiana, and on May 6 he began to write a journal that today takes readers with him on a journey through the war.

Other Civil War diaries have offered insight into the life of the average citizens who took up the call to arms. The foundation of scholarly study on the life of a common soldier in the Civil War, laid by Bell Irvin Wiley, is found in *The Life of Johnny Reb: The Common Soldier of the Confederacy* and *The Life of Billy Yank: The Common Soldier of the Union.* Over the years, other scholars have expanded on life in the ranks as diaries were discovered. Many of these are the writings of common soldiers whose language and writing style reflected the lack of formal education prevalent in that class of rural farmers.

King titled his diary "A Journal of Camp Life as a Private Soldier," and this could lead the reader to surmise that his diary is simply another of the mundane reports of military life, characterized by a sameness of weather reports, hunger, illnesses, and homesickness. While King did include some of those details in his narrative, he offered more: pointed analysis, a private's view of what is happening around him, and an exceptional writing style that makes his journal as readable as a modern-day literary work. It paints a picture of the day-to-day life of an educated man who is a not a wealthy planter or an aristocrat. It is the story of a private in the army of the Confederate States of America who never fired a shot in anger during his service to the nation.

The journal leads the reader to believe that King was extraordinarily bright, inquisitive, and well-read. This private used Latin phrases and complex medical terminology with ease. He demonstrated a keen, cynical wit and an awareness of what was happening around him. King processed information from his personal experiences, newspaper accounts, rumors, and military sources and offered readers a view of his world. King's education was apparent at least to Capt. Smith Kirby, who selected King to be his clerk.

The diary helps to paint King as a frustrated Southern intellectual. His belief in states' rights and the philosophical foundations of secession are clear. Throughout his writing he referred to "liberty" and "rights." He proved himself to be egalitarian and frustrated by the power military superiors and the wealthy exercise over those in lesser positions.

As he prepared to report for duty, King indicated that he must join his friends and countrymen. It is likely that, with the surrender of New Orleans, King realized the war had truly pushed into his home territory. His region was not simply touched but occupied by an enemy he held in disdain: "The enemy are putting forth every effort to make us tribute to their malevolent designs: our cause is bleeding at every pore; the rulers of the different departments of our government are calling loudly for more men in the field; many of my friends have already responded to the call of free, & offered their lives up freely for the glorious cause; and, I can not, I *will* not be a reproach to the name I bear."

King eloquently reported that the enemy was "striving to enslave that they may tyrannize over us." Like many Southerners he believed that the war was initiated by the North, not by the South. "By a series of oppressions unprecedented in the annals of civilized government, they have forced us to seek security against further oppression, from another source." He termed them "the aggressors *ab initia ad finem,*" the aggressors from the beginning to the end.

King was initially part of Marks Guards, which became Company B of Gray's 28th Louisiana Infantry Regiment. The early diary reports his travels across north Louisiana and the deficits in the lifestyle of the common solider, among them inadequate living conditions, ill health, poor diet, and loose morals. He lamented the housing conditions, believing that the common soldiers should be sleeping in tents, not in the open air: "Men accustomed to sleeping in comfortable houses, & suddenly thrust into the open air to sleep are highly liable to contract disease from the exposure . . . a diseased man is not fit to do any work well, & more especially that of a soldier. True a soldier's life is a hard one at best, & he should expect to meet difficulties & trials, but because these *must* come, there is no reason why needless ones should not be avoided."

Illnesses pervade the diary. King related his own medical problems and the illnesses suffered by his comrades, some of whom died from diseases that are easily cured today. He often referred to the neglect of soldiers' medical needs and the treatments he received for his ills. Although he submitted to treatment from doctors, he had little faith in their ability to cure and frequently appeared to be worse rather than better after treatment by them.

The prevalence of illness described in this journal is not surprising. In *Civil War Medicine: Challenges and Triumphs,* Alfred Jay Boulet, M.D., puts illnesses among soldiers into perspective: "Over the course of the war, disease caused roughly *two-thirds* of the 600,000-plus deaths among the troops. Both armies were composed almost entirely of new recruits, who were particularly susceptible to most diseases."[1]

A colonel forced fifty men from each company to go to the saltworks to haul salt at a time when illness had spread throughout King's company. Kings observed: "Three ounces of common sense are sufficient to discern that 25 able-bodied men are more efficient than the same 25 men would be by being encumbered by 25 sick men. May be the colonel intends to frighten the enemy with sick men."

In October 1862 King wrote, "meal, beef, a little sugar & rice, constitute the sum total of the rations we draw." He criticized the quartermaster for buying molasses at fifty cents per gallon, using government wagons to transport it and then selling it to soldiers at one dollar per gallon: "Almost beyond a doubt, Capt. Madden is speculating on money he should pay to us. He has paid the officers, therefore they are quiet." Later he wrote, "our officers have bacon to eat, but there is none for us."

When King was among sick soldiers captured in south Louisiana, his rations were little better. He and the other prisoners relied on the kindness of sympathetic ladies of the area who brought food to the prison at Algiers, across the river from New Orleans.

The diary confirms that King was a moral man, one concerned with duty and honor. Although some might consider war immoral, he justified the actions of his nation as honorable. He held that a country invaded by the enemy had a right and duty to defend itself. He pondered situations that left him uneasy. For instance, King criticized his fellow soldiers for conduct unbecoming soldiers. When women visited the camp to give their regards, he reported, "in shame be it said, many of the men are behaving shamefully—they are crowding around the ladies, staring at them vulgarly." He chastised the officers for failing to control the situation, observing that "if something is not done to improve the morals of our men, I mean the whole Confederacy, I humbly think our cause is lost beyond redemption." Later in the war King voiced concern that vice was "running riot in every direction," though he did not indicate what put him in that mind-set. "It does seem that our people have forgotten that if virtue be lost, *all* will be lost," he wrote.

Although King was a private, he considered himself inferior to officers only in military rank. Early on he suspected the motives of officers not to be honorable. His company members expected to be paid their promised bounties, bounties which they had to sign they had received but did not. Though the officers promised to pay them, the bounties were delayed time after time, and King believed they were being swindled by the officers. He later described the officers as "generally very rash, & ready to make a display of authority."

When King was placed in command of his squad for a day, he reflected on the appointment and wondered if he himself might not be as pompous as an officer. He concluded that his command was "quite ephemeral—it expires with the day. . . . Might not some of our officers learn a lesson worth knowing by making a similar reflection?" He added, "Good sense, & good principles, however require us such reflections. Right principles forbid austerity, though one knew he could command *always*."

King was keenly aware of the difference of class—his as an ordinary private and that of the officers, who were often from wealthy, aristocratic families. He was the very essence of a cry widely disseminated after the New York draft riots: "a rich man's war, & a poor man's fight." In fact, King twice repeated the statement, once while guarding hogs at his Shreveport post in late 1863 and again in March 1864 while serving as a guard to prisoners. The juxtaposition of his duty and the benefits afforded the privileged (officers and wealthy) paints a sharp contrast in class differences, both real and perceived. He admitted that the wealthy commanded a power that allowed them to "escape the burthens of the less fortunate." He was keenly aware that he fell into the latter category.

King observed a guard allowing a carriage on a ferry without looking at a pass, as had been required of him. Having been told that persons riding in carriages were presumed to have their papers, he wrote, "if fine carriages are passes, I am ready to quit fighting for the Confederacy."

While on furlough King saw a colonel at the home of a neighbor. Although he had met the officer previously, they had never conversed. The colonel clearly demonstrated an attitude of superiority. "Does he give me a sympathetic expression?" King wrote. "Not a sympathetic word. His enunciation & mien clearly say, 'It is my business to look after such fry as you, & when your time is up, you had better get back to the army!"

When he heard that Lt. Gen. William Joseph Hardee had succeeded Lt. Gen. Braxton Bragg, he claimed Bragg would make "a fare [*sic*] general for an aristocracy." He left little doubt that he believed the governing styles of republicanism and monarchy (aristocracy) were diametrically opposed.

King acknowledged that the officers were "great men in their way." However, he noted that with rare exceptions the officers "have no regard for the well being of their privates, but regard their own ends as paramount to every right of the soldier." Upon meeting up with friends in another regiment as his company marched across the state, King noted they all "complain at many indignities received from their officers. Indeed, there seems to be a general hatred among the privates against their officers."

When an officer resigned due to bad health, King, whose health was also bad, observed, "if an officer's health becomes bad, with but little trouble he resigns out of the service, but if a private's health becomes bad, to get out, he must *die* out." King thought it shameful his comrades had to suffer due to loose management of officers. He felt officers rated the common soldier at the very bottom of ranking, noting that when a recent shipment of bacon had arrived, the officers had their fill, gave the bacon to the black laborers, and then offered what was left to the regular army.

The officers were not the only men whose behavior King questioned. He also pointed to the wealthy who hired substitutes so they could stay at home. He noted that those who remained at home were frequently speculating, and even claimed there were speculators in the military. "Speculation is rife every where," he wrote. When a speculator charged one dollar per pound for lard, "we are forced to fight in defense of his rights & property for $11.00 per month; we are not furnished with the rations necessary to sustain life in a healthy condition, & our only chance is to purchase them at ruinous prices." He noted in the fall of 1863 that people were speculating on the necessities of helpless women and children and that the nation was drifting to irretrievable ruin.

It was not simply helpless women and children who were going without as a result of the war. Even soldiers were poorly outfitted. In the bitter January cold in 1864, King noted that the Confederate government had not issued the men clothing in "a long time" and some of the men were in great need. Neither had the government paid their wages. The officers seemed little concerned since they had what *they* needed. In mid-February, King finally drew a jacket and a pair of pants.

King found plenty to criticize outside the military. He criticized the state legislators who passed a militia bill calling into service all men from seventeen to fifty but exempting themselves. He criticized Quantrell's Raiders, calling them "a great terror to this country" and noting that he believed even Gen. Kirby Smith was afraid of them. King abhorred bushwhackers and thought their number would only increase unless the average soldiers were treated better.

In north Louisiana, King encountered nothing of the enemy, save the impression that he heard cannons firing at Vicksburg while in camp near Monroe. As his company moved southward along the Red River in January 1863, they arrived at Camp Bisland in St. Mary Parish in south Louisiana. There King learned that the forces had engaged the enemy and succeeded in driving them back. In February he claimed to see the smoke of the enemy's gunboats with indications of battle, but he was not involved. In April, King fell ill once again and missed out on the action. As the enemy neared the encampment, the sick were ordered to move to the hospital at New Iberia. They reached a boat just as it was leaving, and they were ordered to return to camp. There they were taken captive by Union cavalry who "talk very kindly to us, & promise us kind treatment."

The issue of emancipation—a major component of arguments related to the Civil War—is part of King's journal. During his imprisonment, King had an opportunity to visit with Union soldiers. He indicated that Union soldiers told him they did not favor freeing the slaves and would "fight no longer if they knew such to be the purpose of their gov't." He reported that Union soldiers believed it necessary to take slaves from their owners to crush the rebellion but felt the slaves would be returned to their proper owners once that was accomplished. "Such is their delusion," wrote King. "They are caused to believe the Gov't does not *really* intend to free the negro, to encourage them to fight." King did not appear surprised by the inclusion of African Americans in both the Union and Confederate forces. He believed submission on the part of soldiers was a basic tenet of military practice and so therefore black men would make better regular soldiers than white men.

After serving time in a Union prison near New Orleans, King was paroled and made his way northward. By July 1863, he was worried about the fate of the Confederacy: "I may be mistaken, but my humble conviction is, we will certainly have to submit to the domination of Abraham Lincoln." Although issues like the conscription laws made him question the fight, his sense of duty and honor required him to move forward through what he considered deplorable conditions that would not improve.

As a precursor to the Red River Campaign, King acknowledged that Confederate engineers had lowered the water in the Red River, making it impossible for gunboats to pass. Documents of the Trans-Mississippi were removed from Shreveport and provisions were brought into Shreveport, both indicating a preparation for siege by Union forces. In a last desperate attempt to fortify the Confederate army, Louisiana's governor issued an order for conscription of the free blacks, an action King deemed hypocritical.

As the following excerpts from King's diary indicate, rumors were rampant, especially near the time of the Red River Campaign and Battle of Mansfield. Most, however, proved to be false.

> December 28, 1863: The Negroes have rebelled against the Federals at N. Orleans & taken possession of the city. [*King did not believe this.*]
>
> January 12, 1864: Mouton's division has gone in the direction of Gaines' landing in south Arkansas along the Mississippi River.
>
> February 2, 1864: Federal gun boats have been to Fort DeRussy on Red River.
>
> February 9, 1864: Federals have made an attack on Mobile.
>
> February 22, 1864: General Longstreet has taken Knoxville, Tennessee, & put the enemy to flight.
>
> March 17, 1864: Alexandria [Louisiana] has fallen into the hands of the Federals. [*This rumor was true. U.S. naval forces took the town on March 16. Like both Confederate and Union leadership, King realized the importance of the Trans-Mississippi to Confederate victory. Upon hearing a rumor that Union forces were advancing into Texas, he indicated that an invasion of Texas would mean every state in the Confederacy would be invaded.*]

April 3, 1864: Gen'l Marmaduke has beaten the enemy near Rockport, Arkansas.

April 5, 1864: Federals are still advancing; & that they whipped our forces yesterday near Mansfield, in which engagement we lost heavily. [*This rumor was false. The Union column attempting to take Shreveport did not leave its base at Grand Ecore until the following day. The rumor was prophetic, predicting the location of the pivotal battle of the campaign, fought on April 8.*]

April 7, 1864: The Federals are falling back. [*This rumor was false. On that day the Union column was advancing north of Pleasant Hill.*]

April 9, 1864: General Mouton's division attacked the enemy yesterday about 5 miles below Mansfield & drove them back 6 miles, capturing about 2000 prisoners. [*This rumor was true and reasonably accurate.*]

As summer arrived in 1864, King and his cohorts heard rumor of a proclamation issued by Lincoln calling for 400,000 more men. He believed this to be a false report but gave credit to the rumor mill that fostered it.

Despite the positive morale the Red River Campaign victory at Mansfield created, King was a realist. Clearly he wished to have independence from Federal control and its president. However, he realized that this would not occur with the Union advancing, men and artillery being captured, and Southerners taking the oath of allegiance to the Union. King labored on as a private but sought a transfer from the 28th Regiment of Louisiana Volunteers to the Engineer troops. He became a pontooneer, a soldier who handled the portable pontoon bridges necessary for river crossings. Moving down the Red River his sense of morality was stirred as he viewed the ruins left by Union Gen. Nathaniel Banks in the wake of his retreat. King called the general's behavior "wanton cruelty" and argued that Union troops had burned the homes of women and children because they could not enslave their husbands and fathers. King was keenly aware that his country had been invaded and questioned the wisdom of invading the Union rather than simply defending Confederate soil: "There are many who are willing that we separate if we choose, but will be ready at the instant of invasion to take up arms against us."

As the fall of 1864 approached, King mentioned desertions but did not condemn those who left. King's company at this time was in Arkansas, where he found that the people had little more than troops who had to forage for their own provisions. He called the surroundings "one continued scene of desolation" and pondered that the horrors of war "weigh heavily against any cause." By late October the government had not issued pay and offered little in the way of clothing, bread, or meat.

When King received word that a private had been shot for desertion, he remarked that several men had been shot for this act and that he did not believe the "moral standing of the army has been enhanced thereby." He observed that "volunteer service is more reliable and more efficient than coerced service." A note of irony in the diary of this Civil War soldier is his statement that "a slavish servitude is not the servitude of a genuine Christian."

When a preacher in Camden, Arkansas, gave a war sermon, King noted that the church was "filled to packing." This event led King to focus once again on misdeeds of officers, who he believed would benefit from religious activity. He used this venue to return to a discussion of class differences and affirmed his belief that "we are a house divided against ourselves, and could not stand if left to ourselves."

In November, King was finally issued a blanket, the first he had drawn since entering the service. But the news continued to be depressing: men fighting without guns, soldiers without bread for twenty days, and word that Atlanta was held by Sherman. In December, King mused about what he considered to be the inevitable defeat of the Confederacy, which he blamed in large measure on the arrogance of political and military leaders: "I yet heartily endorse the cause we at first espoused, but the present doings of our leaders, both civil and military, I hold to be an abomination." On Christmas Day King recorded that "every day it [war] is continued only aggravates the evils that attend it."

At the beginning of the new year, King received news of Confederate defeats and noted that this was "the first round in the ladder of descent." Unfortunately, large gaps appear in the journal at this point. One passage at the end, however, indicates that the war had ended and that word was coming of plans to reunite the Union and Confederacy. King wrote that he had not expected leniency from the Federals but that he had expected "something of a better beginning." He noted that the "general welfare has been lost sight of in view of selfish interests."

Following Reconstruction, King compiled his daily notes into the volume that is the basis for this work. In 1879 he copied the notes and diary entries to create this journal of camp life. Some of his notes were lost and he had to reconstruct those entries from memory. He insisted that no "grave errors" occurred during this process, though he never indicated which daily notations came from memory only. In the document available today, some of the pages are torn or damaged from ink or water stains, and the last few pages are mostly fragments.

King stressed that he did not rewrite what he observed or believed to be true, that he was faithful to the notes. Even if his perceptions proved to be incorrect in light of the postwar era, he recorded what he knew at the time. Throughout the diary he remained honest to himself and his beliefs, giving the modern reader an insight into his life during the war, because, in his own words, "I have sometimes thought too many of our writers lose sight of the real instead of the ideal."

At the end of his daily notations, King included what he referred to as "Extras," which were poems, songs, and writings of others, usually with his analysis. He felt these pieces exhibited the "true feelings that existed about the close of the war—and the facts as well as the feelings that existed about the close of the war." These extras demonstrate what King felt to be important and also show his sense of humor.

In 1943 the diary surfaced publicly when it was sold to the Texas Library Archives by Mrs. C. M. Armstrong of Seagraves, Texas. No one is sure how Mrs. Armstrong came to possess the work. She is not listed as a descendant in family records, and surviving family members do not know her. Little is known about William Henry King outside the diary. No one knows what education he received or how he earned a living prior to his enlistment in the Confederate army. No additional writings or diaries by King are part of the King family papers, so this work may have been his only literary attempt. The family Bible, oral history, and a letter from King's great-great-granddaughter, Shirley Hampton, are the foundation for this biographical sketch of King.

William Henry King was born July 28, 1828, in Madison County, Alabama, the second of ten children born to William Whitefield King and his wife, Susan Chennault King. His siblings were Charles Rufus, Elizabeth Helen, Mary Merab, Penelope Caroline, Lucretia Jane, Julia Ann, Stephan Corodan, Thomas Whitfield, and Gabriel Davy.[2]

In 1839 William Henry's paternal grandmother, Penelope King, left a trust in her will for "the education & maintenance" of William Whitefield's children.[3] William Henry was eleven years old at the time. Although nothing is known about his formal education, it is likely that he was educated from this trust and that the intellectual writing style characteristic of this diary is Penelope's legacy as well as William Henry's.

The 1850 census for Madison County, Alabama, lists the family as residents, with the exception of the eldest brother, Charles.[4] The King family apparently moved to Bossier Parish, Louisiana, during late 1850 or 1851. They settled in the northern part of the parish at the village of Collinsburgh, about three miles south of the present-day town of Plain Dealing. William Henry moved to Shelby County, Texas, prior to 1854.[5] Marriage records for Rusk County, Texas, show that he married his second cousin, Balsona Elena Kennard, in Rusk County on August 31, 1854.[6] The family Bible lists Balsona as a native of Lownds County, Mississippi, born February 10, 1837.[7] The first three of the couple's eight children were born in Rusk County, and the remaining five were born in Shelby County.[8]

The death of William Henry's father in Bossier Parish on December 6, 1857, created family dissention. Initially, the eldest brother, Charles, was appointed executor of the estate. When he died in 1860, William Henry was appointed administrator and tutor of his minor siblings.[9] His mother sued to have him removed as administrator because the estate had not been settled. In the suit, she indicated that she was destitute from having to feed her children remaining at home and declared that she needed her quarter of the estate.[10]

Other than the suit, there is no proof that William Henry was negligent. Just four months after his father's death, the Civil War began. Attention throughout the South turned to the war and concerns for preservation of their homes, families, and way of life.

Heavily retouched image of William Henry King later in life. Courtesy Shirley Hampton.

Like many men his age, King elected to join the army. At the beginning of the war, he was listed as a resident of Shelby County; however, he returned to Collinsburgh to volunteer his service to Louisiana.[11] His diary indicates that he entered military service on April 30, 1862. Military records show that date to be May 7, the date his company arrived at Bellevue. He was part of Marks' Guards, which became Company B, 28th (Gray's) Louisiana Infantry Regiment.

Marks' Guards was the sixth military company formed from Bossier Parish and the fifth to serve. With a total population of less than four thousand white people, it is surprising that Bossier Parish supplied more than eight hundred volunteers to the Southern cause. That number, approximately 20 percent of the white population, may place Bossier Parish among those parishes in Louisiana that volunteered the most men per capita. In addition to King's service with Company B of the 28th Louisiana, he also served as sergeant in Company H, 4th Engineer Regiment. There he was a pontooneer, a soldier working with wagon-borne portable bridges used by field armies of the time.

Several King descendants believe that William Henry was a medical doctor with a "certificate from New York," but there is no evidence to support this.[12] In addition, his diary specifically states that he was not a medical doctor. He did, however, become a "doctor of phrenology." Although this phrase includes the word "doctor," it is not the terminology used for a medical doctor. Phrenology is the study of the structure of the skull to determine a person's character and mental capacity, a pseudoscience that was very popular during the nineteenth century but that soon fell. King held meetings and lectures on phrenology in Forestburg, Montague County, Texas, where he lived for at least twenty years after Reconstruction. Family members recall that he owned a number of books on the subject.[13] After the war, the 1870 census shows King was living in Shelby County, where his occupation was listed as "selling drugs" (apparently as a pharmacist or druggist).[14]

The family moved to Forestburg in Montague County, Texas, in 1880, where he taught school in the north border area of Texas and practiced phrenology.[15] Balsona died there on December 2, 1883, and was buried in the Hardy Cemetery.[16] Following Balsona's death, King went to Shelby County, where he married his wife's sister, Mary Elizabeth Kennard Tims, the widow of Amos Tims, on July 1, 1886.[17] They returned to his home in Forestburg. The marriage ended in divorce, with Montague County records listing proceedings for the couple on July 20, 1899.[18]

William Henry King (far right), late in life, with his daughter, Marguerite Arabelle King Landers (second from right), and her family. Courtesy Shirley Hampton.

King served as postmaster in Forestburg from November 27, 1899, to September 27, 1900. Shortly after this time he became ill and left Montague to live with his son, William Henry King Jr., in Sappington in Macintosh County, Oklahoma.[19]

William Henry King's death was recorded in the family Bible on September 7, 1903.[20] He was buried in the Sappington Chapel Cemetery near Cowden, Oklahoma. His headstone reads: "William H. King Sr., born July 28, 1828, died Sep 7, 1903 Our father has gone to a mansion of rest. To the glorious land by the diety blest."

The Journal of William Henry King, Gray's 28th Louisiana Infantry Regiment

Chapter 1

Muster, Organization, and Training

For the present, suffice it to say, they have been the aggressors *ab initia ad finem,* as the political history of the U.S. fully proves to all impartial minds.

William Henry King
May 6, 1862

April 30th, 1862.

To-day the oath of allegiance to the Confederate States of America, was administered to myself and many others in the town of Bellevue, Bossier Parish, Louisiana,[1] by J.W. Rabb of the same parish & State, acting under authority from Thos. O. Moore,[2] gov. of the state of La., to raise a company of volunteers for State defense for a term of twelve months, on condition we equip ourselves with double-barrelled shot-guns. He also administered to us the requisite oath to become a soldier in the State service. He then dismissed us until the 6th proximo[3] to make the necessary preparations for the exchange of home comforts for the trials & tribulations of a private soldier.

May 1, 2, 3, 4 & 5, were spent in preparing to march to Monroe on the Ouachita River, the place designated for our rendezvous. Nothing of note connected with this journal transpired during the dates just named.

May 6th, Tuesday.

This morning, the trial of parting from "loved ones at home", with but a dim shadow of a hope of seeing them short of twelve months—perhaps never—was passed; and despite every effort to keep a cheerful appearance, I could not refrain from weeping.[4] I shall ever remember the scene, for I then felt what I shall never be able to express in words. To leave [*part of page missing*] beloved companion & our little infants, [*part of page missing*] only a possibility of returning to enjoy [*part of page missing*] presence & minister to their wants, is, [*part of page missing*] get, the most powerful test my resolutions [*part of page missing*] been subjected to. But why should I hesitate? The enemy are putting forth every effort to make us tribute to their malevolent designs; our cause is bleeding at every pore; the rulers of the different departments of our government are calling loudly for more men in the field; many of my friends have already responded to the call of freedom, & offered their lives up freely for the glorious cause; and, I can not, I *will* not be a reproach to the name I bear. Justice would excuse us were we to treat such enemies as we are now combating, as out laws & highway robbers. They are waging against us a war of conquest & rapine; for plunder & political power they have left their homes & made us special objects of their unholy passions, & with a ferociousness characteristic of a barbarous people, are striving to enslave that they may tyrannize over us. They claim they are only striving to perpetuate the "glorious Union transmitted to us by our fathers"; in answer to which it is sufficient to state, the means they have adopted are utterly subversive of the end they profess to seek. A Republican government—based on the coercion of one third of its subjects, is a misnomer too palpable to require an argument.

By a series of oppressions unprecedented in the annals of civilized government, they have forced us to seek security against further oppression, from another source. Whether the course we have chosen be [*part of page missing*] wise one, the records of time will [*part of page missing*] plain. But we feel assured of [the] fact that nothing good under the [*part of page missing*] government as administered by the [*part of page missing*] now in power, awaits us. The [con]stitution & the Union as they were in the days of our ancestors, were all we could have asked for, but our Northern brethren, (as they should have been) were not content with *them,* claiming, when the subject of African servitude as it existed in the Southern States, was under consideration, there was a "higher law than the Constitution—the law of conscience".

Now, if the Constitution, the great bulwark of the Southern people, was thus over ruled & made subject to the consciences of Northern fanatics, I would ask, where was the safety of the Southern people? & who were the first to rebel against the palladium of civil rights? They not only avowed the "higher law" doctrine, but in many of their States enacted "personal liberty" bills diametrically opposing previous Congressional enactments & the Constitution of the United States. They taught this doctrine of "higher law" to their children in the family circle; in their churches & public schools, & their editors & public speakers accepted the doctrine as a sure hobby for popularity & high places. In fine, it constituted the chief element in both their religion & politics. For the present, suffice it to say, they have been the aggressors *ab initia ad finem,*[5] as the political history of the U.S. fully proves to all impartial minds.

There seems but little if any reason to doubt the ability (so far as talent & resources are concerned) of the South to cope with the vandal hordes of the North, but to my mind's eye there *is a reason* why we may fear, & that reason—I [*part of page missing*] to record it, is, in plain English, dish—[*part of page missing*] which prevails, more or less, in ea [*part of page missing*] the various classes of the South, & in [*part of page missing*] of the more important classes, that [*part of page missing*] ment predominates greatly.

All arrangements completed, & several of us now start for Bellevue. The greater number of us proceed on horseback, with wagons to transport our baggage. At Bodcau Lake,[6] we dismount, send our horses back home, & some cross the lake, & proceed at once to Bellevue, while others (I for one) wait until the wagons come up. After some detention we get across the lake, & drive to Bellevue, about two & a half miles, reaching that place about 2 o'clock, having traveled 22 or 23 miles.

After some electioneering, "wire working" & c., we go into an election for company officers. ———

The election is over & resulted as follows: By acclamation, J. W. Rabb, Captain;[7] by ballot, T. W. Abny,[8] 1st Lt., W. M. Sentell, 2nd Lt.,[9] J. H. Marks, Jr. 2nd Lt.[10]

The election over, all are ordered into ranks. We now proceed to the residence of A. A. Abny, & Miss C. Dalrymple presents us a flag donated by Mrs. C. Dixon. Miss Dalrymple delivers a speech in the midst of which she honors our company with the appellation, *Marks Guards,* in honor to N. Marks, Sr., who has done much for the Confederate cause.[11]

Lt. Abny makes a short but appropriate reply, which is the crowning effort in the way of "putting on airs", & he invites many of us to take lodgings with him for the night, which invitation we gladly accept.

Supper finished, & those who delight to trip the "fantastic toe", repair to the Court House where the "poetry of action" is [i]ndulged in to the exhilaration of many [d]rooping spirits. ———

The dance is now over, having been well conducted, & all are seeking places to indulge in recreative sleep. 'Tis sad to think of, but the question irresistibly forces itself upon my mind, how many of us will again assemble on a similar occasion?

May 7th, Wednesday.

Breakfasted with Lt. Abny, & after bidding adieu, which in all probability may prove final to many of us, to many friends, a squad of us, about 9 o'clock A.M., started for Monroe.

Time may use his effacing hand to the utmost of his capacity, but until he effaces my memory will I forget my parting with Mrs. C. Dixon,[12] Mrs. Beasly,

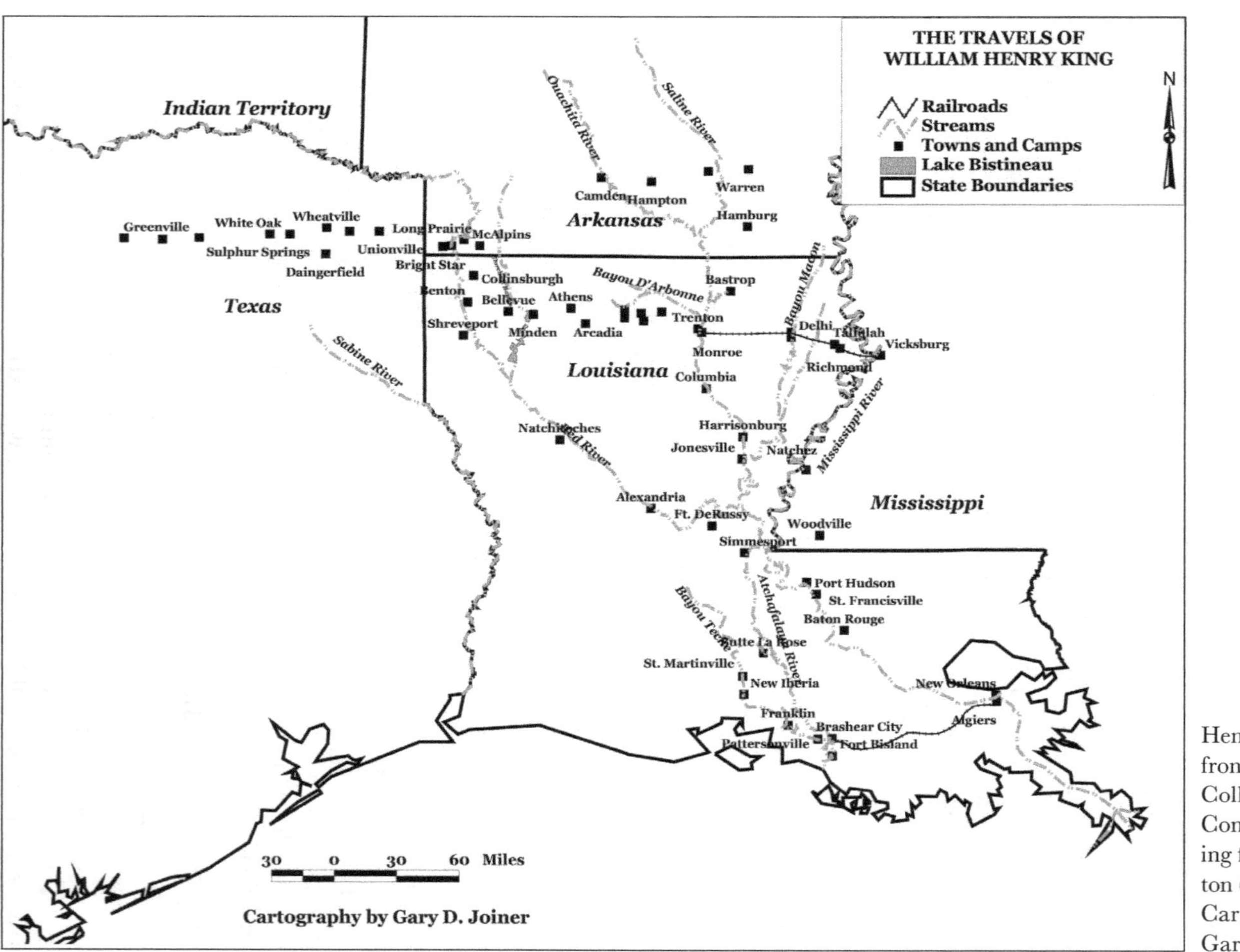

Henry King's route from his home at Collinsburgh to the Confederate training facility at Trenton (West Monroe). Cartography by Gary D. Joiner.

Miss C. Dalrymple,[13] Miss Abny[14] & other lady friends. Their kind & hearty good wishes were expressed so firmly & frankly, that they were indelibly impressed upon my mind. May prosperity attend them through their pilgrimage on earth. I would to God that men entered into this mighty struggle for liberty with the same spirit of devotedness.

We started with good cheer, except an occasional sad thought of "loved ones at home". Our best endeavors were used to dispel sad feelings, knowing well, they could benefit neither our families nor us, but would add greatly to our burdens. If friends at home could have, from some secluded spot, witnessed our actions, no doubt but they would have mistaken the cause of our gayety—we sought to drown trouble in mirth.

We traveled on very lively to J. W. Hudson's, seven miles from Bellevue, where we got a bucket of fresh water, took out our provisions, (having made pretty extensive preparations in that a[rea] before leaving home) & all hands partook [of] it freely.[15]

Six miles further travel, & we fou[nd our]selves at the bridge over Dauchit Bayou[16] thence to Minden in Claiborne Parish, two & a half miles further.[17] There we halted about two hours that I might arrange some business matters, after which we proceeded half a mile further to Shield's Steam Mill, where we found a spring of limpid & well tasted water. Night being close at hand, we halted for the purpose of "pitching tents". Mr. Shields furnished us with a lot, corn & fodder for our teams, & milk for ourselves, free of cost.

After supper, three of our squad went back to Minden, & returned to us with the news that our Company was encamped on the other side of Minden, having traveled two & a half miles further than we expected when we left them in the morning.

Our reception in Minden was quite cool. The first soldiers passing this place were greeted with a cordial welcome, & costly dinners set before them.

May 8th, Thursday

Left the Mill just at daylight with a determination to keep ahead of the main body of the Company, that we might avoid the disagreeableness of traveling with a large company, & thereby enable us to get an egg, a chicken, or pint of milk, *occasionally*. Traveled about sixteen miles & halted for dinner. A pitcher of milk was given to us, & a few eggs having been procured as we traveled during the morning, we feasted highly.

While eating, McGuire,[18] one of the company, came up to us, & informed us the Company was close behind. However, we were in no great hurry, knowing we could, if [ne]cessary, make more rapid headway, and the company would go by Mt. Lebanon,[19] some [*part of page missing*] miles out of the way, to get a [s]upper the citizens of that place had promised the company. Just as the company wagons hove in sight, we started, & a travel of twelve miles brought us to Arcadia, Bienville Parish.[20]

As Arcadia lies ten miles East of Mt. L., we concluded to pitch our tents there, deeming it of no importance whether we traveled fast or slow, only that we kept ahead of the company.

While in the streets of Arcadia, one Mr. Wright, so he called himself, came to us & claimed to be one of our company. Though a good looking man, & to every appearance would make a good soldier, we were unwilling to receive him into our squad, (though glad to see such men members of the company) not wishing to encumber our teams with more baggage. He decided to wait until the company came on next day. He did so, & after arriving at Monroe,[21] framed an excuse & left us, having never been sworn into the company. I was informed he made several unsuccessful attempts to borrow money of different members of the company. May not his intentions have been to make his expenses to Monroe, borrow a little money, & abscond without refunding?

Having disposed of Mr. Wright, we moved to an unfinished house to the East, & in the suburbs of Arcadia, with the view of sleeping in the house as light sprinkles of rain had fallen, & there were still indications of rain. Just as we had got our baggage into the house, & were about kindling a fire, one of our party, J. R. Cavett,[22] cried out, "boys, examine & see if you are not full of fleas!" We complied instantly, & to our great mortification, each man found more or less fleas about his person. We immediately held an informal caucus, & without [hes]itation decided to decamp & seek a mo[re] [de]sirable camp ground. What valiant *[part of page missing] seven of us fled instanter*[23] *from a few, [part of page missing]*
What will we do when we meet the Yanks?

About 300 yards further on we found a situation that promised all we could expect "out of doors". Fully expecting rains to descend upon us during the night, all hands set to work, some cooking, some pitching tents, & others doing whatever was likely to add to the comfort of our situation.

Supper was soon over, after which some of the party went in search of forage for our team. In a short time they returned with plenty that was given to them.

May 9th, Friday

Passed the night pleasantly, no rains falling as was expected.

Traveled about 14 miles, & took dinner near a branch from which we got water. This morning we passed over much better land than any after leaving Bossier Parish.

Some of the citizens whose residences we passed this morning, treated us kindly, but others were indifferent.

Dinner over, we traveled some 6 miles & found ourselves in Vienna, Jackson Parish,[24] at which place we halted about one hour to rest ourselves & team. Thence 5 or 6 miles further, we halted, about 5 o'clock, P.M., to go into camp for the night. Bought corn at 75 cents per bushel, & fodder at 40 cents per dozen.

After pitching tents in a gin-house lot, which we had permission to occupy, one of our party discovered a hen's nest of 16 eggs within 6 feet of our tent. 'Tis needless to say they were appropriated without discussing the morality of the action.

The company came up with us at this [e]ncampment. We expected they would do [*part of page missing*] as we had been traveling slowly that they might do so, not wishing to go into Monroe in advance of our officers.

Saturday, May 10th.

About 2 o'clock, A.M., some one, tired, I suppose, of his resting place, (for our couches were not such as were very desirable) got up, & shouted aloud for all of us to get up. Fully aware that we could not rest unmolested any longer, we arose & got to preparing breakfast. At daylight we were ready to march, & as we preferred being the van of the train, we set off, having no orders to march in order. About 9 o'clock the company came up with us at the "gum spring".[25] From this place we made no further efforts to travel in the lead—some times one ahead, & then another, but all got on quietly to Trenton.[26]

Near 10 o'clock we passed through Douglas, a small village.[27] During the remainder of the day's travel, nothing of note transpired except we were constantly passing & being passed by other soldiers on their way to Monroe.

In the evening we reached Trenton on a beautiful bank of Ouachita River, a fine looking stream, & in an excellent stage for navigation. Trenton is on the West bank of the Ouachita two miles above Monroe on the East bank of the same stream.

The town of Trenton is irregularly laid out, & the houses are triangulated, giving the town a most singular appearance.

The streets were very filthy, & the walks did not indicate a high degree of cleanliness. This, together with the dilapidated condition of the business houses, rendered the place quite undesirable.

The country passed over in this da[y's] travel looks to be very poor, & from ap[pear]ances at that time, there was no go[od] reason to believe the citizens wou[ld] make bread. The land is thin, & [*part of page missing*] weeds & bushes had almost complete possession of the fields. Surely laziness prevailed.

Capt. Rabb, having just returned from Monroe, informed us that we could not be admitted into the service for a short time. This intelligence caused some sensation, as we wished our time to be going on, but we pitched our tents to wait.

After selecting a camp ground, & making all needful arrangements for the night, we began making enquiry as to the terms we were to be admitted into the service. We had by this time learned that the Confederate States had certainly passed a conscript law; therefore, we had become quite solicitous about our terms of admittance. None of us were willing to enter the army for a term of three years as the conscript law required, & from the best information we could gather, there was little chance to be received into the State service, notwithstanding we were sworn into that service before leaving home. We expected to find Gov. Moore at Monroe, but he was not there, neither could any one tell of his whereabouts. All the information we could gather of him was, he had left Monroe with $3,000,000 belonging to the State treasury; that when he arrived there from N. Orleans, he was so much frightened, he did not, for three days, go on shore, & when he did, he had a body guard in attendance.[28] In his Hegira from the city of N. O. it was discovered some boat was following the one the Governor was on, & without waiting to know anything further of the other [boa]t, in a frenzy of thought that it [w]as the enemy pursuing him, he had [*part of page missing*] 00 Bbls. Molasses cast over board to enable him to escape. This was told and currently circulated for the truth, & I have never yet heard it contradicted. What could people expect from such a ruler?

Great confusion prevailed among the soldiers of whom there were about 1600. One hundred brave & well-equipped cavalrymen might have captured many prisoners, and dispersed the remainder. Alas for our country!

May 11th, Sunday.

After breakfast, Capt. Rabb came into camp, (*he* lodged at a hotel) and informed us that if he had known of the conditions of things there, he would not have gone there as our Captain; that all was in the highest state of confusion, & he could not decide as to the best course for us to pursue, but from his whole tenor he was evidently in favor of disbanding. Considerable excitement prevailed in the company. Some were in favor of disbanding, & others were opposed. After considerable discussion in which almost everyone participated to a greater or less extent, it was decided that we remain and be sworn into the Confederate service for a period of three years or during the war. Quite different from our first bargain with the authorities, but I for one acquiesced—not because I believed it justice, or believed the conscript law was legitimate fruit of Republicanism.

Having disposed of this vexed question, another of considerable importance arose. Many of us were getting short of [pro]visions, & we could draw nothing from [*part of page missing*] Gov't until we were sworn in. Final[ly] Capt. Rabb started down to Monroe to [*part of page missing*] into the matter. A few hours after he returned and informed us we could be sworn in in the evening. That information rendered us all quiet for the time. Indeed, we were never otherwise when matters went well.

Between 4 & 5 o'clock we were called into line, & marched to the ferry opposite Monroe. After some confusion occasioned by 10 or 12 of the company refusing to be sworn in for 3 years or the war, the oath was administered to us (officers & privates taking the same oath) by S. W. Odell,[29] deputy mustering officer for Monroe.

The ceremonies of administering the oath were finished, & we returned to camp, but without rations as our orderly, P. V. O'Neil,[30] was in too great haste to get back that he might go to an encampment of several other companies near us, & with whom it was evident we would be united to form a regiment, to electioneer for a position as a staff officer. This electioneering, I fear, will prove of injury to us. Indeed, from facts that have recently come to my knowledge, the spirit of seeking positions of honor & lucrativeness has spread widely through the Confederacy.

May 12th, Monday.

After breakfast we were called into ranks, & one man from each mess detailed to go to Monroe to draw camp equipage & rations. I was one of the detail. We drew meal, bacon, pickled [be]ef, peas, sugar, vinegar & salt ; tents & [*part of page missing*] small share of cooking utensils.

Judging from manifestations then made, [*part of page missing*] was forced to the conclusion that [*part of page missing*] officials then in power in Monroe, were more than indifferent about issuing us supplies. It was difficult to get what we did, & they had other articles we much needed, but could not get them.

After supper, one of our men, M. Matlock,[31] claiming to be a minor, started back home. Men were sent after him, & they brought him back.

As we did not draw cooking utensils sufficient for the organization of less messes, we were forced to form into messes of 15 each. The mess of which I was a member consisted of the following: D. W. Herron,[32] Israel Rodgers,[33] S. J. Herron,[34] J. L. Byrd,[35] B. F. Keeth,[36] A. J. Graves,[37] J. P. Strayhan,[38] A. Dudny,[39] P. C. Broom,[40] G. S. Davis,[41] R. S. Cavett, C. Tipton,[42] Dr. Stroud,[43] J. R. Cavett[44] & myself.[45]

May 13th, Tuesday

"Weather fine, & but little to do. Some of the 'boys' start to Monroe to 'recreate' themselves.

Some are of opinion we will soon be sent to Natchez.[46]

Almost any thing may be heard in the way of news. Many fabricate whatever their brains are capable of producing, & tell it to witness the effect; therefore it is impossible to know what is, & what is not true."

After night a discussion arose relative to which regiment we would unite with, the 29th or 30th. Our Capt. & 2nd Lt. Were in favor of the 29th, & our 3rd Lt. & orderly were in favor of the 30th—our first Lt. had not come up & they discussed the question *ad libitum*[47] after which they called upon us to vote. A majority voted for the 30th, & many of us retired, as we thought, for the night. But some of the particularly [*in*]*terested* parties were not satisfied, & after caucusing a while they called [us] forth & took a second vote. The 30th carried it by a greater majority. Notice was then given us that we must be in Monroe by the rising of the sun next morning, & we were not molested any more that night.

May 14th, Wednesday.

In compliance with the notice given us last night, we were in Monroe early.

While waiting for the mustering officers to finish their morning's nap, I took a little better survey of the town than when there a few days before. It has a very

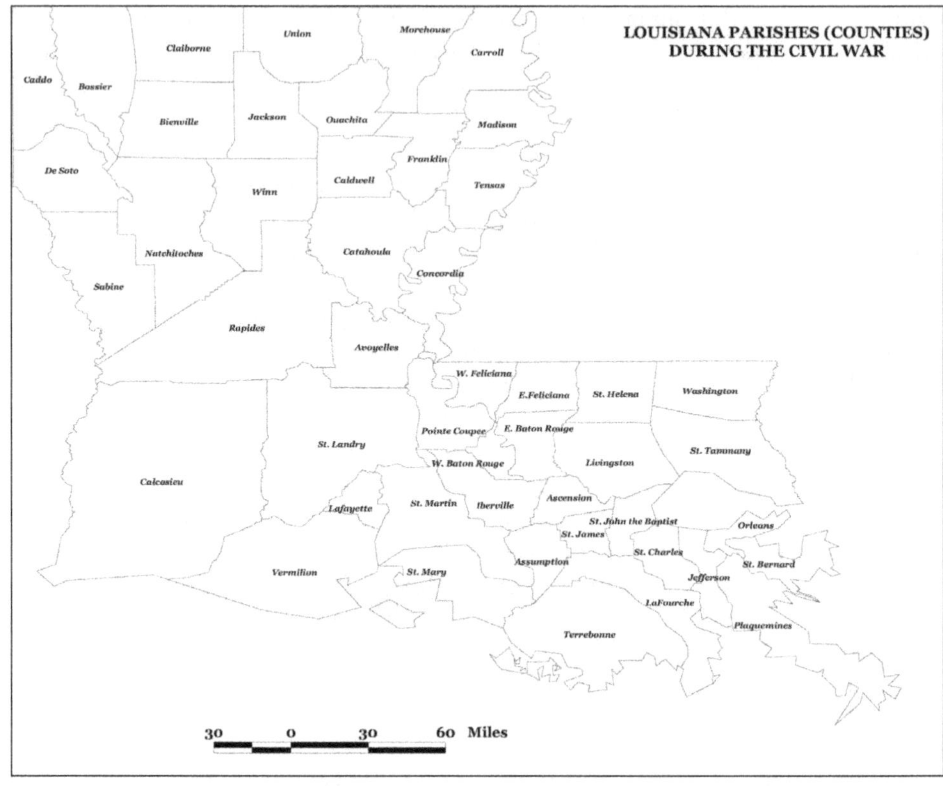

Existing Louisiana parishes during the Civil War. Cartography by Gary D. Joiner.

pretty site, & might be a beautiful town if the citizens had that pride which characterizes a people of refinement. They showed but little hospitality to soldiers.

About 8 o'clock, A. M., the deputy mustering officer appeared, & after a little bustle & stir-around, such as men of his calibre are wont to do on such occasions, we were all called into line, & nine men—myself for one—were selected to take Descriptive Lists of the different members of the company. We were conducted into his office, & the necessary materials furnished us for doing this work assigned us, & we at once set about it. The first Descriptive List I assisted in taking, I asked the gentleman whose it was, if he would sign the receipt for his bounty annexed to the List without receiving the bounty—I had heard they were doing business that way—in reply to which he said, "I am not in the habit of transacting my business in that way." I remarked, "I would not without some assurance of my bounty." We then called Capt. Rabb, who called Odell, the mustering officer, & questioned him concerning the matter. Odell replied, "The conscript law is soon to take effect, & as many are applying to be admitted as volunteers, we cannot stop now to pay over money. As soon as all are sworn in, & the money will be paid over to the different captains of the companies, & they will distribute among the men."

Capt. West,[48] principal mustering officer, then asserted the same, & further stated he had plenty of money. Whereupon Capt. Rabb vouched for the forthcoming of the money. I then addressed myself to Captain Rabb & stated, "Capt., upon your voucher I will sign my receipt." wishing him to *distinctly* understand that upon his voucher alone I agreed to sign my receipt. But, for the life of me, I could not help thinking, why not sign the receipts when the money is received? However, I said nothing more, but proceeded to do the work as directed.

After each man's List was taken in triplicate, & he signed the receipts annexed to each, he then went before the examining surgeon, Dr. Roan, who gave them certificates of ability or disability. And in this connection I will state a noteworthy fact. The surgeon in each certificate certified that he had strictly examined the subject, & found him either qualified or disqualified to discharge the duties of a soldier. Now, I witnessed the examination(?) of several, which consisted in a few careless interrogatories by the surgeon if the subject desired a discharge; if no complaint was made, certificates of ability were signed by the surgeon without hesitancy. Many able-looking men got certificates of inability simply by complaining of some slight infirmity. [*Part of page missing*] of broken constitutions got certifi[cates] of disability by simply manifesting a willi[ngness] to become soldiers. It might be asked, why was Dr. Roan so willing to certify to that which he must have known was false? The only answer I can give is this, he got pay for his work whether he did it honestly or dishonestly.

Our officers decided to unite with the 29th regiment notwithstanding we had voted so decidedly against it. The disaffected were conciliated—better places were given them.

May 15th, Thursday.

Several of the discharged left this morning, which caused some murmuring. Many considered that several of the discharged had shown themselves unpatriotic, & Dr. Roan deserved rough handling for giving exemptions to such.

Some of the company sick of camp diarrhea, but none considered dangerous.

Bad news this evening; reported the gunboats had possession of Natchez,[49] & a boat which left Monroe a few days previous to cross the Mississippi was captured by the enemy.

"For the first time since our arrival here, some sign is manifested to place us in a situation that will enable us to escape if the enemy approach."

There were then no organized troops in the Trans-Mississippi Department except a few about L. Rock, Ark.[50]

Late in the evening we were called into ranks, & orders given us to mark our tents, & put everything in readiness to march at a moment's warning. Evidently a surprise was expected by our officers. At that time nothing would have been easier than the taking of Monroe & the destruction of a quantity of army stores by a single gunboat of the enemy. Their ignorance of our situation was our only safety.

May 16th, Friday.

Dreams of surprise & capture may have flitted across the minds of some last night, but the enemy has not yet approached, and we are all safe. But some of the company found a little job to engage their minds for a short time last night. One of the hotels of Trenton had a sign painted in large letters, *Union Hotel,* & it was determined it should come down. Accordingly a squad organized, went to the hotel, tore down the sign, brought it into camp & committed it to the flames of a fire prepared for the purpose. I was asleep, & did not witness their fun. There are good reasons to suspect that many, in and around Trenton & Monroe bear worse than Union signs—*Union sentiments.*

P. V. O'Neil resigns his position as orderly sergeant, having been elected to serve in the regiment as sergeant major.

Breakfast over, & we receive orders to strike tents, & move to the regiment. A wagon is procured, & our mess, No. 1, moves to the regiment. ————

Here we are in the brush with our baggage lying in a confused mass. None of us know where to pitch our tents, neither can we find a man who can tell us.

Before the wagon got back for a second load, orders were given for it to return, and convey us back to our original campground as Capt. West had issued orders to Capt. Ra[bb] to take a boat for Moreau Landing on [the] Ouachita tomorrow morning ; thence to some point on the Arkansas River, & do[wn] that stream to the Mississippi & across it.[51] We return, pitch our tents in their original positions, & orders are then given us to cook 2½ days rations.

Why order us to move our tents today as Capt. Rabb had previously received orders for us to proceed to Moreau? The truth is, as I think, Capt. West desires to get us away from here without paying our bounties, & as nearly every man in the company opposes leaving here before being paid, our move this morning was devised as a test. Several of the companies of the regiment have signed receipts for their bounties without receiving their money but have not the requisite courage to contend with their officers. Among themselves they complain loudly.

Great excitement in camp concerning our bounties. Many insist publicly on not moving until we are paid.

Capt. West excuses himself to our company officers by saying he has been disappointed in receiving the money. Why they receive the excuse I cannot understand unless it is because they wish to curry favor with Capt. West, for he unequivocally avowed to them as well as to us, he had the money. Now, it is not simply fifty dollars that we are contending for, (although many of us are very needy) but we do not like to be thus swindled. *Against wrong & for right,* we started out to contend; then, why go abroad to correct evils before correcting those which exist in our midst?

After roll call tonight, Lt. Sentell[52] requested all who needed money immediately, to step forward, & Col. Gray[53] would provide for such to the amount of $2500. Many stepped forward, & that proved to be the last of the measure. Several

Brig. Gen. Henry Gray. Courtesy of Gary D. Joiner.

similar propositions were made, but each shared a similar fate except one made by Lt. Marks; he proposed to pay any three men, & take their chances for his pay, & made his proposal good by offering the money.

May 17th, Saturday.

All are ready to strike tents & march to the boat, but lo! Orders are given to move to the regiment. The men are bitterly opposed to going as the ground for camping is a most unpleasant situation.

Our orderly, J. L. C. Graham[54] & several privates, consult Capt. Rabb. He instructs them to search within the limits of the regimental encampment, & if a suitable place cannot be found, we will, for the present, remain where we are. ———They return & say we will not move today, & a call of "fall in" is heard. The object of the call is to place out a guard. Col. Gray has consented that we may remain where we are for a few days on condition we guard the road to prevent the other companies' men from going to town unless they have passes.

This morning Lt. Abney arrived, he having remained at home a few days after our leave to adjust some business. All manifest great joy on account of his arrival, for, since we have been at this place, we have experienced one continued scene of strife. Upon being informed on the state of things, he immediately went down to Monroe to try what he could do. He soon returned with a promise that the money would be advanced to pay the bounties of fifty men. He had the question put whether we would accept the p[rop]osition he had obtained. It was much better than any thing our other officers [had] obtained for us, but we voted, unanimously, [*part of page missing*].

Commenced drilling this evening, which is the first time any attention has been given to that exercise.

Dr. Stroud left us this evening for Corinth,[55] he having obtained a transfer to a command at that place.

May 18th, Sunday.

This day has nearly passed without any thing having taken place worthy of record. Much has been talked of during the day, but nothing decisive done.

The steamer, W. A. Andrew,[56] arrived at this place late in the evening with many articles on board. The officers of the Andrew report an armistice, which created considerable sensation—some giving credit to the report, & others believing it false, & regarding the master of the boat suspiciously.

May 19th, Monday.

Threatened with rain. A refreshing shower would improve things much, for it is now so excessively dusty that it is truly disagreeable to travel about.

For the first time, order has appeared among us. By order from Capt. Rabb we are putting our tents in camp style. I am glad to see it, confusion has ruled supreme since our arrival here, & as there are enough of other troubles to encounter I am rejoiced to see the initial abation of that trouble.

Lieut. Abney has been in good repute since his arrival here, & today stands above par. I hope he may continue so, for I think we have some reasons to fear our other officers will not, in all things, stand to our rights.

Several or our men are sick, but none are considered dangerous.

May 20th, Tuesday.

No guard out today, & I understand the captain expects we will have to move to the regiment. I hope the men will stand firm, *positively* refusing to move until satisfaction for our bounties is given; for I believe this is but another effort to get us away from here without settling our bounties, intending to so tie us into the service we can no longer bother them about the matter.

Orders to strike tents to move to the regiment are now received. Alas! Many of the men obey without faltering. Some of those who made the most positive declarations they would not move until satisfaction for our bounties were given are now the first to strike tents. Indeed, some of them seem to fear they will not be the first to obey the officers. Can men be relied on? Irresistibly comes up.

Just at this juncture, West, the quarter master comes up. He alights from his horse, goes to Capt. Rabb's tent, and after a short consultation Capt. Rabb calls the company to assemble, stating Capt. West wishes to talk to the men. After grinning deceitfully, & using a few sugar-coated expressions, many of the men manifest signs of swallowing the whole dose without an effort. West proposes to pay us twenty-five hundred dollars, & says he can then feed us ; or he will pay the whole & not feed us, & leaves it to our choice. Many seem to think his proposition fair, forgetting he still holds our receipts for the whole amount, having all the while refused to give them up, or making any proper showing that they were unpaid. I suppose he thought he would take the half if he could not get the whole, or perhaps get us off under the belief that half would be paid, & then let us get it if we could.

Feeling that all would soon be lost unless some one interposed, & seeing no indication that any one would interpose, I ventured to speak, & contend for my interest. I told him that I for one was not willing to quit the ground until satisfaction was given. At this he manifested great offense, advanced closely to me, shaking a large roll of money, & exclaiming, "Perhaps you do not believe I have the money. Did you come out to fight for the pitiful sum of fifty dollars?" I replied, "I do not doubt your having the money, I have a family dependent upon myself and friends for a support, & I insist for my dues." He now receded finding he had failed in his purpose of intimidation. Addressing Capt. Rabb he said he would pay him thirty-five hundred dollars, & he wished him to enquire into the circumstances of his men, & pay all in circumstances similar to my own. I then remarked I would not receive mine unless those who did not would say they were willing to wait, for we had all made a strike together, & I would not forsake a friend. He then paid to Capt. Rabb thirty-five hundred dollars, promised more if necessary, & left. This gave satisfaction to a sufficient number of the company to make further resistance useless, so the business of moving went forward but not without some murmuring.

The end so much coveted by our officers is at last consummated—we encamped on the regimental campground but have just finished a tough job of clearing off a piece of ground for our tents. Filth of the most disgusting kinds had to be moved. I am inclined to the belief that in other days had soldiers of the present day been passed upon they would have been reckoned among the "unclean beasts". The company next to us is made up of Louisiana Creoles, & they lack of being the cleanest people I ever saw. The position is rather low, but deep drains are to the East, South, & West. The land does not indicate strong fertility, and the timbers & many banks of clay indicate a mighty tornado some fifty years ago. We have good water, & appearances indicate a healthy locality for this country. Indeed, we are doing well enough except for one piece of bad management. The camp guard is placed very close, & are frequently ordered to let no man pass without a written permit. About 3/4 of the regiment are affected with camp diarrhea, & after a little detention at the guard line, many cannot get much farther. The consequence is filth in the extreme. A breeze from that direction renders breathing an unpleasant exercise.

Capt. Rabb has just arrived from Monroe with $1000 more from Capt. West to be used in paying bounties. Several of the company say they be[lieve] what I said to West has caused him to send out the additional one thousand dollars, and they believe each man of the company should pay me one dollar. I do not, when doing what every man of the company should have done, ask for extra compensation, but I would ask, that in future each man do his duty.

May 21st, Wednesday.

After drill today Capt. Rabb calls for every man who needs his bounty to come forward & receive it. Contrary to the understanding on yesterday, many who were the most noisy about their bounties, & asserted their willingness to "strike" until every man got his bounty, are now among the first to receive it. Others who had boasted they had money enough, that they had no fears of finally getting their bounties, & that *they* would wait on the officials, were also among the first to receive. Some no doubt received their bounties not thinking of what the result would be to their friends who had not. Others received it because they thought the contract to strike for every man's bounty was broken by those who first received, and now every man for himself. Thank Heaven, thirty-six have stood true to the last. We pledged ourselves not to receive unless all were paid, & so long as one man stands firm, all others are bound. If two parties enter into a compact, & the first violates the stipulations the second is released, or, if the second violates, the first is released ; but if three parties stipulate, & the first violates, the second & third are released from the first, but not from each other, & so for a hundred parties.

Pleasant weather, a light rain fell last night, & lowered the temperature of the atmosphere.

May 22nd, Thursday

Great excitement in camp this morning! But our company are but spectators this time, having no part nor lot in the confusion. Many of other companies are asserting most positively they will start home this morning. The Col. makes a speech to them, still they persist, claiming they were promised furloughs before attaching themselves to the regiment of sufficient length to go home & work out their crops. They now claim what was promised them in a fair bargain. The fact is not denied, but the Col. denies his ability to furlough without a commission, & yet says he will treat the men as deserters if they go home. Now, it seems clear to my mind that if he requires a commission to enable him to furlough, he also requires a commission to enable him to arrest & punish. The power to do one necessarily implies the power to the other. They have their knapsacks packed, & are ready to start, but each seems to wait for another. The different companies are now called into ranks to drill & those with their knapsacks hesitate but finally lay them down & "fall [in]".

Drill over, but none have left. [*Part of page missing*] spirit of leaving prevails among [*part of page missing*] but none seem willing to ventu[re].

Capt. Rabb, I hear, has received a letter from Matlock's father informing Capt. Rabb that Matlock is not a minor.[57] It is supposed by some that Matlock will be sent for and arrested as a deserter, but if commissions are required to enable our officers to furlough, they will certainly be required to enable them to arrest.

May 23rd, Friday.

Raining this morning.

Of our mess, Spurlin[58] & Strayhan are sick.

P.M. A party from other companies of the regiment is preparing to start to Trenton, saying they are going there to "press" two Dutchmen into the service because they are guilty of beating their father. The officers seem to wink at the move, & the privates generally favor it. The excitement grows more & more in-tense, & many are falling in to go for the Dutchmen. Getting up as closely as I can that I may the better understand all about the move, I happen to hear one fellow remark, "go on boys, I'll be d----d if there won't soon be so many that we won't get a drink a piece". Methinks I understand the secret of this move now. Whiskey, or cakes & beer are at the bottom of the move, or I am deceived, not much sympathy for the old man. The privates concerned are solely responsible.

Eight men from our company are detailed to start home tomorrow to collect guns. I think the move a bad one, for a great many guns have already been taken from there, leaving a bare sufficiency for home service. Besides, of what benefit can they be to us without ammunition? I am informed there are but ten thousand cartridges in Monroe, & I can hear of none any where else West of the Mississippi.

May 24th, Saturday.

The party detailed to go home for guns started early this morning. I am rejoiced to see them start though opposed to see an effort made to take more guns from our neighborhood. It will prove a gratification to the men as they will be able to meet their families at home, & perhaps attend to business matters now much neglected.

A party, of which I am a member, are detailed for duty on the Steamer Music.[59] We are placed in charge of a Lieutenant who marches us to the boat. He goes to the deputy quartermaster to know what is wanted of us. He returns & informs us we are to clear off the lower deck of the boat. A sense of deep humiliation strikes every one. After many earnest curses are pronounced, we all, with *great* reluctance, go on board & commence the disgraceful duty. Were it a matter of necessity I would not complain, but the captain is receiving $250 per day for the use of his steamer—not using it more than two days each week & the regiment furnishing hands to do all the deck work. Besides, the quartermaster refuses to pay many of us our bounties. We are now at work as carefully [as] a set of fellows well can be taking care of but two things : 1st, don't [do] much ; 2nd, don't do any thing right. The Capt. of the boat, the officers of the regiment, & the quartermaster receive the anathemas of an exasperated set of men by the wholesale. The Capt. of the boat seems to regard his cabin an unsafe retreat, so he comes down & he & two others belonging on the boat go foremost in the drudgery, looking as though they wished us in some other region.

At last done with the Music & returned to camp. While gone to the boat, G. S. Davie of my mess got a furlough of 30 days, & left for home.

Rumored in camp we will soon move some six miles West from this place. I hope so.

Now late in the evening, & all are ordered into line. Seven of our company are ordered to load their guns. —A momentary silence, & then all hands commence conjecturing—some one thing, & some another. Some say they think a steamboat, the W. A. Andrew is to be boarded at Monroe. Some think the party that went for the Dutchmen is to be arrested for they returned without the Dutchmen, & it has been reasoned that *some* party entered the Dutchmen's house, & while there, one of the party purchased 25 lbs. Tobacco, & took it away without footing the bill. At best, we can only guess, & await movements. An officer with orders takes charge of the seven men, & they proceed down the long line—they arrest two men & conduct them to the guardhouse. They are charged with an attempt to desert.

Some of our company are quite sick.

May 25th, Sunday.

Beautiful morning.

Nothing of importance on hand in the way of news.

Spurlin & Strayhan are quite sick. Others of our company are also quite sick.

This evening those arrested yesterday were discharged.

May 26th, Monday.

Fine weather this morning.

I am not well enough for camp duty today, but am doing what I can for J. L. Byrd & J. P. Strayhan of the sick. Strayhan is much better than he has been.

Blackburn[60] of our company got a permit yesterday morning to go to Trenton but failing to return, four men are now detailed to go in search of him. ———

Hearing some excitement, I look out from my tent, & see the detachment bringing Blackburn in. He confesses he has done what he should not have done, promises better for the future; therefore is released.

Reported the steamer Twilight[61] is taken by the enemy near the mouth of Red River.

This morning a deserter is brought in from Winn Parish.

Our officers, both regimental & company, are sharply on the "sprint", each striving to make it appear he is *the* officer. By way of showing off a little this morning, Capt. Cheatham[62] drilled his men in the double-quick step until one of them fainted. Why be in stew about these things. Inde[ed], gradual training is the only kind that will season men to, & duly qualify them for the arduous duties of a soldier. He[re] as in most other instances, "great haste often makes great waste". By it, men are broken down in body & spirit.

May 27th, Tuesday.

Passing the guard station this morning on my way to the spring I observed several men sleeping in the open air on the ground. As tents are not furnished for the guard, they must sleep in the open air, or not sleep at all. Such is well calculated to render men unhealthy. Why not furnish tents? There are plenty in Monroe.

Some argue any kind of fare is good enough for a soldier. I think quite different, & leaving out all moral consideration (which should never be done) there is other argument sufficient to justify the use of tents. Men accustomed to sleeping in comfortable houses, & suddenly thrust into the open air to sleep are highly liable to contract disease from the exposure. Now, it requires but little reason to understand that a diseased man is not fit to do any work well, & more especially that of a soldier. True a soldier's life is a hard one at best, & he should expect to meet difficulties & trials, but because these *must* come, there is no reason why needless ones should not be avoided.

Some of our sick are improving, but others are not doing so well.

The talk of moving has died away, I suppose the officers thought it would please the privates too well.

Ladies have visited our camp this evening, & in shame be it said, many of the men are behaving shamefully—they are crowding around the ladies, staring at them vulgarly. Indeed, many are climbing saplings & trees, & whatever object near that will en[a]ble them to get a view of the ladies. The officers should stop such behavior; for such base conduct will stop true ladies from visiting our camp, & their moralizing influence, to a considerable de-gree, lost. More needed now than any time I have ever seen. If something is not done to improve the morals of our men, I mean the whole Confederacy, I humbly think our cause is lost beyond redemption.

May 28th, Wednesday.

Two other men in the guardhouse this morning. —Miller[63] of our company was put in last night for getting drunk, & threatening to commit murder——of another company was put in under charge of stealing a knife. ———He is taken out & tried, found guilty & sentenced to have his head shaved, & be drummed through the streets of the camp. The latter portion of the sentence if inflicted will be a transcendence of the powers of the officers; for the military regulations provide that drumming through the streets drums one out of camp. ———

The sentence is executed, but as the subject is a young man—not very bright—neither has he property—the punishment is inflicted with impunity. What can privates hope for when witnessing such proceedings? What chance for redress of grievances? The hasty proceedings of the trial, together with other circumstances, render the guilt of the young man uncertain; but were he altogether guilty, the execution of the latter part of the sentence was totally arbitrary. Indeed, whence the power to court martial without commissions.

The deserter is also tried, & sentenced to dig stumps for four days—Miller is released.

During the morning drill, ladies were present to witness our maneuvers: both men and officers made extra efforts. So much for the influence of "[*illegible*] last, best gift to man".

Rumored we will soon move to within twenty-five miles of Mt. Lebanon in Bienville Parish. I hope so, for many are sick here, & a mere change, if to no better place, will be apt to prove beneficial.

Dr. Parham's[64] (Dr. Parham is our company physician, that is, he fills that position, but I cannot say he does do in an able manner) brother from the Army of Virginia is in camp. He passed through Vicksburg last Sunday morning. After passing he heard the firing of guns. No other news.

Four of P. V. O'Neil's sisters were present during our drill this evening.[65] They are "good looking", & the eldest is said to possess a mind of the highest order, & a polished education.

Officers drill this evening. All honor to our lieutenants! They drill the other officers. After the drill Lt. Abny informed us the officers were more awkward than the men of our company.

May 29th, Thursday.

It is now currently talked in camp that the young man who was paraded through the camp streets yesterday is not guilty of stealing the knife, that he is innocent of the charge, & the fact could have been proved, but for the haste of the officers to make an example.

'Tis said Col. Gray will start to Richmond this morning or tomorrow morning to report our regiment ready for service. Why not communicate by express? That would be much quicker and easier.

Alas! One of our company, E. S. Harper,[66] is dead. He died in the hospital of quinsy[67] this morning. He died very suddenly, and from what I hear he did not get the necessary medical attention; the surgeons supposing but little ailed him, neglected his case.

While drilling this evening, I gave out from over-exertion, as the weather is very warm, & I am not well.

Great excitement in camp! News of *peace propositions.* Rumored that Mr. Lincoln proposes to President Davis to give up the cotton States, & let the border states decide for themselves—decide which power they will unite their destinies with. If such a proposition is offered, let every man at once demand acceptance. That is about all we have claimed, & there is no reason to suppose we will ever get peace on better terms.

R. S. Cavett is quite sick.

After supper tonight the remains of Harper were placed in a coffin, & that in a large box, & sawdust packed around the coffin. This being done, the chaplain of the regiment took his stand & pronounced the funeral services. He executed his part well, & the men behaved with excellent decorum. Let us hope the exercise will have a beneficial influence on all who attended. *How solemn it is to witness the funeral ceremonies of a fellow soldier far from loved ones at home!* The thought of dying away from home in camp, where almost none of the common comforts of life can be obtained, & worst of all, without the consoling attendance of one the dearest of all—his *wife,* is, to me, one of the most solemn thoughts I have ever encountered. And what adds greatly to the solemnity of the thought, is the great neglect in a medical point of view with which soldiers are treated.

May 30th, Friday.

Harper's personal friends are getting [*part of page missing*] with all possible haste to carry his rem[ains] back to his wife.

The principle that actuates them deserves admiration, but I doubt the propriety of the act. It can benefit neither the living nor the dead, & at this season of the year, with not half preparations for moving a corpse, the undertaking must prove hazardous to the parties engaged. This body is of the earth, & must thence return, but the immortal spirit may soar in eternal bliss, or grovel in everlasting darkness; yet the practice among men is neglect the part worthy of care, & make much parade over that which endures but a day. The money & time thus spent if appropriated to the use & benefit of Harper's family would be of considerable benefit to them, but as custom among my friends would return the corpse to the bereaved family, I make a small contribution to forward the end. Lest I may be thought disrespectful to the dead—my argument thereby losing its effect—I will pass on after stating I have presented the question for the consideration of those who may read this.

The witness against the man punished for stealing a knife is arrested this morning as he is believed to be the true thief. The one punished has all the while avowed his innocence, & at the instance of some who are friends to him upon the ground of being a friend to justice, he immediately after his trial & punishment, endeavored to get a new hearing, avowing he could prove his innocence & the guilt of the other, but was not listened to. Those of his company who felt that injustice had been done him set about investigating his case, & the more they found out, the more they believed him innocent; consequently they pressed his claim to a new hearing so strenuously that it was granted, & the other party immediately arrested, tried, found guilty & sentenced to dig stumps for 2 days. However, the officers decide he is only guilty of concealing, & the man first tried guilty of the actual theft. Some still hold that the first party is entirely innocent, & that the officers maintained his guilt that they might maintain their consistence. I do not offer an actual decision, but will state there are good reasons for believing the innocence of the first party. Our officers are generally very rash, & ready to make a display of authority.

Received a letter from home today, it being the second I have received since leaving home. All are well, & I am rejoiced to hear it.

One of the soldiers, quite a lad in appearance, requested another soldier to trim his hair. Accordingly a pair of scissors were obtained, & the work commenced. In a short time the hair was taken off, but not in the latest style. Indeed, the most expert sheepshearer could not have clipped the wool closer, but might have clipped it much smoother. This excited much mirth in some who witnessed it, but others were indignant, believing the young man had undertaken to make a laughing stock of the lad. They go to the young man, tell him he has committed a high offence, & to secure his punishment all that is necessary is to report him to the officers. That if he does not compromise the difficulty with the lad by submitting to have his own hair similarly shorn by the lad, they will report him instanter. 'Tis enough; he submits as quietly as a lamb—the lad seizes the scissors & commences his work of retaliation—bystanders laugh to their hearts' content—then go & call others to come & witness the sight. Here they come by the dozen—now they are so thick around him only a few can get a sight—they shout aloud with mirth—a call from the outside of the crowd, "fall back gentlemen, & give us a sight". Those who have seen enough move from the center to the outskirts of the crowd, & others rush forward to get a view of what proves so mirthful to others. As they advance near enough to get a view, the same loud & mirthful laughter rises successively. The young man is perfectly silent except one or two short remarks. When the laughter first commenced, he remarked, "Well gentlemen, if I felt well enough I would help you laugh." The work is now completed & the young man stands up. Being over 6 feet high, all can see him. Some one calls out, "stand up straight & pull off your hat Williams."[68] With perfect calmness, & without manifesting the least shame, he readily complied, & a universal & continued laughter ascended from the crowd. I am not an admirer of such fun, but give this incident a place in my journal that the incidents of camp life may, in some degree, be illustrated.

Today, for the first time, I am detailed on guard.

The lieutenant of the guard, as is customary at the guard station, has been playing at cards, & has miscounted time, & placed the relief (3rd) to which I belong on post at 4 o'clock instead of 5. We protested, but said finally, we would go on if he would have us taken off at 6 o'clock, and he replied that time had been lost & it must be made up. We replied we had not lost any time, therefore we did not wish to make good lost time; that the first relief had lost the time by being taken off too soon, & it should make it good. After some parleying, he agreed to our proposition, & we were then placed on post. Time rolled off about us as usual, but when it became apparent from the sun that our time *must* be out if not more than out, we began to feel somewhat indignant. Time now goes sluggishly—it is near sundown, & we are quite restless—but here we are, & here we have to remain until the relief guard comes around—should that be till midnight. At last we see them coming, & feel somewhat relieved in feelings.

On arriving at the guard station, I asked for the time of day, but could not get it. It seemed to me they were concealing the time; for when we left the guard station, they had two watches. Myself & two others, Thos. Keith[69] and Thos. Love,[70] then went direct to our first lieutenant's tent, & he said it lacked but a few minutes of 7 o'clock. Thence we went to the officer of the day, & reported to him our treatment. He talked very fair—said he would investigate the case, and if we had been mistreated, he would have our grievance redressed. He then went to the guard station; held a caucus with the officers there, & then decided we had been kept on guard 15 minutes too long, & that had happened by mistake, & not by neglect. He did nothing more than hear the plea of the officers at the guard station. Why did he not bring us face to face, & act upon the testimony of both parties? Was he afraid a different decision might be forced upon him?

This circumstance, together with the one concerning the stealing of the knife, & many others not mentioned herein, proves to me that a private has a dim prospect of redressing his wrongs when they come from an officer.

During the night we got but little rest, & that on the ground in the open air. True, a soldier should expect hardships, & should never grumble if they are unavoidable, but when unnecessary, (as in this case, for plenty of tents are at Monroe, but 4 miles from us) they certainly have a right to demur.

May 31st, Saturday

The sick of our mess are improving this morning. —Midday—R. S. Cavett is worse. Indeed he is quite prostrated.

Both good & bad news this evening: Reported that "Stonewall" Jackson has whipped the enemy in Virginia,[71] will invade their territory: & further, that 20,000 of the enemy are marching on us through Missouri.[72] If this be true, what will be our doom? We have but few arms west of the Mississippi, & less ammunition.

Cavett is worse this evening, & I have some fears of his dissolution.

June 1st, Sunday.

Started at daylight this morning to get a place for R. S. Cavett in a private house. I traveled the road back towards home as it was most likely I would succeed in that direction, & it a most earnest request of Cavett, he being averse to going in any direction but towards home. I traveled on enquiring as I went for a situation for a sick soldier, but all seemed to want nothing to do with a soldier, especially a sick one. After some trouble I succeeded in getting him a situation with one Dr. White about 2½ miles West from camp. Returning on foot to camp, not being able to get a vehicle for Cavett to ride in, fortunately I find the chaplain of the regiment has come in with some ladies, & I succeed in borrowing a buggy & horse from him. I go with Cavett, & A. J. Spurlin to wait on him, to Dr. White's. Cavett, I am proud of it, is highly pleased with the appearances of his boarding house, & especially with the appearance of Dr. White.

On my return to camp I find several women have come in to be present at divine service. I am pleased at this, hoping their presence will exert some control over the morals of the soldiers.

Bad news this evening: Reported the enemy is within 16 miles of Richmond, & our forces falling back from Corinth and Confederate money 50 percent below La. Money in the State of Mississippi.[73]

Jas. L. Byrd got a sick furlough of 15 days today, & as it is a good chance I send a letter home by him.

June 2nd, Monday.

No drill this morning as many are anxious to go to Monroe—to-morrow being the day set apart for us to move. Our lieut. passes every one through the guard that wishes to go to Monroe except those on guard. About 40 of us go.

Just before arriving at the viaduct[74] over the Ouachita, we hear the whistle of a car,[75] & make some haste to cross that we may see the cars. —Across, & I propose a trip to the depot to see the locomotive, having never seen one—all assent, & on we go. —At the depot, & I find the locomotive just about such a thing as I expected, except it is kept in much finer polish. —Back on the business street of Monroe—looks like half the reg't is here—crowding among them for some time, & finding nothing that I came for, I retrace my steps to camp.

While in Monroe, I heard that our forces still hold Corinth; that the Yankees are withdrawing from Richmond; that Vicksburg is still unharmed.

Rec'd orders to cook 3 days' rations, preparatory to moving—all respond cheerfully to the order, for we are anxious to leave here.

The guard is now disbanded, & the men are running forth & back across the guard line as if to test the realities of such liberty. —They must all be astir now, for there seems to be double as many as usual.
Cavett is better this evening.

June 3rd, Tuesday

Up this morning before day, & every man seems to be eager to get off. Many of us will be going towards home, therefore we are using uncommon efforts to start. —All is strict bustle, and our orderly sergeant passes along & says we have orders not to strike tents without further orders.

What screw is loose now we know not, but as we have no orders to the contrary, we go on preparing other things, leaving the tents for the last. —Now it begins to be rumored that our company (B) will have to remain here until other wagons can be procured. —Our first lieut. says we must wait till the wagons return for us. This intelligence is by no means euphorious; for we are exceedingly anxious to leave here; more especially when we can go towards home.

Now they begin to move, the men first, the wagons next, & finally the rear guard. The rear guard is halted, & back comes an officer for the flag—our officers having presented it to the regiment. Our men dislike it—they think it unfair to take our flag, & leave us behind. We promised the ladies who presented it, it should never trail in the dust—now strangers have it, & as they do not hold it in the same sacred esteem, but seem desirous of possessing it from the same impulse that a child does a toy—to make one vain display—we feel truly indignant. But, knowing we are no longer freemen, we do nothing more than make a few bitter denunciations of the act, & return to our tents to content ourselves as best we can.

I notice in the Monroe Register[76] that Congress is taking steps to ferret out frauds practiced by quartermasters & surgeons, some 400 having been reported as delinquents. I think some work might be beneficial in this part of the Confederacy. I heard Lieut. Abney remark this evening that he could, & did buy hams at 20 cents per lb., & the quartermaster charges him 25 cents per lb., & swears it is cost.

Went to see Cavett this evening, & found him better.

Some of the men are out on a spree tonight: late in the night they came in, some are intoxicated, but as they behave well for men under the influence of intoxicating spirits, they are permitted to go at large.

June 4th, Wednesday

All are up this morning. Those who were on a "spree" last night look quite drowsy.

About the usual hour we go out to drill. While resting, our drill officers, lieutenants Abney & Marks, get into a dispute (friendly) concerning a face-movement. In the first part of the controversy, Abney seemed to have the better of it, but in the latter part the scale seemed to turn in Marks' favor. None of us are well qualified to judge, but we all agree that Marks is the best drill master in the regiment.

While drilling in double quick time, myself & 2 others break down.

Tipton reports Cavett as not doing well this evening.

Ellis[77] is attacked by quinsy this evening, & seems somewhat alarmed. The officers & all the men show a disposition to do what they can for him. Every one suggests whatever remedy he has known of being used in such cases, & those who take the case in charge adopt such as they think best.

June 5th, Thursday

I am unable to drill this morning as a consequence of my breakdown yesterday in double quick step.

Ellis is better this morning. —Might Harper not have been saved if the same precautionary measures been used with him?

Many are lounging around tents unable to drill.

I attempted drilling this evening, but failed, having not entirely recovered from my breakdown yesterday evening.

Supper is now over, & I hear a stir at the head of the street. On going out to learn "what is up", I find "the boys" are making up a dance—our first lieutenant is one of the number.

As dancing involves a moral question about which there is much controversy, I will make a few extemporaneous remarks, not having time nor space to discuss the question at length.

Wayland in his Ethics says,[78] & I heartily concur with him, an act is resolvable into 4 elements, the intention of the act being the only element in which morality is discoverable. Then, if the intention of the actor be pure, his morals cannot be impeached. Dancing conducted for the purpose of driving away dull cares, & exhilarating the mind, cannot be said to be prompted by bad intentions; therefore, must be innocent. And as such seemed to be the purpose for which our soldiers danced, I necessarily conclude their dancing was innocent. Yea, more—of positive benefit. Our *Creator* saw fit to endow us with certain faculties—one of them mirthfulness—I necessarily conclude the reasonable exercise of them is not only innocent, but positively beneficial.

Further, I approve of the course of our lieutenant; for the men will only love him the more, therefore serve him the better.

June 6th, Wednesday

Pretty morning. —I am still on the list of the sick, having not yet recovered from my breakdown.

Many of the men are complaining, but all are able to be up. Tipton went out to see Cavett last night, & found him worse.

We are now called to "fall in", but for what we know not. Now we are "in", & our first lieut. tells us the object is to march us to Trenton to take a bathe. Some object to going, but are told they will be drilled 2 hours if they refuse to go. I would prefer drilling, though not able to do either, but it would be a punishment, therefore I go to Trenton. I do not object to bathing, I do that frequently, & we have water in abundance for that close at hand.

I with many others return in worse plight than we were when we left, we are worried, & all are covered with dust.

Reported we have defeated the enemy in Virginia, & have retaken Baton Rouge. —Our forces have fallen back from Corinth.

Nat Thompson from Bossier reports that those of our company who went home for guns had appointed last Wednesday to start back to us. He says the corpse of Harper smelt very badly before it was interred.

June 7th, Saturday

Some of our men are still sick, but none of them dangerously so.

We are in constant expectation of the wagons to move us to the reg't, as Thompson reported them not far off yesterday evening. ———2 o'clock, or later, & the wagons have not yet arrived. What can the trouble be? But who would be in a hurry now if paid by the day.

A nice fellow comes over to give our officers the muster roll, & take the names of those who have not received their bounties. Why not pay over? The money is due us, & they have it.

At last the wagons have arrived. Will we go this time? — peradventure.

Another hog, which is the third, has somewhat mysteriously appeared in camp, & is now finding the way into the cook pots, being well divided among the messes. —To speak in plain English, some of our company killed the hogs referred to without making a purchase. I feel that it is not only my privilege to condemn or to justify, but that it is my *duty* to do so. I shall justify.

They inform me, & I believe them to be truthful men, they have tried to purchase them of the owner, but he would not sell them. They have tried to purchase articles of food for the sick from him, but have failed alike in every effort to procure accommodations from him. Now, if one party is in great need of an article possessed by another, & the second party can, for a fair compensation, part from the article without sustaining any material loss; but because he does not wish to accommodate, the second party to some extent losses his tenure. That is, the first party, the one in need, if he cannot have his wants—actual necessities—relieved otherwise, has some excuse for appropriating the article to his own use. At this point I wish to be clearly understood, for it is far from my intentions to at all justify stealing. To appropriate an article to ones own use without the consent of the owner—the need being great, & no other means for satisfying it is one thing, but to appropriate as a livelihood is quite another thing.

Hear to-night that our forces in Virginia under Jackson & Johnson have driven the enemy back; also, that Price has cut off, & taken prisoners, 4000 of the enemy's cavalry.[79]

Chapter 2

Home and Camp Jackson

Nothing save the sacred honor of myself & family, could induce me to separate from them as I have done.

William Henry King
June 19, 1862

June 8th, Sunday.

At last we are on the road to Vienna, Jackson Parish. Many of us have heavy loads to carry—heavier than would have been, had all borne an equal part; but many got off without taking much, & some without any thing.

Called on Cavett as we passed, & found him better.

Eleven o'clock, & we are eight miles from our old encampment, & have halted for dinner, & a rest. I was near giving out on the road two or three times, but being rested frequently, I have held out to this point.

P.C. Broom has been here several days on a pleasure trip, informs me there are tulip or poplar trees not exceeding 3 miles from here, not less than 3 feet in diameter. This settles the question relative to tulips west from the Mississippi.

3 o'clock, & we are again on the road. I am much improved by the rest, but scarcely believe I can hold out till night.

About 4 o'clock we meet Dortch,[1] one of the party that went home for guns. He reports others of the party behind with wagons to haul our knapsacks. This intelligence revives us greatly, ——— we have met the wagons, & having learned all are well at home, we proceed cheerfully.

Our friends report good crops in Bossier; also the organization of a vigilance committee[2] that has dealt with two men. One they give so many days in which to leave; the other is committed to jail to await an opportunity for sending him to Monroe for trial by the military. He proves to be the same man tried in Monroe some time ago.

While in Bossier, Capt. Rabb received orders to enroll the conscripts. We are all more or less rejoiced, for there are those there we would like to see started out from home—those who were very active in securing secession, then urging others into the army, promising to do much for their families, but failing after the men are into the armies; active in joining companies, but just before the companies leave, find some *very* "plausible" reason why they could not leave just then, but, of course will be on soon, but from *some* cause never come on. Now, I *do* feel that conscription is just what they deserve. If I know myself, I do not want any one to receive more than his just desserts, & that I consider he has no right to object to. So let every one receive the fruits of his own sowing—bitter or sweet.

About 6 o'clock, P.M., we arrive at the "Gum Springs", well known on the stage road from Monroe to Vienna. Find the water good, & quite a plenty of it. —We make our beds in the open air in obedience to orders. Would the protection afforded by our tents pay for the labor of pitching them to-night, & striking them in the morning?

June 9th, Monday.

After some sharp words, & perhaps some hard feelings, we get off from camp. Our first lieut. orders the officers' provision box placed in one of the wagons furnished by our friends to haul our knapsacks. Our knapsacks are in the wagon, & we refuse to take them out to make room for the box. At this juncture, the lieut. comes up, & tells us there is room in another wagon for our knapsacks, & then orders two negroes to take off the knapsacks until there is room for the box. The owner of the wagon now backs down, & consents for the box to be placed on the wagon. Seeing there is no other chance, I take my knapsack, go to the other wagon, & find there is no chance to place it on the wagon, except on the pot vessels. Looking around, I see the lieut. coming with a knapsack in each hand. "Lieut.," said I, "this is no place to put knapsacks, just get up here and see for yourself." He replied rather sharply, "throw it in." I replied, "I carry mine on my back first." "Then shoulder it." "I will," it was done quickly. He threw the knapsacks into the wagon, paying no attention to how they fell. A place too filthy for an officer's provisions box, but not for a private's knapsack. Luckily I found a place for my knapsack in another wagon.

After about 6 miles travel, we reach Douglas, 1½ miles travel more, we stop for dinner, getting water from a well. We find the crops much improved along the road since we went down to Monroe.

3 o'clock, & the march is again resumed. By permission of one of our friends, I ride on a wagon as I am unable to march. Both yesterday & today, I ate nothing

for dinner except a little biscuit made in camp. I was so completely worn out, I had no appetite.

Cavett & McGee[3] who were sent for yesterday morning, overtake us this evening.

Camped 1 mile East from Vienna. Lieuts. Sentell & Marks pitch their tents—why not let us pitch ours. Tents for officers—open air for privates.

June 10th, Tuesday.

On the march early this morning, & I am to walk some. At Vienna, we take the Lisbon[4] road, leading N. through a hilly & healthy-looking country. Immediately on the road, the country looks rather poor, but from the appearance of most of the houses, I think the land may be better than it appears.

About 10 o'clock we arrive at the encampment, "Camp Jackson", & I find myself quite worried, having walked all the way—distance, 7 miles.

After lounging about some 2 hours, recuperating in that time, what I could, I make enquiry respecting the chance for a furlough, and find the prospect quite dim. Some not justly entitled to furloughs are making efforts to obtain them with prospects of success, while others who ought to have furloughs, stand a bad chance for them. I am behind in my application, but I will not be out done this time if I can avoid it. I have a just cause, & they have taken the start of me without giving me warning.

I go to J. R. Griffin, Esq., offer him a fee to work for me—he declines the fee, but does what he can for me—it is enough, for he succeeds.[5] Griffin, a private in our company, is a lawyer of integrity. —In haste, I prepare to start, & get off about 2 o'clock—go to Vienna, take in R. S. Cavett, & travel about 14 miles further, putting up with a Mr. Givens who treats us quite hospitably.

June 11th, Wednesday.

Breakfast about 6 o'clock. When Mr. Givens was asked for our bill, he replied, "Nothing; God forbid I should ever charge a soldier any thing—I have never done so yet."

After 4 miles travel, we reach Arcadia. We halt & get a bottle of whisky for the benefit of the feeble who need a stimulant. —7 miles further, we call at a house for water, & for grease to grease our back. Furnished with both, together with plenty of beer, free of charge. —12 miles further, & we call at a house for a "snack", & 3 bunches of oats for our horses. Gentleman of the premises "gone to war." She charges us (5) $2.00 for what we get—conscience seems to condemn, for she falls 50 cents without any remonstrance. —On to Minden, distant 8 miles, thence to Bellevue, arriving there about 8 o'clock at night. —Full eclipse of the moon tonight.

June 12th, Thursday.

Off tolerably early this morning after making a *hard* effort to get off early. Our load is increased this morning, hence more walking. Detained some at

Bodcau Ferry. —Just after passing Ellerson's,[6] I part from my company, sling my saddle bags across my shoulder, walk to J. P. Strayhan's, find no body at home, go to Mrs. Childer's[7] to rest till the cool of the evening, find Strayhan and family there, & for the first time since leaving home, get an excellent vegetable dinner. A short rest after dinner, & I get Strayhan's horse to ride home, accompanied by his little boy to ride the horse back home. —Arriving at home, I find our children at home, all well, & their mother gone to R. S. Cavett's to enquire after me.

June 13th, Friday.

Spent the day most agreeably with my family, eating fruits, reading letters, & writing in my journal. —Just now I feel that I would rejoice to know that those who caused the war had to assemble in one vast field, & fight the battle of their own making—not until one party had whipped, but until the extinguishing of the last man. I want a "Kilkenny cut fight" of it. After such an event, I believe families might retire to their former vocations in peace & quietude—but not till then.

June 14th, Saturday.

Early after breakfast this morning, I start to Bellevue to attend to business connected with a Tutorship I hold[8]—about 1 hour's detention at the ferry at Bodcau, & I cross & go into Bellevue about 12 o'clock. —Conscripts met here today, but none were enrolled, as many excuses (of which one alone was sufficient) were allowed. A man swearing he did not *believe* himself able to bear arms was released. In my opinion the Conscript Law is a blotch on the character of the Confederacy, & this turn in it will produce two fold more disrespect.

Learn today the police jury has passed an act to stop the further issuance of Parish Scrip to pay volunteers the $75.00 previously voted by the Police to all who would volunteer from the Parish. By the act, some of us will receive $37.50 while others get $75.00. Which end of the Seal of Justice preponderates in this case?

Having given attention to my business, I start for home, & arrive at the ferry about 4 o'clock—got across at ½ after 6 o'clock, & having to stop twice on the road, I was till after midnight getting home.

Our legislators, now out of business, & too wise & patriotic to shoulder their muskets to fight in defense of their property & their sacred (?) honors, might find a job in legislating the Bodcau out of existence, or into some condition convenient for crossing. The attempt would be just about as wise, & about as just as the act of voting themselves exemption from all military duty.

June 15th, Sunday.

Attended church at Salem—sermon by Rev. Legett.[9]—Met Spurlin & Cavett—both said they would return to camp at the required time—Cavett had taken a backset—Spurlin looked quite well.

June 16th, Monday.

Went this morning to sell my horse to Lee Carrier, but failed.[10] Spent the remainder of the day in reading, writing & C.[11]

June 17th, Tuesday.

Did but little today except read & write.

June 18th, Wednesday.

Sad to think of—this is my last day at home this trip. I shall try to spend it in the most pleasant manner surrounding circumstances will admit. I do not expect a feast in this way; for one who loves his family dearly cannot, if he be a reflecting man, make merry on such occasions. Went to Collinsburgh[12] this evening to see G.W. Sentell[13] concerning a horse to ride back to camp, he having sent me word he wished me to ride one back for his brother, Lieut. Sentell to ride home. Succeeded in getting the horse—"lucky hit".

A note from Cavett informs me he has relapsed, & is unable to return to camp. The bearer of the note informs one Spurlin is also sick.

A fine rain this evening revives the drooping vegetation.

June 19th, Thursday.

The painful duty of parting from my family is again forced on me. Oh! how can it be with those who separate from their families for weeks, & for months, in search of pleasure; or, even for "fortune"? Give me my family, my beloved family, with but the absolute necessaries to sustain life, & they may have *all* the rest. Nothing save the sacred honor of myself & family, could induce me to separate from them as I have done.

Get along pretty well to Bellevue, making the longest ferriage at the Bodcau. Overtook Strayhan & Gardner 4 miles from Bellevue. Took dinner of our own rations in Bellevue, & after witnessing a game at Billiards, in which Strayhan partook, we traveled on to Mrs. Lofton's, 3 miles E. from Minden, & put up for the night.

June 20th, Friday.

An early start, & a light bill, (3 men & 2 horses) & who would not be cheerful? —Travel on finely with no trouble except the chafing of Strayhan's horse's shoulders. As the sun sheds his last lingering rays on the tips of the tall pines, I get into camp. Find most of our men well—none much sick. Another of our company, James Parker,[14] died last Monday night at a private house below Monroe. Poor fellow, he was taken sick immediately after we got in camp, & was never well afterwards.

After lying down to rest for the night, I was troubled with an affection of my heart, caused by a nervous debility which has, to some extent, troubled me for several years. I could not sleep until under the soothing influence of a pill of opium.

June 21st, Saturday.

Unable to drill in the morning—drill in the evening, & feel much worsted from the exercise.

My first time on dress parade this evening—our music is not of the first quality, but it animates; and it, in connection with something of a desperate feeling, causes me to feel much like making a desperate charge on the enemy, making or losing all at one single dash.

June 22nd, Sunday.

Unable to attend inspection of knapsacks this morning. I suppose there are 150 women, maybe 200, attending divine service in our regiment. Well done for the ladies! I am pleased to see them at any time, but more especially on such occasions as this—they seem to be exerting a potent influence for good on the morals of the men.

Two men are now in the guardhouse for going home without leave of absence. They had intelligence that their wives were sick, & applied for furloughs to go to see them. The furloughs were denied, & they went without them. Others were detailed to go after them, & met them on their return. The detailed men went home to their families, while the others waited for them. They all returned together, & those who went without leave of absence were placed in the guardhouse. Is this a case of desertion? Such is the charge.

June 23rd, Monday.

Better this morning—went on reg't. drill, & am much fatigued—in evening drill, "fagged down".[15] I am ashamed at the confession, but we do not drill as well as we did at the other camp. I attribute this blame to our officers—they have tried to advance us too rapidly besides teaching us incorrectly in many things. None are "first chop" drill masters, & they have been drilled in different tactics.

June 24th, Tuesday.

Peace news today—I have no faith in its resulting in any good to us—believe it gotten up by our enemies to cause us to fall into lethargy, or by our friends to revive our drooping spirits.

Did not drill in the morning—got along pretty well in the evening drill until the double quick movement was commenced—then dropped out, previously obtaining permission to do so.

June 25th, Wednesday.

Not well this morning, but on duty as a policeman, & for the first time in camp, I am placed in command of the squad. Why, isn't it enough to cause me to feel a little pompous? But a little reflection causes me to see that my command is quite ephemeral—it expires with the day. Might not some of our officers learn a lesson worth knowing by making a similar reflection? Good sense, & good principles, however require us such reflections. Right principles forbid austerity, though one knew he could command *always*.

Our first duty as policemen is putting up hospital tents. Just before finishing the work, the regt. officers come in from drill, & being much displeased with the position, they & the surgeon disagree, & the surgeon dismisses us from the work.

Officers are not fond seeing soldiers idle, so a job is soon found for us, & what would you guess it to be? What would *any good* man or lady guess it to be. They might guess, & guess, but I am sure if they were *good* men & ladies, they would never guess. It was cleaning around the tents and cookeries of the officers. It was a *filthy* job, odds & ends, entrails of fowls, & whatever other animals might have been brought into camp; together with feathers, fish heads, scales, & c. & c., had been thrown around indiscriminately, & none removed from their first arrival. Maggots were found in abundance—in some places not less than a quart, perhaps more, could be scooped up at once—and they the biggest of the big, & the fattest of the fat of their kind. All of this, & much more, we had to move out, while the buck negroes of the officers stood around, & grinned significantly. The picture needs no varnish, & my comment is, what could be more humiliating?

Learn that Quartermaster West says we must return to the encampment at Monroe, or we shall not draw wages. Just like the old tyrant—no doubt of its truth if he has the power.

Much sickness in the regiment.

June 26th, Thursday.

The sick are about as yesterday. —Another man of our reg't. died today. Sad to think of, our men are dying in the attempt to serve our country, but are doing it no good.

June 27th, Friday.

The sick of our camp are not improving.

Suppose we heard cannonading at Vicksburg this morning—distance, 110 or 115 miles.[16]

Three of our men who have been home on furlough come in this evening. One of them, B.F. Keith, presents me with a letter from home, containing the news of the good health of my family & friends. Consoling news.

June 28th, Saturday.

Hear sudden & heavy cannonading at Vicksburg, & from the sudden cessation, suppose something decisive has been done.

The sick of our company, except Gibson[17] who is quite sick, seem to be doing better.

Others of our company on furlough, come in, & report the prospects for a corn crop with them not good in consequence of dry weather. Such a drought as that of '60 would do more to defeat us than all the Yankees can possibly do.

June 29th, Sunday.

In company with others, I have taken a bath in Darbone,[18] (I do not vouch for the orthography) about 1 mile North from us, & feel much improved.

The weather is very dry, & we are forced to drill in fogs of dust at which many men complain. Some of our officers say we have no right to complain. This morning we go through the process of wallowing our knapsacks in the dirt, called inspection of knapsacks. It seems to me the officers wish us to be as dirty as possible; for they certainly know we will not have any thing in our knapsacks we do not wish them to see.

Troubled with hiccups.

Almost every man in the reg't. seems disposed to go home, & remain there. Indeed, I solemnly believe there are but few, if any, except officers, and office seekers, who would not gladly accept an opportunity of disbanding instanter. I can not believe men possessed of such a spirit can be effective before an enemy that will fight. Is it because the men are not true men. The majority I believe to be true men—would fight in a just cause & under proper treatment. They are tired, & heartily tired, of being imposed upon by their officers, & no good whatever being accomplished.

June 30th, Monday.

While drilling this evening, Lt. Marks carried us through a wheel differently from any we had ever made before. After the execution of the movement, he commanded us to rest. Several of the men then told him they thought he was mistaken; that Capt. Rabb had always caused them to perform the movement differently. All was said in a polite & becoming manner as far as I was capable of judging, but it appears our young Lt. did not think so; for, after ordering us into rank for a second lesson, he spoke to us in a tone that showed his mettle to be up; & said, *"I acknowledge no man as my authority; Capt. Rabb, nor any one else. I will drill you as I have been taught, & if you don't like it, I will force it."* The words are a comment on themselves. One officer drills us one way, another, another way, & if we are in the puzzled to get through, they are offended. Perhaps double quicked a while for revenge.

July 1st, Tuesday.

Quite unwell this morning, threatened with chills.

A light sprinkle of rain, & from appearances, rain plentiful in Bossier. How hopeful we all feel. But for hope, what would we all be?

The men placed in the guardhouse for going home without leave of absence have been liberated. Suppose the officers could not find them guilty of desertion. The man who ran away from camp at Monroe is now in the guardhouse for deserting this encampment.

July 2nd, Wednesday.

Still unwell. Had I a few liberties, I think I would soon be in fair health. But our Surgeon & officers manifest a total unwillingness to part from their authority, so I must strive to content myself.

Hear from what appears to be a reliable authority, that 15000, or 20000 of our men have laid down their arms at Corinth & gone home without permission.[19] If true, our case is a lamentable one.

July 3rd, Thursday.

Three men from Winn Parish[20] were arrested here today on the charge of being Union men. If they are Union men, honestly & sincerely so, & make no war on us, nor our institutions, I say let them alone.

Some talk of a party being sent in the neighborhood of Delhi[21] to scout.

D.W. Herron of my mess has lost his purse, containing $121.00. 2 men from another company, who have been with our men playing cards today, are strongly suspicioned. I incline to the opinion some of our own men have done it.

July 4th, Friday.

Today is set apart for celebration. It seems to me that as long as every thing else "national" has been discarded by the Confederacy, this should be too. Three men under arrest for Union sentiments, & the arresting party celebrating the birth of the Union. *Consistency!* Many ladies attend the celebration. Speeches from several, & I am proud to learn that J.R. Griffin has the credit of surpassing all others. I believe him to be a sound & consistent man. Surgeon Quinn has blistered me for splenitis,[22] & I am unable to be in attendance.

After roll call tonight, receive orders to be ready to strike tents tomorrow morning at 6 o'clock. Various conjectures as to what will be done.

July 5th, Saturday.

6 o'clock, & all strike tents. Bah! All that is wanted is to sun & air things. To have told us would have been *unmilitary* of course, but it would have saved us much trouble in the way of packing & preparing to move.

July 6th, Sunday.

The Surgeon's blister, "as big as a Spanish saddle blanket"—he thought one less would do me no good—has accomplished no good, but has caused me much suffering. B.F. Keith is quite sick.

Capt. Bradford[23] of our regiment—having been gone for some time—got in today, & gave us a speech on *The future prospects & the present condition of things.* His picture is a glowing one, claiming we have completely routed the enemy in Virginia, & that McClellan with his whole force of 75,000, have capitulated; that our army at Tupelo[24] is in a fine condition; that the surplus corn crop of Alabama (Ala.)[25] alone will feed our army; (how long speaker deposeth not) that the enemy's army is in a disorganized condition. Some one asked while he was speaking, "What will we do for arms, Captain?" Instantly he replied, "we can whip them with pikes." As pikes can be made longer than guns, we could charge upon them, & transfix them to a man. This idea took pretty well. Think one moment—What would the Yankees do while we would be charging? "Stringing us on bullets," of course. Thinks the war cannot last much longer. His speech, as a whole, was not very favorably received.

July 7th, Monday

Last night one of the prisoners escaped.

Today our guns were appraised. Maximum price, thirty dollars—no more allowed. It seems to me unjust for the government to limit the price with no privilege to refuse.

J. E. Wood[26] reports his money stolen from his pocket book. Wonder who got that.

Much excitement! 23 prisoners from Winn Parish brought in, charged with treason. Prisoners all on foot, & guarded by some 50 or 60 men mounted on mules & ponies—quite inferior—& armed with inferior guns. The prisoners are bad-looking men, of but ordinary intellectual endowments, & but little better can be said of the guard. Swap conditions, & it is possible they would look no better. From the behavior of the men & officers of our "good" regt., I believe 2/3 would be in favor of shooting or hanging the prisoners without a trial. How untrustworthy poor feeble man is—ready to take life without pausing long enough to know whether it should be done. Oh! treacherous man, when will thine actions be governed by wisdom & justice?—Eighteen of the prisoners brought in today, & 1 arrested here a few days ago, are sworn into the service, becoming members of a company of this Reg't.

July 8th, Tuesday.

The remaining 5 prisoners are started to Monroe to be put in prison, & await a second trial. It is stated they were tried at home by duly constituted authorities. If so, why try them a second time for the same offense? It is claimed the Confederacy is based on the same principles as those of the old constitution, with the exception that those principles are set forth in plainer, & less equivocal language. The old constitution says, in language unmistakable, that no man shall be twice put in jeopardy of life or limb for the same offense. If we do not observe our own laws, how can we expect others to do it. Until governments fail to accomplish the purposes for which they are created, their laws should be strictly observed. By strictly observing unjust laws of a government seeking just principles, the more likely the unjust laws will be repealed soon; for, by the practical test their evil tendencies can be known.

Gibson died last night. Thus our men are going, & no good being accomplished by us.

Further news, confirming McClellan's capitulation. Believe it is but a sensation.

July 9th, Wednesday.

Another man from Winn Parish arrested. An attempt to rescue the prisoners is expected.

Salinated[27] this morning—done to relieve my spleen—no hope of its doing so. But should it do so, how much better would I be? A bad disease swapped for a worse one.

July 10th, Thursday.

Lt. Col. Walker[28] returned from Monroe last night with orders from General Roane[29] to forward 3 companies to Monroe tomorrow or next day. Many are opposed to going, & it is said Capt. Rabb protests, claiming Col. Walker has no right to place us under Gen. Roane. Many exalt over the Captain's protest. Time alone will disclose the Captain's course, but I have but little confidence. He *has* sacrificed the rights of his men, & I believe he will do so whenever his unjust ambition leads him to do so, or he has not the manliness to contend. —Since writing the foregoing, I learn all the companies have to go, but will go by 3'8; & that Capt. Rabb has "knocked under." He is now something below par.

Lt. Sentell in, from home, today. Reports my family well, & crops needing rain. Reports also, a Brigade of Texas Cavalry this side of Minden on a force march to Monroe; & that McClellan's is 35,000 instead of 75,000. When the truth is known, I do not doubt but it will be, McClellan has not capitulated.

I am very sick.

July 11th, Friday.

Capt. Milton's company have started for Monroe, in great glee, yelling at almost every breath. Evidently their destination is the Miss. swamp where insects, bad water & disease will be their constant companions. As they must go, better go cheerfully.

J. R. Cavett makes an effort to have me discharged, but the surgeon has not experimented on me long enough. He tries this evening to get me off on sick furlough but fails—thinks the officers a little contrary.

Capt. Cheatham's company left this evening for Monroe in high spirits.

Capt. Rabb left last night on 10 days furlough.

July 12th, Saturday.

Very sick today. Lt. Abney informs me several of our company who are sick will be left in charge of one who is able to take care of things. A hospital tent is placed outside of where the guard line will be after they leave tomorrow morning. This seems to be an effort in the right direction.

July 13th, Sunday.

Better this morning, though quite feeble. Just before leaving, Lt. Abney informed me he had advised the surgeon to discharge me, & the surgeon promised to do so.

Our comp. left in good spirits.[30] Grieved to part from them, but glad they go willingly.

July 14th, Monday.

Improving. Surgeon Quinn proffers to furlough me & Byrd if we can get some way to go home. In the evening, Byrd finds a mode of conveyance, gets a furlough of 20 days, & starts.

July 15th, Tuesday.

Dr. T. S. Parkham, another of our mess, gets a furlough with the promise of a discharge sent to him. But 3 of us, including our nurse, J. R. Cavett, are left.

July 16th, Wednesday.

Keith & I are improving. The Heavens are propitious, giving us an excellent rain.

R. S. Cavett arrives today with a substitute. Col. Walker refuses to take him, stating he has been instructed to take no more substitutes. Cavett goes with his substitute to Trenton to try what can be done there.

Surgeon Quinn comes around this evening, & informs me I cannot get a furlough, as the Col. forbids anymore furloughs. Now that I have a good opportunity to go home, furloughs are stopped.

July 17th, Thursday.

T. M. Skinner[31] gets a sick furlough for 20 days. When I have a good opportunity to go home—no more furloughs. J. R. Cavett goes to Maj. O'Neill,[32] & gets him to try the Surgeon & the Colonel for a furlough for me. Tries the Surgeon first, & gets an emphatic denial, but not willing to be outdone, he goes to the colonel & gets him to sign a furlough independent of the surgeon, & then advises me to go home. —After some reflection, I decide not to go without the surgeon's consent. The basis of decision is policy. I will hereafter be subject to his mercy, & feeling assured he has none to spare, I shall strive to avoid effervescence. Send for O'Neill, consult with him, & he agrees my course *may* be best. —Alone today, Cavett & Keith having gone to the hospital at Vienna, expecting me to go home on my furlough. —Being without something to eat, I apply to the Surgeon, & he directs me to go to the hospital for it. Easy enough, & fair enough on his part. If I leave my tent, what I have is liable to be stolen. While soliloquizing on the difficulty, Skinner comes in complaining of being hungry. I propose that if he will guard my things, I will got to the hospital, & get us something. He agrees, & I succeed in my effort. —Late in the evening, while contemplating my condition, Capt. Brice[33] passes on this side of the encampment, & happens to discover me. He enquires after my condition, & after I explain, he proposes to send me some provisions. I gladly accept. He goes, but instead of sending, brings it himself. Many thanks to him. I am told he is very diligent in looking after his sick men. Such was his business when he discovered me. After eating, I get an old gentleman to notice my tent until I go for a canteen of water. After lying down, Capt. Brice brings me a canteen of water—just the captain for me.

July 18th, Friday.

Move my plunder to the hospital this morning, with the understanding that I got to the hospital at Vienna today. —On the road, 2½ miles from Vienna, meet Mrs. E. E. Cavett's[34] carriage sent for me. She & her son's wife have come to see him.

Find the hospital a large & commodious building, but ill provided as a hospital. The floor is quite dirty, & the sick are scattered over the floor with but little reference to order. Lamentable. Better could be done.

Quite to my surprise the Surgeon sends me a furlough for 15 days. Unluckily he dates to begin tomorrow, & I cannot get off before next day.

July 19th, Saturday.

Time goes heavily today. Wonder if I will get off tomorrow. —Heard cannonading all day at Vicksburg.

July 20th, Sunday.

Get off in Mrs. Cavett's carriage in company with Mrs. Cavett & daughter-in-law. About 2 o'clock stop with W. N. Mark for dinner—fare free of charge.

Eight o'clock at night, put up with Mrs. Davidson.

July 21st, Monday.

An early start, & no charge for myself—$2.50 for the others. 12 miles travel, & we are at Minden—7½ miles further to C. P. Thompson's—get dinner, & mules fed.[35] On to Bellevue, & stop with P. Alden's family—Alden not at home, but welcomed by his family, some of whom were sick of bilious fever.[36]

July 22nd, Tuesday.

A late start, & heavy roads. Just after crossing Cypress Bayou, I walked up a hill to relieve our mules. The task was too much for me, & I almost fainted. On to Mr. Childers'—got refreshment, & after a short rest, proceeded home. To my infinite joy, found all well, learned that many of our Texas friends have passed here, bound for the war.

July 23rd, Wednesday.

A little better this morning. After examination, find Mrs. Cavett's crop better than expected, though sorry.

July 24th, Thursday.

In accordance with an engagement with Dr. R. W. Vance, whom I met yesterday evening at B. T. Ratcliff's,[37] I return there this morning to get him to recommend an extension of my furlough. He recommended an extension of several weeks.

July 25th, Friday.

Great fatality in Burnett's Regiment—4 & 5 per day are dying of measles—Hear 85,000 of McClellan's men have been killed & captured, but McClellan escaped.

July 26th, Saturday.

Heard our company has been placed 5 miles E. of Monroe as a picket guard.

July 27th, Sunday.

Nothing for the journal to-day.

July 28th, Monday.

O. R. Hooper, an old Texas friend, took dinner with us today. Enjoyed his company; I regard him an excellent man.

Letter from J. W. Kennard at Austin, Ark.[38]—Men and horses on short rations.

July 29th, Tuesday.

Glowing news this morning. Mason & Slidell have had 7 steel clad Steamers built in England, (having pledged our cotton) & they passed Fort Jackson below N. O. with the view & determination of retaking N. O., & driving the last gunboat out of the Miss., or sink them.[39] Further, that the Citizens of Charleston, S. C., have whipped the Yankees at that place; that the gallant & daring Morgan has taken possession of several towns on the Ohio River, destroying many commissary stores,[40] & taking some arms; that Buell & his forces are completely surrounded, & will certainly be taken.[41] What a sensation! Too much for one time.

July 30th, Wednesday.

Make preparations this evening to go to Washington, Ark.,[42] to get the cards of a spinning machine repaired.

July 31st, Thursday.

An early start, & get on as well as usual, arriving at Lewisville[43] at dark—get directions to Randle's Regiment[44] ¾ of a mile from town—arrive in safety, &

find my friends & relatives well except S. C. King.[45] He complains much of being badly treated by his officers. When he entered the service, they pledged to discharge him as soon as dismounted, or as soon thereafter as ascertained he could not serve in infantry. His health is not good, & has not been for many years; he is dismounted, but cannot get a discharge.

August 1st, Friday.

At Spring Hill, 18 miles from Lewisville, I procure food for my mule, drive about 2 mi. further, feed, & eat a little, & on to Washington about 6 o'clock, & found B. McDonald, the machinist, at work. He said it would be a bad chance to get my work done. Took lodgings with him, & carried mule to livery stable. Washington is a nice town, but streets too narrow for beauty or comfort.

Aug. 2nd, Saturday.

On examination Mr. McDonald finds he has not the materials to do my work, but a Mr. Toland, another machinist, has, & he thinks he can borrow it on Mr. Toland's return home. After some reflection I conclude to wait.

Aug. 3rd, Sunday.

Spent the day in reading.

Aug. 4th, Monday.

Mr. McDonald gets an inferior article of wire of Mr. Toland, & after a day's hard work by both of us, we make an inferior job.

Aug. 5th, Tuesday.

Off before sun up, & reach Randle's Regiment before 4 o'clock. See many of my old friends I did not see as I went up. All, more or less, dissatisfied in consequence of being dismounted, & complain at many indignities received from their officers. Indeed, there seems to be a general hatred among the privates against their officers.

Aug. 6th, Wednesday.

An early start, & reach home before dark. —Hear that Stone of our company has died.

Aug. 7th, Thursday.

Now acknowledged the steel clads have never been built. Will our people ever love truth better than falsehood?

Aug. 8th, Friday.

Reported our forces have whipped the enemy at Chattanooga.

Aug. 9th, Saturday.

Did nothing today to record, neither have I any news to chronicle.

Aug. 10th, Sunday.

Health improving a little. Reported J. C. Breckinridge has taken Baton Rouge.[46]

Aug. 11th, Monday.

Heard today our Regiment has moved to about 10 mi. W. from Trenton.

Aug. 12th, Tuesday.

G. R. Rains & A. Wheeler from Shelby County, Texas, stay over-night with us. They bear the good news that my friends & relations in old Shelby are all well.

They state an effort was made recently in Texas to prevent soldiers from voting; that the attempt was carried in every beat in Shelby except the Shelbyville beat. What next? If becoming a soldier to fight the battles of ones country is to disenfranchise him, what else will it not do?

Aug. 13th, Wednesday.

Reported, probably our forces got soundly thrashed in their attempt to retake Baton Rouge.

Aug. 14th, Thursday.

More sensation news to-day, but I am sick of it for the present.

Aug. 15th, Friday.

In comp. with my wife, spent the night, last night, with R.A. Cavett & family, & returned this evening.

Aug. 16th, Saturday.

Nothing worth writing to-day.

Aug. 17th, Sunday.

Stated, the salt makers at the salt works on Lake Bistineau[47] held a caucus, & decided if any man should sell salt for less than $3.00 per bushel, he should be driven out from the works.

Two men report the lands of soldiers from Texas are selling for Texas. "Force trade & sailors rights," is this? If so, don't want any.

Randle's Regiment is said to be in great confusion, because Randle has abolished the chaplaincy of his Regiment, & forbids preaching within 2 mi. of the encampment. *"Freedom."*

Aug. 18th, Monday.

R. S. Cavett succeeded in getting his substitute in, & is now at home. He informs me that J. L. C. Grayham & the officers of our Regiment quarreled. He told them of their base acts, & they failed to arrest him, though men were summoned for the purpose. Well done friend Joe, you have proved yourself worthy of a freeman's name. Had we a few more such men, we would soon rid ourselves from tyranny from our officers.

Aug. 19th, Tuesday.

Started to Bellevue to see Lt. Abney, but turned back in consequence of my saddle chafing my horses back.

Aug. 20th, Wednesday.

Spent the day at home.

Aug. 21st, Thursday.

Randle's men are still in confusion, & making efforts to have him displaced.

Aug. 22nd, Friday.

Our forces did get the worse of it at Baton Rouge & the Ark.,[48] instead of capturing 2 gunboats, & capturing a third, was *actually* burnt. So things go.

Ben Liverman is placed in camp as a conscript.[49] He is diseased throughout his entire system, & pronounced incurable. Won't he make a good soldier?

Aug.23rd, Saturday.

Cousins P. W. Bryan,[50] & Margaret King of Shelby Co., Texas, took dinner with us to-day on their way to Lewisville, Ark., to see their husbands there in encampment.

Aug. 24th, Sunday.

Attended church at Chalybeatt Springs.[51] Sermon by Rev. Windham.[52]

Aug. 25th, 26th, 27th, 28th & 29th.

Nothing these days of interest for my journal.

Aug. 30th, Saturday.

Mrs. P. W. Bryan, & M. King with us to-night, returning home. Report A. B. Bryan & D. E. King in bad health.[53]

They manifest more dissatisfaction than before they went, having got more correct knowledge of the realities of camp life, especially that which the sick experience. They state but little accommodation can be got from the citizens in & around Lewisville.

Aug. 31st, Sunday.

Quite unwell to-day.

Sept. 1st, Monday.

News to the effect that Congress (Confederate) has a bill up to extend conscriptions to the age of 45 years.

Capt. Rabb has returned home, having tendered his resignation. —Abandons his men on the eve of danger.

Sept. 2nd, Tuesday.

All persons of Collinsburgh beat—all white men—between the ages of 35 & 45 years are required to meet there on the [11th] inst. for enrolling—as conscripts I suppose.

Sept. 3rd, Wednesday.

Prepared to start back to camp this morning, but feeling my health would not admit, & my friends persuading, I declined.

Sept. 4th, Thursday.

A. Pike[54] of Ark. has resigned his position, & comes out in a lengthy letter to President Davis, condemning the acts of Hindman.[55] One step in right direction. If the people will heartily respond to his bold & manly position, something like justice may be obtained. Three cheers for Pike!

Sept. 5th Friday.

Nothing to record.

Sept. 6th, Saturday.

Intelligence from our Regt. at Miliken's bend[56] to the effect that our men are getting better fare. A Joe Grayham to each company, would still improve matters.

Sept. 7th, Sunday.

About 3 o'clock this morning, I was aroused & informed that cousin Thos. King had arrived. At once I expected something serious, apprehending the death of his brother Daniel.[57] As soon as I could arrange, I met with him, & learned to my grief that my apprehension was true; & that he & A. B. Bryan had brought the corpse this far with the view of taking it home; & would be compelled to procure other conveyance from here, & requested my assistance. I promised all I could do, but told him the chance was bad. —Referring the case to Cousin E. E. Cavett, a woman of excellent judgement & discretion, she advised the interment of the corpse here. After some consultation it was decided to comply with her advisement, therefore arrangements were begun immediately to inter at the Cottage

Brig. Gen. Horace Randal, C.S.A.. Courtesy Mansfield State Historic Site, Mansfield, Louisiana.

Grove cemetery.[58] About 12 o'clock, M., the interment was accomplished in a genteel manner—Alas! another fellow soldier & relative has been placed "beneath the sod of the valley." How heart rending it will be to his parents! This is their second son who has fallen a victim to disease in this war.

Dr. Mallory, detailed to attend the sick of Col. Randle's Regt. left at Lewisville, informs me that about 130 men have been left in his charge without any power to furlough or discharge; without medicine; & the surgeon of the regt. was fully aware when he left that but few, if any, of the men would ever be able to overtake the regt. Such is the statement of an educated physician, & he bears an enviable character as a gentleman at home, Panola County, Texas. The picture is sickening to a degree unenduring.

Sept. 8th, Monday.

Dr. Walker of Collinsburgh[59] writes home that he was acting surgeon on the Arkansas[60] when it was blown up, & he feels assured that it was sold. I believed so from the first. The enterprise was too hazardous to be undertaken by one of common sense, with any expectations of success.

Sept. 9th, 10th, 11th, & 12th.

Nothing of interest for the journal.

Sept. 13th, Saturday.

Col. E. G. Randolph[61] of Bossier Parish has been appointed enrolling officer of Conscripts, & Col. of the Militia of the Parish. He has published orders issued from the Head Quarters of Gen'l Taylor[62] at Opelousas, for all men in the Parish who have obtained discharges elsewhere than at Monroe to meet him next Monday at Bellevue for the purpose of marching to Monroe. Has not forbearance ceased to be a virtue?

A letter from J. W. Kennard of the 17th Texas Cavalry, informs me he is near Austin, Ark., & quite sick. He complains greatly of the maltreatment of officers. Says Heindman[63] has been appointed commander of the Indian forces instead of A. Pike, resigned.

Heavily altered photograph of Lt. Gen. Richard Taylor. C.S.A.. Courtesy Mansfield State Historic Site, Mansfield, Louisiana.

Sept. 14th, Sunday.

Attended church at Collinsburgh, Sermon by Rev. Robt. Martin.[64]
No news of importance to my journal.

Sept. 15th, Monday.

A letter from J. R. Cavett informs us that our company, Company B., 30th La. Reg't., has recently been in a skirmish. They fired three times on a party of yankees, & suppose they killed one. The enemy's gun boats being near, several shells were thrown at our men, but no damage was done.

Sept.16th, Tuesday.

Reported that Washington City is in our possession.[65]

Sept. 17th, Wednesday.

Reported our company has been reorganized. Lt. W. M. Sentell made Captain, & J. L. C. Grayham first Lt.. I think this a mistake.

Sept. 18th, Thursday.

B. Bryan & S. T. King with us tonight on their return to the army.[66]

Sept. 19th, 20th, 21st.

Nothing to record.

Sept. 22nd, Monday.

This morning I start on horseback for our Reg't. Just after sundown I reach Murrell's Point,[67] put up with L. Rathbun,[68] & await the arrival of the stage tomorrow morning.

Sept. 23rd, Tuesday.

About 3 o'clock A. M. the stage arrives—Rathbun hails the driver, & as soon as ready I get into the stage. Find 12 passengers & 1 baby on the stage, & now, counting the baby & driver, there are 15 of us. There is a good deal of baggage, & all together we have a heavy load. —At Minden 2 other passengers with their baggage is taken on. Heavy load—much crowded, & expect a hard trip. —A fresh driver & a fresh team, & we make a brisk start. —A few miles brings us to the foot of a hill—a halt, & a call from the driver for all of the men to get out, & walk up a hill; "for", said he, "I have a horse that was never known to pull a lb. up hill." This did not correspond well with a remark he made in Minden while changing the load from the other stage to his. He said, "hand it in, I can pull any sort of a load." To pay for a ride, & then walk did not comport well with our feelings, but seeing plainly that no forward move would be made unless we walked, we readily responded to the over polite (?) driver's request. After several "pulls" he succeeded in getting his balky team to the top of the hill—stage & all safely. —Get on finely to breakfasting stand; 9 miles E. from Minden—a good breakfast at 50 cents each.

One mile east of Mt. Lebanon, Bienville Parish, we met an old negro riding a mule. The mule manifests some shyness, & 2 of the passengers feeling a little mischievous, each blow a whistle whereupon the mule commenced rearing & pitching, & soon laid the old negro sprawling on the ground. He had a bone felon on one finger,[69] therefore could not ride so well. I suppose he was a little vexed at the treatment he had received, & having no better mode of getting revenge, he laid as if dead till the young men of the mischievous disposition, & some others, went to him. They found him but little hurt, & returned manifestly relieved. They made many promises not to be guilty of such deeds any more. So far as I observed, they kept their pledges.

Arrived at Vienna, Jackson Parish, at dark, & the driver from there to Monroe informs us that he cannot get to M. in time to connect with the cars.[70] The passengers set up a general complaint against the stage line. The driver becomes a little exasperated, &, I believe, does his best for a slow drive.

At 11 o'clock we get to the suppering stand, & the passengers finding that abuse does not get us forward, they now adopt the opposite policy—persuasion. —It works well. I am astonished that it is not more generally known that human nature is more easily persuaded than driven.

Having rained heavily in the evening, the roads are heavy, & just after crossing the Coushatta,[71] a stream about 17 miles from Monroe, we are compelled to walk up 2 long, muddy hills. —Heavy work—all in the dark & mud. My notions of justice would make a balance account in such cases. But, what does justice signify when the other party have the money in their pockets? They have it, & whether we walk or ride, they will keep it.

Chapter 3

Eastern Louisiana

I am not anxious to meet the enemy on the battlefield, but I am truly tired of the ennui of stationary camp life—believe it is more destructive to life than an active campaign.

William Henry King
November 7, 1862

Sept. 24th, Wednesday.

Reached Monroe about ½ after 7 o'clock, & the cars, detained from some cause, have not left. Those of us belonging to the army, have not time to arrange for transportation, & must wait for the next train. —Breakfast at the railroad hotel for 75 cents, & the roughest fare since leaving home. —Being much worried, I procure a bed, & court the bliss of sweet morpheus. —Too much exhausted to sleep much, so I search about town for a cheaper boarding place—failing in my attempt, I step into a bakery, buy a loaf of bread for 10 cents, & it suffices for my dinner. By accident learn that I can get board with a Mrs. Jones at 50 cents a meal—see her—make arrangements, & move my baggage.

Hearing a construction train will go out to-morrow, I procure a ticket that I may be ready.

Sept. 25th, Thursday.

On my way to the depot, I meet Lt. Abney. He looks somewhat worsted, & informs me many of our company are sick. —By persuading the conductor a little, several of us succeed in getting off on the train. We ride in a box car containing 2

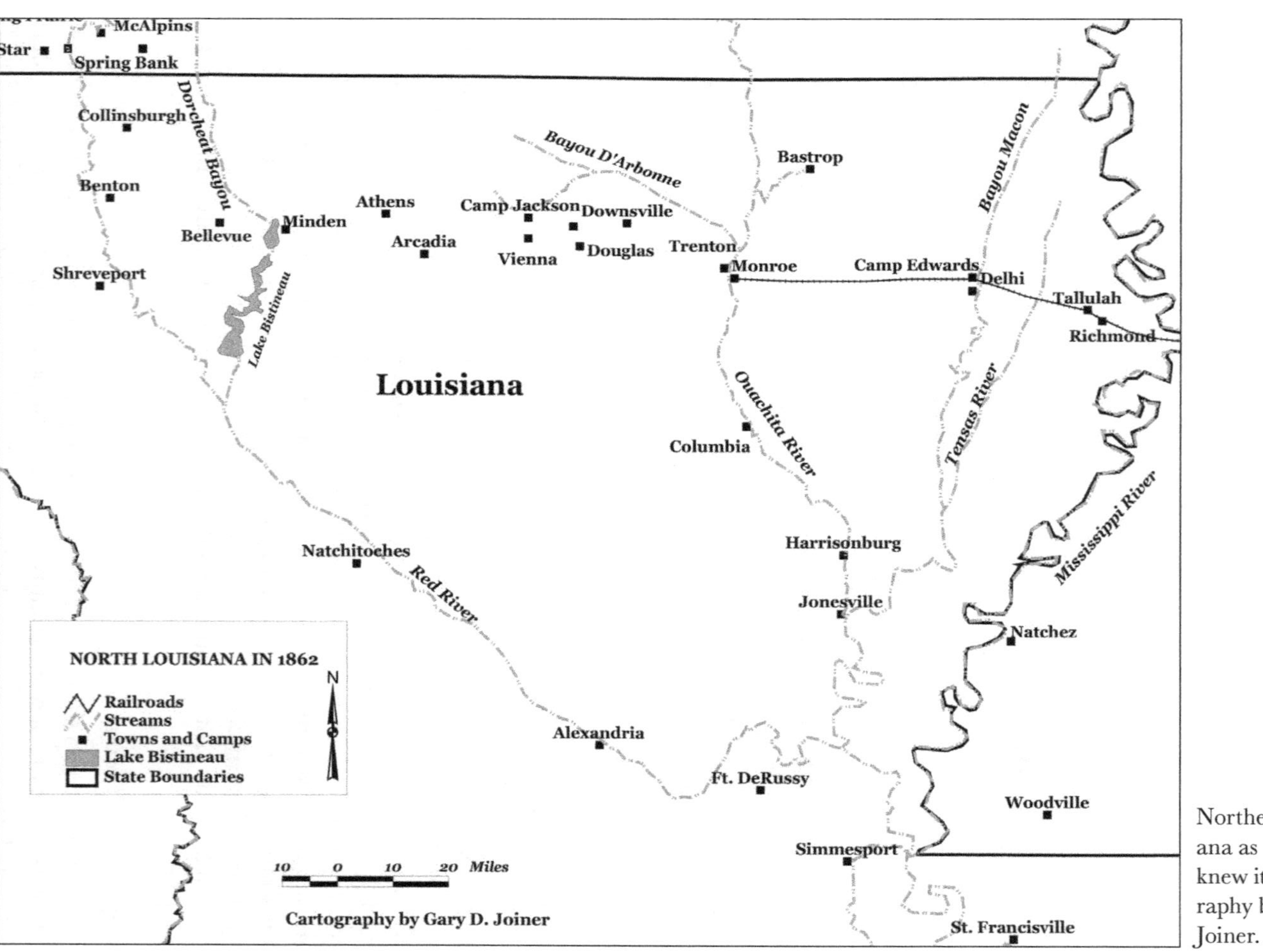

Northern Louisiana as Henry King knew it. Cartography by Gary D. Joiner.

horses & several hhds. of Sugar.[1] My first ride on a car, & I find it much rougher than I expected. Even in a box car, I expected a comparatively easy ride—it is a constant rock & jolt. The horses, with difficulty keep on their feet.

Slow morning, & stopping at each depot to discharge provisions, & adjust business matters, brings 12 o'clock around before we reach Delhi. Here I meet several men of our company—they look badly, fully confirming Lt. Abney's statement. Responding to the invitation of some of company, I take a little whisky, & we start to Camp Edwards, 2 miles N. from Delhi.[2] It is the camp of the sick & unarmed men. The armed men are near Milliken's Bend, guarding the rail road.

On arriving in camp, I meet so many pale faces, I feel the privilege of grunting is not mine, though I am feeble, & worn down with travel.

Camp Edwards is situated on Bayou Macon, about 8 feet above overflow, & the whole country presents the aspect of sickliness. We get water from numerous springs that gush from the bank of the Bayou.

Sept 26th, Friday.

Nothing to interest to-day.

Sept. 27th, Saturday.

Go to Delhi this morning to aid in drawing rations. After getting there, I feel so remarkably bad, I return before rations are drawn. I would not have gone but for the fact that so many of our men are unable to do any thing.

Sept. 28th, Sunday.

Much exhausted this morning.

Sept. 29th, Monday.

Several of our company from Tallulah[3] come in, & they are quite sick. Report our forces preparing to fortify on this side of the Miss. above Vicksburg. Further report the extension of the Conscript law to the age of 45 years. I approve the extension, not because I approve a conscript law—does not harmonize with Republicanism—but because it comes something near making the burthens[4] of all equal. To force men of certain age to do the fighting in this war, while other men, equally able & interested, are allowed to remain at home, & speculate on the necessities of soldiers, & their wives & children at home, is, to my mind, the grossest injustice.

Sept. 30th, Tuesday.

Blank so far as this journal is concerned.

Oct. 1st, Wednesday.

Four men of our Regiment took their everlasting leap today.[5] Not half of our Regiment is fit for duty. Drilling is dispensed with, both in our Regiment, & Shelley's Battalion encamped near us.[6]

Oct. 2nd, Thursday.

Our men are still dying, & our physicians are almost destitute of medicines. Alas! our situation is a fearful one.

Oct. 3rd, Friday.

Men are still dying rapidly, & many look as though they would die soon.

Informed we are to receive no more bacon for a short space of time.

After a brief survey, I present the following variety to illustrate what men will do after becoming inured to troubles. Some are playing at ball; some are playing at cards; some are singing; some blowing horns; some cooking; some eating; some carrying wood & water; some sick; some *very* sick; some dying; some dead; some with spades & axes starting off to dig graves; some hauling off the dead to bury; some stirring around rapidly, prescribing for the sick; some waiting on the sick; some lounging around as carelessly as though all things were "right side up with care," & others at things too tedious to mention. Indeed, this world is composed of a variety. This picture is not overdrawn—not a single coat of varnish is laid on—but more might be said without the slightest drawing out.

Oct. 4th, Saturday.

Commenced the use of Veratrum Virides under direction of Surgeon Quinn.[7] The therapeutic property of Veratrum consists in controling excited circulation: in my case the circulation is too feeble. Just like Quinn. I told him my heart was affected, & he prescribed Veratrum without inquiring into the nature of my case. I take it on the principle of choosing the less of two evils. If I refuse, beyond a doubt, I will be put to duty.

Men are still carrying the dead to the grave yard.

Oct. 5th, Sunday.

Dregs parade this evening, & orders from Capt. Clarke,[8] commander of the regiment here, that all men able for duty prepare to strike tents tomorrow morning at 8 o'clock, preparatory to marching. All unable to march are to report to the surgeon, giving their names, & the names of their nurses.

Oct. 6th, Monday.

Those able to do duty start to Tallula on today's train. —I remain.

J. R. Cavett returned from Tallula tonight, having completed arrangements for substituting. Though opposed to substitution under existing laws, I am glad of it in this case. Cavett is much needed at home; his health is bad; & his substitute, worth but little at home, presents the appearance of an able-bodied man.

Oct. 7th, Tuesday.

Dr. Jackson, physician to our company, informs me that Dr. Quinn got him to go through the Reg't., & take the names of those for whom other physicians are practicing, saying he would never recommend a furlough, or a discharge for one of those men.

Now, I do not wish to interpose in other men's business (having no engagement with any other physician) but I conceive this is a case in which every man of the Reg't. is interested. It is Quinn's duty to give medical aid to every man of the Reg't., but he has fallen far short of this. Many have been compelled to employ other physicians, or go without medical aid. In the name of justice, I ask, who is to blame for purchasing of an individual that which he is in great need of when he cannot obtain it from one who *owes* it to him? Quinn is paid by the Gov't to furnish medical aid to every man of the Reg't, & if any person has a right to complain, the men, who pay from their own pockets for what Quinn is paid by the Gov't to furnish, have the exclusive right to do so. That equal & exact justice may be meted to all, I enter this disclaimer.

It turns out at last, that ours is the 28th Reg't from this State, Col. Gray having just rec'd his commission. Slow work this; nearly 5 months in the service, & the Col. just commissioned! As a matter of course the whole of his business transactions connected with the Reg't are illegal. Why has he had men punished for not strictly obeying his orders? Who are the violators of the law, we or they? No answer is required from me.

Oct. 8th, Wednesday.

My health not much changed.

Oct. 9th, Thursday.

Two men of Reg't died to-day. Had I the power, I would change things immediately. I would have the men leave the ever memorable grave yard—Camp Edwards—as soon as practicable.

I am almost prostrated this evening, having attempted to assist in digging graves. But few of our men are well, & they are worn down digging graves, waiting on the sick, etc.

Oct. 10th, Friday.

J. R. Cavett left us this morning. I am grieved to part from him, yet rejoiced to see him go home.

About 9 o'clock, A. M., the rain commenced descending, & few minutes after, a norther blew up, & we are now so much pinched by cold that I, for one, cannot keep warm wrapped in my bed clothes.

Oct. 11th, Saturday.

Learn from the Vicksburg Whig[9] that Gen. A. Pike's resignation was not accepted by President Davis, as he is entirely satisfied with Pike's management of Indian affairs, & did not choose to trust others with it.[10] I hope Heindman is now without a position.

Recent reports from Bragg's Army, make it appear he has pushed the enemy almost entirely off the soil of Ky.[11] High time that he were doing *something* for the Confederacy. For some time past, he has done but little more than proclaim martial law, & have his men shot. Indeed, he persisted in this course until the people became so much dissatisfied, it was truly necessary he should desist.

But for the efforts of privates, I believe many of our men would die for want of proper diet. No doubt but some have starved for want of diet suited to their conditions.

Oct. 12th, Sunday.

Three of our men, Barr,[12] Skinner,[13] & High[14] are very sick. Men of their own mess utterly refuse to wait on them. But for assistance from others, they could not survive long. This is a time that tries men's souls.

Oct. 13th, Monday.

A letter from home to-day, dated 5th inst., learn intelligence of the good health of my family.

In a copy of the Memphis Appeal of the 9th inst.,[15] I notice some heavy strictures passed upon Lincoln relative to his late declaration of Martial Law. I think Lincoln deserves censure, but I think we should cast about to see if our own moral sky is clear. If I am correctly informed, & I think I am, errors of the same character are now standing against us. The only difference is, martial law, equally stringent as that passed by Lincoln, has been promulgated by generals of the Confederacy, & I have not been able to learn that President Davis has ever demurred. What greater stride has been taken towards despotism than Heindman's martial laws? Yet, not a man of note in this Gov't, as far as I can learn, has raised his voice against the gross assumption, save the hon. Albert Pike. In that case, he stands solitary & alone.

Heindman, in his martial laws, assumes powers that have never been delegated to as high a personage as President Davis himself. Let us cast the beam from our own eyes, then we *may* see clearly to pluck the mote from our neighbor's eyes.

Oct. 14th, Tuesday.

Three men in Capt. Clarke's company deserted last night. Yesterday they traded their claims, for services, against the Gov't., & left some time in the night.

Dr. Jackson informs several of us that he has undoubted evidence that Dr. Quinn is now subsisting himself & mess on bacon drawn for the sick at Vienna. He further states that Quinn has sold of the same bacon to the soldiers at 29 cents per lb.

We are now encamped at Delhi, having moved today. All are rejoiced at leaving that sickly den, Camp Edwards. I do not think we are in a much better situation, but as we have got started, there is reason to expect we *may* find a better situation.

Oct. 15th, Wednesday.

Surgeon Quinn has issued an order for all, who are able, to go to camp near Tallula—excepting a few to wait on those very sick. I am able to go, but not able to do duty. Dr. Jackson certifies that I am unfit for duty, & that I am not likely to be benefited in camp.

It is thought Skinner will not live long.

Others of the sick are doing well.

½ after 12 o'clock & the cars are here. —A little detention, & we are off for Tallulah.

Got to Tallula about the middle of the afternoon, & learn that our camp is about 7 miles distant, near a plantation named Oak Grove. Fortunately a wagon from our Reg't is here, & by some persuasion prevail on the teamster to haul our baggage. The most of us have to walk, especially those least able to do so—not being able to get on the wagon quite as soon as the more vigorous. A little after 6 o'clock, I arrive in camp completely wearied down. The encampment is 2½ or 3 miles from Milliken's Bend. The ground on which we are encamped has recently been over-flown to the depth of 8 or 10 feet; we use water from a small lake; &, all around proves our situation to be unhealthy—extremely so. However, I think the situation a good one for the purpose for which we were ordered here—that of preventing the Federals from making raids from their GunBoats. Too remote from the river to be in much danger from shells. A lake in our rear, & a levee in our front.

4 of Captain Brice's men are under arrest for breaking open a couple of safes above here a few miles.

Oct. 16th, Thursday.

Quite unwell, but drill with a squad of sick. This is an improvement in military tactics. It is intended as an exercise for the sick, & might be a good thing if controlled by men qualified. Men who do not understand Physiology are not likely to accomplish any good in the enterprise. "Guess work is as good as any when it hits", but who does not know it is more likely to miss than hit? And who can estimate the consequences of a miss?

A camp guard is posted this morning—the first for some time past. This misbehavior of a few brings punishment on all. A camp guard restrains in many things that would otherwise be unnecessary, & an extra number of men are required to guard the men who do mischief. The guards are more severely punished than the guarded. It seems to one, justice demands a different punishment.

This evening the prisoners are started to Richmond,[16] the Parish site of this Parish, Madison, to be delivered into the hands of the civil authorities for trial.

Oct. 17th, Friday.

Meal, Beef, a little sugar & rice, constitute the sum total of the rations we draw. "We draw molasses of Q. M.[17] Madden at $1.00 per gal." The sap he has brought the molasses here for the accommodation of the soldiers. Who, that is greedy of gain, with but little or no sympathy for his fellow man, would not be fond of such a mode of accommodating. Molasses he buys at 50 cents per gallon, has hauled on Gov't wagons, & retailed by a man detailed for the business, at $1.00 per gal. Just the thing to make men of his composition accommodating(?) Could not his excessive benevolence be fully gratified by issuing the molasses to us as extra rations? — the Gov't allows it. Bah! There is a peculiar fitness in a man's honest actions & words. Almost beyond a doubt, Capt. Madden is speculating on money he should pay to us.[18] He has paid the officers, therefore they are quiet.

Prisoners who were sent to Richmond are returned to be tried by a court martial.

Got news by to-day's train that Skinner & Barr of our comp. died at Delhi last night. Barr leaves a family in destitute circumstances.

Skinner, I consider, was no less than murdered. It was apparent to all who knew much of the human constitution that he could not stand the duties of a soldier. Dr. Jackson, who treated Skinner for a heavy attack of pneumonia (which well nigh put a period to his existence) when we were at Camp Jackson, strongly recommended the discharge of Skinner, saying one of his lungs was far decayed as to cause a depression in his chest. After it became apparent that he would not be likely to survive his illness, a discharge was given him. Wait until disease will certainly do the work, & then discharge a man—it is an insult, even to a dying man.

The trial of the prisoners has been laid over for completion at some future time. The prisoners are liberated, their captain standing good for them.

Dark, & a cavalry picket brings intelligence that 3 Gun Boats have arrived, & supposes they have arrived at Milliken's Bend. Orders are given for every man of Comp. B, able to march, to gird on their armor. They are not long getting ready, but, sad to tell, only 24, including Lts. Abney & Sentell, can be found able for duty.

Capt. Milton's Comp. follow as soon as they can get ready. An order to extinguish my light puts a stop to my writing for the present.

Oct. 18th, Saturday.

The remaining companies of Reg't were sent out this morning. Our chaplain shouldered a musket, & fell in to the ranks of one of the companies.

Capt. Brice took a musket instead of a sword—that looks like doing work.

After a few hours, all of the companies return. It turns out there is one gunboat, & one transport, bearing white flags. Suppose they are carrying prisoners to Vicksburg for exchange.

I have just got through handling the largest potato I ever saw. It weighs 12½ lbs. Looks to be a yam, but rather white. Judging from appearances it is the only potato to the vine.

Oct. 19th, Sunday.

This morning I feel much better, having thus far escaped the nervous headache from which I have suffered, more or less, for the last two weeks.

Oct. 20th, Monday.

Hear this evening that Jas. Beard of our company died in Monroe the 11th inst.[19] Farewell friend Beard—you were once an able & willing soldier, but no more will you share with us in the trials or difficulties of camp life.

Rec'd my gun, Enfield Rifle, & drilled this morning for the first time since my return to camp. It worried me very much.

Our officers have bacon to eat, but there is none for us.

Oct 21st, Tuesday.

Went through Battalion drill today, & feel much fatigued.

Oct 22nd, Wednesday.

On guard today, but not well.

I observe Lt. Abney is becoming quite austere & crabbed in his manner, but he has thus far treated me very well.

Have just been thinking of the No. of useless offices of the Reg't. Quite a number hold offices that are purely ornamental.

Shoes furnished by Q. M. Madden for our "accommodation" at the tune of $5.50 per pair. —Another slight touch of Capt. Madden's disinterested benevolence. I am not objecting so much against *his trading* with us, but I would have him furnish us the articles we are entitled to, (& his duty to furnish) & pay us our money instead of speculating on our money.

Oct. 23rd, Thursday.

The officers are now investigating the course of Capt. Madden in relation to his dealings with the Reg't., particularly with reference to paying us off. They are "going through the motion", but he has paid the officers, & I am certain they will find an excuse of some character for him.

A discussion in our comp. to-night relative to the propriety of stacking arms to-morrow morning. The object is to demand pay, having never received a dime of wages. Lt. Abney is notified by A. Miller of the design of the men, & he comes among them to consult.[20] I did not hear him, but I am told he says the men have been treated badly, and insinuates they are not to blame; but uses his persuasive abilities to dissuade the men from their purpose.

Oct. 24th, Friday.

This morning Lt. Abney authorizes Sergeant Grayham to not call the roll.

After breakfast Lt. Abney takes Sergeant Grayham to one side, tells him he thinks we had better submit, for he thinks we will be shot if we do not. He further says he, Sentell & Marks will all resign if we do not submit, & leave us to shift for ourselves. He requests Grayham to use his influence to get the men to return to duty. Grayham declines, but says he will stick to the men.

Col. Gray comes into the Reg't. We hear he says he will disarm us. The men take it calmly, and seem determined to meet the worst bravely. I like to see them do so. I was fearful some would back down when the hour of trial came; & for that reason, I would never commit myself until I saw them fully committed. I have seen some of them flinch. When asked my opinion, I would reply, I do not go into the measure unless you intend to fight to the last if necessary.

Col. Gray comes into the company, orders Lt. A. to have the men called into line.[21] Lt. A. orders Sergeant Grayham to call the men into ranks. Grayham calls, but not a man "falls in". Well done "boys". —After a short pause, the Col. turns short off as though he intended to have us dealt with in a summary manner. He calls the officers together, & asks the captains if they think they can raise men to whip us. Capt. Brice advises persuasion, & Capts. Richards & Clarke tell the Colonel their men are all right, & they can soon arrest us. An effort is made to raise the men, & they get the sum total of *seven* men, after resorting to the hobgoblins—"All the men of the Regt. will be shot if they do not obey their officers, they are *sworn* to obey, & of course they must do so", & C & C. —The *seven* volunteers were substitutes.

Failing in all of his *grand schemes,* the Col. now concludes to adopt Capt. Brice's course, and comes among us, & *requests* an audience. All "fall in" unhesitatingly, but I am quite unwell, & feeling assured all danger is over, I retire. —The Col. proposes if all will return to duty, the case shall not come before higher authorities, & he will use his utmost endeavors to get the mony for us—vows most positively it is not here; says he will send Lt Shepard & Capt. Madden to Alexandria for it, & if they fail there, he will then send to Richmond for it; indeed, he will go himself if necessary.[22] —We shall have it in 3 weeks at furthest. The Col. now bestows a few eulogies upon the company, & the company acquiesce—the difficulty being dismissed for the present. I approbate the course of the men, but differ a little from some of them who think the Colonel was all right from the beginning. He showed no disposition to compromise the difficulty until he found he could not apply coercives. So far as I am concerned, no thanks to the Colonel. —All that we have gained is due our own persistence.

Oct. 25th, Saturday.

This morning, ten men from each company are detailed to cut a road from some point on the R. Road to the river near Vicksburg.[23]

Oct.26th, Sunday.

Quite unwell this morning—so hoarse that I cannot speak above a whisper.

Wagons are brought in this morning to move us to Tallula; thence on the cars to Monroe; thence West of the Ouachita to some suitable campground for improving our health. Obtain permission from Lt. Sentell to start in advance. By walking slowly, I reach Tallula, but I am much fatigued. By permission from Lt. Sentell, I go to the Hotel to remain until the arrival of the cars. Finding all of their beds occupied, I return to camp, hire a boy to get me some fodder for bedding, & make the best I can of a cold sleeping place. Lt. Sentell, learning of my failure, brings Dr. McWright to see me. I had been to see him several times, & he acted each time as he thought but little was the matter of me. I think he was only mistaken. He gives me 3 pills, & in due time they afford great relief.

Oct. 27th, Monday.

A heavy frost this morning. —The cars arrive but bring orders for us to remain till tomorrow for a special train for us. A company of 50 men & 3 commissioned officers are to be left to guard the R. Road.

Oct. 28th, Tuesday.

About ½ after 8 o'clock the cars arrive, & we soon load up, & then get orders to take on the comp. detached for a guard. Our baggage is placed on platforms, & we ride on that as best we can. I am close to the edge, & no very heavy jolt would be required to displace me. —Off, & jolling about like a dray, & traveling at slow car rates.[24]

About 4 o'clock P.M. we arrive at the depot at Monroe. The first man I recognize is *Abe Madden*.[25] I am a little surprised, for I thought he had gone to Alexandria.

With difficulty I succeed in getting on the West bank of the Ouachita where camp. I am unable to speak above a whisper.

Oct 29th, Wednesday.

Rec'd a letter from home by the hand of Mr. Doles. All well except J.R. Cavett.

John Beard[26] of our comp. died last night in the hospital. Another good soldier has taken his everlasting leap.

A difficulty occurred today between private Blackburn & Lt. Abney. From what I can learn from those who saw it, Abney is at fault, but as might be expected, Abney is at large, & Blackburn under arrest.

Sundown, & we are here yet, having been prepared all day to move. —Orders to strike tents tonight preparatory to an early start tomorrow.

Oct. 30th, Thursday.

All ready according to orders, but no wagons—just as we expected. At ½ after 8 o'clock the wagons arrive, & we soon get off for the camp ground, South of the old "Monroe camp."

Oct. 31st, Friday.

We are a little west from the Conscript Camp. All conscripts able to travel were started to Vicksburg last night.

Dr. Jackson prescribes diluted nitric acid for my throat.[27] One part acid to 3 of water. Apply with a mop.

Reviewed by general Blanchard.[28]

Nov. 1st, Saturday.

Our measures were taken today to cut our uniforms. The diluted acid helps my throat.

Nov. 2nd, Sunday.

Lt. M. Cavett visits us this morning, & informs us of the death of D.W. Herron of our company.[29] He was a good soldier; an excellent citizen; & an affectionate father & husband. Farewell dear "Wash", oft will I think of you when reflecting on my turmoils in camp life.

Nov. 3rd, Monday.

This morning 7 of our men left for Bossier with cloth to be made into uniforms for us.[30]

Reported Madden brought in money this evening to pay us off. Where did he get it from? *Monroe* or *Alexandria?* Certainly not from the former as Col. Gray *assured* us on the morning of the (to us) ever memorable 24th ult.[31] That the money was not nearer than Alexandria; not from the latter place, certainly, unless Abe Madden possesses the wings of a fairy, & some dark, lonesome night, while all were wrapped in the arms of sweet Morpheus, made the trip to Alex. & back, bringing along the precious stuff. How it all is, I know not, but Abe & his accomplices could tell.

Nov. 4th, Tuesday.

Gen'l Blanchard has issued an order authorizing the enlistment for 4 cooks to each company—either white or black, to take charge of the cooking utensils & C., & do the cooking for the companies. One chief cook to each comp. to receive $20.00 per month; the others, $15.00 per month each.

If the Gov't furnished all of our eatables, cook vessels, & C. & honest cooks could be had, the measure would be an improvement; but, under existing circumstances, it would breed dissension of the most serious character.

Nov. 5th, Wednesday.

Some of the officers have become somewhat exasperated at so much sickness, & even force some to drill whose looks clearly prove them not to be able. I heard Lt. Marks say to Marion Shaver,[32] whose very appearance proves him to be totally unable for duty—"I will take you out, & double-quick you 2 hours, & if that does not cure you, I will give you 3 lbs. of Blue Mass, work you out thoroughly.[33] It is a perfect shame to have 75 men here, & never have more than 25 or 30 for duty." He seemed to be very angry, & was evidently "whipping many of us over Shaver's shoulders." He knew full well that if he personated, some of us would make a rejoinder. Shaver went out to drill, & reliable men tell me Marks forced him to try to double-quick until he was completely exhausted, & cried like a child.

Nov. 6th, Thursday.

Rec'd $75.00 this evening. $3.28 are yet due me. I did not get it for want of change.

Hear that Shaver's legs are much swollen from his efforts at double-quicking yesterday. There *should* be a final reckoning of such cases.

Nov. 7th, Friday.

J.B. Smith,[34] J.R. Cavett's substitute, died last Wednesday in the hospital at Monroe. He sold his life for a negroe woman & $500.00.

Hear that we will leave here soon for Harrisonburg on the Ouachita, 75 miles below Monroe;[35] there take a steamboat for the salt works in St. Mary's Parish.[36] I am not anxious to meet the enemy on the battlefield, but I am truly tired of the ennui[37] of stationary camp life—believe it is more destructive to life than an active campaign.

A stirring time in camp! Dr. Gray,[38] assistant surgeon of the reg't, gives out he will furlough all the sick, & the men are stirring in every direction to get furloughs written.

I hear of none of the sick being refused except Wm. Burns of our comp.[39] Many appear much elated in view of their prospects. I remark to some of the men they had better get *furloughs* before they start. They reply they do not want better furloughs than furloughs signed by Dr. Gray. However, some think it prudent to consult Col. Gray—and it turns out he does not countenance the act, stating it is nothing but a drunken fit of Dr. Gray's. —What a crest fallen set of men!

I did not "nibble" at that bait.

Nov. 8th, Saturday.

Very unwell this morning, having suffered greatly from asthma last night.

Nov. 9th, Sunday.

The Colonel says 50 men from each company *must* go to the salt works. He will employ *all* the ox wagons in the neighborhood to haul them rather than fail in his purpose. It seems numbers, not efficiency, is the desideratum. Three ounces of common sense are sufficient to discern that 25 able-bodied men are more efficient than the same 25 men would be by being encumbered by 25 sick men. May be the colonel intends to frighten the enemy with sick men.

The companies start, one at a time, and I notice one comp. leaves with but 14 men. The Colonel "snapped" this time.

The sun has just set, & wagons arrive for us. Having all things ready, we soon load and start. —Cross the Ouachita, & about one mile below the City of Monroe, we reach the encampment. Our position is soon selected—not very choice—it is late—we are tired, & it is a little too dark to distinguish slight differences. Our fire wood is taken from a fence close by—we cannot find other wood. Supper is soon prepared, & the first time for a month we have—*bacon.* It is excellent, & the "boys" relish it well. I am too unwell to do so—troubled with violent fits of coughing, & nausea.

Nov. 10th, Monday.

Something more than 6 miles from Monroe, we are halted by Gen'l Blanchard's son, bearing an order from the Gen'l to Col. Gray to "turn over" his extra guns.

Dr. Glover,[40] a Comp. physician, but not a soldier, became offended with Blanchard the 2nd for raising a fog of dust by galloping by the company. Glover said something to Blanchard about the matter, & young Blanchard asked if that was a d-d private talking to him.[41] Glover replied he ranked himself as such. After adjusting his business he went back with the Col., that is, to the comp. in which the "d-d" private insulted him, to have the "d-d" private arrested & dealt with for such impudence. On reaching the Comp., Blanchard, with an imperi ous air, enquires for the private who insulted him. Dr. Glover instantly replied, "I am the man,"—drew off his coat & started to Blanchard. Col. Gray interfered, & requested the Dr. to desist from his intentions. Through respect for the Col. he stopped to pause. The Col. then informed young B. that Dr. Glover was not a soldier, but a citizen. That bit of information presented a different phase of the difficulty to young B., placing him & Dr. Glover on a political equality. Blanchard now made handsome apologies, & the difficulty was dropped. Tyrants are never truly brave. The case needs no comment.

Ten miles below Monroe we bivouac for the night. Walked the whole distance today, carrying my gun, cartridge box, with 40 rounds of amunition, belt & bayonet, knapsack & canteen, & I am much fatigued.

Nov. 11th, Tuesday.

I am considerably exhausted this morning. Had fever during the night. On starting, Lt. Abney offers me his horse to ride, & I gladly accept as I feel entirely unable to walk & do myself justice.

After a march of 4 miles, we halt for a rest. Lt. Abney permits us to go to a house by the road to get milk, butter, & C. Find the lady of the house at her dairy dividing her milk among the soldiers, gratis. She has a quantity of milk, & says she wishes to divide it so that all will get some, giving each nearly a canteen full. Some manifest entire satisfaction, taking what the good lady gives, & returning to their positions. Others displayed a greediness characteristic of the brute; receiving what the lady would give, they would turn aside, drink it, & then present their canteens as if they had had none. I soon discovered I would get none unless some of these getting double shares would stand back. I insisted on my right which was reluctantly granted. Receiving my share, I turned away from the disgusting scene—a lady trying to divide her milk equally among the men, but could not do so because of the frauds they practiced upon her.

Ride on a wagon this evening, as I am unable to march further.

Twenty five miles below Monroe we camp for the night between a small lake & the River. One incessant quack, quack, ascends from innumerable ducks, floating on the surface of the lake. Let's name it duck city?

Now in Caldwell Parish.

Nov. 12th, Wednesday.

A little before day the rain descends upon us gently, & bids fair to give us a steady day's rain.

Col. Gray comes around, & gives orders to pitch tents, saying he will not march us in the rain. We soon pitch our tents & turn in.

J.L. Byrd & myself are too ill to sit up, & we spread our blankets on the wet ground, lie down, & make the best of a bad thing. Send for Dr. Jackson, & he says he can do but little good for us here; that we ought to be sent home. Makes the best prescription he can make under existing circumstances, & says the medicine *may* do us some good. Have lain in tent all day, & the rain has pattered down steadily all day. Last night some men were detailed to arrest several rowdies who went among the citizens to do mischief.

Nov. 13th, Thursday.

Cloudy & damp this morning, & Byrd & myself are unable to walk. Dr. Jackson applies for transportation for us, & is refused. Lt. Abney says we *must* walk. But Dr. Jackson will not yield, & an unwilling consent is given that we may ride on a wagon loaded 2½ feet above the bed—an uneasy seat for a well man. Byrd had a hard chill & fever today, & I have had a distressing cough—sufficient to cause vomiting. However, we have held on to our seats.

In the evening the wagons are crowded with sick men, & many of the sick are compelled to walk for want of seats. Distressing. Many are sick; Dr. Gray has but a few sorts of medicines, & is, the most of the time, too drunk to use *them.* Col. Gray is cognizant of the Dr.'s course, yet the Dr. dissipates with impunity.

On this march I notice another trick of our officers: they take it by turns in going ahead to buy butter, eggs, chickens & C., compelling every man to march in ranks until they get what they want. I also notice they have brandy peaches & C. The privates are strictly prohibited from the use of such articles.

Traveled 14 miles today, encamping 3 or 4 miles below Columbia,[42] the Parish site of Caldwell Parish.

Nov. 14th, Friday.

Too sick to travel this morning. Get permission to stop, & as my officers prefer it, I go back to Columbia in Company with a Mr. Huey[43] of Capt. Richard's[44] company. —Now sitting in a street of Columbia waiting for Dr. Gray to procure lodgings & medical aid for us, he having come back with us for that purpose. —No report from Dr. Gray. Supposing he has left us, Wm Moore, a young man from Capt. Richard's company, detailed to wait on Mr. Huey, looks around & finally procures a vacant grocery. Fortunately it has a good fireplace. —Now in the grocery, & after waiting some time for the promised medical aid, Mr. Moore goes in search of a physician. He comes in with Dr. C.C. Meredith, M.D., of this place. Observing the Dr. is a little backward, I ask him if Dr. Gray arranged with him to treat our cases. He replied Dr. Gray spoke to him relative to our cases, but made no arrangement. I remark it is hard for soldiers to pay their own bills, but I need medical aid, & will pay for it rather than do without. Dr. Meredith now takes hold as though he understands our case, & intends to do something for us.

Suppose Dr. Gray came for another supply of whisky, & having got that left us to provide for ourselves.

Nov. 15th, Saturday.

I am worse to-day.

The ladies of this place are very kind to us. They bring & send us a variety to eat, but we are too sick to eat much of it.

Nov 16th, Sunday.

I feel a little better this morning, but I am quite feeble.

Note. —From the above date, I have been
unable to journalize up to the following date.

Nov. 24th, Monday.

I am truly rejoiced to know that I am able once more to resume my journal.

Huey's brother arrives this evening with a hack to take him home. He has no permit to go home, but he is not without a precedent. His Captain is always willing for his men to go home under such circumstances.

Nov. 25th, Tuesday.

Huey & Moore are both gone, & I am very lonesome.

2 o'clock, & I have had nothing to eat since morning. I am not hungry, but I feel that I need something to nourish, & give one strength. —Dr. Meredith comes

in & says he will have something sent to me to eat, & will endeavor to procure a room in some residence for me. —Soon after he leaves, at his instance, Mrs. Varner sends me some soup. I have eaten heartily, & feel strengthened by it. —3 o'clock, I suppose, & Dr. Meredith in a sharp hurry, & asks me if I am ready to move. That sounds quite euphonious, for I am anxious to get out of this old grocery, & the Doctor's manner indicates he has found a conveyance for me to Monroe. He has informed me that Lt. Abney, who has been sick on the East side of the river, & under the Dr.'s treatment, instructed him to send me back to Monroe, as soon as I could travel, with a recommendation to the surgeon at that post to discharge me from the army—A few words, however, settle the question—I am to move to a private house in this place. He has my blankets & knapsack carried, & I walk—distance, about 150 yds. The first time I have been out of doors since entering the grocery.

I find my room up stairs in the residence of Lt. Colonel Boyd of the 12th Reg't of volunteers of this State.[45] My room has a good fire place, bed, & C. A good fire is made for me, & a supply of firewood laid by the fireplace. I am as comfortable as could be under the circumstances.

Nov 26th, Wednesday.

Rested well last night, & I feel that I am improving slowly. —Spent the day pleasantly in reading Robinson Crusoe.

At 8 o'clock P.M. a Steam Boat passed up the River. I did my utmost to stop it, but to my sad disappointment I failed.

Nov. 27th, Thursday.

Improving slowly—the weather fine—but all attempts to get transportation from here to Monroe have, thus far, proved fruitless.

Nov. 28th, Friday.

Two weeks this morning since I arrived at this place.

Dr. Meredith comes in the morning & informs me I can get passage to Monroe on an ox-wagon if I will accept such conveyance. I reply in the affirmative. The wagon will pass here tomorrow morning.

I now settle with the Dr., paying him $15.00 for his medical services. Light bill, & I am much obliged to him for the many extra favors he has done for me.

Nov. 29th, Saturday.

Up early this morning, & ready to start. Wait patiently till about 9 o'clock when the wagon arrives.

Mrs. Boyd did not charge me for board. Many thanks to her.

Have traveled about 11 miles to Mr. Travin's where Mr. Bridges, the owner of the wagon & team, gets corn to feed. I call for provisions enough for my supper & breakfast, & get some bread, potatoes & milk, free of charge. That looks to be liberal, but why did they not let me have a little butter or meat, as I asked for one or the other, & proffered to pay for it? Know it is not creditable to charge a soldier for a little to eat, but cannot afford to give more than enough to save ones credit.

Nov. 30th, Sunday.

Up early this morning, & feel very well, but after traveling a few miles I turn sick at my stomach, caused by indigestion. —Worse in the evening. I am *very* sick—vomiting & purging freely—a clear case of cholera morbus.[46]

I succeed in getting into a house, & with great difficulty succeed in getting to my bed up stairs, for I am sick, *very* sick. The proprietor of the house, Mr. Noble, gives me every attention. After taking some of his medicines, I am slightly relieved.

He remains with me until bed time, & as I am slightly better, & he is an old man, he leaves me to retire to rest, instructing me to send a negro boy, left to watch me, for him if I should need any thing during the night.

Decr 1st, Monday.

I am not so sick this morning, But I am *very* feeble. Mr. Noble comes up early to enquire after my wants. As I wish to travel, I feel that I should take a little nourishment before starting, therefore I request a little boiled milk. He soon has it prepared, & brings it to me. Mr. Bridges comes along with him to see if I am able to travel. Thanks to him; he has treated me as kindly as he could have done. I told him I was very feeble, but I would travel as soon as I could adjust my clothing, & eat a little boiled milk. I soon dispatched what milk my stomach would receive & that was but little—went down stairs, offered to pay Mr. Noble for his trouble & C., but he would have nothing, stating if I chose to do so, I could pay the boy something for his services. I gave him 50 cents for the boy—he said it was enough—I thanked him kindly, & bade him adieu.

Just as I passed out of the gate, I commenced vomiting, & by the time I had reached the wagon, I had disgorged all of the milk.

With a hard scuffle I succeed in getting into the wagon, lie down, & get on pretty well to Monroe, 7 miles. Arrive at Monroe a little before noon; find Dr. Cummings, surgeon of the post, is absent from the hospital.[47] In the evening I succeed in getting an interview with him. After examining my certificate from Dr. Meredith, he certifies by endorsement that he can not do any thing in any case as my regiment had been transferred to another command, general Taylor's.

Having learned from Sergeant Grayham, while waiting for Dr. Cumming, that Lt. Sentell, with a squad of our men, is in Trenton, I at once resolve to report to him. But, how am I to get there? I am very feeble; too feeble to walk so far. Besides my knapsack & blankets are to go. —"Where there is a *will* there is a way," is an old, but trite saying. I have the *will*, & will seek the way to the utmost of my abilities. Go to a livery stable, but the proprietor is absent; thence to the Rail Road

Hotel to engage a seat on the stage that is to go out to-night. Can not find the agent of that line, neither can I find any person about the Hotel disposed to give me any information of him. I leave the place of corruption in disgust. Once before I paid 75 cents for the privilege of a seat at the breakfast (?) table of this Hotel (?), & despite the efforts of a little negro, there were more flies on the table than any thing else. Go to the other livery stable of this place, & the proprietor informs me he has no vehicle. Quite unexpectedly, I meet Dr. McCartney of Panola County, Texas. Having some acquaintance with him, & he, quickly perceiving my condition, offers me the use of his horse, stating, I am going to Trenton & will walk. I accepted the offer with thanks. He remarked there would be some danger as I was very feeble, & his horse was wild. Judging from the appearance of the horse, & the Dr.'s statement, I conclude it is too risky to try the horse. The Dr. said, "If you can get to the ferry I am sure you can get on a wagon bound for Trenton." I resolved to try, but how could I get there? A moments pause, & again, "Where there is a will, there is a way," came to my relief; that is, I could think of nothing more consoling. To accomplish my purpose, I must go back to the hospital for my baggage, & I feel that I am scarcely able to walk there, & then to the ferry; & how can I possibly get my baggage there. On my arrival at the hospital, I meet a conscript hunting the office at which conscripts are enrolled. No one present could say positively, but all thought it was near the court house. To go there, he must pass close by the ferry. Just the thing for me! He is riding a mule, & I get him to carry my baggage, & I pilot him to the place. New vigor springs up, & I get along more rapidly than I thought possible, though it is with great difficulty that I get along. At the ferry awaiting the return of the ferry boat. I drop my knapsack on the ground, seat myself on it, & feel as though it were doubtful whether I will ever be able to rise again. Now the boat strikes the shore, & knowing, from the great crowd that stands around, that if I do not get on quick after the boat is unloaded, I will not be able to get on at all, a new life springs up in me; I arise, take up my baggage, & walk to the further end of the boat, seat myself to await the landing of the boat at the other shore. The boat lands, I step ashore & look around for conveyance to Trenton. The prospect is unfavorable. The wagons are all directed to the ferry except the one that crossed when I did, & that is loaded in such a way that it would be difficult for me to sit on it had I permission to do so. After diligent search I find one other directed toward Trenton, the driver informs me he is not going there. However, he agrees to haul me up the river bank. Up the river bank. & I begin to look for some other conveyance. One general survey, & no prospect presented itself. Behold! here comes a man leading a horse & a mule. I apply to him, & he readily consents to let me have the horse which has a saddle on. With some difficulty I succeed in mounting him, & strike off in a jag of a trot to overtake my benefactor, but find I can not hold on without moderating to a walk.

Now in Trenton, sick, & worn down with fatigue. I put up at the "Turner House" where I find Lt. Sentell. I show him my papers, & give him a full history of my case since parting from the Regt. He is puzzled to say what is the best course for me to pursue. I suggest that if suitable conveyance be furnished I will go with him to the Regt. He concurs.

After supper (I went to the table but could not eat any thing) Lt. Sentell hands me a letter from home, informing me of the good health of all.

Dec'r 2nd, Tuesday.

I am now in a bad condition. My health is very bad, & I have been paying my own expenses since the 11th ultimo, am still paying them without much prospect of a speedy change, & I am held responsible to the Govt. in a way that prevents me from shaping my own course. Bad management.

Crowds of movers are passing here, trying to escape the dreaded invaders. They have left their homes on the Miss., both in this State & the State of Miss., in great confusion, bringing but little with them. Many of them left the most of their corn crops in the fields. A similar train of emigrants were crossing at Columbia during my stay there. The future prospects of many of them are gloomy. They have no particular point of destination, & are almost out of money. Some are proposing to hire their negroes, for next year, for their victuals & clothes. Distressing!

Small pox in Monroe, & the encampment of that portion of our Regt. left behind when we started to the salt works. H. Sears of our Comp. died of it.[48] When the disease appeared, the most of the men were panic stricken, & were furloughed home. Some did not wait for furloughs.

To-night I talk with Alabamians & Mississippians. They think our prospect gloomy; that provisions East of the Miss. are scarce, & that the citizens of the State of Miss. expect to be overrun by the enemy.

I hold that all permanent Republics necessarily have their foundations in the virtue & intelligence of the people. Intelligence, I think we have enough of to serve as a foundation of this Govt., but Oh! Virtue! Where art thou? Hast thou taken an everlasting flight? Speculation has run riot. The only consolidating element I can see, with *rare* exceptions, is gain—the love of filthy lucre—the all absorbing theme of *almost every one*. Every quirk & quibble is now resorted to to speculate on those who are in situations unable to to avoid it. Even the soldiers, their helpless wives & children, do not escape a ruinous per cent.

Dec'r 3rd, Wednesday.

This morning I move my lodgings from the Hotel to the vacant church where our men moved to yesterday morning, believing I can live cheaper there.

John Martin of our Comp. died recently in the hospital at Monroe.[49] 12 men of our Comp. are now dead.

Dec'r 4th, Thursday.

I am not doing so well to-day.

Rainy weather.

A soldier died at Noble's Hotel in this place, to-day. I am told he lacked much for attention. Poor soldiers, many die for want of attention.

Dec'r 5th, Friday.

A letter from home to-day brings intelligence of the good health of all.

W.H. Pinkard of our Comp. came in on the stage to-day, & reports Mitchell of our Comp., & others, in charge of our uniforms & clothing, somewhere between here & Arcadia.[50] We are waiting for them, & it is now probable we will be off soon.

Dec'r 6th, Saturday.

Heavy frost this morning.

I am quite unwell, spitting blood freely. Call on Dr. Gray, brother to the Col., & he recommends heavy drinks of salt & cold water in the proportion of a teaspoonful of salt to a tumbler of water.[51] Tried it, & got relief in a few hours.

The Dr. says I should, by all means, be discharged from the army. He recommends to Lt. Sentell that he send me home. Accordingly Lt. Sentell gives me a recommendation to Dr. Quinn, now at Vienna, to discharge me if consistent with his power; if not, furlough me during the winter months.

Dec'r 7th, Sunday.

To-day I look for an opportunity to start to Vienna, but find none. Mitchell has not yet arrived. Should he not reach here before I leave, & by some chance I miss him on the road, I would be likely to miss some valuable articles of clothing.

Dec'r 8th, Monday.

Mitchell gets the wagons in this morning before day. We open the boxes, take out our clothing, & I am now ready to start home, having made arrangements with Charles Flanagan of Caddo Parish, to ride in his hack.

Nothing lacking now to start but Dr. Shippy who is to go with us.[52]

Lt. Sentell with the men is now ready to start. They have transportation tickets to Alexandria. I bid them adieu, & feel loth[53] to part from them, but I know I cannot stand the trip with them.

Now 9 o'clock, & Dr. Shippy is with us. We are not long starting.

Before leaving this morning, I heard that many of our men were deserting at Little Rock. I could not expect better under the present management. The conscript law gives our officers almost absolute power over our men, & they have used it to the fullest extent—transcending in many instances.

Night overtakes us 24 miles from Trenton where we stop to stay over night with a Mr. Davis. We find him much opposed to taking us in, fearing some of us may have small pox. After much persuasion, & many avowals that we have no small pox with us, he consents. Mrs. Davis is much offended at our being taken in. However, feeling confident we can not get in elsewhere, we are willing to take sour looks & short words if we can but stay. After getting in, & talking with her awhile, she tones down a little.

Dec'r 9th, Tuesday.

Get an early start this morning, & pay a moderate bill.

Luckily I meet Dr. Quinn in the street of Vienna. After examining my papers, he informs me that a furlough from him now is not worth any thing as he is off duty. He instructs me to go home, & says he will send me a furlough from Trenton after reporting there on the 15th inst. I go on home, risking the chance of being taken up, & imprisoned by E.G. Randolph, the enrolling officer of conscripts of Bossier Parish. I can do no better, so I will abide whatever follows.

Twenty one miles from Minden, we call to stay over night with one Geo. Heard, an elderly gentleman.

Dec'r 10th, Wednesday.

A light bill this morning & an early start. Fare rather rough, though a plenty of the substantials of life.

Got dinner with Mr. Lofton 3 miles, or 4, East from Minden.

On to C.P. Thompson's of Bossier, & put up for the night. Mrs. Thompson informs me she heard a letter from A. Miller of our Comp., read, stating our Regt. was then, the 26th ult., at New Iberia. The Federals had thrown some shells at them at the salt works, but did no harm. One shell was found unexploded, & Albert Spurlin & his mess appropriated it to the use of a fire log. It exploded, wounded Spurlin mortally, & Drew Malone slightly.[54]

Dec'r 11th, Thursday.

Off moderately early, & bill very light.

Five miles w. from Bellevue, we stop for dinner with Dr. Marlow. Get a *good* dinner, the best we have had, free of cost. Thanks to the Dr. for his kindness.

On to Mr. Ellerson's a little before 4 o'clock, & his is the last place we will pass before separating. I apply to Mr. Ellerson for conveyance home. He furnishes me a pony to ride, & sends a boy on a mule to lead the pony back. All free of charge. Good luck again.

Arrive at Collinsburgh just at dusk, turn Mr. Ellerson's boy back, & borrow a pony of G.W. Sentell to ride home. At home a little after 6 o'clock, & to my inexpressible joy, I find all well.

Met Col. Randolph at Mr. Woodward's, & he interrogated me closely relative to the time I expect to remain at home, etc. I have met the Colonel many times before, & I can not now remember that he ever spoke to me before. The aristocrat—he is a full blooded one—will not speak to me when I am on a political equality with him, but that I am now a soldier, a private, & his is enrolling officer, he recognizes, & speaks to me though I am in dirty clothes, & look as much like a dead man as a live one. Does he give me a sympathetic expression? Not a sympathetic word. His enunciation & mien clearly say, "It is my business to look after such fry as you, & when your time is up, you had better get back to the army!" A taste of the reception of a soldier at home.

Dec'r 24th, Wednesday.

Nothing of importance relative to this journal to record for the dates omitted.

The Confederacy seems to be in a strait for men just now. Some of its acts to get men into the army recently amount to an attempt to resurrect the dead. E.g., those men who put in substitutes who have died. The substitutes as the representatives of their employers by virtue of a legal contract, authorized by the Confederacy. Hence, the employers are virtually dead in this war. Further, to force any man into the army, that is, any man who has furnished a substitute—because the law includes the age of his substitute, is *expost facto*—a law unrepublican according to the founders of the old Constitution.[55] Why fight against a government that ignores fundamental laws to establish another that plainly disregards *its* contracts?

Dec'r 25th, Christmas.

The *"South Western"* of the 24th inst. says the N. Orleans Delta contains 4 closely printed columns of the names of those in & around N. Orleans who have taken the oath of allegiance to the Federal Govt.[56]

Dec'r 29th, Monday.

Nothing for my journal during the dates omitted.

Marion Shaver of our Company died at home the 25th inst. Farewell poor Marion. Your parents *may feel consoled* to know that no officer "dressed up in a little brief authority" can again compel you to double quick.

Mr. Adams, traveler, informed me this morning that L.D. Evans of Marshall, Texas, is now in St. Louis, Mo., affiliating with the enemy. I am a little surprised to hear it, but recent events lead to the inference that he may be right.

Dec'r 30th, Tuesday.

Nothing to record.

Dec'r 31st, Wednesday.

Blanchard has again revoked his details of conscripts. He should either release those men entirely or place them in camps; it is a great waste of time & money to have them constantly on the road to & from Monroe. Besides, it displays so much want of ability, that the confidence of all is more or less weakened.

Jan. 1st, Thursday. [1863]

Hear that Lt. Marks has resigned in consequence of bad health. If an officer's health becomes bad, with but little trouble he resigns out of the service, but if a private's health becomes bad, to get out, he must *die* out. There is *some* difference, certainly.

J.L.C. Grayham, our orderly sergeant, having been elected third Lt., the resignation of Marks will make Grayham 2nd Lt., leaving the 3rd lieutenancy vacant again.

Jan. 5th, Monday.

Dates are omitted for want of material.

Hear that Capt. Abny has come home to gather up all of our Company now at home; & that he expects to start to camp the 15th inst. If I *must,* of course I will go, but I fear the result will be as heretofore. I will suffer much, & do the Govt. no good. However, I will endeavor to be of good cheer, & take things easy.

Jan. 7th, Wednesday.

The 6th omitted for want of material.

Reported that Shaver's friends talk of having Marks dealt with, believing the treatment of the former by the latter had much to do with the death of the former. There is a good reason for believing so.

Jan. 8th, Thursday.

J.R. Cavett informs me that Capt. Abny has posted an order at Collinsburgh to the effect that all of his Company now in this Parish will assemble in Bellevue the 15th inst. prepared to return to camp. Otherwise their names will be erased from the muster-roll, & they subjected to conscription. If he will give me my choice, I will take the chance of being conscripted.

Joe Bryan,[57] formerly of our Company, but now at home, having put in a substitute under 40 years of age, was recently forced to Monroe by virtue of an order issued by Gen. Blanchard to conscript all men whose substitutes were under 40 years. Bryan told the Gen. that he would test the case—the General's authority—before he would go into camp. The Gen. said he did not wish to have the case litigated, & at once gave Bryan a detail. A man of limited means could have done nothing in the case—not being able to fee lawyers. Money is the best surety for justice in this Govt.

Jan. 13th, Tuesday.

Nothing for dates omitted.

Three Texas travelers staid with us last night, & informed us that flour was worth $50.00 per hundred lbs.; pork, 20 to 25 cents per pound; corn, 1 to $2.00 per bushel; salt, 10 to $12.00 per bushel. Indeed, speculation is rife every where.

Two years ago, had one predicted that salt at this time would be worth 10 or $12.00 per bushel, & other things in proportion, he would have been as non compos mentis.[58] So the world goes.

Jan. 14th, Wednesday.

Some gentlemen staid with us last night who are just from E. of the Miss. They report our prospects favorable.

Jan 15th, Thursday.

Snow on the ground this morning to the depth of 2 in., & still snowing.

Ate "snow bread" to-day for my first. It is splendid, & is made by mixing the snow with dry meal, & baking in a quick oven.

The State Legislature has passed a bill, granting the wives of poor soldiers $10.00 per month, & $5.00 per month for each child. This is another step in the right direction.

It has also passed a bill for raising volunteers for State defense. It proposes to give 50 acres of land, $50.00 bounty, & $16.00 per month, wages. This looks like Republicanism. The sober, second thought, seems to be taking the ascendancy at last—in this State at least.

Jan 16th, Friday.

Have just completed the reading of Gov. Moore's Message to the State Legislature. It 'rings" very well, & but for its involving the Gov. in a *slight* contradiction, I think it is a pretty fair document for the times. In the first part of the Message, he claims to have done a great deal to prevent the fall of N. Orleans, as much as any one could have done under the circumstances. He regarded the holding of the city as of paramount importance, & thought at one time (when the raft was made secure in the river) that all was secure.

After the fall of the city, however, he issued an address to the citizens of the State in which he said, the fall of the city was expected from the beginning. Would be glad to have an explanation from the Gov.

Jan 17th, Saturday.

By examining the acts of the Legislature of the State in extra session at Opelousas, I find they have passed a Militia bill, calling into service all from 17 to 50 years of age;[59] exempting, *especially the legislators,* & a few others. *Patriotic* men—they can pass a law to place others in the army, but their own wise hearts & just hearts are kept aloof by an *especial* exemption.

The *Caddo Gazette* of to-day's issue comes out in a leader, first censuring, them complimenting the Legislature for not exempting Editors.[60] He thinks it quite a blunder to include Editors, but says, not a doubt but it was a mistake—an oversight & that it will be corrected next May, the appointed time for the next session.

No doubt but Mr. Lacy has the promise of some of the members to that effect, & his leader is intended as a hint to others. Exempt me, & I will call you wise & patriotic; otherwise, you are incapable of the trust imposed in you. I cannot make Mr. Lacy's Leader mean any thing else.

A wise & patriotic Legislature is highly essential to a Republican Government—a wise and honest Editor is also an element of considerable importance; but the former, in our Govt. stands paramount to all. Others, though greatly important, may be dispensed with, & the ship of State move on with but little comparative trouble; but dispense with the farmer, & the whole goes down as soon as the farm produce then on hand is consumed. And we hear of no exemptions for farmers except the rich who get exemption on a mere property qualification. "Straws show which way the wind blows," but one need not resort to straws in the political atmosphere.

Gen. Blanchard has revoked the details of conscripts under the age of 35 years. I think the order for detailing was issued the 11th inst. I hope the people will soon get enough of him.

Jan. 18th, Sunday.

This afternoon I went to see J.L. Byrd in relation to the time for our starting back to camp, he having been to Bellevue to see Capt. Abny in relation to the case. Next Tuesday, the 20th inst. is the day set apart. We are to rendezvous at Mrs. Cain's[61] opposite Shreveport.

Jan. 19th, Monday.

Got a letter from my brother, S.C. King, in the army in Virginia, dated the 17th ultimo. He got safely through the battle at Fredericksburgh.[62] He says the Yankees shelled the city, murdering women & children. Indeed, I fear we are fast approaching a war of retaliation.

Chapter 4

Bayou Teche

I may be mistaken, but my humble conviction is, we will certainly have to submit [to] the domination of Abraham Lincoln.

William Henry King
July 19, 1863

Jan. 20th, Tuesday.

This morning I take another parting from my family & friends to return to the army. What troubles & dangers await me there, I know not; but I have had enough of camp life to know that any thing but feasting on the fat of the land, & downy beds of ease await me. However, I can bear all of this with a stern resignation. Hard living I could bear without murmuring If I could enjoy the company of my much beloved family, that I might occasionally impart a word of admonition to my dear little children as well as enjoy the sociality of an affectionate companion.

While waiting for the mail hack, a driver comes along with a wagon, & I drive a bargain with him to take me to Shreveport for $4.00. He has a good team, & I find him to be a pretty fast driver. All suits me well; for I like to go ahead, though I am leaving loved ones behind. —If I *must* go, let me *go*.

After a pleasant trip, for a wagon ride, I arrive at the ferry opposite Shreveport just before sun-down. I take my baggage to Mrs. Cain's, the place of rendezvous, then cross the river & pay a short visit to the city of Shreveport. In due time I return to Mrs. Cain's for supper, Capt. Abney & several of our men, & some recruits—a jolly crowd of us.

Jan. 21st, Wednesday.

To-day we spend in crossing & recrossing the river, & perambulating the streets of Shreveport, waiting for transportation on a steam boat to Alexandria.

Just at night the Capt. & a portion of the men cross the river to Mrs. Cain's to take up lodgings for the night. The remainder of us attempt to do so, but finding it somewhat difficult to do so as the others took our boat & would not return it to us, we returned to the steamer, Texas;[1] the boat we expect to start to Alexandria on to-morrow, get permission of the Clerk to sleep in the cabin on our own blankets, having previously carried our baggage on board.

Jan. 22nd, Thursday.

This morning we find a private boarding house, & get an ordinary breakfast for 50 cents.

Nothing of note to-day except the most of "the boys" got rather boozy, & one of them, E.C. Cross got into a difficulty, & got two pretty severe blows dealt with a stick.[2] A lesson to him I hope, for he has acted rather badly.

Late in the evening we get on board the boat, & just at dark we start for Alexandria. Feeling disposed to be decent when we can, we get Capt. Abney to propose to the Capt., Stinze, of the boat to let us sleep in the cabin on our own blankets, & we will pay for the privilege. The proposition is made, & he asks $15.00 each. Of course we decline.

Jan. 23rd, Friday.

Passed through the poorest country I have ever seen on Red River.

Jan. 24th, Saturday.

About 12 or 1 o'clock in the night, we arrived in Alexandria, & stopped for the night.

After breakfast, we go ashore, & our Capt. looks around for transportation for us. With some difficulty he succeeds, & also draws rations for us.

Jan. 25th, Sunday.

This evening we carry our baggage on board the B.L. Hodge[3] preparatory to starting to Butte Ala Rose[4] on the Atchafalaya. Just as the Hodge gets off, the Vigo starts a little ahead of us with evident signs of giving us a race.[5] They appear to have up a good head of steam, & the black pine smoke rolls up in heavy columns from the smoke stacks. After about one hours run, lose sight of the Vigo, having passed her without much effort.

In the evening we pass Fort DeRusey,[6] pass on to old River,[7] thence down to the origin of the Atchafalaya, arriving there just after night fall, & tie up for the night.

Sketch of Fort DeRussy from the April 30, 1864, edition of *Frank Leslie's Illustrated Newspaper.* The view in this engraving is somewhat distorted by elevation.

Jan. 26th, Monday.

Start down the Atchafalaya this morning, & after passing Simms' Port[8] a few miles we meet the Don Louis,[9] a stern wheel boat, in Govt. employment. Commissary stores & all are changed from the B.L. Hodge to the Don Louis. It is bound for old river to get negroes to work on the fortifications at Butte A la Rose. This change will make it much more pleasant for us, since riding on steam boats is easier than doing camp duty.

Quite a load of negroes is taken on during the day, valued at from $1800.00 to $3500.00 each. After traveling down the Bayou some distance, we tie up for the night.

Jan. 27th, Tuesday.

This evening we reach Butte Ala Rose after some perilous rubs against the banks & timber in the "Devil's ribs", or "Ox bows," in the Atchafalaya.[10]

On upper Atchafalaya we saw some very nice farms, but for some distance above Butte A la Rose, we saw but few farms; the country is entirely too low for good farming. The whole of it is subject to overflow.

Jan. 28th, Wednesday.

Slept on the boat last night, & this morning we get a little bread & pickled beef for breakfast from Capt. Hardy's men who are stationed here as guards.[11]

About 5 o'clock P.M., we reach St. Martinsville after traveling very hard through a flat country of mud & water—first on a flat boat down a small Bayou—

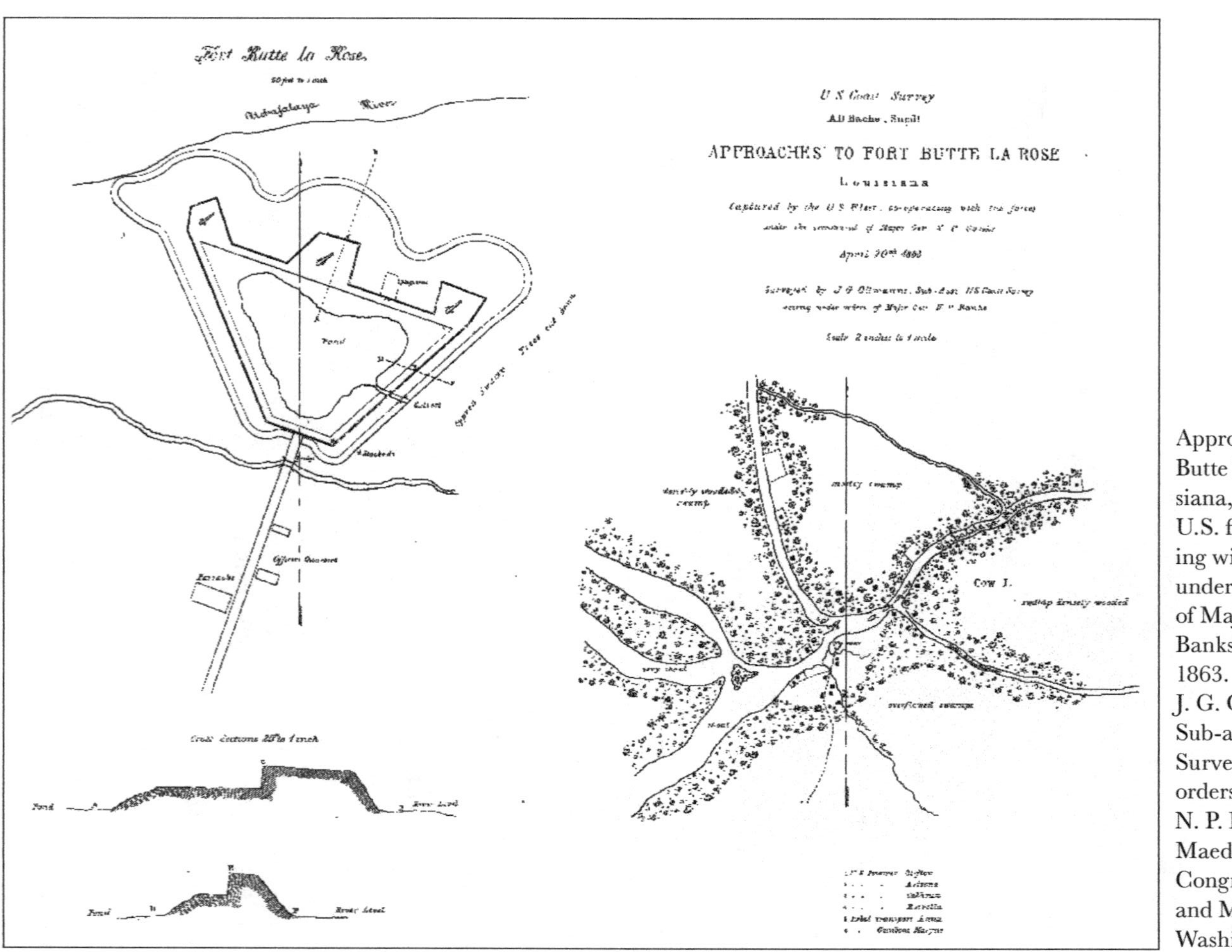

Approaches to Fort Butte La Rose, Louisiana, captured by the U.S. fleet, cooperating with the forces under the command of Maj. Gen. N. P. Banks, April 20, 1863. Surveyed by J. G. Oltmanns, Sub-asst., U.S. Coast Survey, acting under orders of Major Gen. N. P. Banks. J. W. Maedel. Library of Congress, Geography and Map Division, Washington, D.C.

then on foot for some distance—then on wagons 6 or 7 miles.[12] The wagon ride was through one of the most beautiful farming countries I ever saw.

St Martinsville is a very nice town.

The S.M. Darby,[13] a stern wheel boat, in the service of the Govt., has up steam, & is about starting to N. Iberia.[14] Our Capt. finds no difficulty in engaging transportation for us. Bayou Teche, here, is the narrowest stream for navigation I have ever seen. It approaches nearer to my ideas of a canal than any thing I have ever seen.

Start just after sun down, travel till late in the night, & then tie up till day.

Jan. 29th, Thursday.

Arrive at New Iberia early in the morning. After a short detention, start for Camp Bisland where our regiment is stationed.[15] We are rejoiced; for it relieves us of a very long walk.

Jan. 30th, Friday.

Early this morning, we arrive at head quarters of the army at this point. We leave the boat & proceed to our regt., quartered in a negro quarter, near 3 miles below head quarters.

Find most of "the boys" well, & all manifest to be glad to see us.

On the 14th inst., our forces here had an engagement with the enemy, & succeeded in driving them back. Our loss was light. Two of our company were killed, & several were wounded, one of whom died in the hands of the enemy, having been taken a prisoner after he was wounded. The Gun Boat, Cotton, belonging to us was burned by order of General Mouton.[16] From the statements of our men, & the situation of the battle ground, there was no just reason for burning the boat. It is pretty strongly believed the Gen'l had the boat burned to get Capt. Fuller out of the way.[17] The Capt. has done much in the defense of his country, & it is believed the Gen'l wished to dispossess him of his means of operating. Stars can not be seen in the full blaze of a noon day's sun.

Jan. 31st, Saturday.

I have been so unfortunate as to lose my notes from this date to the 11th of Feb. However, nothing of any great interest transpired during the time. There was some fighting between the pickets, & occasionally a man killed.

Feb. 11th.

Yesterday a whole beef was thrown away after having been received by the commissary for us. It looked as if it had died of poverty. Better beef can be furnished, & we should not receive any more such. The officers were much offended at our course, & talked of forcing us to receive it, but we plainly told them we would not eat it, & their trouble would be for naught.

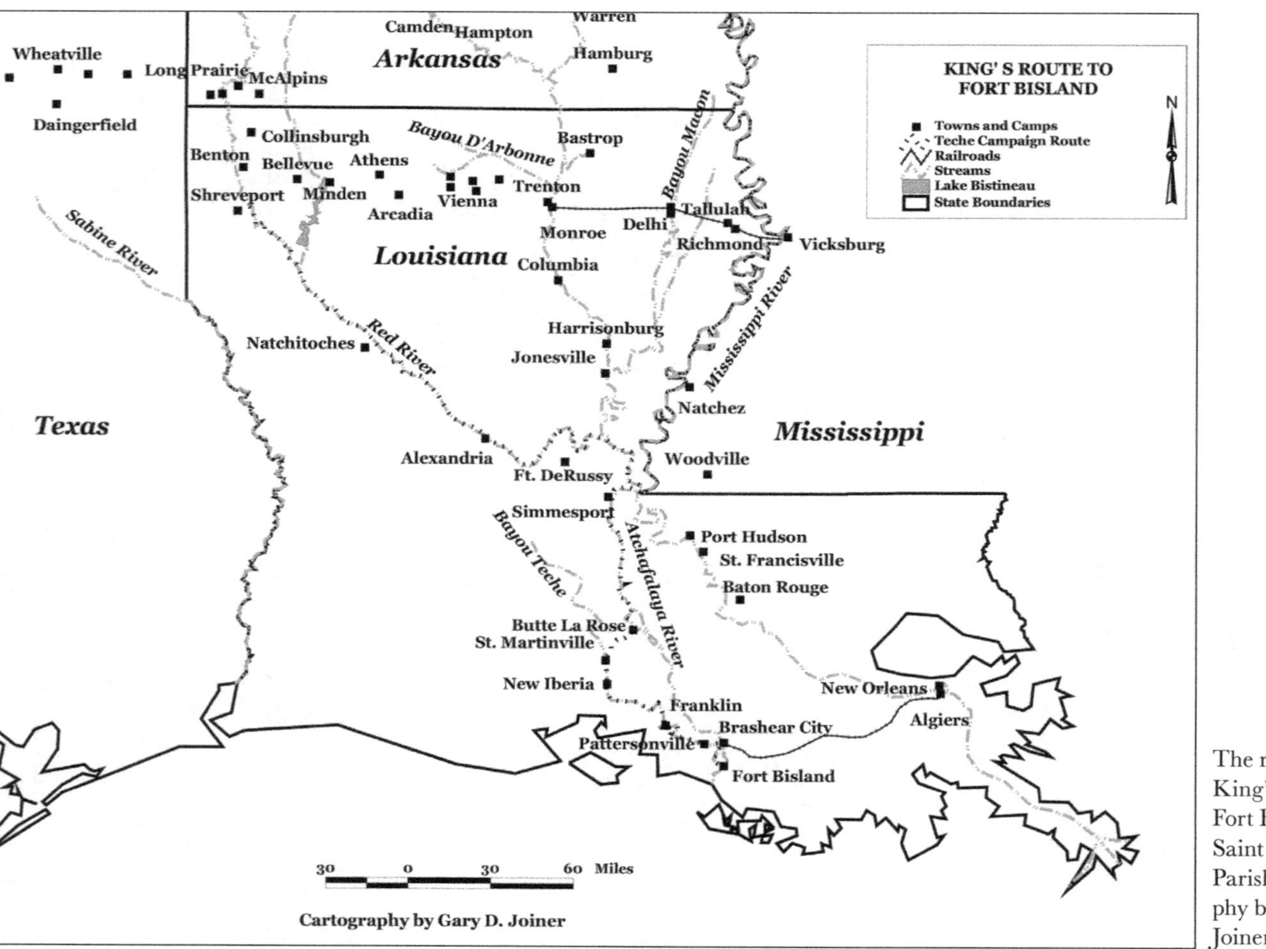

The route of King's unit to Fort Bisland in Saint Mary Parish. Cartography by Gary D. Joiner.

An election on our company was held yesterday for 3rd Lieutenant—vacancy occasioned by resignation of Lt. J.H. Marks. A. Miller received 57 votes, & P.C. Broom 22. An election was also held for 4th Corporal, & resulted as follows: W.J. Cochran, 15 votes;[18] T. Oakley, 13;[19] W.H. Caraway, 8;[20] J. Saulsberry, 3;[21] & myself 11. My name was introduced after several votes were cast that otherwise would have been cast for me. Indeed, I did not wish to be elected, but in answer to the earnest solicitations of my friends, I told them I would serve to the best of my abilities if elected. But, no candidate receiving a majority of all the votes cast, no one was elected. I do not hesitate to believe that if W.H. Caraway had received the highest number of votes, he would have been declared elected. Evidently he is a favorite with the officers. On the 11th the election was re-held. I asked my friends not to run my name, & they consented. The race was between Cochran, 19 votes; Oakley, 31 votes, & Cross, 10 votes. Oakley got the position.

Feb. 13th, Friday.

To-day I take the clerkship of the Company. It suits me well as it exempts me from all other detailed duties.

Mrs. Mugger from Pattersonville visits us almost daily, bringing something for the sick.[22] A short time since she carried all to the hospital. Those who have

Brig. Gen. Jean Jacques Alexander Alfred Mouton, C.S.A. Courtesy Mansfield State Historic Site, Mansfield, Louisiana.

been there sick, testify that Dr. Quinn allowed but little to the sick, & apportioned the remainder to his own "sweet tooth"; hence Mrs. Mugger's change.

Hark! The men are cheering vociferously. —They come in, & state that cheering peace news was read at dress parade.

Feb. 14th, Saturday.

The enemy captured two of our scouts last night.

Feb. 15th, Sunday.

Our fortifications at this place are now completed; at least all work upon them is stopped. They will afford us much protection, but as far as I am capable of judging, the different parts might have been much better arranged, each to the other.

Feb. 16th, Monday.

Last night a portion of our Artillery, a few cavalrymen, & 2 companies of infantry, went down to attack the enemy on the other side of Berwick's Bay. The artillerymen fired 8 times, & drew off. After getting off some distance, the enemy fired at them twice, but did no damage.

Feb. 17th, Tuesday.

Receive 2 recruits to our company to-day. Both—J.P. Vance,[23] & Jas. Robinson[24]—are from Bossier. V. informs me my family was well when he left, the 6th inst.

Wesley Shaver of our company died at home recently.[25]

Including those killed in battle, we have lost 19 men.

Feb. 18th, Wednesday.

Nothing worth recording.

Feb. 19th, Thursday.

Sibley's brigade arrived here last night.[26]

Two privates of the enemy desert, & come over to us to-day. They say others will come if they can.

Feb. 21st, Saturday.

No item for the 20th, but to-day 2 other deserters come to us, & report as the others.

Feb.22nd, Sunday.

Five deserters came to us to-day. They state they think the enemy are preparing to give us battle.

We now see the smoke of the enemy's gun boats. From their movement, there are indications of battle. —Now they commence firing. —After firing 25 times at our pickets, they pass above. Cavalry, artillery, & infantry are sent down, but before they reach the scene of action the enemy withdraw.[27]

Feb. 23rd, Monday.

All quiet at this point this morning. —Hear that our forces repulsed the enemy at Savannah, Ga.[28]

Feb. 24th, Tuesday.

This evening an old Frenchman brings in a lot of eggs at $1.00 per dozen. He refuses to take any money but Confederate money, & will not change money. Some of the men feeling it to be an imposition on the soldiers, play several tricks on the Frenchman.

Feb. 25th, Wednesday.

Seven men are arrested by order of Col. Gray for the tricks they played on the Frenchman.

Feb. 26th, Thursday.

To-day Col. Gray receives an anonymous letter, supposed to be written by a lady, stating the enemy design attacking us next Sunday, at this place, Indian Bend, & Butte Ala Rose.[29]

Feb. 27th, Friday.

An artillery company belonging to Gen'l Sibley's brigade arrived here last night.

The men arrested for the egg scrape are released to-day.

Feb. 28th, Saturday.

We were re-mustered to-day. —Hear the Federals are crossing the bay preparatory to giving us battle.

March 1st, Sunday.

Gun boats are moving about in the bay, & it begins to look a little like the anonymous letter to Col. Gray was not without foundation.

One of the boats came to Pattersonville under flag of truce. I suppose the other boats reconnoitering, as it is customary with them to take such advantages.

Hear the Webb[30] has sunk the Ram at the mouth of R. River, & captured the crew.[31] Good for us.

March 2nd, Monday.

Capt. Abney informs me that Gen'l Sibley has forced Gen'l Mouton to take his post at headquarters. Good: What use have we for officers unless they will remain at their posts? Men failing to stand at their posts are liable to be shot. Why not apply the same rule to officers? Does simply elevating him to a position above us clothe him with superiority of being; or, does it render him more intelligent? If the former, then we should all hold offices; if the latter, so much the more strictly accountable should he be held.

Five deserters come to us to-day.

March 3rd, Tuesday.

P.H. Edwards[32] of our company is appointed forage master of the Regt. Our comp. is now reduced several men by details.

March 4th, Wednesday.

To-day a 24 lb. cannon was planted at our fort. That is *some* improvement at least. But why not bring down those 36 lb. rifle pieces at New Iberia? They are lying there, doing no good, & might be made available to a great extent at this place. Just like our officers; they, in many instances, neglect to use all of the means in their power, & thereby lose many important places.

March 5th, Thursday.

Capt. Madden passed through camp to-day, & the men set up a general cry of, *"Money, Money, Money."*

March 6th, Friday.

I have just finished reading the hon. C.L. Vallandigham's speech.[33] I think it a most able effort, & will be read by future generations as the most patriotic effort made to save a people from destroying themselves.

March 8th, Sunday.

No items for the 7th, but a letter from home to-day, dated the 24th ult., informs me that all are well. Could I be assured of the continued well being of my family, I could bear my own hardships with much more resignation.

March 9th, Monday.

Hear that Terance has ordered the raising of the blockade by the 1st of April. Will do to circulate where all is credulity, but the sound and independent thinker will scarcely entertain it for a second thought.

Hear heavy cannonading; suppose it is the enemy practicing at Brashear City.[34]

March 10th, Tuesday.

The Ram,[35] recently captured by the Webb, has been burned by our own men who were left to guard it. They saw something they supposed to be a Yankee fleet, took fright, set fire to the boat, & left in haste.

March 11th, Wednesday.

The 18th La. Regiment[36] has come to this point. All the better for us here; we may yet need a heavy force here.

March 12th, Thursday.

A letter from home to-day. All well. The intelligence revives me much, for I am quite sick, & much depressed in spirits.

March 14th, Friday.

The 13th is blank in point of an item to record.

The Lincoln congress has passed a conscript law, requiring all married men from 20 to 30 years of age to take up arms. Also, all single men between the ages of 18 and 40 years; allowing each class to substitute or pay to the Gov't $300.00. So it turns out that they are hard pressed for men or money, & are willing to make conscripts of their citizens to supply their wants.

March 17th, Tuesday.

The 15th & 16th are blank in the way of news or camp incidents.

Orders from Maj. Poole,[37] commanding Regt., requiring all stragglers to attach themselves to some Company or they will be arrested immediately. *Very* good if it be strictly executed; but I fear that it will prove as many laws & other orders have proved—*exceedingly* efficacious with some, but with others, vice versa.

Two men belonging to the La. cavalry attached to this division, in playing some tricks with a shell, it exploded, killing one, & wounding two others. 'Tis passing strange that men have no more prudence.

Francis Hungy,[38] J.E. Wood's substitute in our company, having quit the hospital at N. Iberia, & taking a job in a blacksmith shop at $75.00 for his own account, was, by order of the authorities, brought to head quarters by Lt. Miller of our Comp. Lt. Miller thinking him safe, left him in company with McGuire of our Comp. to come down to the Regt. Hungy managed to give McGuire "the slip", got on the boat he came down on, & returned to N. Iberia. As soon as McGuire reported, Lt. J.L.C. Grayham rec'd orders to pursue said Hungy, arrest, & return him to our camp. Lt. Grayham procured a good horse, reached N. Iberia before the boat, met Hungy as he came ashore, arrested him, & to-day returns him to head quarters where he is strictly guarded.

Many of our officers are "blowing" around, asserting that Hungy will be shot, & of right ought to be shot. I happen to recollect that when Hungy was mustered into the service, the officers endeavored to cause all of the soldiers—"& the rest of mankind"—to believe that the Confederate law, in all cases, allowed a substitute to desert when he chose, & the principle alone was responsible to the army. Indeed, that precedent had been established in this Regt. Now, I submit for consideration, whether Hungy is more to blame for endeavoring to evade a fair contract, & thereby injure the other party to the contract, or the officers who, to accomplish a favorite object—prevent further substitution—hold forth the idea that the Confederate law authorized Hungy so to act? *Some* men seem to think it a virtue in themselves to lie & swindle, while, in others, it is a *great* wrong that should be punished with death.

Some of us have just paid $1.00 per lb. for lard. I would be gratified if some ethical writer would explain in what element of the act of the vendor of the lard, the moral quality of the act is discoverable. We are forced to fight in defense of his rights & property for $11.00 per month; we are not furnished with the rations necessary to sustain life in a healthy condition, & our only chance is to purchase them at ruinous prices.

Wesley Davis[39] of our Company passed from the confines of this earth to-day. Alas! A few weeks ago he entered our Company the picture of good health, presenting a fair prospect to live to a ripe old age.

March 18th, Wednesday.

This evening the enemy crossed the bay in small numbers, wounded one of our men, captured 4 or 5, killed 1 or 2 horses, & were then repulsed, with what loss, not known.

March 19th, Thursday.

I am quite unwell to-day. Had a fever last night—am bilious.

March 20th, Friday.

This evening the Yankees cross the bay again. Our forces repulse them without receiving any damage, or doing the enemy any.

March 21st, Saturday.

Hearing this evening the Yankees have left the other side of the bay, except one gun boat & a few men, a small force is sent down to-night to make an attack on them.

March 22nd, Sunday.

Our expedition against the enemy last night proved unsuccessful. Three gun boats were found there instead of one, & it is likely there was a corresponding difference in the number of men.

March 23rd, Monday.

Preparations are being made to make a more powerful attack on the enemy on the other side of the bay.

March 24th, Tuesday.

The artillery return this morning—the other forces are returning—all unsuccessful.

Tipton,[40] Kay[41] & Pochras[42] got in to-day after a long stay at home on sick furlough. Tipton brings me a letter containing the glad tidings of "all well at home."

Our company returned, from last night's trip, wet, muddy & worn down. They had a hard time of it last night in the rain & mud.

Captains Hardy's[43] & Bradford's[44] companies have arrived from Butte Ala Rose.

From the continued moving of troops at this point, our officers certainly expect to make a strong defense at this point.

April 11th, Saturday.

From the last date preceding this, I have been too sick to journalize.

For 2 or 3 days past, the Yankees have been crossing the bay, & making preparations to advance upon us. —This evening they are advancing & driving our handful of advance picket before them.

April 12th, Sunday.

This morning we, the sick, are moved 4 miles back from the breast works. The most meager provision is made for us. Complaining men only are detailed to wait on us. Some of the companies have left the sick to take care of themselves.

Reported the enemy are attempting to land at Shell Mound. —Some thruth[45] in the report I judge, for I see a pretty strong force of cavalry, & some artillery hastening to the place. —Hear occasional firing of artillery during the day, which I suppose to be at Shell Mound.

Heavy cannonading at the breast works this evening.

April 13th, Monday.

Fighting ceased last night about dark, but opened early this morning.

From what I can learn, we received but little damage from the enemy yesterday. I hear of one of our men getting killed, & 2 wounded. As far as I can learn, but little is known of the enemy's loss.

The battle has continued all day with but little intermission. I can learn of but little damage we have sustained. Our gun boat, the Dianna, recently captured from the Yankees, got slightly crippled.[46]

About 11 or 12 o'clock, reinforcements were sent to Indian Bend, where the Yankees are attempting to land instead of Shell Mound.[47] I hear no guns there to-day.

Heavy firing this evening on the battle ground—both of artillery & small arms.

Just before night our firing is slow, hoping to draw the enemy nearer—their cannon are of much longer range than ours.[48]

Just after getting to sleep to-night we are aroused, & told to prepare to move to the hospital at New Iberia; & are informed a surgeon will come to examine us to see who shall go. We rise immediately & make all the preparations in our power, & are now ready. —A few hours longer, & Dr. Jackson comes in, & says all of our crowd must go, & orders us to the bridge on the Bayou, preparatory to getting on a boat. Those who are able, arise cheerfully, & do all they can in assisting us to the bridge. After waiting some time, 2 boats pass without halting. Some one of our men calls aloud, "We have many sick to go on the boat," & the response, "All right," comes to us, but the boat moves forward. —Now comes another boat—the captain inquires if we have any sick to go on the boat. He is answered in the affirmative, & he says he will land above the bridge. From some cause it seems to be difficult for them to land, & the boat, all the while gets further up the stream. Finally it is landed some distance above the bridge. —Wait a few moments for assistance, but failing to get it, B.F. Keith proposes to carry my baggage if I can walk to the boat. I reply, "I do not know whether I can walk there or not, but I have the will to escape the enemy if possible, & I will make my best effort to walk to the boat if you will carry my baggage." He takes my baggage, & I make my best effort. Just before we reach the boat, we discover it is about leaving. Despite our yelling & hooting, they leave, & as there is no other mode of conveyance, the only chance for us, is to return to the cabins whence we came. Dr. Quinn gives orders for all who can walk to leave, & let the sick take care of themselves. Many comply, but B.F. Keith & J.P. Vance refuse to leave us, seeing the wretched condition we would be left in without aid. Not one of us is able to carry our baggage back to the cabins, & some are not able to walk at all.

At last we are all returned to our former situations, & it is now daylight. It being evident that Keith & Vance can not now escape, they set about preparing us something to eat.

When Dr. Quinn issued his order for those who could travel to leave, & leave the sick to take care of themselves, the wind was blowing stiffly, lightning flashed vividly through the skies, & there was every favorable indication of heavy showers of rain. Had they abandoned us at that critical juncture—as they were ordered to do, & as some *did* do—they would have displayed the most reckless disregard of a plain principle of humanity. They *may* be tried for disobedience of orders. If so, I shall strive to prove an earnest advocate in their behalf.

I never was more exhausted, & as I feel fully assured that we will be taken prisoners, I resign myself to my fate, & endeavor to take a little sleep. After many rollings & tumblings, I get to sleep; &, on awakening, I find myself in the full light of day.

April 14th, Tuesday.

An ever memorable day to me. —Another short nap, & I am aroused by the talk of men. I get up; look around, & after hearing the men talk a little, I discover they are Yankee Cavalrymen talking to our men. They talk very kindly to us, & promise us kind treatment.

P.H. Dudney,[49] D.M.High,[50] Rob't Goodwin,[51] J.P. Vance, B.F. Keith & myself are prisoners from our Company, together with others, in all, 23.

The Yankees soon begin to pass us, & they continue to pass all day—infantry, cavalry, artillery, & baggage wagons.

Heard heavy cannonading above us this morning.

This evening a Yankee gun boat passed up the Teche, & a little while after it, a transport passed up.

Late in the evening, I suppose 10,000 or 12,000 of the Yankees passed up on this side of the bayou, & I am told the same number, or about that, passed up on the other side. They inform us they have 15 or 20,000 at Indian Bend. I sympathize with our small army.

Just as we are retiring for the night, we hear another boat passing up. Surely all of our boats in the Teche are "gone up" now.

April 15th, Wednesday.

We are getting along pretty well. The Yankees treat us much more kindly than we expected. As yet, but one has spoken an insulting word to us. He used very insulting & abusive language to some of our men—such no gentleman would

Steamboats *Diana* (left) and *Baltic*. Courtesy Noel Memorial Library, Louisiana State University, Shreveport.

use to a prisoner. He is a quartermaster general, & the privates attempt to excuse him under the cloak of drunkenness—the cover presents no better feature. Tis' sin covering sin.

The Yankees are taking every mule, horse & cart they can find. They kill goats, pigs & beeves without any attempt to conceal the act. The owner of the premises on which we are staying has taken the oath of allegiance, yet the Yankees have taken all of his horses & mules, & are killing his goats, pigs & yearlings to subsist themselves & us upon. Not an envious protection of property.

Other Yankee forces go up to-day.

Our guard inform us their men had a hard fight yesterday. Not quite so good on their side as they anticipated yesterday. When passing here they said they were fully confident of killing or capturing all of our men.

Reported—the Yankees have taken a great many of our men prisoners.

April 16th, Thursday.

About a regiment of the Yankees went below this morning. A few others went up.

One of the prisoners died last night—a stranger to me.

Two or 3 squads of negroes pass this morning on their way to Brashear City. About 20 in one squad—men, women & children—bear evident signs of having been in the marsh.

Many of the Yankees assent they are not on favor of freeing the negro, & would fight no longer if they knew such to be the purpose of their gov't. When the squads of negroes passed on their way to Brashear City, I pointed to them, & asked those of the Yankees who said they were opposed to freeing the negroes, what that meant if their gov't did not intend to free the negroes. The ready reply is, "It is not the *real* intention of the gov't to free the negroes, but it finds it necessary to take the negroes from their owners for the present to crush the rebellion. When that is effected, we have no doubt but the negroes will be returned to their proper owners." Such is their delusion. They are caused to believe the Gov't does not *really* intend to free the negro, to encourage them to fight.

April 17th, Friday.

Other negroes come about us to-day. I heard one sat to the Yankees he did not intend to leave his master—had come among them to see—his master had always furnished him what he wanted, & treated him well in every respect. Lt. York, commanding our guard, said to him, "You are the most sensible negro I have met with."

The Yankees carry a large drove of mules below to-day—Mules they have taken from the citizens. It is outright marauding; an act discountenanced by all civilized nations. Indeed, they respect none of the civilized rules of war except so far as they find it their policy to do so—fearing retaliation.

From the best information I can gather, our men worsted the Yankees yesterday, & day before, though our men suffered much.

April 18th, Saturday.

Orders are given for us to be taken to Brashear City.

This morning the Laurel Hill[52] went down with a number of prisoners on board.

This evening we take passage on a steamer for Brashear City. My knapsack & blankets are missing. I got a negro boy to take them to the boat, & he threw them on with the captured baggage. As my knapsack was very full, I suppose some fellow seized it, thinking it a prize.

Through the aid of 2 Irishmen—one a boat hand, & the other a guard—I recover my blankets & the most of my clothing, though I have lost in clothing & little conveniences to the amount of at least $ 50.00. The Yankees give me a new knapsack. Thanks to them.

Just before we reach Pattersonville, the boatmen commence looking out for a wood pile, & as it is dark, they miss it & get below Pattersonville before discovering their error. They turn back, find the wood above P., take on a large lot of it, & lie over the balance of the night. Their free (?) negroes took on the wood, though the rain poured down in torrents. Each one was thoroughly drenched. Don't think I ever saw a master treat his negroes worse.

Transport *Laurel Hill.* Courtesy Noel Memorial Library, Louisiana State University in Shreveport.

April 19th, Sunday.

Pretty early this morning we arrive in Brashear City in the midst of one of the most severe rains I ever witnessed.

About noon we are moved from the boat to a warehouse, & placed under guard. Those who were very sick were taken to the hospital. Our quarters are good; the floor is covered with straw, & the house, in every way, well calculated to protect us from any inclemency of the weather of this climate.

The present guards we find are much more strict than our former ones; though the most of them seem to be very kind.

Now in the night, & our appetites begin to signify sharply that a little for the stomach's sake would do us no harm. We got a few crackers, & some spoiled beef before leaving the boat this morning, & have had nothing since.

Here it comes at last! I hope there is something good—I know we have waited long enough. But—I am deceived—nothing but crackers & weak coffee. As grumbling will do no good, we can just eat it or let it alone.

April 20th, Monday.

This morning we get the same kind of coffee as last night—the "boys" say, 3 grains to the gallon & crackers enough to last us to N. Orleans.

Between 7 & 8 o'clock we are conducted out & quartered in box cars preparatory to starting to N. Orleans.

About 4 o'clock we arrive in Algiers.[53] As soon as we leave the cars,[54] the ladies crowd around us, & manifest great sympathy, but are compelled by the guard to stand aloof. They seem *very* anxious to converse with us, but are strictly forbidden. One old lady is very anxious to enquire after her son who was in the battle, but even that privilege is denied her. Brutality if I am permitted to judge.

One lady brings a bucket of water, sets it inside the guard line, & says, "here men, is water for you." We partake freely, for we are very thirsty; & as I swallow the cooling draught it seems to one that if all the Southern people were as sympathetic & patriotic as this lady, our Confederacy would to-day be in a much better condition. But, the kindness of the ladies does not end here, for another hands in a few news papers, & a third passes in some sweet cakes. May the benedictions of Heaven rest on them is the prayer of one too wicked, perhaps, to make such petitions.

Notwithstanding it is strictly against orders to converse with us, they give us many hearty good wishes, & some few of us drop a few words to them when not strictly watched.

After a short waiting the city guard come out, & we are delivered into their care. They march us off—to where we know not—the sick in the rear. The van led off in common time, & as many of us are very feeble, it is impossible for us to keep pace with them. Some of the guard hurry us beyond our ability. Unfeeling retches![55] At last one of the guard remarks, "these are sick men, & cannot walk fast; why do you hurry them?" The hurrying then ceased, but one very ungentlemanly guard continued to make all manner of sport of us, saying, "this is a dead march," "This reminds me of a funeral procession," & many other remarks equally unbecoming.

As we passed along, a lady waved her handkerchief at us, & a guard perceiving it, ordered her to take it down instantly, or he would shoot it down. ——

We are in the Belleville Foundry,[56] on the basement floor which is dirty in the extreme. The building is near 200 ft. long; 40 or 45 ft. wide, & is well secured against the escape of prisoners. About 600 of our men are on the upper floor.

The country from Brashear City to this place is very low & swampy, but occasionally there is a place or spot of very fertile land. On this road, a distance of 80 or 100 miles I suppose, I saw what I conceive a fair specimen of Yankee farming with free negroes. They are cultivating a few very small patches, & they are, most of them, very late, & in sorry condition. I noticed these things as well as I could, & do not recollect that I saw a negro at work as we passed. I saw many leaning on their hoes, & gazing at us as we passed.

At sunset, feeling much fatigued & hungry, having eaten nothing but crackers, except a little sweet cake, since leaving Brashear City. "I lay me down to sleep." ———

Near 9 o'clock, I suppose, I find myself awake & very hungry. I move around near the guard at the door, & remark to him, "if this is the way you feed us, I think you will scarcely be able to make Union men of us as many of your men have expressed a hope of doing." He replied it was a shame to treat so, & advised me to kick up a muss about it. I said "no, I am a prisoner & do not wish to get myself into a worse difficulty." Just at this time he was relieved from his post, & told me to wait there, & he would make an effort to obtain something for me to eat. I waited patiently, but finally, feeling so much exhausted from fatigue & hunger, I lay down to rest. However, not long before he brings me some nice beef & light bread with a little vinegar. Never tasted anything that I relished better. He promises me more to-morrow morning if rations are not issued to us.

April 21st, Tuesday.

This morning we are still unfurnished with provisions, & my friend of last night does not comply with his promise. But his absence is easily accounted for. The Captain who has charge of us found one of our men in possession of a bit of meat & bread which he supposed had been obtained from one of his men. He made considerable ado about it, & threatened heavy punishment to those who would furnish us. —About 10 o'clock, A.M., a Mrs. Cobb sends us a basket of provisions—a variety, & of the nicest kind—enough for one meal for all of us. Many thanks to Mrs. Cobb.

The Yankee Captain comes in, & instructs us form into mess by selecting a chief preparatory to drawing rations. We comply readily, for we are hungry in our imaginations. Though we have just eaten a hearty meal, we have been hungry so much, we fear a little.

About 4 o'clock, P.M., we eat our dinner of drawn rations. They have had us here about 24 hours, & this is the first they have given us to eat.

This evening 40 or 50 prisoners are brought in from Butte ala Rose.

April 22nd, Wednesday.

Seventy five or eighty more prisoners brought in.

April 23rd, Thursday.

Further scraps of evidence from prisoners to-day, that our army is not so badly cut up as previously reported.

April 24th, Friday.

Still in prison, & doing as well as could be expected, though we are much more closely confined than any need for. The buildings are composed of 3 large, 2 story houses, forming 3 sides of a square. The 4th, & front side, of the square is formed by a brick wall 12 or 15 ft. high, with gates that are constantly locked. In the center of the wall is a fourth 2 story building—head quarters of officers commanding the prison. We occupy one of the buildings. A second contains the well, & we do our cooking in it. A third is occupied by the Yankee guard. The windows of all the basement floors have iron grates, & are well guarded on the out side, yet have a very limited access to the yard.

Sixty thousand troops are reported as having arrived as reinforcements to the Yankee army. Discouraging to us, but I hope it is as many other Yankee reports—false.

April 25th, Saturday.

The citizens of this place continue to send us delicacies for the sick, & clothing for the needy. Many papers, books, pipes, cigars, & c., are sent in. We have excellent fare in the way of eating. Whether we succeed or not, I believe these people will receive a just reward for their kindness.

April 26th, Sunday.

I am quite sick to-day. My stomach & bowels are much deranged.

Twelve or 15 more prisoners brought in to-day.

April 27th, Monday.

Near 200 more prisoners brought in to-day. I learn from one of them who was taken between N. Iberia & Lafayette, that the last intelligence he had from our forces, they had received not reinforcements; that they were much scattered; that they were making for Texas, & the Federals were picking up our worn out men rapidly. Poor fellows; they have been compelled to fight from the beginning without relief; many times hungry, & many of them without coats, or blankets on which to rest their wearied limbs at night.

The Yankees are now nailing boards over our windows to prevent us from looking at the ladies as they pass. I think the prime object is to punish us as much as possible—both to gratify a spirit of revenge, & frighten us to take the oath of allegiance. They know, though they deny it, that we have a government yet capable of retaliation, & any unnecessary punishment must have an excuse. They know the exclusion of light & air will engender disease.

April 28th, Tuesday.

A Federal paper, the *Era* of to-day's issue, states Confederate money has advanced in the North since the fight at Charleston.[57]

April 29th, Wednesday.

Learn from prisoners brought in yesterday, that gen'l Banks has taken up a complete halt at Opelousas; that 2 or 3 regiments were seen on their way back to Brashear City; that they had nearly completed the demolition of our breastworks at Camp Battery Tuisilier.[58]

Many of the French, called Cagians,[59] are taking the oath of allegiance to the U.S., & leaving the prison. They have partaken largely of the donations of the fair ladies of this place—knowing the spirit in which the articles were given. The object of the donors was to minister to the wants of those engaged in the cause of freedom as espoused by the Southern people. They are of the belief that this oath relieves them from all military liabilities—not taking notice that they take the most solemn oath to defend the U.S. against all of its opposers whomsoever, whether foreign or domestic. Verily, they need enlightenment.

As those who take oath pass out, the Federal officers take much of the clothing & blankets they have received here. The Yankee soldiers report the ladies & gentlemen are taking some of the articles from the Cagians [Cajuns], left to them by the officers, as they meet them in the streets.

April 30th, Thursday.

Many more take the oath to-day.

This evening about 15 more prisoners are brought in.

The ladies have sent in but few provisions to-day. Who would be astonished if they were to withhold their bestowals altogether? So many who have partaken of their donations have proved themselves traitors.

May 1st, Friday.

This has been a beautiful May day, & thrilling reports have been received from our army. As they need confirmation I will not itemize.

May 2nd, Saturday.

Something over 200 of the prisoners are conducted to a boat this evening, & sent up the river: some say to be exchanged, & others say to be paroled, but all is conjecture.

Many more are taking the oath this evening; indeed, more have applied than can be accommodated.

To-night notice is given that to-morrow at 9 o'clock the opportunity for taking the oath will be closed.

May 3rd, Sunday.

Many are taking the oath this morning. I verily believe ½ of the 1200 prisoners brought to this place will have taken the oath before they are done. Others besides the Cagians are taking the oath.

May 4th, Monday.

I had a chill last night, & I suffered much all day.

This evening we are moved up stairs, & 38 prisoners from Baton Rouge are placed in our room.

May 5th, Tuesday.

To-day I feel something better, though I dread my chance for a chill to-night.

Reported this evening we will be paroled to-morrow, & sent to P't Hudson.[60]

May 6th, Wednesday.

Rejoiced to know I missed a chill last night.

Now evening, & we are still here.

From an order issued by Gen'l Banks, & published in the Era, I learn that a Federal Capt. has been killed by some one on bayou Cataubla,[61] & Gen. Banks has therefore issued an order for the arrest of 100 citizens nearest the scene of action to be held as hostages till the one committing the deed can be found. Is that justice?

May 7th, Thursday.

My health is very bad.

Four of our men were taken from among us to-day, & carried over to the city for closer confinement. We do not know the charge. It is said one of them, Vincent, shot a prisoner in Virginia.

May 8th, Friday.

This evening all of us are called into 2 ranks, & the roll called alphabetically. It creates quite a stir among us. Many think we are going to leave instanter. —But it was a mistake.

May 9th, Saturday.

A little better this morning, though I am quite feeble.

Now evening, & the most of us here received paroles.

Just as we finish receiving paroles, the Steamer Iberville,[62] Capt. Dillon, formerly of the Morning Light,[63] arrives. The Capt. who has charge of us comes up stairs, & orders us to prepare to leave. Cheering orders to us! & now a game of true hurly-burly is begun. It seems that each one is trying to render things as confused as possible.

A little longer, & the Capt. orders us to *"fall in alphabetically."* He tries to get the men into ranks alphabetically, but makes poor success—each one is afraid he will be behind some one. At length he tries by having the roll called, & the men fall in as they answer to their names. By this means, he makes a partial success.

After searching us pretty minutely, & taking blankets & other valuables, we are marched to the boat, & as soon as all get on board, the boat puts off at a rapid rate up the river.

May 10th, Sunday.

About 9 or 10 o'clock, A.M., we arrive in the port of Baton Rouge. Here we tie up for the day as the Yankees are shelling Port Hudson. They get no response from our guns.

Here, for the first, I see negro soldiers, all in full uniform.

May 11th, Monday.

This morning we start for Port Hudson. Just before 12 o'clock, M.,[64] we hove in sight of the fortifications—a little nearer, & a signal gun is fired. The Iberville is landed, & awaits the arrival of our transport.

Just below us are 11 gun boats—the Richmond,[65] Essex,[66] & 9 mortar boats.

Our transport, Star Light,[67] conveys us to the landing at Port Hudson, & I manage to ride on a wagon up the steep bluff.

Here I find myself too sick to travel, so myself & others in a similar condition are sent to the hospital. Find the hospital in a deep hollow at the upper end of town, supposed to be mainly out of danger of the enemy's shells, though it is known not to be entirely safe as some shells have been thrown into the immediate vicinity.

The principal growth is sweet gum, water oak, & beech. How I love to snuff the free, pure air, and once more drink of good well water. The very chirping of the birds is relief to my pent-up soul.

How different my situation to-day, & 12 months ago. I was then mustered into the Confederate service.

May 12th, Tuesday.

Last night about midnight, the Federals, as has been their custom for several nights past, commenced bombarding this place. They kept up a pretty heavy

King's route from his capture to his return to Collinsburgh. Cartography by Gary D. Joiner.

bombardment for 2 hours. Some of my comrades got up to witness the scene. They described it as magnificent. I was too unwell to turn out as a spectator. From what I hear this morning, they did little or no damage.

Several of the sick of my crowd are sent to Jackson, La.,[68] about 15 miles distant.

Reported that the Federals are within 7 miles of this place advancing.

May 13th, Wednesday.

This morning Dudny & Monk of my crowd left early.[69] I have no acquaintance left.

The Federals came in sight of the breast works to-day, & then withdrew.

May 14th, Thursday.

I am told this morning the Federals shelled this place again last night, but I did not hear it as I slept too soundly. I am so much inured to trouble & difficulties that I can now sleep while danger is in fearful proximity.

May 18th, Monday.

For the dates omitted, nothing more than the usual rumors & shelling.

Hear this morning that Gen'l Banks has been to Alexandria, & is now descending Red River, supposed to be making for this place.

Hear that Gen'l Pemberton is fighting the Federals at Jackson, Miss., & he is falling back.[70]

Two prisoners brought in—one is a captain.

May 19th, Tuesday.

This morning I obtain a permit of Dr. Harrington[71] to leave the hospital, & start for home. I know that I am in bad condition to start on such a trip; but here they have spoiled corn meal & flour, & but little of any thing else to eat, & as my bowels are in a depraved condition, I find it difficult for me to recuperate on such diet. By abstaining a few days, I improve, but so soon as I commence full diet, I relapse.

There is another important reason why I should leave; the Federals are shelling this place every night, & occasionally in the day. They have been fighting by land, & Gen'l Banks is, no doubt, advancing against this place. I am paroled, hence cannot fight if I were able. Since I am in danger of being killed, or retaken & dealt with as having violated my parole, I think it prudent that I should make my escape if practicable. Indeed, it is only in view of these facts that Dr. Harrington consents for me to leave.

About 10 o'clock, I & Wm Spencer of Claiborne Parish,[72] & belonging to the Crescent Regiment, start. After considerable botheration, we get a pathway said to lead to Bayou Sara.[73] We trudge along, resting every ½ mile, or a mile.

About 2 o'clock, we find a house, (having not yet found the road to Bayou Sara) & call for something to eat. We are denied, & directed to the next house.

After another hard walk for men in our condition, we find the place. The proprietor, Mr. Slaughter, flatly denies us any thing to eat. However, his lady, more kind hearted, gives us something.

After dispatching our repast, & taking a short rest, we start on in company with Mr. Ghaston,[74] a discharged soldier from Port Hudson.

Two miles further on, we take up for the night, completely worn down, scarcely able to drag one foot before the other.

May 20th, Wednesday.

Off early in accordance with previous engagement. Bill high—one dollar each. So sore and stiff I can scarcely travel.

A little Frenchman has fallen in with us who manifests inability to speak more than a few words in English.

About 9 o'clock we are so worn down we cannot go further without a long rest. Stop till after dinner which we get free of charge. Dinner over, & we travel on a few 100 yards at a time. Try every way in our power to get conveyance, but fail.

Three miles from Bayou Sara we call on a wealthy widow, possessing the most magnificent front yard I ever saw. Four negroes were engaged in working this beautiful yard, while two others were engaged in handing water from an artificial pond to water favorite plants kept in a fine glass house. We proposed to recompense her if she would furnish us transportation to Bayou Sara. She replied very decidedly that she could not furnish us transportation, neither could she entertain us during the night. She then gave us some fresh water & some plums; got into her fine carriage, drawn by a pair of fine bay horses, & her driver drove off at a double quick rate.

Had she philanthropy or patriotism, either? I think not. She went in the direction of Bayou Sara, perhaps there, & might have taken us, had she possessed a true heart.

A short rest over, & we start, dragging along as best we can. From the ornamental yard to the main road, we pass through the most beautiful avenue water oaks I ever beheld.

Reaching the road, fatigued to almost complete exhaustion, we stopped to take a few moments rest, & while resting, a negro comes along with a 2-mule wagon, & we engage passage with him to Bayou Sara. We reach our destination just before sunset. Put up at a hotel kept by a widow. Two Federal gun boats are anchored in the river opposite this place, so we are very quiet. Do not stir about town that we may not be found out.

May 21st, Thursday.

Up early, & feel refreshed, though sore & stiff.

The bombardment at Port Hudson last night was very heavy; it jarred the sash of my window. The distance by the road is 12 miles.

Bayou Sara is on the levee, & St. Francisville, in which place we staid over night, is above on an elevated bluff.

We pay our bills, $2.50 each, 50 cents less than custom, & then attempt to reach the R.R. Depot in Bayou Sara, having transportation tickets thence to Woodville, Miss.[75] At the brink of the bluff, we find a guard who refuses to let us proceed further; says the cars do not run since the arrival of the gun boats, & Banks['] encampment on the other side of the river, all of which are now visible. While talking with the guard, a negro boy comes along with a 2-horse buggy bound for Woodville. We propose to take passage with him, but he fails to assent. Learn from him that the buggy & horses belong to a hotel keeper in Woodville, so we take seats without his consent, believing a reasonable fee will satisfy the owner.

Near 5 o'clock, P.M., we arrive in Woodville, Wilkinson County, Miss., after a buggy ride of 27 miles. Settle our fare with the hotel keeper, & put up with him for the night, & engage him to send us to Natches to-morrow for $15.00 each.[76] Today's ride cost us $22.00 each.

May 22nd, Friday.

Our fare for the night, $3.00 each, settled, & we are on the road to Natches [Natchez], in a wagon drawn by the buggy horse, & a sorry mule.

Just before the setting of the sun, we reach Natches [Natchez], distance 35 miles, a day's hard travel. The road is very rough & hilly; the team sorry; the driver sorrier, & the wagon none too pleasant. Several times during the day, Ghaston & Spencer desponded of getting to Natches any time in the evening, or even at night; but I insisted we *must.* "We have paid dearly for the ride, & must have it." "Drive up, driver," and away goes the old wagon, over rocks, chunks, stumps, & hills, almost throwing us overboard many times.

Take lodgings at the Jefferson Hotel.

Hunt the office of the Quarter Master of this Post, but the door is closed, & we must wait. On a second application we procure tickets to Trinity,[77] thence to Monroe.

The Q. M. instructs us not to take less than $7.50 each for our transportation tickets—we have been told they are worth only $2.50 each.

May 23rd, Saturday.

We start about 6 o'clock, A.M., cross the river, & give a negro $1.00 each to take us in a wagon to Lake Concordia,[78] distant 2 miles. On arriving at the lake, we fail to find any one to take us to Trinity. The men of the skiff line are in Natches. We walk on 2 miles further, & being too much fatigued to walk further, we obtain permission of a lady to remain with her until her husband returns home. She said he would sometimes send soldiers about 10 miles. —A short rest over, & the old gentleman comes in. He furnishes us dinner, & sends us, in a cart, 12 miles for $10.00. Cheap when compared to other bills. We accomplish the 12 miles by 6 o'clock, & put up for the night.

May 24th, Sunday.

Pay our fare, $2.00, & set off on foot. Our proprietor owns a ferry, & he ferries us free of cost. —Walk near 2½ miles, & feeling unable to proceed further on foot, we engage with a man to send us in a skiff to Trinity, a distance 11 miles, for $6.00 each.[79] By arguing the question strongly, we prevail on him to take our transportation tickets at $7.50 for the whole.

Between 12 & 1 o'clock we reach Trinity. Find the steamer S. H. Tucker here,[80] but it will not leave here before to-morrow, & will then go no further than Harrisonburg. As there is no other chance for locomotion except on foot, we conclude to wait.

May 25th, Monday.

Near 7 o'clock, A.M., we start for Harrisonburg on the S. H. Tucker. —Arrive at H. at 12 o'clock, M., & finding no boat bound for Monroe, we decide to wait for one. Our tickets paid our way this far, & we still hold them.

Quite sick to-day.

May 26th, Tuesday.

As there is no prospect of a boat soon to convey us to Monroe, we draw 5 day's rations, & engage an Irish woman to cook it for us. She charges $2.00—cheap according to other prices.

May 27th, Wednesday.

Heavy cannonading at Vicksburg at this instant—10 o'clock, A.M.

The steamer Pauline[81] arrived here a half hour since, & I learn from Lee Carrier, engineer, that Lt. Sentell died on the retreat above N. Iberia. I lament his death.

The Pauline has one engine broken down, & the Captain desires to go to Shreveport to have it repaired, but Col. Logan,[82] commandant of this post, orders him into Little River[83] on Gov't business. What it can do in that River with but one wheel, I would like to know. After rations are drawn & taken on board, the order is revoked, & to my inexpressible disappointment the boat starts to Shreveport.[84]

The chance for transportation being uncertain, I start on foot about 5 o'clock, P.M., leaving Ghaston & Spencer behind, & at 9 o'clock, P.M., halt for the night, having traveled 5 miles. When night came on, I would have bivouacked, but I could not find water.

May 28th, Thursday.

My bill this morning is $1.00—the cheapest since leaving Port Hudson. —Heavy cannonading at Vicksburg.

Night, & I have traveled 7½ miles, having ridden one mile. I am much fatigued, & put up for the night.

After supper, a courier who stops here informs me he has a horse to lead to Columbia,[85] & if I start when he starts, I may ride the horse free of charge. I gladly accept the offer.

May 29th, Friday.

At 2 o'clock, A.M., I pay my bill, $1.00, for a small piece of meat & bread that I got for my supper—I slept on the piazza floor on my own bedding & start with the courier. —At 8 o'clock, A.M., I arrive at Columbia very much worried. —Learning the stage stand is on the opposite side of the river[86] at Mr. Fluit's, ¾ of a mile distant, I walk to that place, & await the arrival of the stage which is due here to-night, & goes on to Monroe to-morrow.

May 30th, Saturday.

Start in the hack this morning, & ride to Mr. Butler's, 20 miles, & being too sick to travel further, get permission to remain here till the hack passes to Monroe again, next Tuesday.

Spencer & Ghaston came up with me last night, on the stage; here they leave me, & I presume I will see them no more on this trip.

May 31st, Sunday.

I feel a little better this morning, having obtained a little medicine last night of Mr. Butler, which now seems to be acting finely on my system. Slight fever this evening.

June 1st, Monday.

Up this morning, but I feel that my system needs further medical treatment.

I engage a young man who is going to Monroe in his buggy, to take me for $2.50. I am not able to travel, but I am anxious to get where I can have medical aid.

11 o'clock, & I am now in the hospital at Monroe, awaiting an interview with Dr. T. M. Cavett,[87] an old acquaintance. —He comes to me, & finds me with a hot fever. Prescribes citric acid as a drink, & a wet cloth to my head till my fever abates. My fever is very high, & my system in a wreck of misery. Late in evening, fever abated much.

June 2nd, Tuesday.

Took several doses of quinine in the morning, & have escaped fever till late in the evening, though it is light.

June 3rd, Wednesday.

Take more quinine to-day, & escape fever.

June 4th, Thursday.

More quinine, & no fever. Much better.

June 5th, Friday.

Feel pretty well this morning. A pill of opium to keep my bowels in check, & occasionally a whisky tody[88] to act as a tonic.

June 6th, Saturday.

This morning I procure a transportation ticket to Minden, & then get permission of Dr. Cavett to leave the hospital to-morrow evening.

For about 2 hours this evening, I have been quite sick. Suppose I have used too much citric acid.

Meet S.W. Weaver of Col. Roberts' regiment of Texas infantry.[89] Weaver is here for medical treatment.

June 7th, Sunday.

Much better this morning.

Just after sundown we leave Monroe—4 passengers, 3 white men, & 1 negro.

June 8th, Monday.

Breakfast this morning 20 miles from Monroe, having had a slow & uneasy ride during the entire night, without any supper. —Get along at a slow rate to-day.

June 9th, Tuesday.

Arrive at Bellevue this morning at sun up. Get breakfast with Mrs. Smith,[90] & give her $8.00 to send me to Mr. Childers' —17 miles. Arrive at Mr. Childers' at dinner time; take dinner with him, & then a siesta which lasts till late in the evening.

At home after 7 o'clock, P.M., & find all well except J.R. Cavett, & my little son Jimmie. Neither of them is much sick.

Greatly fatigued, though I stood the trip better than I expected. Small grain from Monroe here, looks very fine But corn crops are not as good for want of rain. There has been no lack of rain here.

June 14th, Sunday.

Nothing for the dates omitted.

The "Bossier Cavalry" are returning home, having obtained a transfer to this department of the Confederacy.[91]

June 16th, Tuesday

Yesterday blank in point of items for my journal.

Unwell this morning—have some fever.

Read in the papers to-day, that Gen'l Smith[92] has crossed the Miss. River to P't Hudson with 18,000 men, & a plenty of bacon—a false report I fear. Many reports I omit, both for want of space, & confidence in them. So many prove false; I would not mention any but for the fact that those reading this in after years, could not form just estimates of the doubts & uncertainties that constantly attend us. These false reports are so numerous that we never know when to believe our own high officials. It is evident they will report any thing that serves the present, utterly disregarding future consequences. Policy, leaving out all considerations of right, dictates a different course.

June 19th, Friday.

The 17th & 18th are without items.

We, the paroled prisoners, are ordered to Camp Pratt preparatory to exchange.[93] No such preparation is necessary, & the order is unjust in the extreme.

June 28th, Sunday.

Dates omitted for want of suitable material.

Yesterday I visited a camp of instruction West from Shreveport,[94] & on my return to-day, I was taken up by the guard at the ferry, & taken before the provost marshal for a pass to cross the river. I show my papers—a pass is issued—I go back to the ferry, & as the boat lands on the side, the guard proceeds to examine the papers of the travelers. The corporal says to them guard, "You need not bother those folks in the carriage." I asked "why?" and he replied, "the presumption is, persons riding in a carriage have their papers all right." I replied, "if fine carriages are passes, I am ready to quit fighting for the Confederacy." He instantly seized his gun; assumed the attitude to thrust his bayonet into me, & ordered me to silence. Not being accustomed to comply readily with such imperious & unjust commands, I refused obedience. Many sharp words were passed, even to the passing of the lie. I told him he was a liar, & a coward also—that no brave man, having the advantage of being on duty, & the other party totally unarmed, would behave as he had done. He drew down his bayonet, & I left unscathed. So much for "up-starts"—"dressed up in a little brief authority."

June 29th, Monday.

Learn to-day that Lt. Miller of our company, died yesterday in Bellevue. Miller was a good soldier.

Dates omitted for want of items.

June 30th, Tuesday.

Obtain from Dr. Smith a certificate of disability to return to the duties of a soldier for 20 days[95]

July 9th, Thursday.

Omitted dates blank in point of items for any journal.

Hear that B.F. Knight,[96] & R. Slack[97] of our company died recently.

During 4 days just past, I have been much annoyed by diarrhea

July 19th, Sunday.

For many days past we have been much exercised about the downfall of Vicksburg. First reported taken by the enemy, & then contradicted—we remain in suspense for several days—but now it is a fixed fact that both Vicksburg & P't Hudson have been surrendered.

I may be mistaken, but my humble conviction is, we will certainly have to submit [to] the domination of Abraham Lincoln. The day may be stopped for a season, but I think it will surely come. Time will decide as to whose judgment is correct.

August 1st, Saturday.

From the best intelligence we can gather, our armies are retreating in almost every department. Gen'l Holmes has been badly beaten in the Miss. Above Helena

Lt. Gen. Edmund Kirby Smith, C.S.A. Courtesy Mansfield State Historic Site, Mansfield, Louisiana.

& has retreated to L. Rock, having lost many men.[98] Many have deserted him. No doubt but heavy desertions will prevail throughout the entire Confederacy. Many of the citizens will take the oath of allegiance, & general discouragement prevail every where. These facts will greatly encourage the enemy, both citizen & soldier. Our condition is deplorable, but despondence works no good, so we should bear patiently whatever evils may befall us.

August 6th, Thursday.

Items wanted for the dates omitted.

Gen'l Smith has issued an order for ¼ of the negro men of this department between the ages of 18 & 45 years for the purpose of fortifying Shreveport.[99] Very good if justly executed, but I shall expect it to prove as most of such orders issued for some time past—a fat job for favorites.

August 9th, Sunday

I am omitting dates again for want of material.

I am informed that another order is issued for the paroled prisoners to assemble at Camp Pratt. It is now between our lines, & the lines of the enemy—not a *very* suitable place for a camp of instructions, I think-especially of paroled prisoners. — ——Learn the order was issued before the breaking up of Camp Pratt. Of course the order is annulled.

August 11th, Tuesday.

Nothing to journalize on the 10th inst.[100]

News to the effect that France & Spain have recognized the independence of the Confederate States. Some are exulting over the news, but I should like to know the virtue there is in the simple act of recognition uncoupled with any direct interposition. True, recognition is the first step, but if it benefit us, something must follow quickly & purposefully, for ours is a desperate case.

August 16th, Sunday.

From the 11th to this date, nothing of interest to this journal.

Hear in a way that causes belief, that the Federals are advancing on Little Rock.

Confidence in the stability of the Confederacy is failing fast, & unless something is done soon to restore confidence, I see no chance for us. Citizens & soldiers, as far as I can learn, are losing confidence—the great pillars of the Confederacy are shaken to their centers.

John H. Morgan has recently been taken prisoner.[101]

W. L. Yancy is dead.[102]

Chapter 5

The Cattle Drive and Home

Surely we are drifting-drifting to irretrievable ruin.

William Henry King
September 26, 1863

August 18th, Tuesday.

The 17th furnishes nothing to record. From this time on, omitted dates will not be mentioned.

President Davis has made a further call for conscripts, extending to the age of 45 years.

To-day I start to Texas in company with J.R. Cavett, G.S. Davie, Bruce Cavett & A Jones, all of this Parish, for the purpose of purchasing beeves for ourselves and neighbors. We travel by the way of McAlpins;[1] thence through Long Prairie;[2] thence down R. River 8 or 10 miles, & camp for the night.

August 19th, Wednesday.

Start early this morning & travel on to Spring Bank;[3] cross the river; travel about 7 miles further, & stop for dinner. One mile further travel, & we are to Bright Star.[4] Fourteen miles further, & we halt for the night in Davis County, Texas. Prior to the war this county bore the name of Cass; but the citizens of the County, not liking the course of senator Cass, in honor of whom it was named, took in relation to the war, changed it from Cass to Davis. [Since the war went

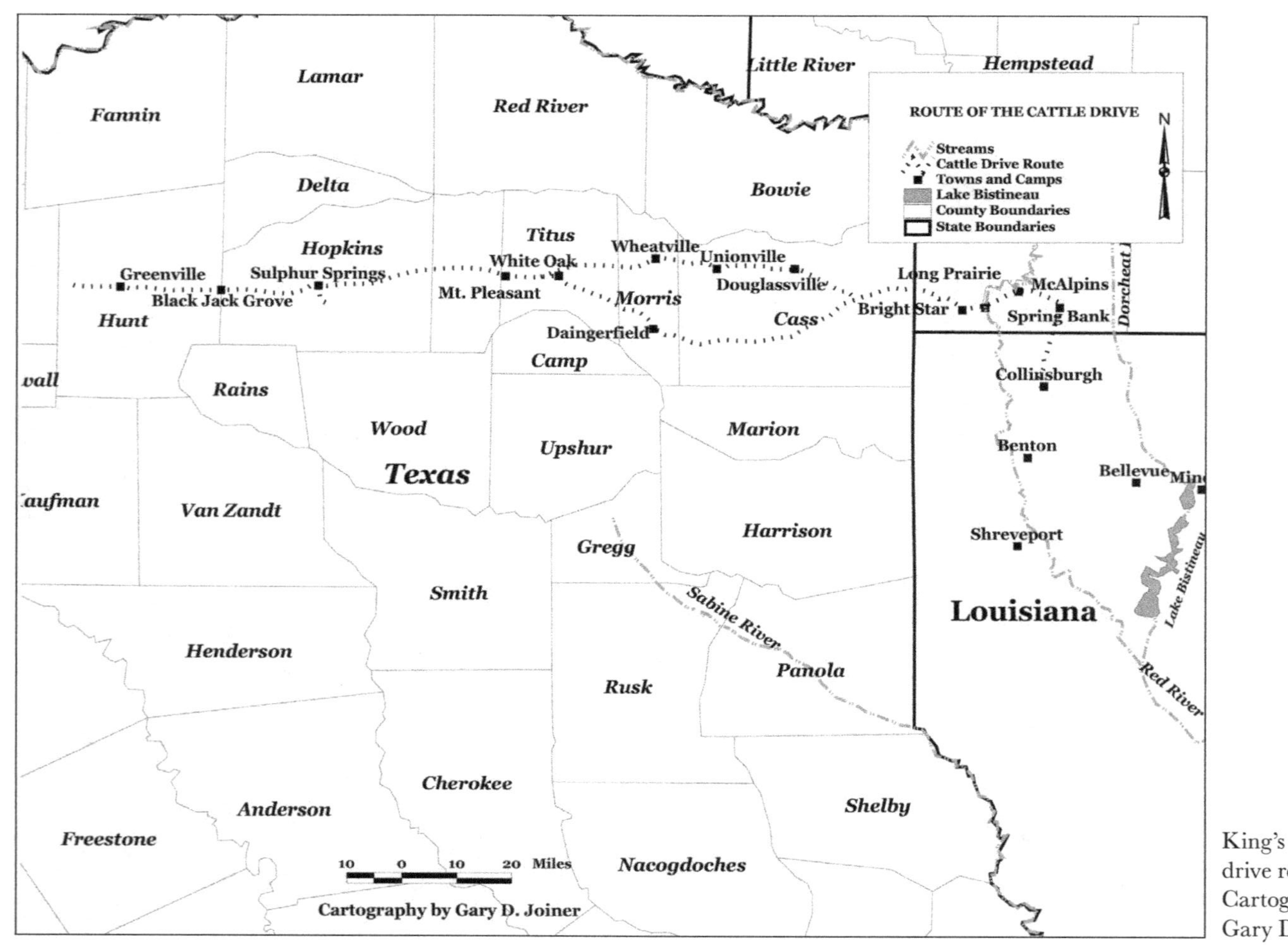

King's cattle drive route. Cartography by Gary D. Joiner.

against us, the name of the County has been changed from Davis back to Cass.] Verily, people will float with the current.

August 20th, Thursday.

This morning we pass through Dangerfield. Stop for dinner 2 miles west from Dangerfield,[5] having traveled 17 miles. — About 10 miles further, & we camp for the night.

G.S. Davie is very sick.

August 21st, Friday.

Davie is too sick to travel on with us, & he turns back. — Camp 3 miles East of Mt. Pleasant, Titus County, Texas.

August 22nd, Saturday.

Pass through Mt. Pleasant, & find it a sorry looking country town. Travel 10 miles further, & take dinner in the suburbs of Gray Rock. —Just before night we get into the Prairie, & cross the line between Titus & Hopkins Counties.

August 23rd, Sunday.

Took dinner in Sulphur Springs[6] with Dr. Davis, the gov't beef agent. He says we can drive beeves out of the State if we will file affidavits setting forth that we want them for family use. — Ten miles further, & we camp for the night.

August 24th, Monday.

4 miles travel, & we are at Black Jack Grove.[7] 13 miles further, & stop for dinner. — Three miles further, & we are in Greenville, Hunt County. — Travel 8 miles further to S.K. Cheney's & camp for the night. Quite a change in the weather this evening—the fire feels very pleasant.

August 25th, Tuesday.

About 10 o'clock last night, the rain began to descend, & we got but little more sleep during the night. Jones & Cavett are both sick this morning—too-sick to travel, hence we are halted.

After many intercessions, we prevail on Mrs. Cheny to take us into her house. Mr. Cheny was favorable, but his lady, whom he had recently married—and his second wife—was rather tenacious. A veritable norther, & we find a big fire altogether comfortable.

August 26th, Wednesday.

This morning we return to Greenville, having declined a further western travel, & learn Jones, with two of the negroes, at Dr. Young's, as he is too sick to travel further.

Travel 8 miles south easterly from Greenville in search of beeves. We called at every house on the road, & many off the road, to get corn to feed, but failed until just at night, & then we used much persuasion.

August 27th, Thursday.

Failed to find beeves; return to Greenville, & find Jones & one of the negroes very sick. Cavett is also sick. We now travel East 9 miles to Rasson Sovell's; pitch tents at his well to await Jones' recovery. We have excellent water, a rare thing in this country.

August 28th, Friday.

We have not yet found any beeves. Many of the citizens regard us suspiciously, thinking we are speculators, against whom they are greatly prejudiced. Others regard us as speculators for the Gov't; against Gov't agents they have much antipathy.

The Gov't agent of this county told us yesterday, that he would not let us drive beeves from this county, but said if we would wait until he can take a small drove To supply the market at Marshall, he will then sell to us as many beeves as we want.

August 29th, Saturday.

Still waiting for the sick to recover.

August 30th, Sunday

This morning we start for Sulphur Springs. Jones & the 2 negroes still remaining in Greenville.

About 7 miles from S. Springs, we commence enquiring for corn to feed on, & fail, completely fail till we have passed 3 miles from S. Springs in a S. Easterly direction. Here we stop with a Mr. Goodson of whom we get corn.

August 31st, Monday.

I am loitering about camp to-day, spending a portion of my time with Mr. Goodson. Cavett started yesterday to search for beeves.

Sept. 1st, Tuesday.

This evening Cavett returns, & informs me he has bought 50 beeves, paying 37½ dollars per head.

Sept. 2nd, Wednesday

This morning we send for Jones, Cavett goes in search of Dr. Davis, & I, in charge of the remainder, proceed to Mr. Lindlay's, the gentleman of whom Cavett bought the beeves.

Sept. 3rd, Thursday.

Spend the day in hurding the beeves.[8]

After night Jones comes in, & decides to take a third of the beeves, & go home with us.

Sept. 4th, Friday.

Start for home this morning, travel 16 miles, & camp at Dr. Moore's.

Sept. 5th, Saturday.

All right this morning, & we start off in big glee, expecting an interesting day's travel. Jones goes ahead to get dinner ready by the time we come up with him. But, as is his custom, he gets off "on the wrong foot," takes the wrong road, & our calculation in this particular is completely upset. Proceed till near 4 o'clock, P.M., & get dinner at White Oak.[9] We get a good dinner, & eat like hungry men—both white & black. Indeed, we apologize to our landlady, acknowledging she may make an extra charge.

Put up to-night with a Mr. Cheny Having traveled fifteen miles.

Sept. 6th, Sunday

Put up to-night with a Mr. Wagoner, having traveled 18 miles.

Sept. 7th, Monday

Traveled 14 miles to-day, & camp at Wheatville.[10]

Sept. 8, Tuesday.

Pass through Unionville this morning.[11] Travel 17 miles to-day, & put up with a Mr. Lachly.

Sept. 9th, Wednesday.

Pass through Douglasville this morning, a travel of 17 miles, & we halt for the night.[12]

Sept. 10th, Thursday.

Travel 20 miles to-day, & arrive at Spring Bank.

Sept. 11th, Friday.

Attempt to cross the river this morning, but fail. One beef, got entirely away, & we sold the chance of him for $15.00. Having been told that cattle will not "take water" readily early in the morning, especially after hard travel the previous day, we defer further attempt at crossing the river until evening.—Evening, & we make a second effort to cross the river.—Succeed in crossing all but one which we chase until he dies from fatigue & heat. Sell him for $40.00. He would have been worth 65 or $70.00, had we got him home all right.

Had we stopped 5 miles from the river yesterday, & drove to the river this morning, it is reasonable to conclude the beeves would have "taken the water," without much trouble—worn & thirsty, they would not have feared the water so much. But, we *must* learn, though it be in the *severe school—experience.*

Camp on the East bank of the river.

Sept. 12th, Saturday.

Travel 15 miles, & camp at the head of Long Prairie. Now we begin to feel at home.

Sept. 13th, Sunday.

Travel on to Dooley's; halt, & divide beeves with Jones. Find him unwilling to settle fairly. He is not willing to lose his third of our losses at Spring Bank, & is unwilling to bear his part in traveling expenditures. I have told Cavett he was dealing too loosely with Jones.

On to home just at dark, having traveled 22 miles. Find our folks up, but some of them have been very sick.

Sept. 14th, Monday.

From the best information I can obtain, I am yet unexchanged.

Sept. 15th, Tuesday.

The Federals are gradually advancing on us. Many are fleeing for a place of refuge.

Sept. 24th, Thursday.

Current news again that France & Spain have recognized our independence. In my judgment, we have heard that news too often for our best interests. But, in our drowning condition, we seize at whatever presents itself, though it be a phantom. In this way people are led by crafty leaders into the ~~the~~ most dangerous extremes. Their passions are aroused, & stimulated by degrees until any thing is received with avidity that promises the accomplishing of the desired end.

Sept. 26th, Saturday

Gen'l. Mouton has promulgated an order, releasing all paroled prisoners belonging to his command from their paroles. From what source he derives his power, I would like to know. If capable of filling the station he occupies, he *must* know the right of the paroled prisoner is inalienable. No earthly power, however stupendous, can set aside the sacred right of a paroled prisoner. I yield to the order, but I do so reluctantly. First, because I am not exchanged; & secondly, because Gen'l Mouton has no power to cancel my parole. I yield because I know I *must* do it; not because it is right that I should do so.

I believe we are at last overpowered, & all of our efforts will prove unavailing. Our people have become so corrupt, that they gladly seize the opportunity of speculating on the necessities of helpless women & children. Things are changed so much that I have become measurably indifferent as to which party triumphs. The war is not what it was when it commenced. At first, it was, on our part, a war for equal rights; now it is a war for the aggrandizement of a certain few at the expense of the masses. The wealthy have got out of the army or into office. Some have put in substitutes, & others have got details to take care of their *property*—it, in the estimation of our civil & military authorities, being of far more importance than poor men's families.—Surely we are drifting-drifting to irretrievable ruin.

Oct. 4th, Sunday

Had a short interview with Capain Abny to-day, & he informs me we are not exchanged; that Gen'l Banks disregarded the paroles of prisoners taken at Brashear City, not long since; & for retaliation Gen'l Mouton had ordered us to duty. A parole is a sacred contract between the party paroled, & the government paroling—a contract that neither party has the right to abrogate, neither has a third party the right to abrogate it; therefore, the disregarding of a parole by Gen'l Banks, or any of his soldiers, does not, in the least affect our paroles; & Gen'l Mouton violates a most sacred principle in attempting to set aside our parole. Besides, Gen'l Banks had previously given notice that all paroles of prisoners not held a specified length of time, would not be recognized as paroles. This was to prevent the paroling of prisoners before the issue of the battle in which they were captured, could be determined, & applied to both parties. The prisoners captured & paroled at Brashear City, were captured by a small body of soldiers who could neither hold that post, nor take the prisoners away. Hence, they were paroled before they were held the required length of time. Viewing the questions in the most charitable manner, I am constrained to condemn, unequivocally, the course of Gen'l Mouton. Admit his course, either on the ground of principle or policy, & the whole contest that had better be abandoned. Lincoln's programme could be no worse.

It is hard indeed, but I have promised to meet Capt. Abney in Shreveport next Friday, the 9th inst., & to make my word good, I will do so.

Oct. 8th, Thursday

Learn to-day that the balance of prisoners is against us. This explains the whole secret of our being ordered to duty. That fact, together with our great reverses, makes it probable that we will not be exchanged soon, if ever, & as Gen'l Mouton is in great need of men, he is willing that sacrifice our lives, & even our sacred honors to save himself—yea, for the merest chance of saving himself. If this is the freedom we are fighting for, I want none of it. Alas! how corrupt our leaders are.

Oct. 9th, Friday.

To-day I go to Shreveport to meet Capt. Abney for an investigation of my case at Head Quarters. By inquiry, he learns that nothing is known there of the order promulgated by Gen'l Mouton, & that we are not exchanged. He sees clearly the situation we are in. But as he is a subordinate, he is afraid to say to us, "Go home." He says, "I will not say for you to go home, but if you do, I will write to you from Alexandria after I reach there & make the necessary inquiry." I at once inform him I am going home, thereby clearly telling him he may write from Alexandria.

On arriving at the ferry, a little after 1 o'clock, we find a crowd of refugees. They continue to cross till late in the evening, & crowds are still waiting to cross. Such heavy immigration will certainly cause great scarcity of bread stuffs in Texas. Indeed, I fear it will cause intestive war.[13] Many of the citizens of Texas are opposed to refugees upon the ground that bread stuffs will be too scarce if so many go there.

Hear that Bragg is in front of Rosecrans; Longstreet on Look out Mountain;[14] & Wheeler[15] & Forrest[16] on Tennessee River in rear of Rosecrans;[17] & Rosecrans' men on quarter rations of corn bread; no chance for him to escape, &c. I shall wait for further news, believing I will finally hear a different report. The style now is, brilliant successes are removed when we are defeated.

Hear that 30.000 Federals have crossed Berwick's Bay, destined for Texas.[18]

Oct. 17th, Saturday.

To-day I visited D. T. Cavett who is recently from Gen'l Holmes' Army. He says Holmes' army is greatly demoralized, & that the Federals are gradually advancing & driving our broken down army before them.

Oct. 25th, Sunday

Gen'l Holmes' Head Quarters are now at Lewisville, Ark.

Gen'l Rosecrans is not yet captured as was reported about 2 weeks ago.

Hear that 35,000 Federals are now coming up in the direction of Alexandria from Berwicks Bay.

The Federals that crossed Berwicks' Bay, & reported to be bound for Texas, came up near Washington, La. & returned.

Federal forces now occupy Camden & Arkadelphia, Ark. Our forces have fallen back to Washington, Ark.[19]

J.P. Strayhan Of our company told me yesterday he was in Shreveport recently, & was there taken up.[20] Finally he got off by getting a pass to return to his regiment. But, instead of returning to his Reg't, he returned home, to which place, he had the paper permits from his officers to go, & there assert his broken down health. When he left his wife & 3 little boys, to go to fight the battles of his country, he was an ablebodied man. He has fought in several hard battles, & now that he is almost hopelessly diseased, & with the proper papers from his officers, he cannot even go to Shreveport without being imprisoned. Such, I fear, is a foretaste of the liberty we are fighting for. I still hope a day of just retribution will come. Yea, I know it will come, though it may not come in this life.

Nov'r 8th, Sunday.

The Port Hudson prisoners are exchanged, but no news yet of our exchange. Perhaps the papers were overlooked.

Gantt, a South Arkansas Congressman, has turned against us. No doubt but he will command a heavy influence against us as many are ripe for such a move, & have, for some time past, been waiting for some one to bolt.

Nov. 10th, Tuesday.

Wm Jones[21] of my company informs me to-day that P. H. Edwards[22] of the same company died recently in or near Alexandria. Alas! Edwards was young and promising, & might have been useful but for this unholy war.

Jones also informs me that Captain Abny failed to get our men (8) who had been taken up in Shreveport as they attempted to pass there on furlough.[23] They were assigned to provost guard duty. I learn from other sources, that men with discharges, paroles, & other permits to pass to & fro, are frequently taken up in Shreveport, & confined or kept in prison 2 or 3 days, & then released or put to duty. If this be the freedom we are fighting for, I, for one, want none of it. The truth is, 2/3 of us are fighting to keep up the remaining 1/3 as an aristocracy of the most abominable class. Our portion of that class composes the officers our army; another portion composes the civil officers, State & Confederate, & the remaining portion remain at home; the greater majority of whom are speculating on the necessities of soldiers' wives & children. How long soldiers will thus suffer themselves imposed on, yet remains to be seen.

Nov. 11th, Wednesday.

Late yesterday evening I received intelligence of the demise of J.W. Shields,[24] a member of my company; & last night sat up, in company with others, with his corpse. Some ten months ago he was detailed to work on the gun-boat then in process of construction at Shreveport.[25] Since the completion of said boat, he has been employed at other work. But his health becoming bad, he obtained a sick furlough, & at the time of his death was at Mrs. Dalrymple's near Collinsburgh. His physician decided that he was laboring under a chronic disease which was pushed to maturity by pneumonia. His earthly career is now terminated, & with it the jeers often cast at him for reporting sick. Soldiers are so uncharitable as to sneer whenever a one reports sick unless his sickness partakes of great violence. There is no such thing as avoiding the troubles of this war.

Nov. 15th, Sunday.

Again, I read in the papers of the exchange of prisoners, & from the reading of the exchange notice, I presume that I am exchanged, though there is some ambiguity in the reading of the order. As a matter of cause, I yield obedience, but I frankly acknowledge that obedience is not the result of free will, but the result of coercion. To leave any dear little family to the cold mercies of the world; to brave the dangers of a soldeir in this most unholy war, simply to keep despots in power yet a little longer, is a trying scene beyond description. Those who hold the rule Of our gov't can prate[26] of liberty, "all that is worth living for," since it is that delusive argument that enables them to keep their power. But, to us who are compelled to leave our families, all that is now near & dear to us, & fight for $11 per month; that in a bloated currency that is scarcely worth the paper on which it is stamped; the gov't feeding us on *poor* beef and musty corn meal; some of us occasionally receiving a garment from the gov't, while other receive none; submitting to the most humiliating behests of officers who have not the capacity to control a flock of geese, but whose wealth or parentage has secured to them their position; the ultimate end of all our sacrifices being the perpetuation of an abominable aristocracy instead of true freedom as that aristocracy would fain have us believe; to us, this, this boasted freedom, is any thing but desirable. 'Tis my earnest prayer that a healthy reaction will soon take place.

Learn that the Federals have taken Brownsville on the Rio Grande.[27] I cannot say that I am grieved at the news, since the capturing of Brownsville may put a stop to the great swindle of the cotton agents of the Confederacy.

Learn that small pox, of a most malignant character, prevails in San Antonia: Also, a disease called black measles.[28] And it is said the small pox is in Arkansas.

Nov. 17th, Tuesday.

Hear that Lt. Grayham, & many others of our company, have embraced Christianity. Since man by nature is fitted to be religious, & since Christianity presents the best system of all religions, I am glad to hear of it.

Yesterday I received a letter from J.W. Kinnard by which I learned he had been transferred to Gen'l Mouton's division. Some consolation to me since I shall have some opportunity of being with him occasionally.

A call for 1/3 of the negro men now remaining on the plantations is now ~~called~~ made. They are wanted to raft Red River.[29] Another fat job for some pet.

Nov. 20th, Friday.

The Gov't now demands that the citizens of this vicinity haul the gov't cotton to Benton about 14 miles above Shreveport. Indeed, the day is beginning to dawn in which there is some consolation in having nothing unless one could have a vast fortune. To possess property to manage it for the benefit of military commanders the owner sustaining all losses, but the great military reaping all the profits-to say the least of it, affords but little comfort. Those vastly wealthy command a power that enables them to escape in some measure, the burthens of the less fortunate.

Unless some new light dawns on my perceptive faculties, I think I shall ever after this stand in opposition to military institutions as conducted at the present time. The whole throng & practice of military education at present teaches the most abject submission on the part of subjects; & the most oppressive tyranny on the part of commanders. "Bone & muscle, (the mental & most faculties standing in subordination,) are the all important elements of a "good soldier". Sufficient intelligence to comprehend, & to execute an order, is all that is needed in the way of intelligence for a "good soldier." And, the less the virtue, the "better"; for when a mean thing is to be done, all questioning of the *right* to do it, is an impediment in a military sense. Negroes will make better regular soldiers than white men for the reasons stated.

I have been informed a squad of cavalry passed through this neighborhood, recently with my name, & the names of other paroled prisoners, intending to arrest us if found.

However, some of our neighbors presuming a portion of us had gone to the army, & that others were too sick to do so, informed the cavalry of the facts, & the cavalry-men passed on without seeing any of us. I have but little doubt that our names were furnished to them by men at home. Col. Randolph recently informed me he saw the cavalry men with my name hunting me.[30] I replied, "all right. Col, & if you see them again you may tell them I am generally about home, & they will be apt to find me there if they wish to see me. I have not yet skulked in the bushes, & do not expect to do so. As you are fully aware, I have a perfect right to be at home." To the latter statement, the Colonel made some evasive reply. He also said his information to me was not official, but an act of friendship. Of course I thanked him, but I most frankly confess no thank sprang from the depths of my soul; for I half suspicioned the Colonel to be he who had given our names to the cavalry-men. There are those among us who feel too patriotic to go to war, claiming a higher sphere in which to act—see that others do not remain at home whether they are entitled to do so or not. Patriotic fellows! Good & true to a fault. If one comes home from the army, after the ordinary salutations by "friends at home," the following interrogatories ensue: "Have you got a furlough" "How long will you remain at home?" &c. &c. At the next meeting-time not more than half out, perhaps-such as the following may be expected: "Why, I thought you had gone back;" "You have had a good stay at home." Nothing is plainer than many are ill at ease when they see a soldier at home.

Hear that Capt. Abny has written for us to report to camp immediately as all have been exchanged. Next Tuesday, the 24th inst. is the day set apart for starting. 'Tis a hard task, but since I *must* go, I shall endeavor to go like a man.

Nov. 21st, Saturday.

Received a letter from Capt. Abny, today, in which he says for us to report at camp near Alexandria, & to do so immediately.

He writes that the enemy have fallen back to N. Iberia; that our forces have captured about 1500 prisoners, & killed from 300 to 500.

The Captain is still engaged in court martial. It does not speak well for our army there. The Court was opened some time in August last.

Nov. 22nd, Sunday.

From the reading of the Caddo Gazette of last Friday, I have apprehensions of an early defeat of Bragg's army.[31]

Travelers report a battle is expected to take place soon near Washington, Ark. If it take place, I apprehend our army will be defeated; because our army there is greatly demoralized, & can not be urged to do good fighting. If the head of affairs would displace Holmes,[32] and give Price command of that army, some efficiency might be expected notwithstanding the deplorable condition of that army.[33]

Nov. 23rd, Monday.

Tomorrow morning, if not providentially hindered, I shall take leave of my family & start to the soldiers' camp. Knowing the troubles that await me there, & feeling confident all will prove unavailing so far as the good of our people is concerned, I go forth reluctantly. But, if fall I must, I shall endeavor to fall honorably.

Chapter 6

Shreveport

Hear various rumors to the effect that General Banks is advancing in Western Texas. When Texas is invaded, every State in the Confederacy will be invaded.

William Henry King
December 19, 1863

Nov. 24th, Tuesday.

Waited for the stage till near 10 o'clock, & then learning it had passed early, I started early on horseback, & about dark I arrived at C. Wallace's.[1] Mr. Wallace is the father in law of Leander Hamilton of our company.[2] Hamilton having sent an invitation to us to meet at his residence that we might all be to-gether; & he living close to Mr. Wallace, we, at the suggestion of Mr. Wallace, put up with him. He lives about 6 miles above Shreveport.

Nov. 25th, Wednesday.

Came out to the main road this morning at Cizer's,[3] there sent the boy accompanying me back with my horse. Luckily we fall in with a corn wagon, & I get permission to put my baggage on it, and after a walk of near a mile & a half, all get on another corn wagon, & ride to the ferry. Applied to the guard at the pontoon bridge[4] for permission to cross on the bridge. Found it against order as a pass from the City of Shreveport was required. After a moment's pause, the guard remarked, "this is a gov't bridge, & you are soldiers of the gov't; there can be nothing wrong in your crossing on the bridge, so if you will not report me, you

Model of a pontoon bridge at the Richmond Battlefield Center, Tredagar Iron Works, Richmond, Virginia. Photograph by Gary D. Joiner.

may pass over." We crossed over, & of course, have said nothing to the authorities about it.

On application for transportation to our command, it is denied, & we are assigned to post guard duty.

Nov. 26th, Thursday.

Hear that the famous Quantrell[5] is stationed near this place, & that one of his captains rode into a church last Sunday while Parson Tucker, a Baptist preacher, was preaching to negroes, & insulted the parson's wife. As soon as parson Tucker could procure a gun, he shot the captain.[6]

In the forenoon of to-day, I have been engaged in hauling wood, & in the evening placed on guard to relieve a sick man.

Nov. 27th, Friday.

I saw a poor lady yesterday evening from Smith County, Texas,[7] having come the whole way by herself to see her husband in prison. From the best I can learn he is innocent of the charges preferred against him: I observe she is treated coolly by the officials, & gets no satisfactory reply. A soldier, seeing the coolness with which she is treated, becomes enlisted in her behalf, steps forward, urges her claim, procures a permit for her to visit her husband in prison. He is very destitute in the way of clothing, & the main object of her visit is to suppy[8] his wants in that particular, having brought many articles of clothing for him. She manifested carlsness,[9] yet there was evidently resolution to do what she could for her husband, or die in the attempt to do for him.

Nov. 28th, Saturday.

Yesterday evening a rain came up, & early in the night it commenced sleeting. Fortunately I found Wm Bowdon, & got into his shanties to rest during the night. Bowdon is in the Louisiana militia. I became acquainted with him, several years ago in Texas.

Nov. 29th, Sunday.

I attended the Catholic Church to-day, the first time I was ever inside of one. The exercises partook large of the theatrical, & widely different from any religious services I ever witnessed. 'Tis something remarkable that all of the religious denominations are traveling by the same way-bill, yet some of them are traveling to one point of the compass, & others to another point. Indeed, some are journeying to every conceivable point. Who can judge as to which party is right? *All* may be right in *some* things, but *all can not* be right in *every thing*.

Col. William Clarke Quantrill, C.S.A. Courtesy Eric J. Brock, Shreveport, Louisiana.

Nov. 30th, Monday.

Last night I took the place of a Mr. Cox who reported himself sick. My post was at the arsenal door on Texas Street.[10] To-day I feel badly in consequence of loss of sleep; & exposure to the cold. Much better arrangement, & at little cost, might be made for us; both at the guard station & at the regular posts. There is no clemency for a soldier, he must meet whatever troubles arise without favor or affection.

Quantrell's men are still in this section, & I much fear they will do more serious mischief before they leave us. They are a great terror to this country. Last night they paraded the streets of Shreveport in gangs of from 2 to 4. They were quite boisterous, & made heavy threats against Gen'l Smith, provided he should attempt to place them under any other command. Each carried 2 or 3 six-shooters. We are allowed an empty musket to each post, & must not, under any emergency, load them. Nothing is plainer than Gen'l Smith & his staff are afraid of these men.

Dec'r 1st, Tuesday.

One of the men liberated from prison a few days since, left yesterday morning.

Hear that new orders are now issued for all of the paroled prisoners of the 28th Reg't of La. Volunteers to hasten to report at Regt'l head quarters. I suppose we are safe, though we may have some trouble about it.

There seems to be a general impression among the news paper editors, that the decisive battle of this war will be fought at or near Chattanooga.

Dec'r 2nd, Wednesday.

This evening I am detailed to guard a lot of hogs brought from the Mississippi bottom.

The negroes in the service of the Gov't at this place, are furnished with plenty of bacon, & we draw none. Evidently, they are held in higher esteem by the authorities than white men. "The rich man's war, & the poor man's fight," is verified in this act.

N. Lawrance,[11] one of our company, went into the Quarter Master's office this evening to draw his pay, & was ordered by the Quarter Master's clerk to pull off his hat. Hearing no power to resist, of course he obeyed. A reaction *must,* beyond a doubt, take place, if it result in the downfall of this monstrous despotism. To all intents & purposes, it is now what we at first opposed the Federal gov't for.

Dec'r 3rd, Thursday.

S.M. Self[12] of our company came in to-day, & he is also placed on duty here.

Never, during any soldiering, have I witnessed so much profane swearing, & vulgar language; & what renders the practice more shocking, is to see that its prevalence is most among the young men. A company of militia, mostly boys, is encamped near us, & they are all adepts in the use of profane & vulgar language.

Dec'r 4th, Friday.

Hear the Federal prisoners that have, for some time past, been kept at Tyler, Smith County, Texas,[13] will be brought in here to-day.

Hear that an order form Col. Gray, approved by Gen'ls Mouton & Taylor, has been sent to Col. Shiners, Commandant of Post at this place, for all of our men at this place. I would rather remain here, but if go I *must,* I will yield. Here, I am less exposed to the vicissitudes of the weather, & I am much closer to my family.

The Federal prisoners were not brought in as was expected, but have been placed in camp near this place. About 20 of our own men were brought in this evening. All are from Texas, & were taken up by Parson's men.

A letter from home to-day, dated yesterday, informs me that all are well there.

Dec'r 5th, Saturday.

On guard to-day, & my post is at one of the doors of the prison. While on post, I used the opportunity of conversing with one of the Federal prisoners, & I find him both intelligent & pleasant. He is an officer; was on the gun-boat Dianna when it was captured, & at that time became a prisoner. He is a Missourian, & says he is a pro-slavery man, & is fighting for the old Union—would have no crowned heads on this continent-would invade Mexico to free it from its invaders. Corporal Madingly is well acquainted with this prisoner, & says he knows the prisoner's father is a slave holder in Missouri.

From recent discloures, I am now fully assured that many of our men are wrongfully imprisoned. There are reasons for believing that Parson's men have been receiving pay-extra-for the prisoners they have been bringing in; hence they sought numbers, regardless of the circumstances under which they were at home.

To-night I am informed that one Crawford, a lawyer of Columbia, Louisiana,[14] who was arrested & brought before Gen'l Smith under charge of entertaining Union sentiments, but released because the charges could not be sustained, has raised a company of about 65 men from Jackson & Winn Parishes, & has joined the Federals. So much for persecution. From respectable men I learn that during the agitation of the question of secession in the State of Louisiana, Crawford made Union speeches, & did all he could honorably do to defeat Secession. Failling in his efforts, he became quiescent, yielding entire obedience to the new order of things, making no effort to impede, but all the while standing firm in his Union proclivities—yielding a strict obedience to laws he did not approbate. Since he could not quietly enjoy his opinion, he took as many as he could, & joined the enemy. Who can blame him? Obedience to law is all a Gov't has a right to claim of its subjects; their opinions are their own, & the gov't that would deny the right of opinion, is intolerant, & not worthy of the love of its subjects. A gov't with laws highly objectionable, yet tolerating freedom of thought & of speech, is worthy of a patriotic feeling.

Dec'r 6th, Sunday.

Quantrell's men left here to-day. They crossed R. River at the ferry opposite this place, & took the Washington road.[15] Their destination, I have not learned, but as the road they have taken leads directly through the neighborhood of my family, I entertain some strong apprehensions.

Have news to-night, that Bragg is one the retreat; that Lee has fallen back to Richmond; that Texas has ordered all of the negro men, of that State, from 17 to 40 years, into the service.

Dec'r 7th, Monday.

Hear one report to-day that Bragg has beaten Thomas desperately; & then hear that Thomas has beaten Bragg. An alkali & an acid, when mixed, neutralize each other. Such reports, for a short time, neutralize each other.

Dec'r 8th, Tuesday.

On guard to-day, & my post is at a gov't cow pen.

Rumored that Gen'l Smith will take the place of Gen'l Holmes & Gen'l Polk will take the place of Gen'l Smith. I supposed some changes would be made, but was not looking for the displacement of Gen'l Smith. Guess Gen'l Holmes will be put on retired pay now, as that is the style. If an officer fails to fill the measure, he is put on retired pay, but if a private fails, he is put on roots.

There was a row at the houses of two women of ill fame. At one, three men were severely beaten, but fortunately, from the best information, no life was lost, notwithstanding 7 pistols were discharged. Such behavior should be severely dealt with.

I have been unwell for several days-afflicted with bronchitis, but I am better to-day.

Three men deserted us last night.

Dec'r 9th, Wednesday.

I feel much debilitated this morning, having just come off guard duty.

Dec'r 10th, Thursday.

Have just read a Caddo Gazette, Extra, of yesterday's issue, from which I learn that Bragg has fallen back to Chickamauga after a hard contest with Thomas.[16]

The News, Extra,[17] of to-day says that Bragg has beaten Thomas severely, & that Longstreet has captured the most of Burnside's men. Some how, it seems to be hard to get the true history.

Dec'r 11th, Friday.

Yesterday, 5–8 prisoners, deserters from our army, were brought in here. Seven of our men deserted last Wednesday night, instead of 3, as was reported.

Three of the prisoners brought in yesterday are hand-cuffed. What a wonderful comment on the prosperity of our cause, desertions are common, though they are constantly being caught & returned.

I hear our Gov't stores are being moved from San Antonio to Austin, & that Austin is being fortified—all of which indicates a falling back to the interior.

Dec'r 12th, Saturday.

Gov't stores are being moved from this place to the Sabine River. Sugar & other articles, to, or below Camden; the Cotton to Elliott's Bluff.[18] Another move towards the interior. "A blind man might see" what is expected.[19]

I have just learned that the Confederacy demands the tax, to be paid on Gold or silver; if paid in Confederate money, must be six dollars for one of gold or silver. So much of their opinion of the currency they give us—will not receive it at par themselves, but if a private refuse it at par, he will be in danger of being shot for so doing.

The Gazette, Extra, of to-day makes it appear that Bragg is badly beaten; that it is quite likely that a general engagement has taken place between Meade & Lee.[20]

Dec'r 13th, Sunday.

Hear that Gen'l Smith left here yesterday, for what purpose, I know not.

I am told the heavy guns at this place, are being removed to some point on R. River below here—supposed to be Alexandria.[21]

Cap. Jackson, commanding post guards, informs me there is some talk of Gen'l Holmes' army moving in the direction of Little Rock. As moving may improve the health of the army, it may be well enough, but as to any other good resulting from the move, I shall wait in breathless expectation of hearing—"no good accomplished."

Dec'r 14th, Monday.

On guard to-day. My post is at the gun boat.[22] Conversing with some of the hands on the boat, I learn they are very much dissatisfied on account of receiving short pay; no clothing; & not enough to eat. They draw no bacon. Indeed, there is an under current of dissatisfaction in every class of soldiers I have access to. True, if asked bluntly, their feelings will not be fully expressed. The fear of unpopularity, & even the charge of treason, as has been in some instances, will prevent soldiers from fully expressing themselves, unless approached with sympathy, & in confidence. Not unfrequently, when first asked, they will express the most sanguine expectations, but a little closer examination discloses an undercurrent, though not in sight at first, it is *deep* & *broad*.

I find the gun boat to be a massive piece of work, &, if of the right kind of workmanship, capable of withstanding many heavy shocks. But, as I am not a competent judge of such a thing, I shall withhold.

Dec'r 15th, Tuesday.

A prisoner, by the name of Kitts, escaped last night.

The Gazette, Extra, of yesterday, comes out relative to the late fight between Thomas & Bragg. I do not now doubt that Bragg was badly beaten.[23]

The Federals seem to be striving for a general engagement with Lee.

Dec'r 16th, Wednesday.

Received, to day, a letter from home, dated the 13th instant. It contained information of the good health of all.

Hear that Colonel Sandidge[24] sent into Shreveport a load of cabbage: The choice heads for the officers as presents; the inferior heads to the soldiers at fifty cents each. I did not believe the report at first—having a more exalted opinion of Col. Sandidge—I tried to explain it away, but the testimony was so strong I was forced to yield.

Thirty of the prisoners at this place, are started under guard to Gen'l Walker's Division. If there is not a change soon, it will not be long before one half of our army will be guarded by the other half.

Dec'r 17th, Thursday.

On guard to-day. My post is no. 2—inside of the guard house.

My position on guard to-day, has afforded me a good opportunity for observing the manner in which the prisoners at this prison are treated, & I consider it a disgrace to our cause to treat prisoners as our authorities do. They are badly fed; are almost naked; covered with vermin, & wallowing in dirt & filth unavoidable on their part. The cook is as filthy as a hog. No one but a *hungry* man could possibly eat his cooking. True, many men imprisoned here, do not merit much, if any thing, but common respectability, & justice demand that they be not punished in this way. Indeed, some innocent & true men are thrust in here. If a man deserves killing, treat him kindly while he is held a prisoner, & then execute his sentence in mercy. Justice may, & should be done in mercy.

This evening a genteel looking fellow is committed to prison. He says he had a furlough of twenty five days, but it was disregarded. His statement may be false, but there are good reasons for believing it.

Hear the Federals are advancing rapidly into Texas. Whether true or false, time will develop. The Heavens resound with wars and rumors of wars.

Dec'r 18th, Friday

I bought a Gazette this evening, expecting to get some extraordinary news (which news I did not expect to be true) as one of the men concerned in publishing the paper has been heard to say that the best news since the commencement of the war would appear in this issue of the paper. I *did* expect some *stuff* would appear, but I was mistaken, even in that.

It is stated that John Morgan and six of his men have escaped from the Columbus, Ohio, penitentiary, on the 28th of Nov. last.[25] The escape was accomplished by digging through the floor of the cell into the sewer leading into the river. I fear Morgan & his men have been otherwise disposed of—reported escaped to avoid suspicion of their true fate.

The Federals claim they have 35000 negroes bearing arms.

In the Gazette of to-day, I notice an extract from the Atlanta Appeal, advising the people East of the Mississippi River to live on milk, butter, vegetables & bread, & sell their meat to the government for the soldiers.[26] If complied with, the soldiers will get none unless the officers get much more than they want; for they must feel they have enough, & some to waste before they will consent for the soldiers to have any. The officers first, the negroes next, a little to waste, then, if there is a surplus, the soldiers may have a little.

Dec'r 19th, Saturday.

Hear various rumors to the effect that General Banks is advancing in Western Texas. When Texas is invaded, every State in the Confederacy will be invaded.

Dec'r 20th, Sunday.

On guard to-day. Post at the commissary.

Parsons' scouts brought in 78 men to-day. Captain Stewart, officer of the day, says Parsons' scouts bring in innocent & honest men. Such work will react if continued.

This evening I witness horse-racing through the streets in front of Gen'l Smith's head quarters.[27] I am surprised to see such conduct going on with impunity.

Dec'r 21st, Monday.

Blankets are being issued to-day, but no man can draw without a descriptive list. When pay or clothing is to be issued, a descriptive list is demanded, but if duty is required, no descriptive list is needed. The pretext is, the pay or articles drawn, must be entered on the descriptive list that the Government may know what the soldiers have received. According to this rule, if a soldier is so unfortunate as to lose his descriptive list—and many of them do lose their descriptive lists—he can never draw any thing more. It is all a pretext—a simple—a foolish—excuse to evade doing justuce. A soldier who is so unfortunate as not to possess a descriptive list—no matter what accident has befallen him—he may go cold, yea freeze, for want of a blanket but such is no excuse against a detail for duty. If I could not frame a better excuse, I would boldly say, "it does not suit my inclination to do justice in this matter, & that would save me from the perplexities attending a palpable contradiction.

Dec'r 22nd, Tuesday.

This morning there is a change in issuing blankets. Men are drawing without descriptive lists. I have no faith in the attempt, but I shall make an effort to draw a blanket for the sake of a test. I try, but fail. Captain (?) Jackson says he can not let me have one, as I already have one. Others have drawn one, who had two. They tell me Captain (?) Jackson did not ask them whether they had any blanket. He is just a little too verdant to fill the position he stands in, & since I do not treat him with more than common respect, he turns the cold shoulder to me when I apply for my rights. I think you are a little mistaken Captain (?). If you have no accomplices sharper than you are, I apprehend no fawning will be extorted from me.

Oscar B. Sherwin, a detail, working in the foundry, tells me men are deserting from the arsenal.[28]

J.D. Vance of our company, reported for duty to-day.[29] He says he has intelligence to the effect that Dick High and Bob Goodin have both taken the oath of allegiance to the Federal government.[30] They were inclined to do so before they were separated from us in prison in Algiers. Vance & I had several arguments with them to prevent them from doing so. Finally they were taken from the prison, & taken to the hospital. We then agreed they would turn Federals.

About 10 o'clock to-night, the government saddle shop, in Shreveport, came down with a terrible crash. Eleven men were in it. Two were killed dead; others were horribly wounded, & others escaped with but a few scratches.

Our whole camp was soon astir, as every man, but a few to guard the camp, was called on to go to the ruins to rescue the dead & wounded. But after detailing 8 men to act as guards, the remainder of us was sent back to camp as there was nothing we could do.

While there I was forcibly impressed by the manners of the men. Many were standing around apparently unconcerned, joking as though nothing serious had happened. The officer directing the operations was using the bitterest oaths over the bodies of the dead & the wounded.

Dec'r 23rd, Wednesday.

Too unwell for duty to-day, the first day I have missed since I have been here.

Longstreet, so says the Caddo Gazette, Extra, has raised the siege of Knoxville.[31]

Our congress has met, & the Secretary of war recommends the abrogation of the right of substitution; and the conscription of all, allowing no exemptions. He says we will, at the expiration of our 3 years enlistment, be allowed to join some company under existing organizations. He admits that nearly 2/3 of our army are straglers, deserters, or absent from the the [*sic*] army, in some other way.

Scarcely a paper, or an extra, is issued but the price of gold in N. York is quoted at high rates. But I *never* see the price of gold in Richmond.

Dec'r 24th, Thursday.

I have just read an Extra,[32] of yesterday, which contains the substance of the Presidents message to Congress. He admits the war has continued much longer than he expected; that our foreign relations are altogether unsatisfactory; that our currency is well night broken down; & recommends the repeal of the substitue[33] law, & the conscription of all who have substituted.

Now, here we find the President of our Confederacy proposing to violate a sacred contract. Should a citizen refuse to yield to this violation, should it become a law; or, if a substitute, whose age is above Conscription, should consider his contract broken, & return home, such acts would be treated as treason, desertion, &c. "It is a poor rule that will not work both ways."

Hear that our Reg't is on its way to L. Rock.

The paroled prisoners in paroled camp near L. Rock are deserting heavily.

Twelve Federal prisoners were brought in to-day. Two deserters also came in.

Dec'r 25th, Christmas.

On guard to-day. My post is no. 2, at one of the prison doors.

An Irishman, belonging on the gun boat,[34] turned out into the city for a gala day, & having got a little too much whisky, became more boisterous than suited the authorities. Accordingly, he was arrested, &, with considerable difficulty, was forced into prison. I was at the door through which he was passed into the prison. For a few minutes after he was placed in the prison, he was very quiet, appearing to be in a deep study. All of a sudden, as if seized by some sudden & powerful emotion, he started to the door, affirming vehemently, & with powerful oaths, he would not remain in the prison. It was my duty to prevent any one from passing in or out at the door, unless they had permits, & before he arrived at the door, I ordered him to halt, at the same time drawing my bayonet down in a thrusting attitude. He did not halt, & upon the instant, I thought he did not value the threat of a bayonet from me. He was a very large man, in full vigor of life, & could have fended off a thrust from me, & passed out. Instantly, I stepped back, cocked my Enfield Rifle, which was well loaded, leveled it on him, & again bade him halt. He obeyed, having just reached the door sill. I suppose he stood there for five minutes, hurling the most bitter oaths at one. He said I was a coward, or I would have thrust the bayonet through him when he first started; that he was no coward, & was not afraid of dying. Evidently he was chagrined because I did not make a thrust, but relied on the firing of my gun. He advanced upon the bayonet, but the instant I was ready to give him the contents of my gun, he halted, nor advanced any further. He had not advanced to a position that would justify my shooting him, & nothing he could say was a sufficient excuse. Indeed, I felt no inclination to shoot a man who was intoxicated, & a prisoner. I felt that shooting should be my last resort. Several said I should have shot him, but I observed none were willing to encounter him. Indeed, *all* seemed to be afraid of him. Several men & the officer of the guard, were required to force him into the prison, & he was all the while making powerful threats against the officer who, immediately after the committal of the prison, went below, & would not return, though solicited by many to do so. When the officer was solicited to come up, the Irishman would speak abusively of him, & defy him to come up. Evidently, the officer was afraid of him, & the Irishman knew it. I first requested the calling of the officer, from which the Irishman judged me afraid, & he became more abusive in language and threatened to walk out. I remarked as calmly as I could speak, that he might say what he pleased, but must remain inside of the door. With my gun well presented; cocked, & my finger on the trigger, I looked him steadily in the eye, & notwithstanding his repeated assertions that I was a coward, he kept within limits.

All is over now: the Irishman was kept within limits; no body was hurt, and I am very glad of it.

Seven prisoners escaped last night, & 1 man deserted from this company a few days ago.

A News, Extra,[35] is issued to-day, claiming to contain the substance of Lincoln's message to the Federal Congress, on the settlement of our difficulties. He says all below Colonels in the Army, Lieutenants in the navy, & some other ex-emotions, can, on taking a prescribed oath, be restored to their constitutional right.

Dec'r 26th, Saturday.

Off guard this morning, & no prisoners having escaped, I presume there is no danger of my being put in the guard house for escape of prisoners, as was done yesterday morning.

Dec'r 27th, Sunday.

On guard to-day. The weather is cold, cloudy, & drizzling, & we are not allowed to go inside of the guard house to shelter as we have heretofore done.

Twenty-two prisoners brought in from Texas to-day. One is manacled with a log chain. This constant hunting down one portion of our men by another, is a wonderful comment on the prosperity of our cause. If our government is right, the men deserting are wrong; &, if the men are right, the government is wrong. So, let it be as it may, it is a deplorable condition.

Dec'r 28th, Monday.

We were marched from camp to town,[36] and drilled about two hours this evening; then marched back to camp & dismissed. To go through the whole, it required nearly the entire evening.—Early in the morning we are called into rank, marched to the guard station, and, when it suits the convenience of the officers, we are mounted on guard for 24 hours. In the open air all the while; traveling the circuit of more than one mile at the time of relieving; & all the rigmarole

& circumstance required of us, makes it near noon the next day when we arrive at camp. About 1 hour's rest, & then for a drill till near sun down. Can men bear up under such treatment for any considerable length of time?

Rumored that the negroes have rebelled against the Federals at N. Orleans, & taken possession of the City. Good if true, but I do not believe a word of it.

Dec'r 29th, Tuesday.

On guard to-day, acting as supernumerary.

Three prisoners brought in to-day from near Camden, Ark.

President Davis says our army is in better condition now than at any previous time. The secretary of war says 2/3 of our army are absent without leave—conflicting statements.

The great rebellion of the negroes in N. Orleans turns out to be a small difficulty in Fort Jackson, in which about 30 Federals were killed.

Hear the Federals are landing at Niblitt's Bluff[37] on the Sabine River.

To-night a party of men & women of ill fame assembled in building near the guard house, & a difficulty arose between them on one side, & the guard & prisoners on the other, but nothing serious resulted therefrom.

Dec'r 30th, Wednesday.

A prisoner escaped yesterday, & this morning Col Shivers orders all of the supernumeraries to be put in the guard house for the escape of the prisoner. Lieutenant Kidd, commanding the guard, reported the escape of the prisoner, but could give no explanation as to how he escaped. Shivers, as is his custom, was both drunk & in an ill humor, & determined on revenge, ordered Lieutenant Kidd to place the supernumeraries in the guard house. No investigation was made, & there was no reason to conclude any of the supernumeraries more guilty than others, nor that all of the supernumeraries were more guilty than all of the other guard. But some body must be punished, & it mattered but little with Col. Shivers who should bear it.

When Lieutenant Kidd told us of Col. Shivers' order, I never felt more indignant. Indeed, the high handed injustice from President Davis down to the meanest corporal, both inclusive, loomed up before me in mountains of great magnitude. I vowed in my heart that if thus punished, I would never again entertain a spark of sympathy for the Confederate Government. Already I had suffered injuries (& my companions with me) until I was powerfully indifferent, & if executed, this sentence will *force* me to be what I have often thought I *never would be*—an enemy to these *Confederate States.* Of course I could not fully avow these sentiments, for my life would have been demanded as a forfeit; but I talked very strong to Lieutenant Kidd, & having cultivated some intimacy with him, he said he would not execute the orders until he had another interview with Col. Shivers. He said he was fully satisfied of my innocence, & did not suspicion any one in particular. Said he told

Col. Shivers he did not know how the prisoner escaped; that possibly he escaped from one of the supernumeraries when conducted to the rear. ——— After a short waiting, Lt. Kidd comes in, & reports the sentence will not be executed.

It might be objected that I should not take such strong ground against the Gov't on account of the act of one of its officers. I do not. Such acts among the officers of the Confederacy are common—they constitute the rule—and there is no chance to get such grievances redressed.

The prisoner escaped, as was afterwards found out, by writing himself a pass, and passing through the door by one of the guards. He had been in but a few hours, & was better dressed than the most of the soldiers—was dressed like a citizen—& as many both citizens & soldiers, were passing in & out on passes, he had no trouble.

I appreciate the kindness of L't Kidd, & here take occasion to state, that as far as I have seen him tried, he is one of the few exceptions among the officers.

I heard a man say last night that our currency in Houston, Texas, stands $25.00 against $1.00 in silver.

Dec'r 31st, Thursday.

Snowing to-day, & very cold. I am on guard at the spring. This is one time I am in good luck. I could not have got a more favorable position. This Spring is well sheltered, & within 100 yds. of the camp.[38]

Jan. 1st, Friday [1864]

A few nights since the aristocrats of this place held a party on a steam boat, & had three men detailed to guard the boat while they practiced their chosen dissipation. This is the way things go in this Confederacy. The masses are servants for the few, & must minister to the wishes of that few, though it be degrading in a high degree, & even destructive of the establishment of that aristocracy.

Hear the Indians are making considerable depredations in Cooke County, Texas.[39] This is a favorable time for their operations. But few men are left on the frontier to oppose them, & they are stimulated, & backed, by the Federal government to the most horrible deeds of cruelty.[40]

We have news now that the Confederate Congress has conscripted all from the age of 15 to 55 years, both inclusive, exempting none, not even those who have substituted. Will the men, who have substituted, certainly have to go into the army? I venture, as an opinion, that those who are wealthy will find a loop hole through which to get out, but those who have paid largely of what they possess to have substitutes, will find some trouble to get out. I will wait, & see.[41]

Jan. 2nd, Saturday.

Weather very cold; as cold, I think, as I ever experienced in this latitude.

This evening I go down to the fortifications on R. River below the City of Shreveport. I find some tolerably strong fortifications.[42] At the old fortification I found 7 men guarding the carriage of a heavy gun.[43] It seems to me 3 men would be enough, & better distribute burthens. Couldn't two men do all the guarding necessary? But few would have any use for any part of the carriage, & no one for the whole of it. No one could take any part of it without considerable labor to detach it; so two-men would fill every requirement. It is no uncommon thing to see more men at some post than is necessary, while at others there are not enough. That a fair and equitable distribution in all things is difficult to attain, I freely admit, but that is no reason why some effort should not be made in that direction.[44]

Jan. 3rd, Sunday.

On guard to-day. My post is supernumerary.[45] New orders are issued, requiring the guard to go the whole around when a relief is posted. Post number one is at one of the prison doors, & when a guard at that post is relieved, he must fall in behind the relief guard, & march the whole round of posts. Counting all the meanderings, it must require a travel of near two miles to make a round. Now, to accomplish this round in the night, through mud, & allowing for the necessary hindrances, requires nearly 2 hours of fatiguing travel. From every one, the question spontaneously arises, what is the use of all this? There is *no* use in it, & it is required to gratify the taste (?) of Major Schaffer. He thinks it does not look well to see a corporal going a round without a full quota of guard following at his heels. If looks are all that is desired, the order might be suspended at night, as at that time the Major & most, if not all, of his tasty fellows are at home asleep. If not, they generally stroll in "dark" places where they neither see much, nor desire to be seen by others.

Jan. 4th, Monday.

Major Schaffer is at guard mounting this morning, making a *big* splurge, having things done up the "scientificest." Bravo! Major, I would like to see you encounter some on a political equality. Methinks you would figure a little different.

After the new guard was mounted, he caused the old guard to be called into line, & there remain until the first relief was put on, which required about 1 hour. A little more bombast, which is a heavy tax on the poor soldier.

Learn from a friend that a Lieutenant has just arrived from East of the Mississippi. The reports are abundance of provisions there, & all quiet. There are some desertions, & there are many "bushwhackers" in Tennessee.[46] They are Tennesseans, and many of them have been in our army. If treated in that Department as we are in this, no doubt but many more will be "bushwhackers."

Jan. 5th, Tuesday.

Two men deserted last night, & one deserted a few nights since. Sixteen prisoners escaped but a few nights since. A great many are brought in, but others go to fill their places.

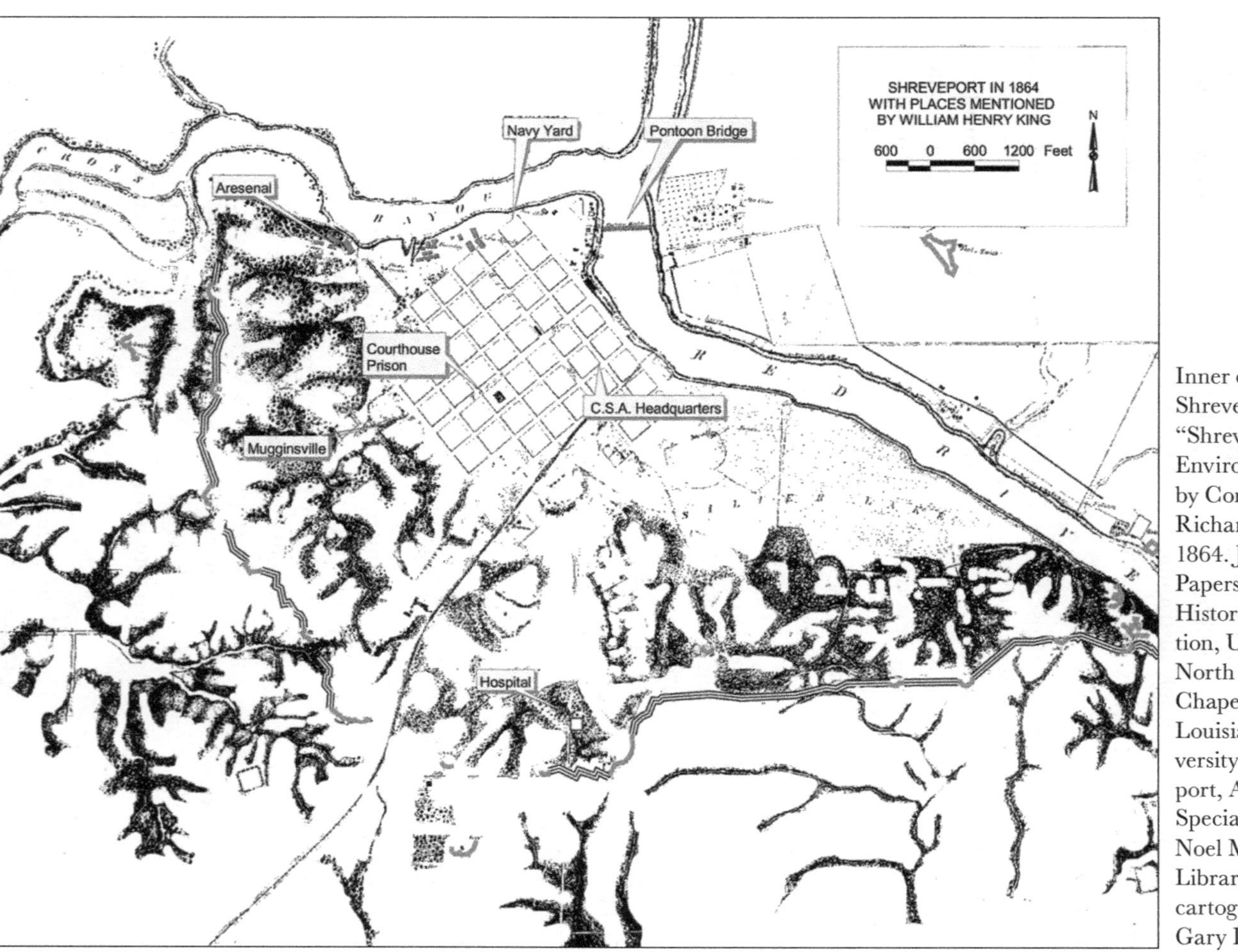

Inner defenses of Shreveport, entitled "Shreveport and Environs," drawn by Confederate Maj. Richard Venable, 1864. Jerome Gilmer Papers, Southern Historical Collection, University of North Carolina, Chapel Hill. Copy at Louisiana State University in Shreveport, Archives and Special Collections, Noel Memorial Library. Additional cartography by Gary D. Joiner.

It is now considered certain that General Hardee[47] has superceded General Bragg. Don't know much about Hardee's merits, but feel quite certain the Confederacy is not worsted in the exchange. Bragg would make a fare general for an aristocracy or a monarchy, but not for a people battling for independence. Republicanism is one thing, & Monarchy another—they are antipodes—& material that suits the requirements of one, don't suit the requirements of the other.

I am too unwell for duty to-day.

Jan. 6th, Wednesday

I am still unwell, & can not do any camp duty.

The shoemakers of this place have been conscripted to-day in consequence of extortion. Well, extortion is highly censurable at any time, and under any circumstances, but when so prevalent among the high officials of this Confederacy, there is, at least, some palliation for the poor shoemakers.

Learn from the South Western that Gen'l Lovell has been tried for the surrender of New Orleans, & has received an honorable acquittal.[48] Of course; he is one of President Davis' "pets," & *must* stand clear.

Jan. 7th, Thursday.

On guard to-day, though not well. I would not report for duty when not well, but if able to do duty, I find it preferable to the ennui of camp life. If not able to do duty, our officers do not like to permit us to go beyond the narrow confines of our camp.

My post is at the back gate of the hospital yard.[49] It is a new post, & as I have no gun, nor any evidences but my word that I am a guard, I find my post a troublesome one. When I halt men, who are constantly passing, they question my authority, & some pass along, believing it a "sell." Indeed, the attending circumstances requires a great deal of passing through this gate. One department of the hospital is on the north side of an alley, & the other department on the south side of the same alley. Through this gate is the way for all to pass in passing from one department to the other. The object of the post was to prevent those who had no business from passing; & those who would occasionally pass down the alley into the town rather than procure a pass, to pass out by the guard at the front door. There is no use for a guard at either place for the last named purpose as none but the convalescing are thus to be hindered from going out, & there is a provost guard to pick them up. The idea of this post originated in the brain of some one who had not enough brain to see it would cause more trouble than benefit.

Jan. 8th, Friday.

The News Papers are harassing us again in relation to the peace party in the North. I hope it will not turn out as formerly—the harbinger of some defeat on our part. In these matters it seems our leading characters have lost sight—if they ever knew it—of an important fact; that a bitter is all the more bitter when contrasted with a sweet.

Jan. 9th, Saturday.

On guard again to-day, though not well. My post is No. 1 in the guard house. When I first commenced duty at this place, we drew rations enough, but now we could eat at one meal what we draw for a day. If we had no other means of subsistence, our suffering would be intense. All of my mess have some money with which we buy something to eat, & occasionally we get something from home. Those who have no money, or friends to furnish them, follow what is well known among the soldiers "pressing"; that is, they take it, whenever they can find it. Is it stealing? At any rate, it is not unmitigated theft.

Several of our men are put in prison to-day. They are committed for different offences. One man was committed a few days since for expressing himself too freely. He was not pleased with the proceedings of our officials, & giving vent to his feelings, was decreed a sufficient offense to put him in the guard house to await trial. I have always regarded freedom of speech as an essential element of a Republic. He should be allowed to express himself freely; if he falsified, the falsehood will recoil upon him, & if he tells the truth, he does no more than should be done.

The weather is yet intensely cold.

Jan. 10th, Sunday.

I am quite unwell this morning. Last night I had two "sick spells" that rendered me unfit for duty, but rather than cause disturbances, I held out till morning. It is troublesome to make details in the night to fill the places of sick men, & prefer to hold out if practicable.

Three prisoners, who had been sent to the hospital for medical treatment, escaped last night for which some of the guard were put in the guard house. In view of all the attending circumstances, it is grossly unjust to imprison a guard for the bare fact of the escaping of a prisoner. There are numerous ways by which one can easily escape from the hospital without, in the least involving the responsibility of the guard. It is shameful that our men must suffer so much of punishment, & of disgrace, on account of loose management by our officers.

Jan. 11th, Monday.

I am too unwell for duty to-day, and must content myself with whatever medicines may be prescribed for me.

Jan. 12th, Tuesday.

I learn from good authority that "bushwhackers" are operating in Sabine Parish in this (La.) State. They are operating at this time in the States of Tennessee, Georgia, Arkansas, Louisiana, & Texas. A sad state of things. Unless men are treated better, "bushwhacking" will increase.

Hear that Mouton's division has gone in the direction of Gaines' landing on the Mississippi River.[50]

A prisoner escaped from the hospital to-day.

Only 3 men over 2 reliefs could be furnished to-day. A few men were detailed from Montgomery's Cavalry Company, but others were still wanting to complete the 3rd relief, and a portion of the first & second reliefs were chosen to serve in the third relief; alternately. Unless our burthens are lighted, we will soon be unable to muster a Corporal's squad.

Jan. 13th, Wednesday

I am very unwell to-day, though on guard.

Last night one of our men died in the hospital. He sickened since the commencement of this spell of bad weather.

After standing guard 2 hours at the hospital, I reported sick, & returned to camp.

Maj. Gen. Sterling Price, C.S.A. Courtesy Mansfield State Historical Site, Mansfield, Louisiana.

Jan. 14th, Thursday.

I am quite sick to-day.

Jan. 15th, Friday.

I am now an inmate of the hospital.

Hear this evening that Gen'l Price is in this City, & his army is on its way here.[51]

Jan. 16th, Saturday.

Hear to-day that some of the business houses of this place are refusing to take Louisiana State money. Whether from some bad management in the financial affairs of the State, or because of the positions the Federals hold in the State, I have not been able to learn.

Jan. 17th, Sunday.

I do not suffer so much pain to-day, but I find I am slightly salivated.

Jan. 18th, Monday.

To-day I find that ptyalism[52] is increasing.

Learn that some others have deserted from our camp.

Jan. 24th, Tuesday.

Since the 18th instant, I have been too sick to pay attention to passing events, but from what few items I have been able to pick up, the same downward tendency, so far as our cause is concerned, is plainly discoverable.

Last night a poor soldier named Berry died in a room adjoining mine. Night before last he came into the room to wait on his brother, then very sick. That night he was not on duty, & he obtained permission to wait on his brother, knowing those detailed to do so were neglectful of their duty; During the night he was taken violently ill, & died last night about 12 o'clock, midnight. His disease was pneumonia of a most violent form. He was forbidden the use of much cold water as a drink but a scorching fever occasioned an insatiable thirst for it. The chief nurse who was on watch left the room, & Berry, who was fully able to walk, went to the water bucket, & took a hearty drink of cold cistern water, & returned to his couch, where he died in less than five minutes, I think. I had, for some time, been taking cognizance of his breathing which was exceedingly laborious. I had also heard him go to the water bucket, & take a hearty draught of water, & I do not think it was exceeding five minutes before his breathing ceased. The nurse soon came in, & talked very abusively to him for taking the water. But, alas! Poor Berry heard not a word of the abuse—he was no more. Oh! What feelings of horror came over me to hear the dead man thus rebuked; & that by one whose constant duty was to minister to the wants of the sick; and should, of all men, be the most tender and patient. He claimed as an excuse, Berry had acted highly indiscreet in drinking the water, not seeming to recognize the fact that Berry's intense suffering had dethroned his reason.

Jan. 25th, Monday.

My health is improving slowly. I was badly salivated; so much so, that for several days I could not talk, nor could I eat any solid food. But for the kindness of Wm G. Monroe, a Missourian, & second nurse in this ward, my suffering would have been much greater. Soon after my admission into the hospital, he became interested in me, & acted the true friend to me from that time to this. My physician, Dr. Riggins,[53] a Missourian, manifests but little interest in any of his patients, & has all the while refused to prescribe a diet suitable to my condition. Though unable to eat a particle of solid food, it has invariably, been furnished me with little that I could possible eat—sometimes nothing. Monroe was, & is yet, vigilant in procuring whatever he could that I would eat. Many times his efforts have been fruitless, but I would furnish money, & he would go, or send, to the market, & buy something that I could eat. For these acts of kindness I shall ever feel grateful.

Hear diverse rumors to-day, but nothing reliable in the way of war news.

Seven or eight Federal prisoners are brought in this evening.

Sent to the market for a bottle of milk this morning. Louisiana State money struck at this place was refused.[54]

Recently, I have heard some boasting that the soldiers East of the Mississippi have not been deserting more than is common in armies. I see that Gen'l Smith has issued orders to prevent them from coming to this Department; all in consequence of heavy desertions there.

Jan. 26th, Tuesday.

Warm weather for the season.

I am improving slowly

Jan. 27th, Wednesday.

A note from J.R. Cavett this morning, dated the 24th instant, informs me that my family was well.

Gov't Stores; Sugar & Cotton, are still being moved from this place to some point westward.

Jan. 28th, Thursday.

About 140 Federal prisoners escaped from the camp of the prisoners near this place.[55] Some of them have been retaken, & brought back.

Major Schaffer is having the post guard uniformed. Perhaps his pride will result in some good, one time. All of us are in need of clothing, & some are in great need, and the Gov't has not given us any for a long time; neither has it paid us our wages. Spur up, Major; we will not owe you any thanks for the clothing if we get it; for it is our due, & you are promoted by no principle of justice, but by an ambitious pride; but let us have the clothing, & we will applaud you a little.

Jan. 29th, Friday.

Another squad of 62 prisoners from Texas, were brought in to-day.

More than two weeks ago, A. J. Groves,[56] and S.M. Self, both belonging to Co. B, 28th La. Vol's, left post camp. I hear that Self is at home very sick, but I have not been able to learn any thing from Groves.

Groves I never knew until I went into the army. He was a messmate of mine from the first. Some of my intimate friends, and messmates, had known him, & seemed to appreciate him. He proved an agreeable messmate, & a soldier always ready to do his duty. Indeed, I have seen him drill with a scorching fever on him, & have known him to go on guard though very unwell. For some time previous to his leaving, I had loaned him different articles of clothing when he went on guard; for he was so destitute of clothing that he could not possibly have borne the intense cold without additional clothing. A few days before he left, he made efforts to obtain clothing & money, the Gov't being considerably behind with him, both in clothing or money; but failed in every attempt. He stated to the officials, that he had no money, and was almost destitute of clothing; that he had no relations to furnish either; that his old father had been stripped of all he had, by the federals on the Miss. River; that his only brother had lost his wife, & now had a large family of little children to provide for; that if the Gov't did not furnish him he would be destitute. These facts were patent to all who were acquainted with Groves & his circumstances, but they availed nothing. They brought neither money nor clothing. But the calls for Groves to do duty remained unremitted, though the weather was bitter cold. He responded to each demand without murmuring until the constant exposure so much impaired his health that he could go no longer. The night before he left in the morning, (he left just after breakfast,) he related his troubles to me, & said, *emphatically,* he would not stand it. I had never heard him utter a word against any treatment he had before received, so I thought he was only in a fit of passion, & would feel differently when that subsided. However, there was an earnestness in his expression, that renders it not easily forgotten. Can I call him a deserter?—I can not find it in my heart to do so. In addition to all I have claimed for him, our comrades in arms state no one proved himself more gallant on the battle field. When rehearsing his troubles to me, he was so hoarse he could not speak above a whisper, and seemed to be in profound trouble. This is not an overdrawn picture, & by no means an isolated case. It is but an example of what is occurring daily. Yet such men are called deserters, & if caught, are brought here, or taken to some other point, & incarcerated to await a trial for life by a Court

Martial composed, perhaps, of men who have but little thought of justice, or even ability to comprehend it. Men who would sacrifice principles of honor & justice to forward their own ends & aims. The picture is heart rending, therefore let us turn from it.

Jan. 30th, Saturday.

I am not so well to-day, but think my bad feelings are only temporary.

The State Legislature is now in session in this place, & one can scarcely look upon the streets at any hour but some "spirit" can be seen. Don't know whether they are legislators or not, but from the character of the lesislation We have had of late, I judge they are.

Jan. 31st, Sunday.

I feel that I am convalescing this morning.

Last night a man died in this room.

I learn from a source I can not doubt, that the matron of this hospital is a woman of ill fame, & for that reason good women will not visit the hospital except in emergencies. "Birds of a feather flock to-gether," & base men & women as naturally seek each others company.

Feb. 1st, Monday.

There are men in this hospital of debilitated constitutions, sore legs & chronic diseases who have been taken up by Parsons' men, & brought to the prison at this place. Why bring such men here? Able men are required to wait on them; guard them, &c. To the Confederate army made any stronger by their presence; or is the cause of justice in the least vindicated by their presence?

My health is improving slowly. I would do better in camp, if I could be exempted from duty until I had gathered sufficient strength. But no; one must be restricted to the narrow limits of a hospital if he can not do all that is imposed on him in camp. The only way I know of to keep even with such requirements, is to be certain to remain in the hospital long enough.

Feb. 2nd, Tuesday.

It is rumored that Federal gun boats have been to Fort DeRussy on Red River.

"The number of slaves killed by neglect and brutality of the enemy will equal the loss of life of white in both armies." This I extract from the Gov. Moore's Message to the General Assembly of the State of Louisiana now in session at this place. That I have no definite means of knowing the correctness or incorrectness of this statement, I freely admit, but I have no hesitancy in believing it incorrect; & that Governor Moore knew it when he wrote it.

Feb. 3rd, Wednesday.

The wheat crop of Texas has been severely injured by the recent cold spell.

Parson's Brigade is now passing through this place on its way to Texas. The sick, the lame, & the blind; the deaf, & the dumb of Texas may look out now; for Parsons' men will soon be after them. There are two Parsons' brigades in this department-one from Missouri, & the other from Texas. It is the Texas brigade that has been so efficient in bringing men from Texas to the prison at this place.

Feb. 4th, Thursday.

This evening I got a partial view of Colonel Parsons, commanding Parsons' brigade of Texas Cavalry. He looks to be 30 years old, or upwards; of medium stature, light hair, & florid complexion. He was dressed in the most fantastic style, with many little notions of ornament, both on his person, & saddle & bridle—the whole presenting the unmistakable declaration, "I am *the* man of this Department." The old adage, of, "All fuss, & feathers," seems altogether pertinent here.

Feb. 6th, Saturday.

A letter from home to-day of the 31st ultimo informs me of the good health of all at that time.

Brig. Gen. Mosby Parsons, C.S.A. Courtesy Mansfield State Historic Site, Mansfield, Louisiana.

Capt. Abny was in town this evening. I tried to get an interview with him; but failed. He gives intelligence that our Division is now on the march to Alexandria.

Feb. 7th, Sunday.

This morning, for the first time since I have been in this hospital, I took a walk through town. The walk fatigued me, but I now feel that it will prove beneficial.

Feb. 8th, Monday

In my perambulations through the city to-day, I find the streets crowded, & the department of officers is well represented.

From an advertisement of Col. Wm Harrison,[57] I infer that men who have furnished substitutes, will, by an act of the Confederate Congress, be compelled to enter the Confederate Army. If true, who can have any confidence in a contrast with the Confederacy.

Feb. 9th, Tuesday.

Hear to-day that the Federals have made an attack on Mobile.

About 60 prisoners are brought in from Texas this evening.

Hear that Gen'l Price has fallen back to Spring Hill, Arkansas.[58]

Several days ago, one W.H. Jones of Houston County, Texas, proffered to show me his papers, claiming he had been wrongfully imprisoned by Parsons' men. I declined doing so, thinking there was no need of evidence more than his own statement; for his whole behavior bespoke truth. Since that time, I have spoken of the circumstance to others, & the whole was flatly contradicted. That I might be more certain of what I affirmed, I, to-night, asked for an inspection of his papers. He readily complied, and I unhesitatingly pronounce them all right., & his furlough not out until the 18th inst.[59] He was furloughed from his command to go home to recuperate his health. His furlough being almost out, but his health still bad, he went to his County town to get an extension according to provisions of law. A competent physician made the extension, & the whole certified to by the County Clerk, with seal affixed, as directed by law. Just after the completion of the extension, a squad of the ever memorable Parsons' Brigade, came upon him; seized, & carried him before one of their own physicians for examination. The physicians would not examine Jones' papers, nor investigate his symptoms, but giving Jones a single look, directed the officer of the guard; "put him down for light duty," & he was soon on the march for the prison at this place. They brought him within three miles of his home; &, being unprepared in the way of clothing, & his wife in a delicate situation, he requested the privilege of going by home to get clothing, & give some directions relative to family affairs—but no—"onward, direct, to the prison at ~~at~~ Shreveport was the order of the day." But his health being very bad, he was brought from the prison to the hospital. He has tried several times to have his cause investigated, but has each time been treated with silent contempt. There seems to be general derangement of his system, & he is afflicted with haemoptysis[60] From which none of the physicians, in the army or out of it, who have had charge of his case, are able to give him more than temporary relief. Ye, who prate of the liberty we are fighting for; and the tyranny of the Federals; please give us a solution of this case. If this is freedom, away with it.

Feb. 10th, Wednesday.

Last night, the action of my heart was very much deranged. Within the last four years, I have had several such spells—some of them very alarming—& the advice of good physicians is, be as quiet as possible, & use but little medicine. This morning I stated the case to Dr. Rigging. He smiled significantly, & said, "be quiet a while, & see what it will come to." Evidently, he thought I wished to prolong my time in the hospital, but I had a good witness to the state of my pulse at the time of the spell. To me, neither position is desirable, but if well, I would much rather be in camp doing duty. Health & camp duty *always* before sickness & hospital fare.

One of Parsons' men, recently brought into this hospital, says our men are taking all of the horses from the citizens in the vicinity of Pine Bluffs, Arkansas;[61] done by order of Gen'l Holmes. He says he saw the last horse taken from a woman whose husband was in our army. She wept bitterly, and besought the officer to spare that horse to her, & her little children, as their sufferings would be greatly increased if he were taken away. But the hard heart of the officer was unyielding.

He further states he saw a young lady dismounted in a muddy road, 6 miles from home, and her horse taken. This man acknowledges the injustice of such deed, but believes we will yet come out all right.

Feb. 12th, Friday.

To-day I left the hospital to try the duties of camp life again. I do not feel able to do a soldiers' duty, but as I can not get the requisite exercise to gain strength while confined to the limits of the hospital, I return to camp.

Feb. 13th, Saturday.

I am informed to-day from a reliable source, that cotton is being shipped from this place to New Orleans. This is done by the officers, and, of course, counted all right. If a private or citizens, engage in such business, the act will be regarded as a high crime. To sham the act for a little while longer, it is now rumored there is a 90 days free trade between the Confederacy and the United States. To further quiet matters, a great many men are being furloughed.

I regard these acts as forebodings of a finality of this desperate difficulty. The officers will be apt to get large sums of money for the cotton, & I believe it is mainly in view of this that the struggle is further protracted.

Feb. 14th, Sunday.

I learn from the Caddo Gazette of the 12th inst. That Alfred Barbow, Jo. Johnston's Quarter Master, has absconded, leaving a deficit of $15000000.[62] 'Tis said he was in the habit of getting drunk, gambling, & engaging with houses of ill fame for himself & friends. There are many Barbours in this war—some *might* be found in Shreveport—even at Gen'l Smith's Head Quarters. If they do not embezzle public funds—& I am not fully assured they do not—they get drunk, & engage with houses of ill fame.

Feb. 15th, Monday.

Drew a jacket & a pair of pants to-day for uniform.

Hear that M.J. Johnson of Texas got an agency in the Cotton business at Brownsville, sold several thousand bales for specie, & absconded with the money, taking his whole family with him. The report may be false, but I give it for whatever it may be worth.

Feb. 16th, Tuesday.

I learn to-day that more than sixty prisoners were brought in yesterday from Texas, and that others were brought in the day before.

On guard to-day. My post is at the hospital.

Learn from the News, Extra,[63] of to-day, that the Federals, 30000 strong, have retaken Jackson, Mississippi, & that they are concentrating on Mobile.

Gov't stores are still begin moved from this place; one bhd. of Sugar to 3 yoke of oxen. That does not seem like there is much hurry.

A very sudden change in the weather—from warm to cold.

Feb. 17th, Wednesday.

We were drilled this evening, & it fatigued me greatly.

Feb. 18th, Thursday.

I am quite sore and still to-day, caused by the severe drilling yesterday.

Hear from what is considered reliable authority that senator Wigfall has written home that the institution of slavery must "go up;"[64] that the world is against us, & we can not prevail.

Too unwell for duty in the morning, but drill in the evening. All are uniformed, & we made something of a display. I reckon that will do now about as well as any thing.

Two Steam Boats arrived at this place this evening, bringing a considerable lot of Sugar and molasses.

Hear a store of fresh goods has just been opened in this place. Connected in some way, I suppose, with the Cotton trade. To all intents & purposes, so far as the cause we set out for is concerned, this war is at an end, but it will be protracted as long as possible if speculation continues to be tolerated.

Feb. 20th, Saturday.

Hear to-day that Gen'l Lee (not R.E. Lee) has driven back the Federals from Jackson, Mississippi, to Vicksburg, killing, wounding & taking prisoners, to the amount of 6000.[65]

Feb. 21st, Sunday.

Learn from a Washington, Arkansas, paper, that the Raleigh, N.C., Standard advocates returning to the Union.[66]

Preparations are being made to take more cotton below.

Ten Federal prisoners escaped from the prison last night. Six were caught, & brought back before night.

Feb. 22nd, Monday.

On guard to-day. My post is at the gov't corn pens.[67]

We now have news that General Longstreet has taken Knoxville, Tennessee, & put the enemy to flight. In exultation, I see flags streaming before the breeze. If they would hoist a flag over the cotton they are preparing to take to the Federals, I think the scene would be complete.

Feb. 23rd, Tuesday.

Last night some person bound a rag around a stone, set the rag on fire, cast it on the warehouse opposite to the guard house. It fell into the gutter, & before any damage was done, it was discovered, & removed. I can not conceive of any thing to be attained by the attempt except some one desperate, & determined on mischief, did it, not caring who was involved as mischief was done.

During the night a set of drunken rowdies kept up their rowdyism in the basement story of Gen'l Smith's Head Quarters. In one apartment there is a drinking saloon, & in the other, a gambling saloon. I frequently pass, & see drinking & gambling going on, & from all I have seen, & hear of this place, it is frequented mainly, if not exclusively, by officers & professional gamblers.

Last night two of our men left. Both were good looking men.

Feb. 24th, Wednesday.

On guard to-day. My post is at the guard house.

To-day, for the first time, I asked Col. Shivers for a 2-day pass. He flatly refused. Others have never failed, though they apply once a week.

This evening James Dunn of my company was brought in a prisoner, & put into the guard house.[68] His health becoming very bad, he was furloughed. He went home, & after his time was out, remained there.

From the best information I can gather, the late reported fight at Knoxville is a mistake.

Feb. 25th, Thursday.

We were taken out at 2 o'clock to drill, & continued till about 5 o'clock. It was near 4 hours from the time we left camp until we returned. Such duty as we go through will soon wear out men—especially when fed no better than we are.

Fear our uniforms will not profit us in the end. The Major is now determined to "cut a figure."

Feb. 26th, Friday.

Twenty five men have just been brought here from Galveston, Texas, to serve on the gun boat.[69] After arriving at this place, they were required to take an oath to serve for 3 or 5 years. They refused, & were sent to our camp. Last night 10 of them took "French leave of absence;" that is, they left without permits. They were willing to serve on the gun boat the balance of the time they had agreed to serve the Confederacy, but vowed they would not now make engagements.

Feb. 27th, Saturday.

To-day my post is at the guard house.

In the evening, the coroner of this place was killed by Gen'l Smith's orderly. From all I can learn relative to the case, the deed was unjustifiable.

Feb. 28th, Sunday.

Last night 14 Federal prisoners escaped. I hear that 4 escaped from camp below here.

The great victory reported to have been gained by our forces at Jackson, Mississippi, turns out to be a mistake.

Major Schaffer informed us we are now Gen'l Smith's body guard, & he, Smith, is second president of the Confederacy. Are we not conspicuous characters? Major Schaffer evidently thinks so.

Feb. 29th, Monday.

Ten of us are now detailed as a continued provost guard. We flatter ourselves that it will prove something easier than former service.

A very cold rain to-day.

March 1st, Tuesday.

There is a considerable sleet on the ground to-day.

This evening we are entertained by the famous Sam Williams.[70] I do not think I have ever heard his performance on the violin surpassed. For melody & softness of tone, I am sure I never heard any thing more pleasing.

March 2nd, Wednesday.

Under orders from Col. Shivers, we have arrested Mitchell, a drummer at this place, & conducted him to the guard house. I learn the charge preferred against him is, he was discharged from the hospital at this place by Dr. Catlett,[71] with order to report to his command. He went to Col. Shivers for transportation, & Col. Shivers assigned him to duty here as post guard. In obeying the orders of one, he disobeyed the orders of the other, & *vice versa.* What course could he have taken to escape?

March 3rd, Thursday.

Arrest a Mr. Kempe[?] under charg[e] of being a conscript. He was sent to the guard house, but not placed among the other prisoners. We had charge of him for some hours at our quarters, & he manifested comparative contentment. But our duties were to arrest, not guard prisoners, & having plenty to do in our special line, our officers complained at the extra duty imposed on us, & had Hope sent to the guard house. On arriving at the guard house, he protested bitterly against going in among the other prisoners. It now became apparent that the officers were disposed to deal lightly with him; afraid, from some cause, to deal decisively with him.

March 4th, Friday.

Nothing of peculiar interest transpired today in our new sphere of soldiering. The like will not, probably, happen often; for our situation is such, that exciting events will be apt to come before us often.

March 5th, Saturday.

Another day blank so far as any thing of interest is concerned. The fact is sufficiently noteworthy to fill this space.

March 6th, Sunday.

Currently reported to-day, that the Federals are in strong numbers in Monroe & Harrisonburg.

March 7th, Monday.

Parsons' brigade is dismounted for want of corn in Texas. I judge they will not now prove so terrible to many of the citizens of Texas.

Further rumors that the Federals are in Monroe & Harrisonburg.

There is a report that there has been a big fight in Mississippi, & the Federals were completely routed. Gotten up as a counter irritant, I suppose.

March 8th, Tuesday.

I have just had an interview with a gentleman from East of the Mississippi River, & he says there are no exchange of prisoners there. It seems the Federals & the Confederates are too contrary to agree to *disagree,* & fight the dispute out.

March 9th, Wednesday.

Gen'l Green is ordered back to this State.[72]

From good information I learn that provisions, in Western Texas, are very scarce, & there are serious apprehensions that many will suffer from want of something to subsist upon.

From the tenor of the news papers, they are bolstering up for heavy fight the ensuing spring. More blood must be spilled, & valuable lives lost, that more speculation may be indulged in to the amassing of wealth on the one hand, & a consequent poverty on the other. What a reckless disregard of consequences!

March 10th, Thursday.

Learn from a gentleman just from the East of the Mississippi River, that of the great battles, resulting in our success, reported to have been fought recently, have never been fought. More props from unknown, Messrs, Editors; so you may prop again.

Gen'l Walker's men[73] are greatly disaffected on account of the trade now being carried on between the Federals & our officers. Hoozah for them! That this is "a rich man's war, & a poor man's fight," needs no further proof.

I have just seen a gentleman who is direct from Austin, Texas, & he says all are whipped out there. Of course there are *some* exceptions, but I do not doubt his statement as true in the main.

Maj. Gen. John G. Walker, C.S.A. Courtesy Mansfield State Historic Site, Mansfield, Louisiana.

Chapter 7

The Red River Campaign and Aftermath

That this is no longer a struggle for the rights of the *people,* but for the aggrandizement of a certain few, is a clear case.

William Henry King
July 12, 1864

March 11th, Friday.

A portion (110 feet) of the obstructions in R. River at Fort DeRussy has been forced from its place by high water.[1] Great engineering! When this water is low, & gun boats can not pass, obstructions are put in the River under the supervision of "Competent Engineers," but as soon as there is plenty of water for the gun boats, it sweeps the obstructions out. Consummate folly!

March 13th, Sunday.

Nothing in the way of news for to-day, nor for yesterday. It is truly surprising, and I think it worthy of note.

March 14th, Monday.

It is said that Randal's brigade has stacked arms on account of the trade now carried on with the enemy.

Another gentleman from Western Texas says board in San Antonio is $60.00 per day & in Austin, $40.00 per day. He further states many are coming East to get provisions.

Day before yesterday, Wm Strayhan of Bossier Parish was arrested in Colonel Harrison's battalion, & forced to take the oath of a soldier. Strayhan is very lame, & has been unable to get about without a crutch for many years. The officers are in need of numbers to complete the battalion, & they are willing to resort to a trick as low as forcing a lame man in. If there was such a thing as redressing the grievances of a private or poor citizen in this Monstrosity of a government, Strayhan could have those officers severely punished. But, in an attempt to do so, he could accomplish about as much good as the dog that bays the moon. A government that will thus suffer its subjects imposed upon, giving no redress, is not worthy of support at any time, or under any circumstances.

March 15th, Tuesday

My wife visits me, & informs me that family & friends are well at home. I find some trouble in procuring lodgings, but finally arrange with Mr. Mofield, the stage driver.

March 16th, Wednesday.

Various rumors are afloat this evening in relation to Fort De Russy having fallen into the hands of the enemy.[2] It is spposed by some that cotton buyers originated it. It is highly probably they have done so; for there is little they will not dare to do, when a bargain is at stake.

March 17th, Thursday.

This evening we get intelligence to the effect that Alexandria has fallen into the hands of the Federals.[3] The intelligence occasions a great stir. Thirty volunteers are called for to do temporary service on the gun boat, Missouri. Eleven of the post guard volunteer, but that lacks 19 of the required number. That 19 is not lacking long, for the guard house is called on, & the deficit is made at once. Some of the men were brought in & imprisoned to-day. That is the way it works.

Men are constantly deserting from this post.

March 18th, Friday.

On yesterday, Shingles (herpes)[4] appear on my side, & on application to Dr. Catlett for medical aid, he prescribed a dose of salts (sulphate of magnesia)[5] for several mornings in succession. I am not a Doctor, hence, do not pretend to know much about diseases, or remedies for them; but, like most of men, I have my opinions, & will express them and, regarding this prescription, I can not see the point. Salts, as I have been taught, are cooling & purgative, good to move the bowels, & especially when the system is in a feverish condition. Though my disease is painful, I have not the slightest fever, & my bowels are in a soluble & healthy condition. But, however inappropriate, I must submit—kill or cure, it is all one with Dr. Catlett.

It is now believed, beyond a doubt, that the Federals are in Alexandria. The "impregnable" Fort De Russy was taken with light struggle.

March 19th, Saturday.

Quite a stir among the authorities to-day. From some cause we do not see so many "authorities" (officers) in town to-day. I recon[6] Gen'l Smith has stirred among them with a long pole. That's the way to do them, Gen'l—send them to the front when the enemy approaches.

From certain manifestations it is presumable that Gen'l Smith is endeavoring to provision this place for a siege.

March 20th, Sunday.

We have just learned that our forces fought about 1 hour at Fort De Russy; that Walker's and Taylor's commands are below the Federals.

The steamer, M. Relf,[7] has arrived with all the sick from Alexandria.

March 21st, Monday.

Much excitement prevails in the city, both among citizens and soldiers.—Learn the archives of this department are being removed from this place, but to what point, evidence is lacking.

Herpes continue to grow worse on me, though Dr. Catlett's prescription has been followed to the letter, & I apply to Dr. Riggins for treatment. On exhibiting the eruptions, he asks significantly, "is that all?" Believing from the manner of his interrogatory that he supposed I wished to get quarter in the hospital, I remarked, "I have not come for a place in the hospital; I am doing duty every day, & expect to do duty every day unless I grow worse, but as this eruption is painful, & has, for several days, been growing worse, I would like to have it relieved before it becomes serious." He then promised a prescription, but after attending to other cases, walked off & left me. As there was nothing better I could do, I returned to my quarters, and resigned myself to chances, with a pretty strong conviction that Doctors were some thing of a humbug any how.

March 22nd, Tuesday.

Gov. Allen of this State has issued an order for the conscription of the free negroes of this place.[8] When the Federals received negroes into their army the Southern press, & the Southern people in general, made a great ado about the matter. Now negroes are conscripted in the South, & I reckon that if the South urges any thing against the Federals on that score, it will be the "pot saying to the kettle, you are black."

This morning, D.Z. Elder of the place,[9] commenced the job of conscripting the free negroes of this place by placing a guard around the market house with instruction to let all negroes in, but let none out.[10] A squad of our men acted

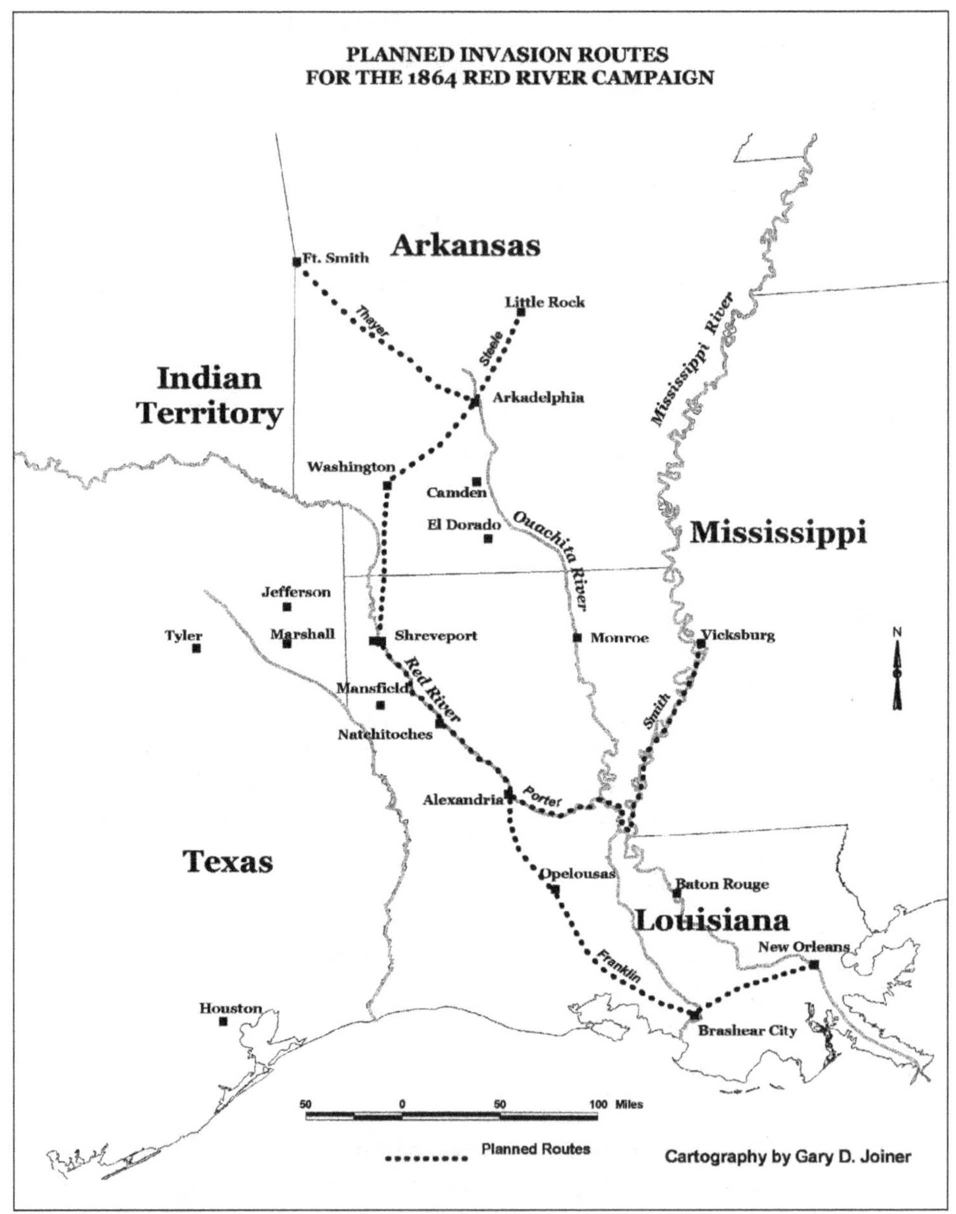

Union plan of invasion in the Red River Campaign. Cartography by Gary D. Joiner.

as guard, & I learn from them the move occasioned a considerable sensation. Negroes that had been sent to market for rations for the breakfasts of their masters, were detained beyond ordinary breakfast time of day, & their masters came after them, making heavy threats against the guard. But the guard was composed of men who knew their duty, & were not easily frightened out of it. They had been turned over to D.Z. Elder to execute his orders, & they knew full well that he was responsible if any thing wrong was done. Pending a considerable dispute between a portion of the guard & a few citizens, Capt. Elder stepped forward, & acknowledged his responsibility.

The trouble was finally ended without any serious casualty; but Cap. Elder had to go to Gen'l Smith's head quarters to explain himself. Capt. Elder has the requisite vim for such emergencies, or it is probably he would not have got off very lightly. Officers are a little jealous of authority in others.

Gen'l Banks infantry are now in the vicinity of Walnut Hills, Arkansas. Our space for action continues to narrow down.

Provisions are being brought to this place, rapidly, preparatory to siege. In some things, & at some times, our commanders are heavy on preparations; but most frequently, the time is just too late to accomplish much; & the thing done had about as well been left out, & something else done in its stead.

Maj. Gen. Nathaniel P. Banks, U.S.A. Courtesy Mansfield State Historic Site, Mansfield, Louisiana.

March 23rd, Wednesday.

A passenger on the stage from Mansfield, reports Gen'l Taylor 40 miles below Mansfield; & 7 gun boats, & 27 transports on this side of the falls above Alexandria.[11] We are still narrowing down.

See some of the commissary stores are being moved from this place.[12]

Some are fleeing to Texas with their property. It may avail all that is desired, but I consider it will prove but a short postponement.

March 24th, Thursday.

A portion, perhaps all, of Gen'l Price's train passed through here this evening.

Orders are issued for starting the Federal prisoners, to-morrow morning, from this place to some portion of Texas.[13]

See other refugees passing to-day.

Ten Federal prisoners brought in to-day. Five negroes brought in with them, but not taken from among the Federals. While guarding them, many crowded around, and declared the negroes ought to be killed. How inconsistent! It is but natural for them to desire to be free, & if they do nothing but runaway from their masters to obtain their freedom, certainly they do not merit death. I believe a state of social subordination is the negroes political status, but we should deal with him in a humane manner; that we are strictly responsible for any abuses, and will have to render an account for our dealings with them.

March 25th, Friday.

All of Gen'l Price's infantry, (about 5 thousand,) except one brigade, arrived here to-day.

Now reported the Federal gun boats have not crossed the falls above Alexandria.

March 26th, Saturday.

Martial law is proclaimed within the entrenchments of this place.

The Federal prisoners sent from the guard house at this place, have been returned. Our officers are "business" men—something has to be done if it must immediately be undone.

March 27th, Sunday.

Several Confederate prisoners escaped from the guard house last night.

The mail matter for Texas has been returned to this place, & an effort is being made to prevent the circulation of rumors. The attempt will prove futile; a rumor circulates more rapidly under the restrictions of secrecy than without any restraint. This originates from the constitution of man. Each has one or more confidential friends, and if a rumor gets afloat under restrictions of secrecy, each feels it his especial duty to make it known to his particular circle; and as these circles lap over, & anastomose,[14] the rumor is soon scattered broadcast throughout the entire limits it is intended to affect. Remove the secrecy, & no one but tattlers will busy themselves about the matter; & tattlers are always busy, more especially when they have a secret to carry.

I am now almost well of herpes & have done better without medicine than I did under Dr. Catlett's treatment, & I have but little doubt that I have done better than I would under Dr. Riggins' prescription. At any rate, I am satisfied with my course.

All of the surplus baggage of Gen'l Prices' army is now being put on a boat to send it to Jefferson, Texas.

I have just seen 2 of Price's men in [*illegible*]. From all I can learn of them, many are reckless & desperate.

March 28th, Monday.

The convalescent are being moved from this place to Jefferson, Texas.

Learn from good authority that many of Price's men deserted on the march to this place. From evidences worthy of credit, many of them are in the army here because they could remain no longer at home, on account of personal difficulties.

March 29th, Tuesday.

Last night we patrolled the streets of Mugginsville,[15] suburbs of Shreveport, & found numbers of Gen'l Price's men without passes. Some of them "skedaddled" when we halted them, but others stood their ground. We found them congregated around houses of ill fame in great numbers, disclosing the most lamentable degradation.

March 30th, Wednesday.

It is now reported a fight is going on at Alexandria.[16] If more fighting be necessary to end this struggle, let it come soon.

March 31st, Thursday.

Hear that Gen'l Green has had a fight with the enemy near Alexandria, and defeated them.[17] I suppose he fought only the advanced guard. Hear also the Federals are engaging Marmaduke near Arkadelphia, Arkansas.

April 1st, Friday.

Yesterday, three Englishmen were arrested in this place, supposed to be spies. A citizen by the name of Ragsdale was also arrested, supposed to be leagued with the Englishmen.[18] At this time we are guarding them at the Verandah Hotel,[19] at which place they pay for their own lodgings. They are men of fine appearance, & take their imprisonment rather easy, though they manifest some surprise at imprisonment, having shown their papers all right, & proved by several officers of good standing, of the Missouri army, that they are high toned gentlemen, & only engaged in buying cotton.

April 2nd, Saturday.

No thrilling reports to-day. All quiet as if nothing of importance was pending.

April 3rd, Sunday.

The Englishmen have a city parole to-day, & Ragsdale is confined in the guard house.

The Federals are above Natchitoches, advancing slowly.[20]

Last night a mob of the Missourians broke into the house of Mrs. Kelly in Mugginsville, & stole a lot of cakes, eggs, candy, &c.

Gen'l Parsons (Missouri) with all of his forces, has left, destined for our army near Natchitoches.

Gen'l Marmaduke has beaten the enemy near Rockport, Arkansas.[21] So says dame rumor notwithstanding the efforts to suppress her labors. Her duty, she will perform, though Gen'l Smith issue ten thousand orders for her labors to cease. While these are things possible, there are also things impossible, & it is the height of folly to attempt a palpable impossibility.

This morning I applied to Col. Shivers for a 2 days' pass to visit my family, & adjust some business affairs that I think should be attended to, & especially so as the Federals are expected to over run the country soon. He gave me a positive denial, saying he had positive orders to grant no more passes pending the approach of the enemy—just as though it were possible the enemy could come to this place within 2 days.—However, he has since given L. Hamilton a pass to visit his family. His plea was sufficient at the time, but it has not lasted a day. Had he told me at once that he did not see fit to grant me a pass, but would grant a pass to some favorite, I could have have [*sic*] respected him in his manly, though partial, decision. "Theft will out;" so will falsehoods.

April 4th, Monday.

Now hear the Federals are advancing from below, & the gun boats are above the falls.

Gen'l Parson's (Texas) men are rendezvousing at Marshall, Texas, & many come without their guns, seeing the government has failed to pay them for their guns, & they have carried the receipts until they have worn out. So much for dishonesty.

April 5th, Tuesday.

Reported this morning that the Federals are still advancing; & that they whipped our forces yesterday near Mansfield, in which engagement we lost heavily.[22]

Captain Hawkins says the Quarter Master General's report gave the amount of bacon burnt when Little Rock was evacuated, 323000 pounds. That is the way much of the bacon of this Department goes. It is massed in the fortified towns & cities, and the officers consume, or appropriate in some way, what they want, & when the place is evacuated, the balance is burnt. The poor soldier trudges off through mud, perhaps, without a morsel; & probably has not had a ration of gov't bacon for months—some times no meat, or beef so poor that it is blue. Such will consume the patriotism of any people.

Last night several lewd women were arrested, & lodged in jail. Our guard had an interesting chase after some of them.

This evening a considerable number of our prisoners are taken from the guard house, & started under guard to their command to go into the anticipated fights. I am told if these men survive the battles, they will, at an appropriate time, be tried by a court martial, & probably shot. I fail to discover any justice in such treatment.

April 6th, Wednesday.

Some of the minute men are fishing for our position—prefer it to going into a fight.[23] Brave "boys"—don't blame them for wanting a "good thing," but doubt the equity of ousting others to get it.

April 7th, Thursday.

Hear the Federals are falling back.[24]

An attempt is being made to raise a company among the citizens of this place and vicinity. As yet, it has not taken well. Would like for the fighting to go on, but wold rather leave the job to some one else.

April 8th, Friday.

Gen'l Walker's command is this side of Mansfield. They are still furloughing men from that command.

To-day is *fast* day, appointed by president Davis. It is mocking. How can a nation expect the smiles of "Providence" when the people are so wicked? Will the President himself utter a solitary prayerful expression to-day?[25]

April 9th, Saturday

Hear this morning that Gen'l Mouton's division attacked the enemy yesterday about 5 miles below Mansfield, & drove them back 6 miles, capturing about 2000 prisoners, about 200 wagons, 20 pieces of artillery, and quite a number of small arms.[26]

Hear this morning that Gen'l Taylor's whole army, together with Gen'l Parsons' & Churchill's brigades, attacked the enemy this morning, & put them to flight.[27]

April 10th, Sunday.

Hear that we have lost heavily in the late fights, but gained a complete victory. Lieut. Col. Walker is certainly dead.[28]

Brig. Gen. Thomas J. Churchill, C.S.A. Courtesy Arkansas History Commission and the Old State House Museum, Little Rock, Arkansas.

It is feared our forces cannot pursue the enemy effectually, owing to our heavy losses. Losses on both sides reported heavy.[29]

April 11th, Monday.

Reports from the army are still favorable to the Confederates, though it is evident we are lost heavily.

Goodwin,[30] Ben Richardson,[31] & Johnston[32] of our company were killed; & McGuire[33] wounded.

L.B. Hendricks[34] of our company died recently. His father I regard in high esteem, & heartily condole with him in the loss of his son.

April 12th, Tuesday.

No news from the army below to-day.

Hear the Federals have taken Camden, Arkansas.[35] Gain at one point, but lose at another.

More whisky taken from the whisky sellers to-day. From good evidence, I believe it is used by the "brass buttons." If so, I am opposed to taking any more from the whisky dealers. It is not right to rob one drunkard to accommodate another; & it seems to me worse for an officer to get drunk than for a private to do so. I do not think I have ever found Col. Shivers clear of the fumes of whisky; yet, in great dignity, he will order a private to the guard house for getting inebriated.

Major Tucker has been pressing horses for several days past. Why not take some of the horses belonging to the "brass buttons," instead of all from poor men & farmers who are in great need of their horses?

Gen'l Tappan's brigade passed through here to-day, going below, I suppose.[36]

Though the enemy has been driven back, it has been at a heavy cost.

April 13th, Wednesday.

Another day of tranquility; no rumors, no news to thrill us.

April 14th, Thursday.

Gen'l Green has been killed in an engagement.[37] He was gallant and dashing, though hasty & inconsiderate.

'Tis said the Federals are hardly pressed—their gun boats having not yet got to Campti.[38]

Hear that Gen'l Steel is advancing from the direction of Little Rock.[39] They are retreating on one side, but advancing on the other.

April 15th, Friday.

Gen'l Walker's brigade passed through here to-day,[40] proceeding up the river. It is supposed they are to reinforce Gen'l Price. In this brigade, I met many of my old friends; the most of them are heartily tired of the war, & none are inclined to justify the acts of our leaders.

Hear that a dispatch, arriving here to-day, from Gen'l Taylor to Gen'l Smith, gives intelligence that Gen'l Taylor holds Grand Ecore & Natchitoches, & the gun boats & transports of the enemy are above, sustaining heavy losses from our forces.[41]

April 16th, Saturday.

Gen'ls Tappan, Parsons & Churchill passed through here to-day, proceeding up the River with their commands.[42]

Capt. Bradford of our regiment has presented a requisition from Gen'l Taylor to Gen'l Smith for all of his men at this place.[43] I learn that Gen'l Smith has complied; & that we will all be removed as soon as other men can be sent to take our places.[44] The intelligence is not greeted with a hearty welcome by us; but if go I must, I shall do so with as bold a front as possible—this is not time for cowering.

April 17th, Sunday.

To-day is another day of quietude. Rumor has ceased for a rest spell, and news agents have run short of material. But they will not be idle long; for they are of a restless & impatient disposition, & besides, cannot bear to see us in a state of rest.

April 18th, Monday.

Gen'l Price has had a fight with Gen'l Steel between Washington & Camden, in which Price was victorious.[45]

Hear the Federals have visited Monroe again, & burned the court house, the rail road depot, & all of the rolling stock thereat.[46]

April 19th, Tuesday.

Hear that Gen'l Price has recently whipped a foraging party of the Federals, between Washington & Camden, killing several hundred negroes, & capturing about 200 wagons—the whole party was put to flight.[47]

April 20th, Wednesday.

It is supposed Banks is retreating in the direction of Harrisonburg.[48]

I am informed that Capt. Bradford of the 28th Louisiana Volunteers, says we are not exchanged. I concur with him, for I have never seen any conclusive proof that we have been exchanged, though our officers have said so.

April 21st, Thursday.

No news upon the breeze to-day. Well enough; for such storms as we have recently had, if continued daily would exhaust any people.

April 22nd, Friday.

We still get news favorable to our arms at Grand Ecore; & also at Camden.[49]

April 23rd Saturday.

In drawing our last rations, we drew all bacon; the first time we have done so for about 15 or 16 months. How we do rejoice! A swap of "Buck & Rowdy", tough as tough well can be, for a bit of "Old Ned," we'll be hailed by all with many shouts. Let the swap be made occasionally, & we will yield more *obedient* service if not more *efficient* service.

Last night two supernumeraries—a mistake, but one supernumerary—conducted two prisoners to the wharf; they both fled, & have not been heard from since. One man guarding two in the dark-bright idea.

Men are still deserting from Capt. Jackson's Camp.

Hear that Gen'l Banks has burned Grand Ecore, and retreated.[50]

April 24th, Sunday.

Another calm. Today, we must feast on previous days' news.

April 25th, Monday.

Learn that our cavalry had a fight, recently, with the enemy near Grand Ecore, in which engagement our forces got the better of them, sustaining a loss of 600.[51]

To-day, a soldier came in & reported that he belongs to Churchhill's division; that he was taken a prisoner in the Mansfield fight, & has been exchanged. He was placed in the guard house—cool comfort if his report be true, but there are some reasons to doubt his report.

To-night we have to guard a captain at the Verandah Hotel to prevent his escape. Were he a private, our only trouble with him would be to take him to the guard house, & turn him over to the guard there. Surely there is a difference.

April 26th, Tuesday.

Again we have a quiet. What is the matter? What has become of the sensation characters? Verily, it does seem they are growing beautifully less. But for the fact that they have, at all time, & in all places, existed—the fact affording a possible evidence of their existence being necessary—I would wish them out of the present time, that we might frequently breathe more easily. But as they seem to be a concomitant of all people, I reason we would not have our complement without them.

April 27th, Wednesday.

Learn from an official report from Gen'l Tappan, that our forces have captured at Marks' Mills, Arkansas, 1000 prisoners, 300 negroes, 6 pieces of artillery, & killed & wounded 500 Federals.[52]

One of our men, captured recently, but who has been exchanged, informs me that about 50 of our men took the oath of allegiance to the United States.

April 28th, Thursday.

Hear further news to the effect that Gen'l Steel is suffering heavy losses by the active & energetic efforts of Gen'l Price.[53]

To-night I receive an extract of a transfer from Gen'l Smith's head quarters. I am thereby transferred from the 28th Regiment of Louisiana Volunteers to the Engineer troops of this Department, under Capt. J.L. Smith Kirby,[54] commanding pontooneers at this place.[55]

Feeling assured I can not stand infantry service; and that it was probable I would not be permitted to remain here much longer; I, a short time since, sought this transfer. I did not have to consult any officers, but simply present myself to Captain Kirby, who, being pleased with my appearance, applied to Gen'l Smith's head quarters for my transfer, & forthwith it was done. No doubt but my officers will be a little displeased, but since I have done nothing dishonorable, but have only sought my own interest, I have no pardons to ask, nor apologies to make.

April 29th, Friday.

This morning I report to Captain Kirby.

I feel very much debilitated from biliousness, so my entrance into the company is unfavorable. But Capt. Kirby assigns me to a mess, & says he has nothing especial for me to do. He also has the company physician see me.

I am now mainly among strangers; B. F. Keith of our old command is along with me, & a few others with whom I have recently become acquainted.

April 30th, Saturday.

To-day I am taking quinine & Dover's powders,[56] directed by A.M.H. Bills, hospital steward, which seems to be the medicine I needed. Bills is not, as I thought yesterday, a doctor, but has practiced medicine.

I have assisted sergeant Wiggs in making a new muster roll.

May 1st, Sunday.

Have news that Gen'l Steel has been routed from Camden with heavy loss.[57] Also hear that Gen'l Lee has defeated the Federal forces near Richmond, Virginia.[58]

May 2nd, Monday.

Our company will not leave to-day, as has been expected.

Hear that our forces have had a severe fight with the enemy near Camden, & it is claimed our forces gained an advantage.[59]

May 3rd, Tuesday.

We are still stationary, not having started on the anticipated march. We are well situated for soldiers, & believing all efforts on our part will avail no good for

Pontoon boats on their transport wagons. Courtesy Naval Historical Center, Washington Navy Yard, Washington, D.C.

us, I am, not careing whether we start soon or not. I do not crave for any more active duty in this service. An occasional move, I shall not object to, as constant inactivity is not conducive to good health.

May 4th, Wednesday.

I judge our army is not doing well in Arkansas, as we have not heard from them for several days.

I am now feeling very well, having been strongly threatened with fever for several days.

Now have orders to leave here immediately, but we have not the requisite teams. Why issue orders that can not be executed?

On guard duty to-night, guarding our mules.

May 5th, Thursday.

A mule was stolen from us last night. They are so much scattered that it is impossible for one guard to protect them; all a mistake to suppose one man can guard mules & horses scattered so widely apart that not half of them can be seen at once.

May 6th, Friday.

We now have news that our forces in Arkansas have routed Gen'l Steel, capturing 800 wagons, 1300 prisoners, & are now pursuing Steel, rapidly.[60]

Receive orders this evening to start to-morrow with our boats.

May 7th, Saturday.

Our forces have fought the enemy at Jenkins' Ferry, Saline River, Arkansas, & our loss is reported, 100 killed, & about 200 wounded.[61] Gen'ls Scurry & Randall were both killed.[62]

We have not yet started to Arkansas. [*Illegible*] said we will start to-morrow, —Learn the order has been countermanded.

May 8th, Sunday.

I have seen a report from Gen'l Smith, dated the 4th inst., in which he states we have in one month, in this Department, killed & wounded 8000 of the enemy, taken 6000 prisoners, 34 pieces of artillery, 1200 wagons, 1 gun boat & 3 transports. A brilliant success, but there is a reverse side of the picture. Our losses have been heavy.

The Gen'l holds forth that if all do their part, we will soon be relieved from this Yankee despotism.

May 9th, Monday.

To-day 1230 Federal prisoners, captured in the Jenkins' Ferry fight, were carried through here.[63]

May 10th, Tuesday.

Lieutenant Crosland, 1st Lieutenant of our company, says we will leave here to-day.

This evening we take our pontoon boats to the river, & put them on the R. Blanton,[64] a small stern wheel steamer to go down the River; 24 of us are to go with them; the remainder are to go down with the train to meet us at Campte.[65]

I learn from an Extra[66] that our forces have taken Plymouth & Newbern, N.C.;[67] that Lincoln has called out the militia for 100 days.

May 11th, Wednesday.

About 10 o'clock, A.M., we start

Go on very well to-day, nothing of any particular note happening.

Take up about 10 miles above Loggy Bayou,[68] & remain over night. There are not enough hands on the boat to run at night.

May 12th,Thursday.

At about 7 o'clock, A.M., we start, and just above the mouth of Loggy Bayou, we pass the wreck of the New Falls City,[69] sunk and then buried to obstruct the passage of the federal gun boats.

This evening we pass the Oceola.[70] It was snagged & sunk recently.

Late in the evening we meet the Countess with about 200 prisoners on board.[71]

Confederate steamer *New Falls City*. Courtesy Howard Tilton Memorial Library, Tulane University, New Orleans.

During our travel to-day, we saw the ruins of several houses, burned by the Federals. Arrive at Campte just before night. Find it almost entirely burned down.[72]

Soon after landing, while walking on the guard of the boat opposite to the engine, my foot slipped, & despite the best effort I could make, I tumbled into the water.[73] My first impulse was, to swim up to the stern of a pontoon boat which was lashed to the steamer just above me. As soon as I got my head above the water, I perceived, with the most powerful effort I could make, that I was going down stream instead of up—it was impossible for me to ascend. I whooped aloud, & the engineer, the only man on board, all others having gone ashore, heard me, & came hastily to my relief. But he was so much frightened, that he could do but little, & his efforts & suggestions were as much against me as for me. I resigned myself to the current, aiming to keep my head above the water and catch to the wheel as I passed the stern of the boat. The boat is square sterned, & the construct caused a curve in the current sufficient to carry me under as I passed. With a desperate effort, I seized one of the paddles of the wheel. At this instant the engineer cried out in a fearful tone, *"do not climb on the wheel!"* Pausing, but holding on to the wheel, I asked, "why?" He said my weight would cause it to roll over and drown me, & at the same instant thrust out a long pole for me to seize, & let him draw me by the side of the boat until I could climb out on the pontoon boat. Now, I had slipped off the guard without any thing to bother me, and there would be a good chance for him to tumble in with me—pole and all—making a worse state of things than already existed. I argued the case with him, & finally persuaded him to hold on to the wheel until I could climb out, all of which was accomplished in a little while, & in perfect safety. Coolness & presence of mind is worth every thing else in such difficulties. After getting on board, I learned the engineer could not swim, & had his plan been attempted, he would, almost beyond a doubt, have slipped overboard at the place I did; for the guard at that place was perfectly wet,& about as slippery as it could be. And as there was no one else present, he would certainly have drowned, &, in all probability, would have caused me to drown. But, many thanks to the engineer, for he did the very best he could, & rendered some efficient aid, & I am now on board, all safe except my hat. However, some of the men have returned to the boat, launched the skiff, and picked up my hat. Many hearty laughs as I stand dripping wet. —I have exchanged my wet clothes for dry ones, & feel resolved to be more careful in future as to how I walk on the wet, slippery, guard of a steam boat.

May 13th, Friday.

We are now lying by, awaiting further orders

I have taken a survey of the ruins at this place.[74] It is shocking to the senses of any person of refinement, disclosing the worst state of the passions. Such deeds will blot the pages of our history for all time to come. It is wanton cruelty.

May 14th, Saturday.

We are still awaiting orders.

The Vigo and Trixie passed down this morning with stores for our army.[75]

Hear that Gen'l Banks has left Alexandria.[76]

May 15th, Sunday.

A courier from Gen'l Walker informs me that he will be here to-morrow or next day.

A courier from Natchitoches informs us that Gen'l Banks has left Alexandria, and is attempting to cut his way out on the East side of the River; supposed he intends to go by Harrisonburg.[77]

Reported an attempt was made a few days since to reinforce Gen'l Banks, & the reinforcement was driven back, & 8000 captured by our forces—800 would do very well, & I would be more inclined to believe it if 800 instead of 8000 had been reported.[78]

The courier also informs us that our forces captured, a few days since, 4 transports & 1 gun boat; that Gen'l Banks had succeeded in getting all of his gun boats except one below the falls.[79]

May 16th, Monday.

This morning we moved down to Grand Ecore, & are now awaiting further orders. On our way down, we met Era No. 7,[80] & learned the Federals burned Alexandria just before they left.[81] What a better revenge for one who boasts of civilization & refinement. I do believe none but a black heart would be guilty of such deeds! *Burn the homes of women & children because they can not enslave their fathers & husbands!*

We meet our train here, & it will return to Shreveport. It had better been permitted to remain at this place.

Find Grand Ecore burned down![82] Alas! Must this was degenerate into a war of retaliation?—That our rulers, both civil & military, with some exceptions, are base men, there is no just excuse for thus punishing innocent women & children. Such severe punishment, without a just cause, will engender hatred of the bitterest character, & cause those, who, otherwise, would be tolerant in their feelings, to become violent opposers of the Federal cause, & warm advocates of the Confederacy—not hating the Confederate impositions the less, but hating the Federal impositions the more.

May 17th, Tuesday.

Traveled over the Federal camp ground at this place, to-day, & found many things, though not of any particular value, they left—burnt guns, &c. All they could not carry away—that was of value—they damaged until it was valueless. Don't blame them for that, but burning the property of citizens is savageism.

Yesterday evening, 120, or 125 gun boatmen were brought in from Fort De Russy. They presented, in the main, a sullen appearance.[83]
I learn that 2 gun boats have been sunk—also 3 transports—near Fort DeRussy.[84]

To-day we move down 12 or 15 miles to St. Maurice.[85] Don't find the people so clever here as at Campti. Some of them have a strong tincture of negro blood, &, as a matter of course, there is but little affinity between them & free white people—that is, in a social point of view.[86] A white man, of true dignity, can not consider a negro his equal. From manifestations I judge the mixed breeds here received some favors from the Federals while they were here.

May 18th, Wednesday.

Gen'l Banks has effected an escape, & Gen'l Walker is ordered to select a camp near Natchitoches.[87]

Capt. Kirby, with a portion of our men, started yesterday on board the Blanchard after the remainder of our boats.[88] They were sent some time ago to Alexandria.

We have put down a bridge as far as we have boats, balks, chesses, cables, anchors & lashings, and are awaiting the arrival of the remainder of the material to complete the remainder of the bridge.

This evening Gen'l Walker receives orders to proceed to Alexandria with his men with all possible haste.[89]

We take up, in obedience to orders, the portion of the bridge we have laid down, & are now ready to start on the steamer Trent tomorrow morning, for Alexandria.[90]

May 19th, Thursday.

This morning we attach our pontoon boats to the Trent, and start for Alexandria.

Several invalid of Gen'l Walker's command are on board, & among them, John Shedd of Texas, with whom I have formerly been acquainted. He was wounded in the Jenkins' Ferry fight. He had twisted his blanket, tied the ends to-gether, & was carrying it shot-pouch fashion. A ball from the enemy struck his blanket in front of his breast, passing through the folds of his blanket & clothes but did not penetrate his skin. But the concussion was so violet as to stun him severely, & render him unfit for duty, & that to a degree sufficient to disqualify him for duty to the present date. He informs me that we lost heavily in that fight; that he does not claim a victory for us in that fight.

About noon, or a little thereafter, we meet the Blanchard, with Captain Kirby & the men on board, but without any pontoon boats—the boats having been used in making a bridge at Alexandria.

We reship on the Blanchard, & start for Shreveport. This trip is likely to turn out to us something of a gala time in the way of soldiering—*"dum vivimus, vivamus,"*[91] is the motto of some, & who cares if we adopt it for the remainder of this trip?

In stopping the Trent by the Blanchard, 2 of our boats got badly injured.

After getting all things safely on board, we travel a short distance, & tie up for the night. The Blanchard makes slow progress up stream, towing our boats.

May 20th, Friday.

All take things easy this morning, so we are a little late in starting.

We pass Grand Ecore this evening, & find our train just leaving for Shreveport; they have been to Natchitoches instead of Shreveport as was expected.

A few miles above Grand Ecore, the Blanchard is landed opposite to an old field, and a pretty "draw" made on the fence for fuel for the furnace of the Blanchard. Captain Kirby first ordered all of us to assist in bringing on the rails; some responded cheerfully, but others paid no regard to it, going in the river for a bathe. Some of us argued that to assist facilitated our progress, and we would the sooner reach Shreveport, an end desired by both officers & men. Soon all, the officers not excepted, were engaged, & the job of "wooding" much sooner ended than otherwise would have been, & we were again on the travel.

While bringing on the wood, some of our men argued they could take the skiff & beat the boat. To one who had never given attention to such a race, it did seem so. Some of us took issue, & a race was agreed on. Accordingly, three took the skiff & started that they might have a fair start. We were longer finishing the job of "wooding" than was expected when they left, but after starting, we were not long coming in sight of them, & they were soon willing to swap skiff riding for steam boat riding, though some of them tried for a while to keep up appearances.

Just at night we reached our former landing at Campte, & tied up for the night.

May 21st, Saturday.

Off again at the same old rate—slow, *very* slow. However, believing we will reach Shreveport some day not *far* in the future, we cheer up, & take things easy, though we find our pile of wood is growing "beautifully" less.

Here we are, "wooding" again, though it seemed yesterday that we had enough wood on to last us to Shreveport.

While we are busy with the wood job, three of our men take the skiff & go ahead to a farm to procure butter, eggs, milk, or any thing in the way of eating. As we come up, they run the skiff before the boat for the purpose of getting on board, as we run along. Captain Crooks turns the boat sufficient to cause the skiff to strike a little to the left of the bow, striving to stop them by ballooning. Finding a collision unavoidable, for they were too intent to get on the boat to observe him, he stopped the wheel of the boat. The instant they struck the skiff went under. Two of the men anticipating their danger, sprang from the skiff on to the boat, being aided by men on board; the 3rd man went under, & was carried by the current under the pontoon boats, a distance near 50 feet. He was then pulled into one of the boats in a stragling condition.

May 24th, Tuesday.

About 2 o'clock to-day we arrive at Shreveport, nothing more of interest occurring, except our passage through the cut off at Scopini bend.[92] Before reaching the cut-off, we provided well in the way of fuel, and steam was raised as high as safety would allow; we then pushed into the stiff current of the cut-off, & with all the effort that could be brought to bear, we finally passed the cut-off. At times, it was scarcely discernible that we advanced. Upon the whole, the trip was a tedious one—such as "gets away" with ones patience.

On our arrival at Shreveport, we got intelligence that Lee has defeated Grant before Richmond.[93] Also learn that Banks has crossed the Atchafalaya.

The crops on the River as far down as we went, are backward, but if seasons continue late, much more grain will be raised than I expected after Gen'l Banks' destroying visit.

May 25th, Wednesday.

Our train comes in to-day. We did not beat them much, considering we came by steam power.

May 27th, Friday.

Have news that Gen'l Lee has outed Grant, & Gen'l Johnston has whipped another force—commander not named—near Chattanooga.

May 29th, Sunday.

Eighty four prisoners were brought in this morning from below. They were taken in a fight on Yellow Bayou.[94] In the fight we lost 300 or 400 men.[95] It is claimed the Federals got the worst of the fight.

Confederate money is now selling here at $100 Confederate mony for $1.00 in gold or silver.

May 31st, Tuesday.

I have just read the Gazette Extra of yesterday.[96] The news from Virginia is still favorable to the Confederates, but as yet, nothing decisive has been effected.

June 1st, Wednesday.

We had a refreshing shower last night, & a cloud is now arising that promises a good shower. Indeed, it does seem that we have been blessed of Heaven this year. We should feel thankful.

A law has been passed by the Confederate Congress, requiring the bonding of Confederate money, & it is creating no inconsiderable sensation. It seems to

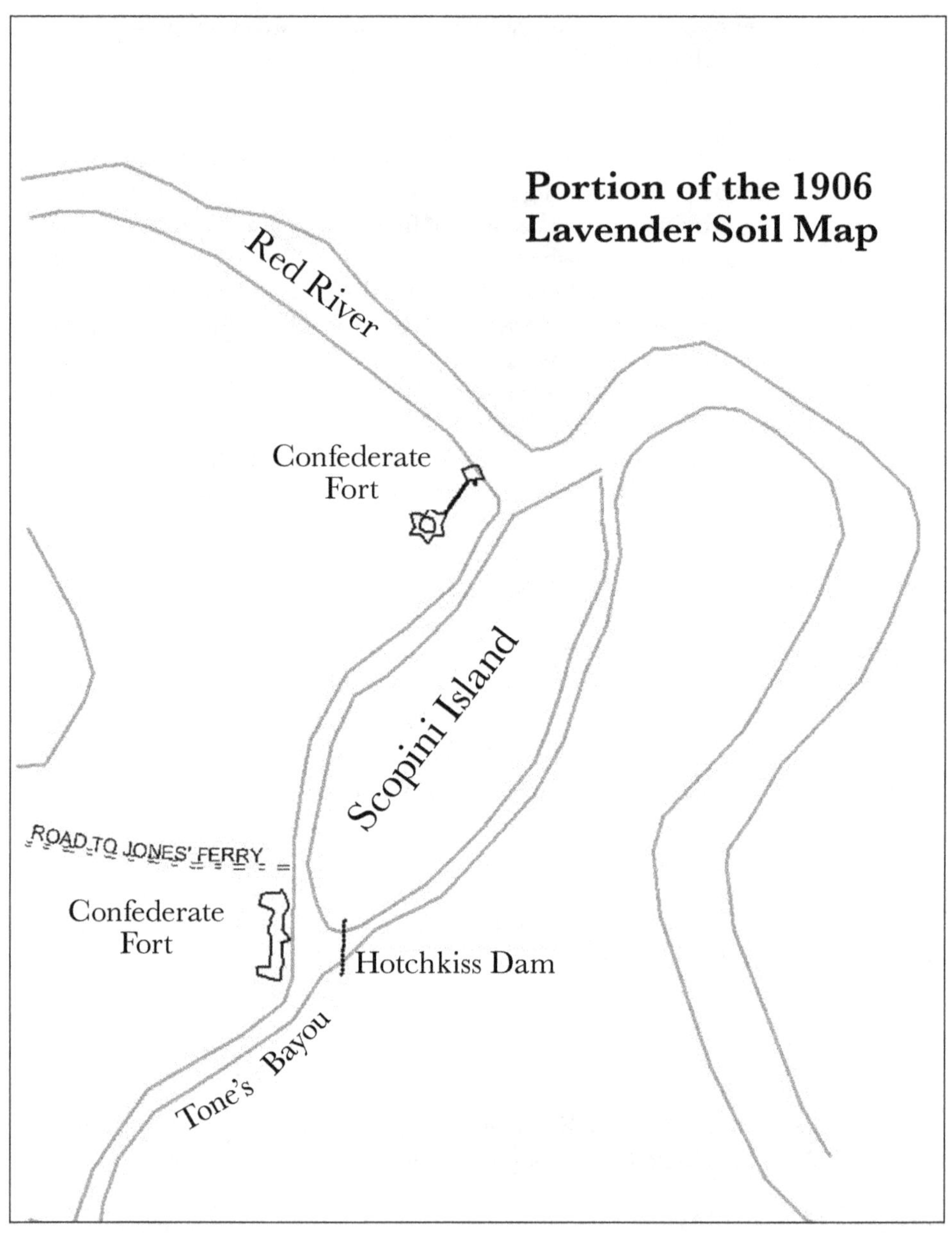

Confederate defenses at Tones Bayou in southern Caddo Parish, based on the Lavender Soil Survey map of 1906. Original in Archives and Special Collections, Noel Memorial Library, Louisiana State University, Shreveport. Cartography by Gary D. Joiner.

me that something should be done with the money since it has become so nearly worthless.

June 2nd, Thursday.

This evening a heavy shower passed over, and a very strong wind accompanied it. Some of the steam boats were greatly injured by it. The pontoon bridge was blown to pieces. Some of the old houses sustained some damage.

June 3rd, Friday.

Another proclamation is going the rounds, purporting to be the product of A. Lincoln, in which he has called for 400000 more men. The "proclamation" bears primafacia evidence of not having emanated from Lincoln; evidently it is not his, or, at any rate, has been garbled. False reports are liable, when cautioun is exercised, to get afloat; but when no effort is made to suppress them, but they are fostered & made all that can be made of them, they are numerous & enormous.

June 5th, Sunday.

Another Extra is out to-day from which I learn that Gen'l Johnston has fallen back to Atlanta, Georgia, but is certain of an overwhelming victory. Yes, our reporters and news mongers are always "certain" of some grand achievement whether it be achieved or not. I have great confidence in Gen'l Johnston, but I fear this is one "chicken counted before it hatched."

June 6th, Monday.

Rained to-day; encouraging to farmers.

June 7th, Tuesday.

Raining to-day. Now we are beginning to fear there will be too much rain for the best interests of the farmers, but from intelligence from all parts of Texas, there never was a better prospect for crops there. The wheat crop of Texas is made, and is pronounced excellent. A good crop in the Confederacy is now a *desideratim.*[97]

June 8th, Wednesday.

We still have wet weather, & Red River is in fine boating condition. First class Red River boats now pass up & down the River, meeting no obstructions.

From scraps of evidence picked up in different ways, I infer that Gen'l Banks is on the East side of the Atchafalaya, awaiting the advance of Gen'l Taylor.

June 11th, Saturday.

Obtain a pass of 4 days duration to visit my family. On arriving at home, I find all doing as well as could be expected.

June 15th, Wednesday.

Last night I returned from home, having enjoyed my 4-days leave of absence. I left my family all up, but not well.

The news for several days past tends to prove that Lee has the advantage of Grant, & that Johnston has defeated Sherman.

Gen'l Taylor has been relieved of his command by order of Gen'l Smith, to await orders from President Davis. I hear the charge is insolence.[98] Well done for Gen'l Smith. I consider he has done more to reinstate confidence in this department than most of the men would have done, & if he will now purge the department of officers, I can not but believe he will have done much for the honor of our cause, if not its success—which I now scarcely think probable.

From information from different sources, I am compelled to believe that Gen'l Taylor showed but little respect to Gen'l Smith, knowing he is a favorite of President Davis, which favoritism amount to great privileges. It is now well known that President Davis' specials *must* have position, even if better men must be displaced to give them room. So well established is this fact, that Gen'l Smith was not misrepresented, & I believe he was not, that he would not take all responsibility for the dismissal of Gen'l Taylor.

June 19th, Sunday.

We have further news to the effect that Gen'ls Lee & Johnston have again whipped the enemy.

The river is now rising, & is fuller than at any time during the winter.

The weather is excessively warm.

June 20th, Monday.

A Gazette, Extra, is out to-day which gives further encouraging accounts of our successes in Virginia.[99] It also reports Morgan operating in Kentucky.[100]

June 23rd, Thursday.

The last intelligence from East of the Mississippi River is favorable to our arms.

A member of our company received a letter from home, Dallas County, Texas, a few days since, learning therefrom that many houses had been robbed in the County. Now is a favorable time for the perpetrators of such deeds—a vast majority of the men are in the army, & the women & children constitute the chief defense at home.

On the 16th inst. I was assigned to the duty of writing for the Company—constituted clerk of the company, & exempted from all other duty. In some respects it is favorable to me, keeping me from many exposures, but in others, unfavorable, confining me very closely, requiring almost constant engagement. If I could bear fatigue, guard duties &c. with the ease that some do, I would greatly prefer it.

An Extra is out this evening with intelligence to the effect that Grant has approached to within fifty yards of Lee's works, close neighborship for such vast armies bent on the destruction of each other expect to hear of something terrible soon.[101]

Have news that our forces have whipped the Federals at Tupelo.[102]

Reported that Morgan is in Kentucky, doing considerable damage to the enemy.

June 26th, Sunday.

An Extra (this is a time favorable for Extras—suppose the editors find it profitable) of yesterday furnishes some encouragement, though I shall feel anxious until I hear that either Johnston has whipped Sherman, or Lee has whipped Grant, & I scarcely expect to hear either.

Red River is now in *fine* boating condition; it is several feel higher than it was at any time during the past winter.

There never was a better prospect for a grain crop in Tran Mississippi Department. The prospect is good for more grain than the grain of any two previous years.

June 28th, Tuesday.

Hear the Federals were driven back from Petersburg, Virginia, by the Militia & "dead heads."[103] The expression, "dead heads," is both current & significant among the soldiers. By it is meant those who have some position, or office that is of no utility to the Confederacy, but created solely for their benefit—to keep them from active duty. Of course this is not conceded, but since the offices are not useful but ornamental, the soldiers, that they may express themselves briefly, call those who fill the offices, "dead heads," we judge the tree by the fruit it *actually* yields, not by what it *pretends* to yield.

We also have news that Johnston has driven Sherman back.

It is now pretty currently believed that Generals Scurry & Randall were killed by our own men. Scurry killed, purposely, and Randall accidentally.[104] Horrible to contemplate! A general killed purposely by his own men. If he merited death at the hands of his murderer, it is a sad affair; if innocent, it is still more sad.

Red River was rising yesterday—remarkably high for the time of the year.

June 29th, Wednesday.

The Crescent City Regiment is now encamped at this place to do post & provost duties.[105] The change is quite a breaking up to some.

Hear that General Taylor has preferred charges against General Smith. At present the enemy is pressing us rather closely to undertake the adjustment of a so grave a difficulty. In fine, Gen'l Smith has not only abilities, but a high order of ambition, and he is now too near isolated from the power of President Davis to be tampered with—would, in all probability, attempt a confederacy of his own.

Diarrhea and flux[106] are strongly prevalent in our company, though, we have yet had but one bad case. For a few days, I have been sharply annoyed with diarrhea. A dose of calomel[107] & opium have done much to relieve me. Our diet is well calculated to derange the functions of our bowels. Instead of meal, we get what is familiarly known as "chops," that is, the grain is only broken into from about 8 to 12 parts; perhaps more, perhaps less. Meat & bread, both good, do not afford a sufficient variety of diet. Man is omnivorous, & can not, for any considerable length of time, be healthy with out a greater variety than meat and bread afford.

July 1st, Friday.

For 2 days just passed, we have been hearing very favorable news from General Johnston. We hear that he has defeated Sherman; and that Forest has done much in the way of cutting off Sherman's supplies.

One of our sergeants, J.W.M. Thomas, died to-day of flux. I believe his case was badly treated. He was young, & had sufficient abilities to do well. I learn he leaves a young wife & a little babe to mourn his loss.

July 4th, Monday.

Have news to the effect that Lee has driven Grant back 40 miles from Richmond. 'Tis said that Grant acknowledges the campaign against Richmond broken up, and he is now going to reinforce Sherman. "Going to reinforce Sherman" is guess work, I think.[108]

July 6th, Wednesday.

This evening I was taken ill very suddenly. For about 2 hours, I was *very* sick —vomit—bile, & purging. For a while I was almost collapsed. Perspiration was profuse, & breathing was exceedingly difficult. Our hospital steward, A.M.H. Bills, was of opinion that I had poisoned myself by drinking an infusion of the root of a weed. He may have been correct, for I was mistaken in the weed—did not get the weed I wanted, but got one, the properties of which I know nothing. The circumstance shall prove a caution to me. I never felt more certain that I was getting the right weed, though I was *really* getting one that I know nothing of. —"Wild Indigo."[109]

July 8th, Friday.

I feel much better this morning, though I am yet somewhat debilitated.

July 10th, Sunday.

My health is improving slowly, and I think I shall be able to discharge my duty before many more days elapse.

We have had nothing definite from Richmond for several days. I am in constant expectation of something thrilling.

July 12th, Tuesday.

No recent news from Richmond that is highly encouraging. From the last Northern accounts secretary Chase has resigned; gold advanced, & other things of about the same tenor.

Rumored that General Smith has been relieved from the command of the Trans Mississippi Department.[110] If so, I am of opinion he will hold on to the command despite the President's orders. General Smith has a position united to his tastes, & he knows that President Davis has more in the other Department than he can give attention to; that if the President lets go there to attend to General Smith, he, the President, will certainly go under. That General Smith will attempt to hold his position contrary to orders, is only inference. However, it is deduced from facts that clearly point in that direction. That this is no longer a struggle for the rights of the *people,* but for the aggrandizement of a certain few, is a clear case.

July 14th, Thursday.

Quite a cheering dispatch was received yesterday, stating that General Lee has captured 4 divisions of Grant's army; that 20000 of Grant's army have laid down their arms; that General Beauregard has routed General Burnside from the Weldon Road; that there is a peace convention in New York City. The dose is rather large, & he who can swallow it must have strong credulity. I shall expect to hear of some heavy disaster to our arms, soon. Such reports are frequently the preludes of some heavy reverse on our part.

July 16th, Saturday.

A thousand or fifteen hundred prisoners were sent from here to-day, to be exchanged at or near the mouth of Black River. The most of them have been prisoners a long time, & they are now dirty & ragged. Many have no shirts, & almost all are barefooted. It is a topic worthy the consideration of all. What a desperate enmity must exist among men that measures are pushed to such an extreme. The Federals treat our men equally bad, if not worse.

July 20th, Wednesday.

News to-day to the effect that a portion of Lee's army commanded by Ewell, Breckinridge & Rhodes has invaded Maryland, and are threatening Washington City. I doubt the policy of invading. There are many in the North who are willing that we separate if we choose, but will be ready at the instant of invasion to take up arms against us. We set out upon the defensive, & now to assume the aggressive would give the Federals the advantage in the way of a pretext for prosecuting the war.

July 23rd, Saturday.

Several Extras have appeared for the last 2 or 3 days, giving favorable accounts of the invasion of Maryland. The invasion, so far as its present successes are concerned, may be all right; the final results will be apt to be against us—the mighty spirit that will be stirred in the North by it, is that which may be feared.

July 24th, Sunday.

Have news now that General Breckenridge has taken the City of Baltimore, and that General Lee has taken the breast works of the North side of the City of Washington.

Last night was a cool night for the season; I slept under a blanket, & was rather cool then.

My health is not yet good; my bowels are yet much disordered.

July 26th Tuesday.

An Extra out to-day, stating our raiding party in Maryland have left there. Of course they could not remain there long.[111]

July 28th, Thursday.

To-day I am thirty six years old. How swiftly time flies! Once in life I thought but little of declining years, but the surrounding circumstances are now so different! I have an indigent family that much need my attention, & I am held here without any opportunity of doing any thing for them. The thought that my children may grow up in ignorance weighs heavily with me.

Vice is running riot in every direction, & there is but little effort to suppress it. It does seem that our people have forgotten that if virtue be lost, *all* will be lost. Science, Literature, Wealth, Fame, all sink to naught if unaccompanied by Virtue.

July 29th, Friday.

I hear an Extra is out to-day, giving an account of the fight now going on between Johnston's successor & Sherman.[112] It says our army is giving Sherman a good whipping.

About 12 o'clock to-day, we received orders to march from this point tomorrow at 4 o'clock A.M. I suppose from circumstances we are to go in the direction of Alexandria.

July 30th, Saturday.

To-day Capt. Kirby notifies me that he will keep me here to continue to serve as his clerk. He is Judge Advocate of a Court Martial now in session at this place; and I have up to this time acted as his clerk. The intelligence relieves me very much; for the weather is very hot, and the trip would prove exceedingly fatiguing to me. I now think I may safely rejoice at being transferred to this company. That I will have to do my duty, there is no mistake, but when it is done, I think it will be appreciated.

Late this evening, the train starts in bustle & confusion.

To-night Lieutenant Crosland and his detail got back from Houston with our clothing—some consolation amid so many troubles.

July 31st, Sunday.

The most of the day, I have been engaged in copying the proceedings of the Court Martial. My day's work is completed, and a portion of the day remains. The work is congenial to me, & I will be able to render more service in this department than the field service, but I question the propriety of doing it on Sunday. But my papers are required to be ready for to-morrow morning.

The hands in the government shop near our encampment have worked all day to-day. In my humble opinion more, in a pecuniary point of view—to say nothing of a moral character is lost than gained by such proceedings. Nothing is more evident than men, and the inferior animals, must have rest, & experience has well established the fact that periodical rest is best. What is gained to-day, will be lost in the end, will be lost with interest compounded. The men are now much less qualified, physically, mentally & morally, to do the ensuing week's work, than had they rested to-day.

Aug. 5th, Friday.

For the last 3 or 4 days we have been receiving news to the effect that General Hood, General Johnston's successor, has driven Sherman back.

It is currently believed here that the Infantry of General Taylor's old command have crossed the Mississippi River. Certainly nothing will be gained by sacrificing one department in the interest of the other; for it seems that nothing can be more evident than if one Department be lost, the other will be as a consequence. If, by crossing our men from this Department to the other, the Northern army there could be annihilated, there would be good reason to cross every man from this Department to the Eastern Department—such can not be expected.

Aug. 7th, Sunday.

For some time past we have been hearing at short intervals that the Federals have been whipped back from Richmond and Atlanta. Indeed, according to the news, they should have been demolished by this time, but they are still close around Richmond and Atlanta. If rumors &c. would prove sufficient, we might rest easy, feeling assured the work would be accomplished.

Aug. 11th, Thursday.

We now hear that General Taylor has orders to take ten thousand men East of the Mississippi River.

From the most reliable accounts, there is some good reason to believe that Gen'l Hood has been worsted in his engagement with Sherman on the 29th ultimo.[113]

Among us some interest is now felt concerning a party of men who recently left Tyler, Texas, and started for Mexico. Another party started in pursuit of them, but on coming up with them, they joined them. A larger party was then sent in pursuit, & at last accounts an engagement was expected.

A few days since, the Crescent Regiment was brought out against Smith's Battallion to dismount them, and assign them to duty with the Crescent Regiment. We now hear the most of Smith's men have deserted.[114]

Our officers are great men in their way, but it does seem to me that matters could be better. If it be desirous to enlist men in a cause, an incentive must be presented. Cause a man to feel interested; cause him to feel that to act is honorable, profitable and honest, and you are certain of his cooperation. But, cause him to believe you care nothing for his welfare; that for his own debasement & your own aggrandizement, and there is nothing more certain than you have lost him. Our soldiers—a vast majority of them—*know,* from sad experience, that our officers, with rare exceptions, have no regard for the well being of their privates, but regard their own ends as paramount to every right of the soldier.

August 12th, Friday.

The Crescent Regiment is now ordered from here in haste. Their destination, we know nothing of.

August 16, Tuesday.

From the latest intelligence our forces are not doing well at Mobile, Alabama, and Petersburg, Virginia.

August, 18th, Thursday.

To-day I receive an 8-days furlough, and visit my family. I find all well except my wife. I have had a wet, muddy travel, owing to the rain that fell yesterday & to-day.

August 26th, Friday.

Returned to camp to-day, leaving all well at home.

We have had no reliable news for several days. Rumors have been afloat, but were too vague & indefinite to take much notice of them. It is now regarded as certain that the order to cross ten thousand of our men East of the Mississippi River, has been revoked. Some *suppose* the men would not cross. The supposition is, evidently, correct. The men deserted (I do not think deserted the right term here—think left would be preferable) heavily. and most of those who did not leave, did no more than they were compelled to do to forward the end of crossing. There are some good reasons for believing the move was intended to narrow down General Smith's power, and also to reinstate General Taylor. As far as discoverable, General Smith's efforts to execute the order were simply passive—no prompt, energetic, decisive measures were taken to execute the order.

A friend, D.T. Cavett, informs me that his company of cavalrymen, and some others, are now engaged in collecting cotton in the vicinity of the Mississippi River above Vicksburg to trade to the Federals. If an individual trades with the Federals he is severely dealt with, but the officers carry on a wholesale traffic with perfect impunity. Surely circumstances *do* alter cases.

September 3rd, Saturday.

Fort Morgan at Mobile has fallen into the hands of the Federals.[115]

General Forest has recently made a dash into Memphis, Tennessee.[116] His men procured a supply of good clothing, and then escaped.

Red River is now in fine boating condition. In that particular, we have, all the year to this date, been singularly blessed.

The desertions from our army when attempting to cross the Mississippi River, were considerable, and at last accounts were still deserting.

By a General Order from Head Quarters of Trans Mississippi Department, General Magruder is to command the District of Arkansas. General Buckner is to command the District of West Louisiana, and General Walker the District of Texas.[117] Much of the swapping is done to afford occasion for the display of pomp and circumstance—an element of no small importance in this horrible war.

September 7th, Wednesday.

We have received orders to join our company at Monroe, Louisiana. So after all we must take the field. But the weather is now much more pleasant, & the stay we have had affords considerable consolation.

Besides our stay, there is another comfort for me. Captain Kirby so maneuvered things as to get, or enable one to draw, ninety three dollars extra pay for my services as Clerk of the Court Martial for thirty one days. Ninety dollars of the money was "new Issue," which is more valuable than the "Old Issue." The maneuvering was not the least interesting, & is of sufficient interest to give in this connection. A draft signed by Captain Kirby as Judge Advocate of the Court Martial, was prepared, and he accompanied me to the Quarter Master's (Maj. Herd) office. On presenting the draft to the clerk, he stated that he could not pay it unless General Boggs would sign it.[118] "All right" says Capt. Kirby, taking the draft, starts out, & calls to me to follow. I went with him to General Smith's Head Quarters, and at the outer door he directed me to await his return. After some 20 or 30 minutes, perhaps, he returned, saying "all right now," & we started to the Quarter Master's Office. On our arrival there, Captain Kirby says in a sharp tone, "Jacobs, General Boggs says if you send another paper to him to sign, he will order you under arrest." Jacobs—the clerk—manifested slight irritation, and said he didn't care if every dollar in the office had to be paid out, or language to that amount, and without hesitancy paid over the money. There is nothing in the army regulations authorizing such pay, but Captain Kirby is a cousin to, and pet of, General Smith, & that beats army regulations.

Although such pay is not authorized by the Army regulations, I have never thought I did wrong in receiving such pay. By receiving it, I did not get that which some poor soldier might have got. What I got only lessened the pile to disburse among "pets." Besides, the government owed me more than I got.

It is rumored that General Shelby has captured 2800 prisoners near Little Rock; that General Price has started for Missouri; that Vallandigham, and Seymour of New York, are nominated for the presidency by the Chicago convention.[119] Enough for one time, true or not true—but if *all* be true, there is but the dimmest shadow of a prospect for good for us to result from it. Nevertheless, thousands are *feasting* on the news, & it is but to get one's self into trouble to speak disparagingly of it. Indeed, it is not safe to "think so too loud." So, if such *will sell* at a high price, just let it sell, & I judge the purchaser, if any one does, will get full benefit of his purchase.

September 11th, Sunday.

It is now generally understood that Moreland and [*illegible*] Pennington[120] are the nominees of the Chicago convention.

I am informed by what seems to be good authority that L.T. Wigfall of Texas, now Confederate States Senator from Texas, has been making speeches in Texas advocating a central government, denying the rights of the States to organize a militia &c. It is said that "straws show which way the wind blows." L. T. Wigfall is not a straw, but a beam of great weight & strength,

In fine, he is a man who has made, and will continue to make, "his mark," and that he is one of those ultra "fire eaters," whose platform is "rule or ruin," is patent to all. His general character comports well with the report just received, & this coupled with much of the legislation of the Confederate congress, tells.

Sept. 13, Tuesday.

We have news that McLeland's platform is quite liberal,[121] and a reconstruction of the States is advocated, granting to the Southern States all of their Constitutional rights, & much more that is liberal—more, I fear, than we could get after surrendering.

News from the Federals to the effect that Atlanta, Georgia, has been taken by the Federals.[122]

Sept. 14th, Wednesday.

The fall of Atlanta is now confirmed.

We have further orders to proceed to our company which is now at Trenton.

Chapter 8

Arkansas

I suppose we may regard this as the first round in the ladder of descent—a pretty long stride.

William Henry King
January 1, 1865

Sept. 15th, Thursday.

About 12 o'clock, M,[1] we start to Trenton to join our company. Our start has been a tardy one. Indeed, not one has manifested a willingness to hasten, & some have maneuvered to stay the starting as long as possible. Our route is up the river to Benton; thence easterly to Bellevue.[2] After crossing the river, in company with sergeant West, I proceed ahead of the train to Benton where we will get forage for our stock. Having obtained a permit to go by home, I invite sergeant West to accompany me, and after a short pause he consents to comply if I will await the arrival of the train[3] that he may supply the necessary forage—he is the proper authority to draw—Captain Kirby having remained behind. Late in the evening the train comes up, and when we have finished drawing forage, night is close at hand, but our will is, go, & off we start. Near 9 o'clock, P.M. we arrive at home; a supper is soon set for us; we heartily partake of it, & in a short time we retire for a night's rest, that we may be ready for to-morrow's travel.

Sept. 16th, Friday.

After breakfast this morning I travel some 3 or 4 miles with sergeant West to get him in the right road that he may be able to overtake the company without getting lost. He has consented for me to remain at home for 2 days longer, as I can then easily overtake the company before it reaches Trenton.

Having reached the proper point, & given all necessary instructions, I return to my family for the further enjoyment of their company, which, though always preferable to soldiering, now is far more pleasant than a soldier's life. I have, from my first acquaintance with him, found him generous, & this act causes me to appreciate him more.

Sept. 18th, Sunday.

This morning I once more bid my family adieu to start to my company at Trenton. I got on finely through the day, except about 12 o'clock I became so sick that I was forced to halt and rest awhile. Feeling greatly refreshed, I proceed on my journey without an interruption, arriving at the bridge across Douchit Bayou,[4] just after the setting of the sun. I apply for lodgings over night, but fail to get accommodations. Proceed on to Mr. Weldon's, and apply there for entertainment but fail; thence to Minden, & finding no hotel I go to C.B. Sherwin's, but find no one at home; thence on to Shields' mill—applying at different places to I proceed, but "no" is the response every time. At Shields' mill I find Michael Smith encamped. He is from Bossier Parish, and has charge of a train of wagons loaded with wool. He has no corn, and I am in trouble about feeding my horse. Finally I drive a bargain with one of Mr. Smith's teamsters (a negro) to go to Mr. Shields' house for corn for my horse. The negro gets fifteen ears for which I pay one dollar and fifty cents—ten cents an ear. What say you who are over burthened with philanthropy? Wouldn't you like to try ~~try~~ it a while? Get $11.00 per month and pay ten cents for an ear of corn? As far as I have seen it tried, it dissolves patriotism, and I would like to see it tried with some of those possessed of a superabundance of the element. Here it might be objected that I have from a single instance deduced a conclusion, but it should be borne in mind that I have previously given instances of a similar character, & that these are but a few only of those that might be given. The truth is, we have Shields all over this Confederacy, and instead of being the exceptions, they constitute the great mass. Ye who doubt it, try it as I & others have done, and you will find your ardor dissolving like mountains of snow subjected to the melting rays of a mid summer's sun. The wool with which Mr. Smith's wagons are loaded, is said to be destined for Georgia, but I should not be surprised to hear it has fallen into the hands of the Federals as our cotton is going. Let us wait and see.

I find Mr. Smith very clever, offering me whatever accommodations he can afford, but having just left home this morning, I am pretty well supplied for a soldier. However, many thanks to the old gentleman.

Sept. 19th, Monday.

Just at the break of day, I start—travel to Mr. Lofton's a distance of 2 miles; get my horse fed, & a breakfast for myself—all for $2.00. This is a little better than the corn bill. I have stopped with Mr. Lofton different times before this, & I have always found him as reasonable as circumstances would admit.

Breakfasting over, I take the Athens and Terryville road, and a little after sunset, I get lodgings for the night within 6 miles of Vienna. I am very much fatigued.

Sept. 20th, Tuesday.

I start at the break of day this morning, though I am poorly able to travel, having a fever last night. But, learning last night my squad is not far ahead, I push forward, and after passing Vienna about one mile I find the encampment, but all have left except sergeant Joiner. I am greatly relieved in mind, for I am so much worn down that I almost apprehended yesterday and this morning, that I would not be able to overtake them.

We travel on leisurely, & soon come up with the squad. With customary incidents of traveling, we arrive at Tookville a little before night, where we draw forage for our horses and mules, and a little to the east of Tookville we pitch tents for the night.

After the ordinary routine of encamping, some half dozen, perhaps, of the men conclude they need a little pork, & as it had not been issued to us, they would "press" it. Accordingly, it was not long before a gun was heard, and then the squealing of a hog. —A little while longer, & several men are busily engaged in dressing a hog that under ordinary circumstances would not be fit for the table. But they are very busy at the work, and some are grumbling heavily because they are not getting more help. Whatever my inclinations would, otherwise, have been, I am now too sick to be more than an attentive observer. Finally, portions of the hog are prepared, and many partake of it with a gusto, and ere long we are wrapped in the arms of sweet morpheus.

Sept. 21st, Wednesday.

About 12 o'clock, M, we arrive at Trenton, leaving the wagons at our (the 28th Reg't La. Vol's) old camp ground, about 1½ miles back. We soon make arrangements for the necessary repairs of our wagons; drawing forage & rations.

Just as sergeant West and myself are about starting, a man of fair appearance meets us, & desires to know if sergeant West has command of our squad. Being answered in the affirmative, he claims a damage of $50.00 for the hog that was killed by our men last night; stating he will have all of us arrested; confined in prison, & tried by a court martial; at the same time stating good evidence he has for establishing the fact that it was done by some one or more of our squad. Sergeant West knew, & I knew, that the hog had been killed by our men, and we knew some, if not all, of them. Sergeant West knew his knowledge of the fact made him culpable, and evidently was ill at ease, though he made a good effort to maintain his equanimity. Knowing my own innocence, and feeling there was no chance to place guilt upon me, I was perfectly easy concerning myself, but for

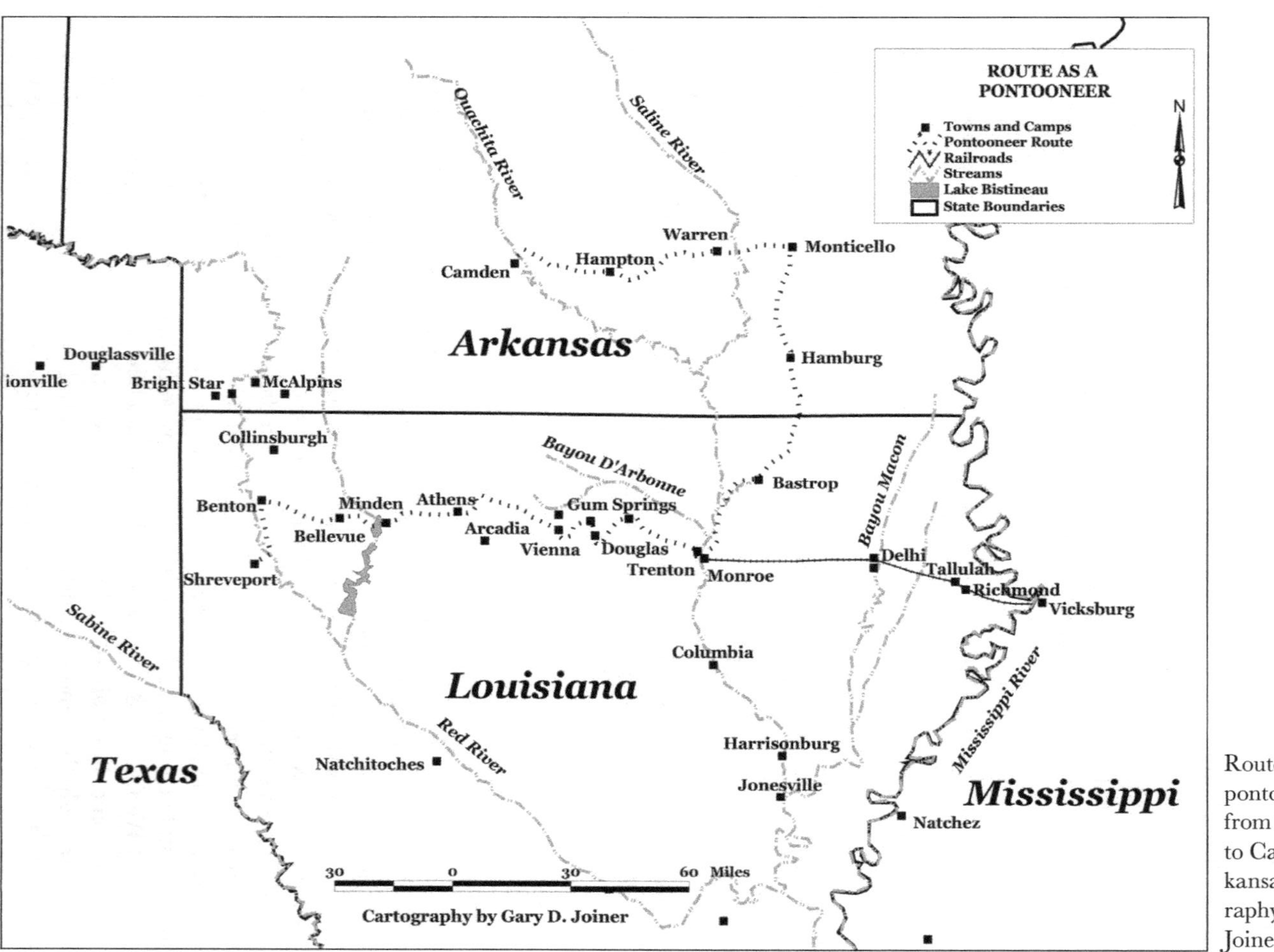

Route of King's pontooneer unit from Shreveport to Camden, Arkansas. Cartography by Gary D. Joiner.

sergeant West, I did feel concerned. After a short discussion, he paid the $50.00, & we returned to camp. He stated the case to the men, & they came promptly to his relief—each paying his prorate. The men killed the hog, not for the pecuniary profit, but because they were hungry, & had no other means of getting the meat.

Hear this evening that General Sherman has completely routed General Hood. I have been expecting something of the kind, for I could not believe Hood equal to Johnston who has conducted such an admirable retreat; or, rather, a series of retreats.

Sept. 22nd, Thursday.

We cross the Ouachita this morning at Trenton, proceed down the river to Monroe; take the Bastrop road; travel about 14 miles, and camp for the night.

The last day's travel before reaching Trenton, & to-day's travel; present one ~~one~~ continued scene of devastation, occasioned by this unholy war, Every thing presents a gloomy aspect. The question irresistibly comes up—how much further will we go backwards.

Sept. 23rd, Friday.

Fifteen miles travel brings us to Bastrop, the Parish Site of Morehouse Parish. Here we turn square to the left, (Westward,) go 2½ miles to Point Pleasant on Bayou Bartholomew to get corn. Thence back to Bastrop, and take the road to Monticello, Arkansas;[5] travel about 2 miles, & camp for the night. After leaving Monroe for about 10 miles, the road led through a low bottoms land. After that to Bastrop, we traveled on a low ridge with some pine growing on it. Bastrop presents the appearance of having been a nice little town prior to the war, but like all other little towns I have seen since the war, its aspect is not inviting.

Sept. 24th, Saturday.

A few miles travel this morning brings us to the ferry—over Bayou Bartholomew, and we find it hazardous because of an old, and much damaged ferry boat.

Having crossed into Arkansas a few miles this evening, we halt for the night.

During our whole travel from Shreveport, we have found it difficult to procure accommodations of any character. Many are unwilling to accommodate us; some totally unable to do so, & none fully able to do so.

The necessities for a war should be great before arms are resorted to.

Sept. 25th, Sunday.

Thirteen miles travel brings us to Hamburg, the county site of Ashley County, Arkansas. It is the nicest little town I have ever seen in the State of Arkansas. Here we expected to draw rations and forage, but we were quite mistaken; for we can not get either. Hunger for ourselves and horses is now staring us in the face. But we have overcome many seeming impossibilities, & there is no doubt but we will make desperate efforts to surmount this ere were yield the point. On enquiry we learn that our army has consumed nearly all the people can possibly spare; therefore, to follow the road they have traveled, it is almost absolutely certain that we will get nothing before reaching Monticello. We soon learn that but few soldiers have traveled the road from here to Longview,[6] and we immediately determine to go by way of Longview. We travel about five miles, and camp near a Tanyard with considerable persuasion, we prevail (of course we pay for it) on the proprietor to sell us one bushel of sweet potatoes & a few collards. The collards we boil with our last piece of meat—about one pound, quite a small bit to divide among fifteen hungry men. In selling the one bushel of potatoes, I think the old gentleman miscalculated—thinking it would prevent us from "borrowing" a few. Some of the "boys" here provided for to-morrow. Getting enough of the bushel to suffice for my supper & breakfast, I am willing to take chances for my dinner to-morrow. Indeed, I shall never resort to the practice until driven to it by sheer necessity. It shall be to gratify absolute hunger—not to make a profit.

Sept. 26th, Monday.

Our breakfast consists of potatoes only, and whether we will have any thing for dinner is a question. Before starting we hold a council, & decide that all of us who can leave the wagons go ahead; not stopping for several miles, leaving that space for the teamsters and the [wagons].

We couple off in twos; feeling assured that not more than two can get accommodations at the same place. A.B. Treson & myself go together. Some 8 or 10 miles travel we find some of our men who, having got ahead of us, have found accommodations. Lucky fellows! Can't we get in here too?—We try, but don't succeed. Now we commence trying at every house we find, & to Longview inclusive, the uniform response is, "no." Passing Longview, we quit the main road, taking a "neighborhood road," travel about five miles, and finding no house, we retrace our steps near 2½ miles, oblique from the road into a pathway, leading, as we suppose, into the main road. Lucky "strike" for us, for about one mile from the intersection of the main road, we find a house, & the "good" people (we don't know whether they are good or not) tell us we can get dinner. I have said dinner, but it can not in fairness be called that; for it is now as late, if not later, than 2 o'clock, and must be cooked. Call it what you may, we are rejoiced at the prospect, & will take it as soon as we can get it, asking no questions as to time of day, or whether it is supper, breakfast or dinner. —Well, we have finished our meal, paying fifty cents each, & we must confess the fare was good for the charge and the times. We are rejoiced to learn that we are not far from the main road, and having got the necessary instructions, start to rejoin the squad, & render an account of our travels since morning. We expect some interesting accounts when we all get together. The bare facts themselves will, no doubt, be interesting, but all are more or less skilled in polishing such things, we expect something extra.

We find no difficulty in regaining the main road, & fall in with some of the squad. A little further one we encamp near a house, and purchase of the land lord one bushel of sweet potatoes, and with 2 chickens procured by some of the men in their travel to-day, we have quite a feast. Two or three of the men get accommodations with the proprietor, and that leaves a better share of the potatoes and chickens for the remainder of us. The old gentleman manifests every disposition to accommodate us, but his surroundings clearly indicate his inability to do so. This, Drew County, is a poor county as far as we have seen, & almost destitute of provisions. I think it impossible that our army can remain here long. Indeed, I doubt the propriety of its remaining here any longer; for the people have not a sufficiency, & if the army continues here much longer, great destitution will prevail.

Sept. 27th, Tuesday.

All are hungry, and anxious to get to the company, believing we will get something to eat when we get with it.

This evening we arrive in Monticello, Drew County, Arkansas. We have not yet seen any but the poorest country in the county, & if all of the county is like what we have seen, it is certainly poorly able to support an army at any time.

We find our company in pretty good condition—getting far better rations than prospects indicated.

I suppose the object of sending the army to this regions is to subsist it on the tithe tax of this section as it would be too far to haul it, granting the Federals would not get it, nor interfere to prevent our trains from hauling it. But why rob a people of a portion of what they have when they barely have a sufficiency to subsist upon? —It is "robbing Peter to pay Paul." Yea, it is worse, for it is taking from old men, women and children what they positively need.

On inspection we find Monticello a much larger, & a much nicer town than the appearance of the County, as far as we have seen it, in any wise indicates.

Sept. 28th, Wednesday.

We had a heavy rain last night. It was much needed, for water was very scarce, and the roads very dusty.

Sept. 29th, Thursday.

Another rain last night. Water is plentiful now, & the dense clouds of dust that a few days ago were constantly floating in the air, are seen no more.

Kelly, one of our company died last night. Thus they go, one at a time.

Sept. 30th, Friday.

In the night last night, we received orders to go with a portion of our bridging, & bridge the Saline River near Warren.[7]

Up early this morning, & a detachment of the company start in obedience to orders to bridge the Saline River. I am one of the detachment, & am proud of it, for I had much rather travel than remain stationed here, especially when traveling in the direction of home. We get off in considerable glee, but ere we get far we find that our travel is likely to prove a hard one, in consequence of the recent rains.—The roads are very muddy, and showers of rain are falling at intervals. At almost every hill we have to "double team," or "all hands" get to the wagons and push, thus aiding the team to ascend. Our teams are but little more than half sufficient, and that frits the teamster & in their over efforts to make up the deficiency by whipping, they make matters worse—worrying the mules to almost exhaustion. But, all manifest a desire to travel on, hoping to find some spot more suitable to our circumstances, & what the teams can not do, is done by the men without much hesitancy, though with no little grumbling. —Almost night, and we have halted to encamp for the night, but before we get all arranged, the query comes up from all, "What shall we do for something to eat?" Lieutenant Crosland, commanding the detachment, immediately proceeds with a few men to a house near by to find a beef, intending to impress it if found. He failed in his purpose, & learning there are no other houses near us, returns to camp, & says we must for the present content ourselves with what we have—bread. The intelligence occasions some sensation, but that which can not be cured, *must* be endured. During this perplexity one of the squad, Crutchfield, solicits me to admit him into our mess as he is alone, all of his messmates remaining behind; and after a consultation with my messmates it is agreed that he be received. I report to him, and he at once brings forward his camping implements, rations, &c. What wonder! What joy! We all feel at seeing him draw forth a shoulder of nice pork. For the present we are all right; but what for the others? To divide would not simply disfamish [?] us, but disappoint them, for each would get just enough to sharpen his appetite feeling. There will yet be other occasions on ~~on~~ which we may have to run the gauntlet for rations, I decide at once now is the time to make Lieutenant Crosland a party to this peculiar method of "drawing rations." Accordingly, I suggest that Crutchfield present a piece of the meat to Lieutenant Crosland. Without hesitancy he replied, "I shan't do it; but you may." I accepted the opportunity, and taking a nice bit, I presented it to the Lieutenant who received it no less gladly than we did, asking no questions relative to where, or how, we got it. Again, I will state that sometimes we must *take* whatever we can get to eat, or suffer great hunger, & that it is under such circumstance, only, that I admit justification on the part of those who take it.

The roads, otherwise rough enough, are, by the excessive rains, rendered almost impassable, & two of our wagons broke down to-day.

Oct. 1st, Saturday.

After much labor, cutting away logs, bridging, lifting & pushing the wagons from mudholes &c., we arrive at the Saline River, McDade's Ferry, 16 miles West from Monticello. Immediately we set about bridging the River, and accomplish the job in time for a portion of General Churchill's men to cross over before night. Eight of our boats span the river which can now be forded on a tall horse.

Now is the gloomy season of the year, & it seems to me this is a gloomy looking country at any season. The people show to be unhealthy, possessing so little energy that nothing more than a sufficiency to "keep soul and body together" is regarded by them as worthy of attention.

Oct. 2nd, Sunday.

Nothing of special interest for to-day, except we still have great difficulty getting rations for ourselves, and forage for our stock. We suffer much, but our mules & horses suffer more. General Forney,[8] commanding the army here, has instructed Lieutenant Crosland to look out for his own subsistence, that it can not be furnished from the army supplies. Now, this furnishes a text from which a chapter might be written. Here we are in a land of destitution; no rations furnished but a little corn meal, and no sieve with which to separate the bran from it, and if a man takes a pig or any thing with which to satisfy his gnawing hunger, he is subject to be dealt with by a court martial. If he pleads inability to do efficient service, he subjects himself to insulting and abusive language; perhaps punishment. And to refuse to do duty would almost be certain to be punished by death. The Army Regulations are executed to the letter against the private, but for any wrongs he receives he has no redress—he "must give and endure." Oh! Justice! Where art thy council chambers? For them we have sought in vain.

Oct. 3rd, Monday.

Now late in the evening, and most of the troops have crossed the River. I presume our stay here will not continue much longer. The prospect of leaving soon cheers us. It would be relief to us, and great relief, perhaps, to women & children, for the evidences are clear that they must suffer.

I hear we are ordered to Prairie DeAnne[9] where we may procure subsistence.

The weather changed very suddenly from warm to cool this evening. In our present condition, much wet and cold weather would cause us to suffer heavily.

Oct. 4th, Tuesday.

It rained a little last night, and heavily to-day.

This evening all of our train came up except one wagon that broke down.

We cross the River, encamp, and proceed to take up the bridge.— Night, and we have all of the bridge up except five boats which we leave in the River till to-morrow, ceasing from all labor for the day.

Oct. 5th, Wednesday.

The job of loading is now completed, and we start with eighteen boats, leaving all of the balks and chesses. Pass through Warren, County site[10] of Bradley

County, and encamp for the night, having traveled 3½ or 4 miles. Here we draw some rations.

We have orders to proceed at leisure to Camden. Such an order under existing circumstances, is agreeably received.

Late in the evening we learn that General Price's men have been skirmishing with the Federals above Monticello.[11]

Oct. 6th, Thursday.

About 4 o'clock this morning we are aroused, and put on a forced march to Camden. We have reports to the effect that the Federals are trying to cut our entire army off from Shreveport. That which promised yesterday evening to be an easy thing in a soldier's life, now promises to be an arduous task. No one can tell one day what the next will bring forth, therefore soldiers—and they more so than others-should never count any thing allied to the future as certain.

We camp about 18 miles from Warren a pretty good day's travel. The Federals may overtake us, but we are determined to make the best race we can. If caught, we intend to be caught in a struggle to get away since we are totally unarmed.

Oct. 7th, Friday.

Just after the rising of the sun we start, and a travel of about four miles brings us to Hampton, the County site of Calhoun County. Hampton is about such as the other little towns of Arkansas that I have seen—not of any great importance.

Camp in the evening, having traveled—according to the best reckoning we can make 18 miles. As the roads are, we think the Federals will scarcely be able to come up to us before we reach Camden.

Oct. 8, Saturday.

With the usual difficulties, we arrive at Lone Rive Ferry[12] on the Ouachita near Camden, about 2 o'clock, P.M.

Hear to-day that Polignac's men are gone on to Washington, Arkansas; that the Federals are advancing from Fort Smith and Little Rock.

Petersburg, Virginia, has been taken by the enemy.[13]

Oct. 9th, Sunday.

We now have a bridge stretched across the Ouachita River at Lone River. Ferry, one mile from Camden. The bridge spans two hundred and fifty feet.

From Vienna, Jackson Parish, Louisiana, via Monroe, Bastrop, Hamburg, Monticello, Warren, Hampton, on to this place, the country presents one continued scene of desolation—enough to convince any reasonable man that the provocation must be great to be sufficient to justify a war. When contemplating these horrible scenes I sometimes doubt whether a nation is justifiable in going to war under any circumstances. The horrors of a war weigh heavily against any cause.

Oct. 10th, Monday.

I visited the town of Camden to-day. It presents the appearance of once having been quite a business little town, but like all other towns I have seen since the beginning of the war, it presents features of decay.

Oct. 11th, Tuesday.

Some refugees have passed to-day. That their conditions will be bettered by the move, is a question of doubt. But, like a sick man, tossing from side to side of his couch for an easy position, so are the people of this Confederacy—seeking that which is no where to be found in the limits of the government. That some places are preferable to others, is a fact beyond dispute, but no change will afford temporary relief for a great length of time. — Permanent relief is beyond our reach.

Oct. 12th, Wednesday.

About 200 men are now engaged in cutting down the timber on this, the North, side of the River. As the timber is very heavy, it would afford great protection to the enemy in an attack on this place. On the South side of the River, and a little ways above the Ferry, Fort Lookout, on a high bluff, is situated and the cutting away of the timber gives great range to the guns of the fort.

Oct. 15th, Saturday.

This evening, my ears were greeted with the report of guns that terminated the existence of Captain Guynes of General Walker's division.[14] I once thought of witnessing the scene, but as the time drew nearer, and I learned more of the circumstances, I felt less like seeing it, and finally I concluded it was too heart sickening to contemplate, & to witness it was more than I could stand. But for the fact that justice to his memory demands a defense should be made, I would willingly blot it from my memory. If facts have not been grossly misrepresented, it is a foul murder, powerfully involving the honor of General Magruder, though he has the decision of a Court Martial to excuse him. Captain Guynes was charged with encouraging his men to desert at the time of attempting to cross the army over the Mississippi River. He had been arrested under the charge, and released without a trial. Feeling he was aggrieved on account of so base a charge, after arriving at this place he demanded a trial that he might prove himself innocent. In the trial his guilt was attested to by men whom he had previously had punished for violations of the army regulations. Others testified they would not believe these men on oath. With this testimony, the Court Martial thought it to be the duty of said court to find Captain Guynes Guilty, and sentenced him to be shot. A reprieve was gotten up, and approved by every officer of the Brigade, and General Forney, but General Magruder would not grant a reprieve. In the petition for the reprieve were set forth the facts—that the witnesses against Captain Guynes were his personal enemies—that other witnesses of good standing made oath they would not believe an oath said witnesses against Cap. Guynes—that Captain Guynes bore a good character in the army as a soldier and a gentleman—that his character at home was unimpeached—that he was an old man, above the age of conscription, and could at any time have resigned and gone home. But General Magruder was relentless—he had an opportunity to make an example and he could not let it slip.

The whole of General Ransoms' brigade, and a few pieces of artillery were in requisition to prevent the release of Captain Guynes by force. No demonstrations were made to release him, but there is a general belief that no ordinary guard could have retained him.

I have searched diligently for the facts in this case, and I am now fully confident they are correctly given.

Can the Federals do more in the way of tyranny?

Oct. 19th, Wednesday.

General Magruder is pushing forward the fortifying of this place. I am not an engineer, therefore my opinion would not be received by the authorities as worthy of consideration, but my opinion I have, and I am willing to give it for whatever it may be worth. It seems to me this place could be strongly fortified for a large army. There are too many points to be defended for a small army. The small army we have here could defend the place against a very superior force. It there is any probability of a fight here, let us fortify by all means. Though I believe no fighting we can *now* do will bring our independence, but I also believe if we make good fights we may get better terms in the final settlement.

We have some very thrilling news from Richmond; from General Price's army in Missouri, and from our army in Georgia. I apprehend that the news has been enlarged upon—that some of it has been gotten up as a counter irritant.

S.W. Weaver of Col. Roberts' Regiment informed me last night that his brother, L.H. Weaver, soldiering in Western Texas, receives half of his pay in specie. Why not divide it that all might get a little? It would be acceptable in a high degree, and justice would certainly give us a shove. But, the scales of justice are lost or mislaid just now, and it is probable they will not be recovered while this horrible war lasts.

Oct. 20th, Thursday.

It is now reported that General Price is in Jefferson City, Missouri, with thirty thousand men.[15] If the actual number of his army could now be known here, I would willingly venture the assertion that his army whether in Jefferson City or elsewhere does not exceed in number 12 or 15000, and do not believe it numbers as high as 10000, —Some things look best when inflated with gas, and I am of opinion this Confederacy has a full benefit in that article. They have ceased to pay us any thing; almost ceased to clothe us, or give us meat & bread to eat—substituting "gas" in whole or in part for all.

Oct. 22nd, Saturday.

Reported that McClellan has withdrawn for the Presidency—that Seymour is out as a peace candidate. There is always something good in prospect, but little or nothing good for us is every attained.

Oct. 24th, Monday.

Hear that a party—about 250 Federals—appeared insight of Col. Logan near Princeton; that Logan and his men fled &c.

Yesterday I visited General Polignac's Division, & found many of his men in a destitute condition—some without shoes, and many very thinly clad. Winter is close at hand, and if something is not done soon to relieve the wants of the men, many will suffer greatly. But little concern is manifested for their welfare, and at this near approach of winter, the best effort possible that can be made will not be in time to save many from great suffering.

Oct. 26th, Wednesday.

Reported that General Lee has captured 18000 of Grant's men; that General Hood and Sherman are on a race to Dalton, Georgia.[16]

A brigade of infantry crossed the River at this place this morning, going in the direction of Princeton to do out-post duty.

Yesterday A.B. Treson and John Gaytor of our company were arrested and sent to prison to await the trial of a court martial. The charge is a refusal to obey orders. On the march from Warren to this place, Lieutenant Venable ordered them to each drive a team, and they plainly refused. This would seem sufficient to secure a sentence against them, but there are circumstances that greatly modify the crime, if there is any, of Treason. As to Gaytor's excuses for non compliance, I am not sufficiently posted to make a defense for him, but unhesitatingly state that I believe Treson to be a gentleman, having messmated with him, and in every particular in that association I found him true to right principles. Treson was transferred to this company as an artificer;[17] and others as laborers, teamsters. For some time past but little regard has been paid to the different duties for which the men were transferred to the company to do—detailing men transferred for one line of duty to do that of another, & *vice versa.* There was no necessity for this, in many instances at least, for men of one line of duty were taken to do that of another when there were men of that other who could have served as well, & even better. Observing this, Treson remarked to me one day that he anticipated trouble in that matter; for he could not drive a team, and would be compelled to refuse if called on to do so; that he had never harnessed a horse in his life, & did not know how to do so; that he had worked at the mechanic's trade from his boyhood, having never ploughed a day; that he knew he could not now manage 6 of these Spanish mules attached to one of these large wagons; that if ordered to drive, he would state these facts to the officers, and if they were not sufficient he would then refuse. He did so in a respectful manner, but they were not sufficient, and he then stated respectfully he would not drive. On the other hand it is claimed that the army regulations make no distinctions between men; that it is the duty of men to do any duty assigned them by their officers. But, be it remembered, that army regulations, like all other rules gotten up by man, cannot fill every requirement, and under many circumstances, unreasonable, and even impossible, things are required by the regulations. Is there a man, officer of private, of the whole army of this Department, who, in every particular, conforms to the regulations? The answer is emphatically *no.* In the case of Treson, the *letter* of the law was violated, but not the spirit. His refusal was not a refusal to obey law, but a refusal to do that which he *could not do.* Again it is argued he should have tried. That on first thought is feasible, but amore mature thought suggests the following questions: If he complies, does it not acknowledge ability to do? And does not acknowledgment of ability imply responsibility? Besides he would have endangered not only the wagon and train, but his own life. And why all of this? Was there no other teamster at hand? There were other teamsters, fully able to drive, but the order had been made, and it must be complied with, or Treson suffer a penalty for noncompliance.

In defending the cause of one, let me not be unjust to another. Though I think Treson has been unjustly treated, I am not at all disposed to place the whole blame on Lieutenant Venable. The army regulations make it his duty to do as he has done, though I think the circumstances would have justified a modification in his act. I believe Lieutenant Venable to be a high toned gentleman, and that he has done what he thought to be his duty. He is not a spirit after the usual style of the officers, and never attempts a pompous display of authority. He is second Lieutenant, and seldom in command of the company, and perhaps for that reason is a little more sensitive regarding the disobedience of his orders. Indeed, I believe him to be the most scrupulous regarding questions of right of any officer I have yet soldiered with, and that scrupulousness has rendered him unpopular among the men, and his knowledge of the fact causes him to be more particular.

Oct. 31st, Monday.

About 15 negroes have been placed in our company, not as soldiers but as laborers, and they are now employed in hauling corn fifty miles. It seems to me it would be cheaper to move to the corn, for the want of rations will soon cause us to evacuate this place if the enemy do not.

We now have news confirming the report that our forces hold Atlanta, Ga.

A private was shot a few days since for desertion. Several men have been shot recently for desertion, but I am not able to see that the moral standing of the army has been enhance thereby. Punishment may serve a good purpose when judiciously applied, but when adopted as *the* remedy, it will almost invariably fail. The subject is worthy the most profound consideration of Statesmen & Divines. Who that has tried it does not know that volunteer service is more reliable and more efficient than coerced service? The Saviour plainly taught that service to be acceptable must be an act of willingness. A slavish servitude is not the servitude of a genuine Christian. Let us hope this subject will be carefully considered by the wise men of the world.

Nov. 4th, Friday.

A letter from home to-day, dated the 31st Ultimo informs me of the good health of my family, &c., but it also gives the sad intelligence of the loss of my youngest brother in the army in Virginia.[18] It is not known whether he is dead, taken a prisoner, or has died. All we have learned is he is missing, and we are left in suspense regarding his fate.

Nov. 7th, Monday.

Reported that General Smith is under arrest for dealing in cotton with the Federals.[19] Since privates and citizens are not allowed to trade with the Federals, I think it is a greater crime for an office, especially a General, to do so. But I doubt whether an order for his arrest has been issued; and if it has, I venture the assertion that General Smith does not submit to the arrest. While the present state of things exist, he has a little sovereignty, and can with impunity carry on a profitable trade.

Preparations for escaping the horrors of the war are going on among the citizens in the way of refugeeing.

Last night Rev. Winfield (of Camden I suppose) was to preach a war sermon in Camden, and having preached one in Monticello in which he remarked very caustically upon the conduct of the officers and many citizens, the church was filled to packing, and many could not get in. Ordinarily churches are now poorly filled. To my understanding, this fact speaks in tones of thunder. Nothing is more evident from this sort of men than they are ripe for any measure that inveighs against the officers. They are heartily disgusted with the doings of the officers, and many of the citizens, and are ready at any moment a leader, in whom they have confidence, presents himself to make a strike for their rights. The truth is, we are a house divided against ourselves, and could not stand if left to ourselves. Should the Federals withdraw, leaving us alone, we would soon have an internecine war of our own. We are now composed of heterogeneous elements—elements that will not unite when all external force is withdrawn. The instant external pressure is with-drawn, elements will begin to fly off in a tangent with a deafening whiz. The most sanguine of our final success that I have conversed with relative to the trouble, admit its existence, and when asked for a remedy in the event of our success, they suggest physical force,—the very same we have for nearly four years been battleing against—strange inconsistency. They are not willing to receive the remedy themselves, but readily seize and apply it to others. When will we learn wisdom's ways? When will we be willing to do unto others as we would they should do unto us. Oh! Justice! once more visit us, and let us feel thy comforting influence.

Oct. [November] 10th, Thursday.

Yesterday, our detail who have been gone to Shreveport for blankets returned, and the blankets are now issued. I have drawn one, the first I have drawn since I have been in the army service.

Last night Rev. Winfield preached his war sermon. I am told he spread himself in regular "spatter gun" style—firing heavily into the ranks of both officers & privates. I do not doubt but he hit stinging marks in both ranks. Let him fire again, though I think his battery will not more than bruise the outside bark. However, that is the first work to be done, & I hope others will come to the rescue.

Reported that General Price has been defeated at Kansas City.

Nov. 14th, Monday.

Have undoubted evidence that General Price has been badly defeated in Missouri, having lost Generals Cabble And Marmaduke, & many others, all having been taken prisoners.[20] When last heard from, he was at Cane Hill, Arkansas,[21] with quite a number of unarmed men. Before he went to Missouri, it was reported that a great many armed men would flock to his standard if he would take a sufficient force there to assist them. Now his defeat is attributed to having so many unarmed men that he could not effectually use his armed men—the unarmed men were a burthen to his armed men.

Nov. 15th, Tuesday.

This evening eight men came into our camp, stating they have made their way from North of Missouri River. They report a hard time in getting out from there; that they attempted to go to Price, but the Federals cut them off, routing the whole company—forty eight men.

Day-before-yesterday, Fagan's[22] Division moved from this place to some point on Red River to get subsistence for the Division.

Nov. 17th, Thursday.

To-day we get news from a man from Price's army twenty miles from Fort Smith. He states the men are in a destitute condition; that they have not had bread for fourteen days, and at the time of his leaving they had but 2 day's rations of beef; that Price had lost all of his cannon but [*illegible*] pieces, and they were drawn by oxen; that he is cutting his way to R. River, following and [*sic*] old trace.

Nov. 18th, Friday.

Reported the Federals were at Tulip in Davis County,[23] day before yesterday.

Last night it rained heavily, and is still raining—now in the evening. We are very much exposed to the inclement weather, and unnecessarily so I think. We have no tents, & we have to make the best shifts we can.

Brig. Gen. James F. Fagan, C.S.A. Image in the collection of the Mansfield State Historic Site, Mansfield, Louisiana.

Nov. 22nd, Tuesday.

For some time past, we have had bad weather; first raining, then cold, and the earth muddy. The River here has risen until the banks are almost full. The drift has parted our bridge, and the wind and strong current of the River prevent us from replacing it.

With the news in our possession from men from General Price's Head Quarters up to about the 11th inst., I judge he has reached Boggy Depot.[24] The men state that they were about 20 days without bread, and 3 days without any thing to eat. They state that General Price lost many men; that he had received many recruits; by the time he would reach a point of safety, they did not think he would have more men than he started to Missouri with. Evidently his move into Missouri has resulted in disaster—more demoralizing than had he remained away. Like a drowning man catching at straws, our officials are constanly making moves without counting the final cost—in a fit of desperation seizing any thing that presents itself.

Nov. 24th, Thursday.

General price is now in Washington, Arkansas, and has scarcely as many men as he started with, and those with him are badly demoralized.

The citizens of Washington, Arkansas, have petitioned the removal of General Parsons's Brigade stationed there.

Nov. 27th, Sunday.

From the Washington, (Ark.) Telegraph,[25] I learn that Sherman still holds Atlanta, and that Hood is near Chattanooga. I now believe that Sherman has held Atlanta from the time he first took it. I also learn from the Telegraph that two members of the Legislature of Alabama have introduced resolutions, proposing to adjust the present difficulties with the North on the Chicago platform; that Vice President Stephens, H. V. Johnson of Georgia, and W.W. Boyce of South Carolina, are disposed to compromise with the North.

President Davis in his message states the public debt is 1.120.000.000 dollars. We *may repudiate* it, but we will never pay it, for we can not.

Citizens of this State are constantly passing here, going, mostly, to Texas, but some to other counties in this State, to find provisions. There is not a doubt but many children will cry for bread ere another crop is made; and if this war continues, the crop of next year will not be sufficient to supply real necessities until the next crop can be made.

Dec'r 2nd, Friday.

It is reported the largest fleet ever known is now at City Point. Supposed it will be moved to some point South.[26]

California and the Territories are reported as having given large majorities for Lincoln. For nearly 2 years our News Papers and leading men have been persuading us that they, together with many other States, were opposed to Lincoln's administration.

From a man who has been with General Price, I learn that the recruits General Price got stole the arms, ammunition, and horses of many of his men, and then deserted. It is an undeniable truth that his recruits was composed, mainly, of desperate and devilish men who could not remain in any civil community that had power to eject them.

General Price's men are at Boggy Depot instead of Washington, Arkansas, as was reported not long since.

Dec'r 5th, Monday.

Captain Kirby informs me that the news now posted on the Bulletin Board in Camden is that the United States Congress are preparing to send peace commissioners to the Confederacy to adjust terms of peace; that Sherman is progressing through Georgia, on his way to Savannah. The last item explains the first. The depressing effect of Sherman's march needs a counter irritant, and to be certain of the efficacy of the remedy, it is sent along with the disorder. No doubt but many will *feel* cured for a season—until the gas bag explodes.

From a speech, from President Davis, recently delivered at Augusta, Georgia, I learn there are croakers[27] on that side of the Mississippi as well as this; who censure the executive as well as the Generals; that General Grant has caused the destruction of great quantities of grain in the Shenandoah vally, and that he has taken all the cattle that could be obtained, and destroyed many houses and mills.[28]

Dec'r 8th, Thursday.

Sherman is still progressing through Georgia, devastating the country as he goes. Having divided his army, one division is striking for Beaufort,[29] and the other for Augusta.[30] The *peace plaster* has not stopped Sherman's career.

General Beauregard is reported to be at Corinth, and General Hood is reported as threatening Nashville and Paducah.

Reported that Brazil and the United States are now in opposition; from what cause I have not learned.

Dec'r 10th, Saturday.

Instead of General Lee having killed, wounded, and taken prisoners to the amount of 72000, and having driven Grant with his remaining forces, pell mell into the City of Washington, it now turns out that Grant is still closely investing Richmond. "Somebody" will not tell the truth every time.

Sherman is still in Georgia, & Hood is in Tennessee.

Refugees are still crossing at this point, going Westward.

I have been told that many of the men who went to Missouri with General Price, deserted him while there.

General Parsons' men are drawing Potatoes, sugar & rye. Why is it they get more than we do? They get the same of meal and beef that we do, and the potatoes, sugar and rye extra. They can desert, go home and remain there, bidding us defiance, and for that reason, I suppose, they are fed better. They are also much better clothed. All of this *may* be justice, but if so, I can not see the point. That one should be well fed while the other is partially starved, I am sure will never be recognized as justice by the party whose share is lacking.

The fortification of Marshall, Texas,[31] has been commenced. So further, and still further back we go.

Dec'r 13th, Tuesday.

Reported that Lincoln has issued a proclamation in which he offers pardon to all who will lay down their arms by the 8th of January, A.D., 1865, and return to their former allegiance. But upon those who do not, he will wage a war of extermination. I do not believe he ever saw the proclamation.

General Magruder has issued an order prohibiting any more citizens of this State, Arkansas, from emigrating to Texas to escape from the Federals. It is certainly a hard thing. One is prohibited from moving from one section of the country to another, still they claim this shall be the freest of free governments.

Dec'r 16th, Friday.

General Magruder has issued a circular to the citizens & soldiers of the District of Arkansas, in which he manifests quite a conciliatory spirit, evidently bolstering up for another 4-years war. He contends that election of Lincoln to the presidency secures infallibly our independence. He also thinks it quite certain that a financial crisis will take place soon in the United States. The same old hobby revived again. It is curiously amusing to retrospect the different reasons why the United States could not prosecute the war against us much longer. In this connection I will give a few of the most important reasons, such as foreign intervention which would take place soon from various causes—a financial crisis in the United States—divisions among the people of the United States, &c. All the while, there has been no good reason for supposing that foreign intervention would be for us rather than against us; that a financial crisis was more likely to occur in the North than in the South; that the people of the North would be more apt to quarrel among themselves than the people of the South. Indeed, the reverse of all these, might now be pretty safely assumed. Foreign governments are mainly monarchical; in some instances with a tolerably strong element of aristrcarsy, and in some instances a small element of democracy, but always subordinated to the first two. The former are always opposed to the latter, having from the birth of the U.S. opposed it; all the while striving to infuse elements of discord, supporting every tendency to centralization. Our effort in the beginning was to cast off a centralized power, assuming better democratic proportions. Hence, the sympathies of foreign governments were mainly with the North. Some have thought foreign nations would aid us for the purpose of securing our cotton trade. The advantages that might accrue to them in the cotton trade in the event of our independence, would not be sufficient for them to go to war. If one nation should assist us, other nations would not then permit it to monopolize our cotton trade. Relative to a financial crisis, there were better reasons from the beginning of the war to apprehend such a crisis among ourselves. They had a well organized government—a unit on the prosecution of the war. We could claim a unit regarding the defense, but we had no government; it had to be formed, if not from chaos, from a variety of elements characteristic of chaos. Though we were a unit regarding the defense, the different modes of doing this were multitudinous. The sequel is, they have an unprecedented war currency—less depreciated, perhaps, than ever before known and ours is scarcely worth the paper on which it is stamped. To-day we stand a worse divided people than they. The soldiers are ripe for a revolt against their officers, and a vast majority would willingly have President Davis and his cabinet into the middle of the Atlantic Ocean; there is but little good feeling between citizens and soldier. Indeed, no department harmonizes well with any other. The whole superstructure will, ere long, be crumbled, and every effort at bolstering will prove futile. Mark what I have said, and remember I am not the cause of what I predict; nor am I rejoiced at it, only, since it *must* come, let it come quickly. Understand me; I yet heartily endorse the cause we at first espoused, but the present doings of our leaders, both civil and military, I hold to be an abomination, and unhesitatingly say, down! with them. Not that I hate Federal oppression any less, but that I hate Confederate oppression the more. The Federals from the beginning proposed to subjugate us, and the Confederates proposed to save us from that subjugation. But in saving us they substitute oppression as bad if not worse. If oppression I must receive, I prefer it from an open enemy—deliver me from the sway of a *pretended* friend.

Dec'r 19th, Monday.

Sherman has reached the coast in Georgia on the Savannah River, and it is supposed he will strike for Richmond.[32]

Rumored that Lincoln has adopted part of the Chicago platform, offering to guarantee to the state composing the Confederacy all of their constitutional rights, returning all of the slaves as far as practicable.

The above paragraphs stand in opposition to each other. We need not look for any concessions from Lincoln while victory perches upon his banner. If concessions are obtained they will be obtained under different circumstances.

Rained yesterday, and is raining again to-day.

Dec'r 20th, Tuesday.

This morning we move across the river to cabins built by our men for our winter quarters. They are situated to the North of, and at the borders of the town of Camden. They are very comfortable arrangements for soldiers.

Evidently the River will overflow soon, for it has been raining for three days, and the River is rising rapidly. Our move is just in good time. Our stay on the bank of the Ouachita has been a disagreeable one, truly-wet, muddy & severely smoked.

Learn the Federals are collecting at the North of Red River.

Dec'r 21st, Wednesday.

It is very cold and unpleasant to-day, and the River is still rising. This is one time we are in good luck. What would become of us if we were still out of doors?

Three mules of our train died to-day, and one died last night. They were almost starved, and the cold, rainy weather finished the work for them. On our march from Monticello to this place, I made several allusions to our own sufferings with hunger which so much engrossed my journalistic exercises that I said but little regarding the suffering of the poor mules. They were the most hungry animals I ever saw. They would eat the timbers of the wagons. In several instances they ate the hounds of the wagons, and the spokes of the wagons, in pieces. When tied with coarse raw-hide to prevent them from straying, they would eat the raw-hide "in two," and browse on whatever they could find. That the right of an animal is extinguished in that of man, is, I believe, generally if not universally conceded. But all unnecessary punishment of the inferior animals is, beyond a doubt, a great crime. That the suffering of the mules just alluded to was unnecessary, is inferred form the fact that no good was accomplished by it, but much suffering of animals and men was involved. Yea, the suffering of women & children has been, and will be, considerable in consequence of the trip. There was no good reason for supposing any benefit could accrue to us from it, and the evils were patent to all.

Reported that 5000 of McClellan's men at Little Rock mutinied, burned a portion of the town and proceeded to Duval's Bluff, at which place an attempt was made to bring them to terms, but they prevailed, and burned a portion of that place. The report may be true, but I think it doubtful.

Dec'r 23rd, Friday.

Reported that Wisconsin and Iowa have seceded from the United States. I do not believe a word of it, and the rumor weakens the little faith I had in the report relative to the mutiny at Little Rock. "They" don't seem to understand well the business of misrepresenting—making it just a *little* bit too big to be believed on a sober, second thought. Sometimes the dose is so extremely nauseating that it vomits before it can be swallowed.

Dec'r 25th, Sunday.

Another Christmas is now upon us, and this civil war still rages. There is some consolation in believing it is now in its dying struggles. Every day it is continued only aggravates the evils that attend it. Men are growing more and more demoralized; property is being consumed by the million; the awful chasm that separates us in feeling from the Northern people is daily becoming broader and deeper, and scarcely a faint gleam of hope of our political separation remains. The prospect is too gloomy to contemplate—let us learn from it.

Yesterday an extra guard was posted, & I see they are on post yet. Why this was done I can not say unless it was done to prevent them—or all of us—from enjoying a Christmas commemoration.

Ouachita River is *very* high, lacking but a few feet of being as high as ever known, and it is still rising.

Last night there were many guns fired by the soldiers. I did not think the authorities here would allow it. Judging from indications I believe the soldiers have done it to express their contempt for the posting of the extra guard. As soon as the extra guard was posted, the men began to manifest restlessness, and have been more boisterous than I have ever known them.

Dec'r 27th, Tuesday.

Last night there was a heavy firing of guns, whooping and so forth, among the soldiers. I learn this morning that very stringent orders have been issued against the firing of guns, and hallooing after night. Evidently last night's demonstrations were in defiance of said orders.

By order of General Magruder, Major Rowley is now moving General Magruder's Head Quarters to Washington, Arkansas.

All ordinance stores are also being moved from this place. These operations are rather significant.

Dec'r 28th, Wednesday.

There are divers[e] reports extant as to the probabilities of an early peace—such as the Lincoln and McClellan move, the same having a violent opposition among the people of the North,—the assembly of peace commissioners from the Confederacy; the United States, and Europe. If one thing does not quiet the anxieties of the people, straightway another is applied.

Dec'r 31st, Saturday.

The soldiers, and the community generally, are now in a fever of excitement regarding the news that Sherman, with his whole army, has been taken prisoner, that Hood has been able to take Nashville, Tennessee; that the Western States have seceded. By virtue of the news of the 28th inst., we have been able to make a greater ascent—to a height that makes one dizzy. The question unavoidably comes up; How are we to descend? A vast precipice lies just before us, and into the vast abyss—broad and deep—that lies just below, we must descend either by gradual descent, or by long and ruinous leaps. How it will turn out, time will disclose. To my perceptives, nothing but crazy points in dim distance present themselves. But those who prepared the lofty peak will, doubtless, with the same unscrupulousness, prepare a ladder for us to descend on.

I have just finished my fourth consecutive meal without any meat. Yesterday my dinner consisted of corn bread; my supper last night, of flour mixed with water and baked, and my dinner to-day, of corn bread. The corn meal from which our bread was baked, is not sour only, but actually *bitter.* If we continue the use of it long, it will certainly cause sickness. Historians of the Revolutionary War bestow high commendations on the patriotism of soldiers who subsisted on potatoes. With us a good potato would be in high esteem, and we would *willingly* exchange meal unfit to feed dogs on for potatoes; or for the acorns on which the noble old chief, Andrew Jackson subsisted in the Indian War of 1812. Let us not be understood as, in the least, undervaluing their hardships. Ours are felt the more acutely because they could be avoided—better could be done, and it is not done because commissaries can not make so much money if they furnish us good meal in lieu of the bad. They can buy damaged meal at a much reduced price, and receive full pay for it from the Government. The evidence on which this statement is based

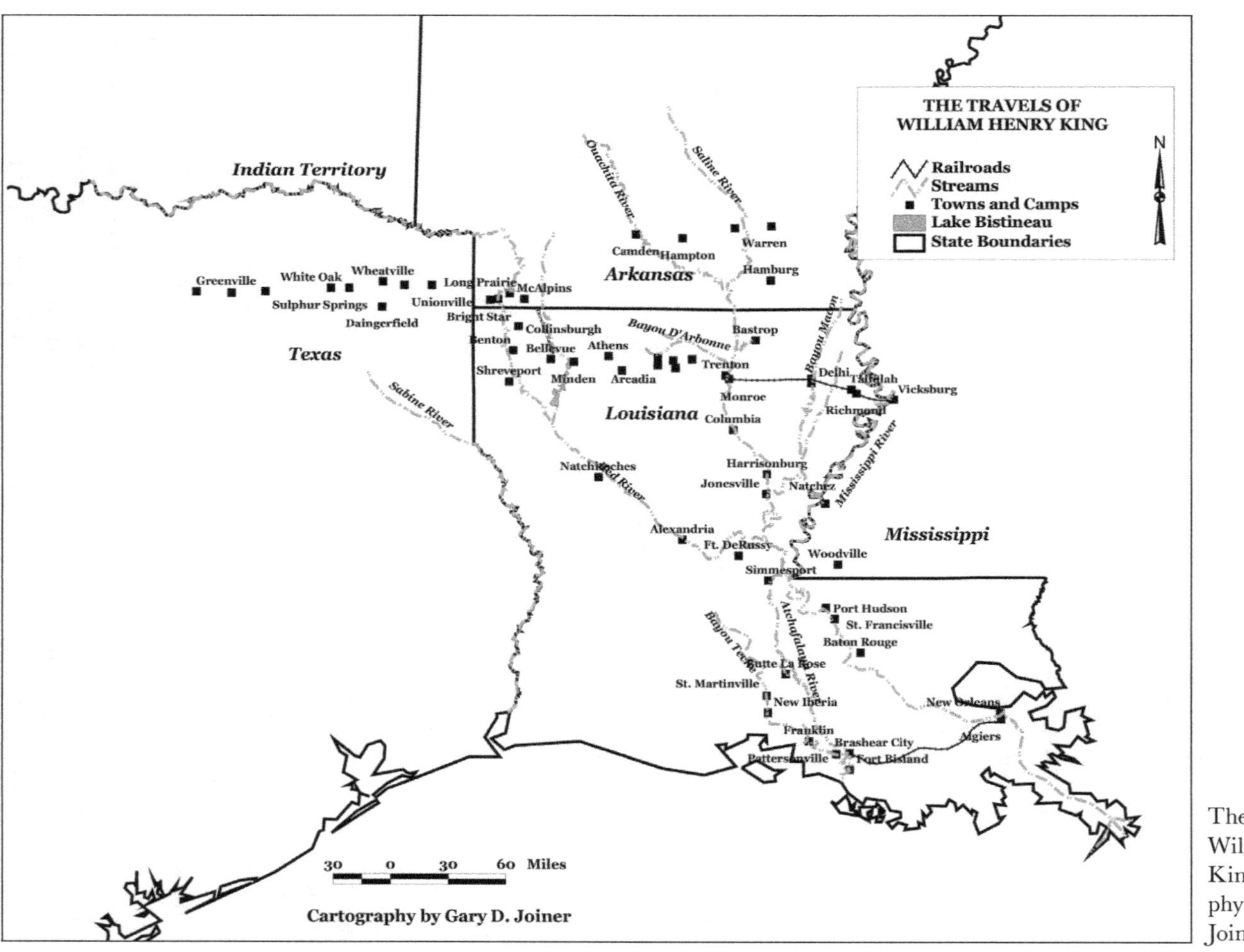

The travels of William Henry King. Cartography by Gary D. Joiner.

is good, though I can not say that it is so beyond a doubt. I have never been able to test these transactions in a way to place them beyond a doubt, but I feel well assured of the truth of it. The best evidence I have is, inferior meal is furnished when good meal can be furnished. I leave the story to the future historian, hoping it will receive justice.

Jan. 1st, Sunday. [1865]

The first day of the week, the first day of the month, and the first day of the year—a coincidence that would occur every seventh year but for the occurrence of leap year.

The latest news is, Hood has been defeated before Nashville,[33] and is in full retreat; and Sherman is investing Augusta, Georgia; Price relieved from his command, and Tappan appointed in his stead. I suppose we may regard this as the first round in the ladder of descent—a pretty long stride.

Jan. 7th, Saturday.

I have reliable news to the effect that General Thomas has beaten Hood at Nashville; that Bainbridge has beaten Breckenridge in Western Virginia; that Sherman has taken Fort McAlister on the Savannah River just below the City of Savannah, and is closely investing the City of Savannah, and . . .

[*missing pages*]

. . . not, in any true sense of the term, and called a freeman. Thus we get an early [*illegible*] of the faithfulness of the Federals to their declarations. Is this restoring us to our "former relations to the Union"? a phrase so much in use by the Federals since the beginning of the war. Is it justice to the negro to sever his claims upon his former master, and then throw restrictions around him which are inconsistent with freedom in any just sense of the term?

I have not expected any thing lenient from the Federals, but policy, and the best interests of both the North and the South so clearly indicate mild measures, that I expected something of a better beginning. The general welfare has been lost sight of in view of selfish interests.

———

This is the end of my journal, and I have stated it is not equal to my desires. I have had many difficulties to encounter. Some of the notes taken have been lost, and their place had to be supplied from memory, but I think no grave errors have been committed. The style is not equal to a critic's requirements, but my aim has been to to [*sic*] present facts and events more as they occur in real life, than as idealistic. I have sometimes thought too many of our writers lose sight of the real instead of the ideal. In transcribing, and commenting on my notes, I have been compelled to do so at short intervals, suddenly turning my mind from the pressing duties of active life; not thinking, perhaps, of the subject from one writing to another.

Arkansas

Experience and observations have taught me that if one refuses to under take a job because imperfections may as ever must arise, he had as well abandon the stern duties of life. Every effort of man is more or less a departure from absolute perfections and nothing that man does can justly be claimed to be perfect only as many is perfect. If one desires to do right and strives to do right, his failures, if grave, should be viewed in sympathy rather than in censure. I do not make these allusions as a mere extension of my own failures but more to show the importance of their general application. That imperfections exist in this journal, I am fully apprised, and I ask no more than a fair criticism. Having used stringent remarks concerning the acts of others, I claim a spirit sufficiently liberalistic to allow a like stringency of remarks.

Epilogue

To the End of the War

William Henry King's diary ends abruptly with the last entry on January 7, 1865. From that point to June 1865 and his parole as a prisoner of war in Shreveport, his story is shrouded in mystery. This is due to the lack of diary entries and to the general lack of known facts about specific troop placements and movements in the Trans-Mississippi during that period.

According to records, King was made a sergeant in Company H of the 4th Regiment, Engineer Troops, sometime after the diary ends.[1] Little is known about the unit, which was a part of the Confederate army and not in state volunteer service. Correspondence in 1911 between former officers and archivists in the Confederate Archive Section at the National Archives indicates that it is probable that all engineering companies paroled in the Trans-Mississippi Department in 1865 belonged to the 4th Engineers.[2] The same correspondence indicates that the 4th Regiment was originally the 1st Battalion, Engineer Troops, Confederate States Army.[3]

The 4th Regiment included at least eleven companies, some which were lettered and others named for their commanders. Not all of the companies were listed in the correspondence mentioned above. Among the missing was Company H.

Portions of companies A and E were stationed at Galveston, Texas, and appear to have surrendered with Kirby Smith in late May 1865.[4] Dickinson's Company was stationed at Camden, Arkansas, as late as February 1864, and Company H is likely to have been with them.[5]

Company H was apparently formed when King joined it on April 28, 1864. Since King does not mention his promotion, it is most probable that he received it after January 7. The company also apparently operated as an independent bridging unit attached to forces in Arkansas at Camden. There is no record of it operating jointly with companies of pontooneers, but it is likely that it served with Dickenson's Company of the same unit. According to King's diary, Company H was commanded by Capt. Smith Kirby.[6]

From the conclusion of the Red River Campaign to the surrender of forces in the Trans-Mississippi, the Confederates perceived threats along four lines. Each posed different problems for the defenders. The first consideration was a movement by Union forces from the north out of Little Rock, Pine Bluff, or Fort Smith. Kirby Smith spent an inordinate amount of time fretting about this possibility. Late in 1864 he moved four divisions to southern Arkansas. King's unit was stationed on the Ouachita River at Camden to assist in countering this threat. The second potential problem was another thrust up the Red River from the Mississippi River. Federal troops were stationed at Morganza, just below the mouth of the Red and the Mississippi Squadron, and heavily patrolled the great river. News of Union troop buildups were constant, but the intent of the massing of troops was completely conjectural. The third area of potential threat came from southern Texas, with the possibility of a successful landing by Union forces at Galveston or Matagorda Bay. The fourth area was closer to home for the commanders in Shreveport. This was a danger from the Mississippi River in the event of a successful landing at the DeSoto Peninsula, opposite Vicksburg, or from across the river at Natchez, or from southeastern Arkansas, perhaps from Chicot County.

During the early months of 1865, Kirby Smith became convinced that the greatest threat to the department was from the coast of Texas. He was also apparently preparing to take his army into Mexico and fight from there if the Confederacy collapsed around him. After the Red River Campaign in 1864 and continuing early into 1865, Smith made some major reassignments among his district commanders. Most prominent was his transfer of Maj. Gen. John Magruder to the command of the district of Arkansas, which freed Maj. Gen. Sterling Price to conduct his raid into Missouri. He promoted Maj. Gen. John G. Walker in June to Richard Taylor's position as the District Commander for Western Louisiana.[7] (Richard Taylor had been promoted to lieutenant general over Smith's objections and given command east of the Mississippi River.)

The Texas Division, the largest Confederate unit west of the Mississippi River, was not pleased with Walker's replacements.[8] This division was told that it would transfer east of the Mississippi River, and, when it became impractical, it was sent to Arkansas and finally into Texas. The 4th Engineers were part of this general movement into Arkansas, first to Monticello, then to Camden. In November, the Texas Division, under Maj. Gen. John Horace Forney, was moved to Spring Hill, Arkansas, in the southwestern part of the state. Other units, including the engineers, stayed at Camden. In February, the Texas Division moved south of Shreveport, and, in March, they were moved into Texas, supposedly to counter the threat of an invasion.[9] In May, Walker was given command of his division again, but by this time it had all but ceased to exist.[10]

On April 21 Kirby Smith announced that Robert E. Lee had surrendered. He then held a meeting with the Trans-Mississippi governors to determine the next actions. They voted for surrender, but he did not agree. Conditions in Shreveport grew worse as Smith detached units to move into Texas and central Louisiana, with the idea of carrying on the fight farther south. On May 13 the 3rd Louisiana Infantry Regiment, stationed in Shreveport and at that time almost intact, was rumored to be on the verge of mutiny and prepared to loot the government stores. A Missouri regiment was ordered to surround them and, for a short period, it appeared that open warfare between Confederate units would break out within the fortifications of the capital.[11] Nothing came of the supposed mutiny. Instead, government warehouses were opened, and soldiers from both states took what they could carry off. No one tried to stop them. On May 21 the Missouri troops began to restore order. Kirby Smith had no knowledge of this. On May 18 he left Shreveport, placing Lt. Gen. Simon Bolivar Buckner in charge.[12]

Smith and his contingent surrendered at Galveston on May 26. Confederate commands in Louisiana surrendered piecemeal, and the terms of surrender were signed by Smith on June 2.[13] On June 3 C.S.N. Lt. Comdr. Jonathan Carter surrendered the CSS *Missouri* to U.S.N. Comdr. W. E. Fitzhugh, making this the last viable Confederate unit to surrender within Trans-Mississippi and perhaps the confines of the continental United States.[14] Union forces entered Shreveport on June 6, and Confederates soldiers began surrendering by unit or individually.

At least a cadre of the members of Company H surrendered to Federal authorities in early June. Many of the engineer troops appear to have surrendered at the nearest sight to their homes. This indicates that some companies of the 4th Engineers may have informally disbanded and reported to parole stations most convenient to them. Varying dates listed for parole status, from as early as May 10 to as late as June 28, support this.[15] King was paroled on June 13, which was later than most of the others in his company by almost a week. This may be explained if he was at home in Collinsburgh. Perhaps he heard about the surrender and then traveled to Shreveport to sign the papers. Some soldiers surrendered at the places where they were detached. Surviving records indicate that members of Company A surrendered at Shreveport and Meridian, Mississippi. Companies B, D, E, G, and

H surrendered at Shreveport. Company C surrendered at Natchitoches. Company F surrendered at Natchitoches and Shreveport. Company I surrendered at Shreveport, Alexandria, and Natchitoches, and Company K surrendered at Shreveport, New Iberia, Natchitoches, and Alexandria. No information is known about the surrender site or the number of troops that surrendered in Company J. One member of Company H surrendered in Monroe.

Appendix 1

Bossier Banner, May 6, 1862

"On Wednesday, May 7th, the Marks Guards, 125 men strong, with John W. Rabb captain, and T. W. Abney, W. M. Sentell and J. H. Marks as lieutenants, left Bellevue. This company was the fifth company organized in the parish, and was officially designated as Company B, Twenty eighth (or 29th) Regiment, Henry Gray Colonel, and became a part of Mouton's Brigade, Polignac's Division. "On the previous evening Miss Clara Dalrymple presented the company with a beautiful banner. She addressed the company from the front porch of the residence of Hon. A. A. Abney at Bellevue."

> "Marks Guards, Citizens, Soldiers and Patriots.
>
> On this, the eve of your departure to the tented field, there to conquer or die in the defence of our liberties and our rights, I present you this banner in the name of its donor, Mrs. Callie N. Dickson. It is made and presented by the hand of woman, and bears upon its silken folds the stars and bars of our glorious young Republic, with the motto, "Our Southern Homes," and floats aloft unstained by crime.

As often as you look upon it, whether in the camp, or on the march, or amid the storm of battle, you cannot fail to remember that you are fighting for your homes, your wives, mothers, sisters, daughters, your honor and all for which men delight to live or dare to die—all imperiled by an insolent and vandal foe.

Take it; we commend it to your strong arms and brave hearts—to the battle and the breeze—confident that while one of you survive it will never trail in the dust, though blackened by the smoke and torn by the shock of battle, no stain of dishonor will ever blur its fair folds; but that pure and unsullied it will be returned to us and be received with a holy thrill, hallowed, as it will doubtless be, by heroes' blood.

Our hopes and our fears go with you (not fears for our cause) and constantly shall our prayers ascend to the God of battles and the God of our fathers, to protect you from the leaden rain and iron hail of our enemies, and from the still more dangerous diseases and pestilence which sometimes brood over camps, and pray for your speedy and safe return to your homes and firesides, when you will receive the welcome and congratulations of a free and grateful people.

Tis sad to think that we may never more behold some of your manly forms in our midst; that you may never more gladden the sight of those to whom you are near and dear, but your memories will be cherished in our heart of hearts, and you will have a monument in the affections of all true lovers of liberty, more lasting than ever was niched in stone or marble.

We part with you in sorrow, but with pride, because you are in the path of duty—'thrice armed, for your quarrel is just'—fit companions of a cause as glorious as soldiers ever fought for or woman prayer for. With such defenders we have no fears for the result, for we know that.

Whether in victory exulting, or in death laid low, Falling, you will leave not a blot on your name With your backs to the field and face to the foe You'll look proudly to heaven from the death bed of fame.

Our cities may be burned and our fair fields made desolate by vandal hordes, but we can never be conquered—never subjugated."

Freedom's battle once begun

Requethed from bleeding sire to son,
Though baffled oft is ever won.

The blood of Albert Sidney Johnston, Felix K. Zollicoffer, Ben McCulloch, McIntosh and a host of other noble spirits, which has been so freely poured upon the altar of our liberty, has not been offered in vain. Should you be called upon to mingle yours with theirs, we know that it will be given as freely.

In the name of your neighbors, your friends and your kindred, I bid you a kind and fond adieu."

Bossier Banner, May 6, 1862

Appendix 2

Extras—1879

Though through writing my journal, I have material connected with the war, which will be inserted here. Such compositions will, some of them, scarcely be found in standard works, but as they exhibit so forcibly the pure feeling that existed about the close of the war—and the facts as well as the feelings I do not think a true understanding of the war can be given without the facts and feelings they contain. More elegance might be desired, but I doubt whether a better expression of popular sentiment could be given.

The first is an "Extra" which, if viewed independent of the circumstances existing at the time, would be out of place here, and *should* have been out of place every where. At the date of its issuance, all were eager for news, and every soldier who had any care about the war would spend his last fifty-cents for an "Extra," hoping to get some news of consolation. Remember too, the soldiers were serving for eleven dollars per month, and to many 23 and to some 18, months wages were due. Further, the soldiers mainly clothed themselves; and sometimes the lack of a dollar to purchase some article of diet when sick, was the occasion of suffering. And a few dollars to satisfy the fee of a physician, was often necessary to have medical aid.

Standing on the sidewalk in front of the Verandah hotel on Milam Street, Shreveport, Louisiana, early in the morning I observed a news boy coming down the street calling aloud, "here's your Extra!!!"[1] A few moments more, and he was in front of me. The price was fifty cents, and I handed him a dollar for two, and hastened to the second story of the hotel to read before my turn to take a post at a door to guard some prisoners, three of whom were Englishmen. As I passed the door, one of them asked me if I got an Extra—he having heard the news boy. I told him I had two; that it was common with many of us to do so, and let others have one. He desired one, and handing it to him he asked the price. I replied, "fifty cents." He handed me one dollar, but I could not change it, and he insisted I should keep the dollar. As soon as he commenced reading, he exclaimed, "April fools." I examined, & found it so. I had not read a word of it, and had no suspicions of any character. I felt beaten, more because I had sold the Extra to the Englishman than because I was beaten. I immediately offered him the money, but he declined an acceptance. I vowed innocence, but there was a good reason to believe I designedly defrauded him, having to pass into a hall, and up a flight of stairs before I reached his apartment, giving me time to examine, and discover the "[*illegible*] Jolly" but I had not. So it was, I got an "Extra," and the Englishman paid for both his & mine. An objector may [*illegible*] that boys are excusable for April fooling. So they are to certain limits, but neither men nor bys can have a just excuse for swindling a man out of his money, not even a copper cent. Here it is. —

Extra.
Friday, April 1st, 1864

By Telegraph.
Latest News from the North
Another Draft.

Lincoln Calls For
900 000 000 000 000 000 000 000
More Men!!!

Arrival of The China Fleet!!
Great Excitement.

Resummonia, April 1 — Through the kindness of our friend, H.P. we have been enabled to lay before our readers the following official dispatch received at a late hour last night.

Kennsyltucky, March 30 — Forty thousand rebels are advancing. Great excitement prevails. Lincoln has called out 900 000 000 000 000 000 000 000 more men to repel the advance.

The steamship Great Eastern arrived at Campti last night with special dispatches for Dr. [*illegible*] from his *old friend* Louis Napoleon, giving a full account of the sailing of the Cina fleet and the recognition of the Confederacy by his Imperial Majesty J.W. O.B.E. Kihjjyvovooooony Emperor protector of Buzzard Island.

There is not a *shadow of a doubt* according to the Dr's conviction of the truth of the above.

The following highly important dispatch from the Tycoon of Japan in relation to the Alabama being near overlooked, should be read by all.

> ☞ *Signdd e galgdud o n tha inoot almn of h un rP vo H W hi weddut*
> leryoiiieocthjl easithe aiaeoPo Nain anf tann Ml Tingupa ir snhoif
> P hus ie enloc instlffo L hEero osonp otannun nVa vflleaeo Tipnens
> Si Geda immr mieabosap we, aowhrtlneck.
>
> ☞ We also call the attention of our readers (officials especially) to the following notice in relation to the extensive manufacture of brass buttons.
>
> io Bhr eainnBonesripr f col oenio plvore a shh it wafe, I e st Pyo D
> Num giierd t gtr hKanl ihrcrips obgid otiva addobae ou; r o vM
> scysu receens lvd s.s v htuirsShruhe aep bSee lto L saffi a ciave b
> wrssicwete z'otona ihilcae, eoh a Toodl-oan ounon iEee

Mobile, March 26. — Mr. Potts, a very reliable gentleman, seen Mr. Snorts, who seen Mr. Snooks, and he conversed with Col. Srognenecor, who is a staff office of Gen Gochenmasher, told him just to hold on a few days and he would hear of biggest battle every fought on continent.

Mugginsville, La., April 1. — The "Mugginsville Reporter" say, bedding, kitchen furniture, hogs, poultry and other necessaries are very scarce since the last raid our ill-fated city.

Mugginsville, April 1. — Great preparations are being made in Treajce Islands to receive Dr. [*illegible*] Ambassador from Muggins. The ladies of the court have prepared a beautiful petticoat for his own use. He has arrived at Heagti, Expected in the next flatboat at Treajce Islands. A chicken house was consumed by last night. Loss of life terrible. Two respectable old hens and ten dead rats were killed. Total loss of property amounts to $10!! No insurance.

Buzzard's Roost, April 1. — Official information that the muskettoes are advancing. Their lines extend to black bayou. Severe skirmishing at night. General engagement expected. The enemy have been reinforced by their old allies the Theos An attack on Muggins is rumored to be their intention. The garrison is preparing for a gallant defence. Great demands for musketto bars. No news from the rear.

The steamer *Atlantic* arrived from China and reports that great excitement exists on account of the Confederate Currency Bill. Bonds rose from 30¼ @ 87½. Great demand for 8 per cent bonds. The Emperor recognises the Confederacy.

Texmapol.lo, March 4. — The excitement is increasing. Brass buttons advancing $1230 a set. Great battle expected.

Rip Reakin, April 1. — Red river is to all appearances, still running downstream with but little prospect of its running up.

Alligator Bayou March 20. — It currently rumored and generally believed in highly official circles if it don't rain soon we'll have a might long dry spell.

The steamboat Overland arrived at our wharf on an ox wagon loaded with corn shucks for the C.S.

Here's Your Mule You April Fool.

Such is the dish of has prepared by those who have exemptions from the service of soldiers, for the especial purpose of furnishing news. Ye, who are fond of such combinations, can satiate your appetites, and when you have done, please inform us whether you find it wholesome. If so, we will claim your mental faculties to be abnormal.

The following is of a different character, and contains so much truth it should be preserved, though the composition is not elevated in style. It was composed in the last years of the war, and is an excellent index of what then existed between the different classes!

Just How They Do It.

—

Air — Southern Wagon[2]

O, Soldiers, I've concluded to make a little song
And if I tell no falsehood, there can be nothing wrong.
If any be offended at what I have to sing
'Twill be because his conscience applies its bitter sting.
Chorus. — Oh, how'd you like the army,
the brass mounted army,
The highfalutin army, where
eagle buttons rule.

Of late I've been thinking of this great army school,
With iron regulations and tyrrant's rigid rule;
But chosen words or phrases I need no long seek—
The facts as soldiers know them no stronger language speak,
Then how'd you like the army,
the brassmounted army,
This highfalutin army,
where eagle buttons rule.

Whisky is a monster and ruins great and small,
But in old Kirby's army, Headquarters get it all.
They drink it where there's danger,
although it seems too hard,
And if a private touch it they pop him under guard.
Then how'd you like the army,
the brass mounted army,
This highfalutin army,
where eagle buttons rule.

And when we are marching there's order No. Blank
which makes the private soldier forever stay in rank.
Although its rather cooling as soldiers often say,
It is a general order which privates must obey.
Then how'd you like the army,
the brass mounted army,
This highfalutin army,
where eagle buttons rule.

We sometimes get so hungry we're bound to press a pig,
Then the biggest stump in Dixie we're sure to have to dig.
And when we fret those who wear long-legged boots,
With neither judge nor jury, we're put on double roots.
Then how'd you like the army,
the brass mounted army,
This highfalutin army,
where eagle buttons rule.

At every big plantation or negro-holder's yard,
Just to save his property the General places a guard;
The sentry's instructions to let no private pass;
The rich man's house and table are fixed to suit the brass.
Then how'd you like the army,
the brass mounted army,
The highfalutin army,
where eagle buttons rule.

I hate to quit this story so beautiful and true,
But the poor men and the widows, must have a line or two,
For them no guards are stationed, their fences oft are burned
And property molested as long ago you heard.

Then how'd you like the army,
the brass mounted army,
This highfalutin army,
where eagle buttons rule.

The army's now much richer than when the war began,
It furnishes three tables where once it furnished but one,
The first is richly laden with chicken, goose and duck,
The next with pork and mutton, and third with good old Buck.
Then how'd you like the army,
the brass mounted army,
This highfalutin army,
where eagle buttons rule.

Our generals eat the poultry and buy it very cheap,
Our colonels and our captains devour the hogs and sheep;
The privates are contended, (except what they steal,)
With buck and corn bread plenty, to make a hearty meal.
Then how'd you like the army,
the brass mounted army,
This highfalutin army,
where eagle buttons rule.

These things and many others are truly hard to me,
But still I'll be contended and fight for liberty.
And when the war is o'er, Oh! what a jolly time;
We'll be our own commanders and sing a nicer rhyme.

And thus we'll leave the army,
the brass mounted army,
This highfalutin army,
where eagle buttons rule.

We'll see our loving sweethearts, and sometimes kiss them, too;
We'll eat the finest rations, and bid old Buck adieu.
There'll be no generals with us, no orders to compel;
Long boots and eagle buttons will take a long farewell.

And thus we'll leave the army,
the brass mounted army,
This highfalutin army,
where eagle buttons rule.

Simon Soapsuds, 16th La.

This ballad is all we know of this "Simon Soapsuds," but in this he has given prima-facia evidence that he knows something about how the war has been conducted. At the time he wrote, I was not so sanguine of our success as he, but I had previously experienced his expectations.

From his last stanzas it is evident that he was not "weak in the knees,"—his step was firm and elastic. It has been common with those whose faith has held to, to characterize those who foresaw our defeat as "weak in the knees," "knock howdy" limber jointed etc. Poor arguments, but the rash are often forced to use them.

"ON SPECULATION."
Air — Taxation of North America.

Come gentlemen and ladies all, and listen to what I say
Concerning this interruption in North America.
We once was a happy people, and a glorious nation too,
But now we are torn asunder, and bursted into two.

We once did live in peace and plenty, with all the world below,
But now it is quite different, as you already know.
For Demagogues of the North and politicians too,
Have enforced some laws upon us, they had no right to do.

We told them of their evils, and they must make amends
To those obnoxious laws, or they could not be our friends.
They only laughed at us, and said we must obey,
Any laws they chose to make in North America.

We only asked for our rights that were guaranteed to us.
We wished to be let alone, for we did not want a fuss.
They would not let us go with what we considered right,
And now they forced upon us an awful bloody fight.

We are now engaged in a bloody war with friends and kindred
dear,
That has made the widow and ophan weep, and brought from
them a tear;
It tells us in plain English, that we may understand
Now is the time that every one should prove himself a man.

This is not time to stay at home, and "Speculate" you seek,
While soldiers are on the battle field to fight for you and me.
Be careful how you "Speculate or you may see the day
You will have to settle with the soldiers of North America.

Although you stay at home, exempted by our laws,
From fighting for our liberty, in this our noble cause;
You have a duty to fulfill, I am sure you must obey,
Or you never will enjoy the blessing of North America.

While soldiers are on the battle-field, exposed to cold and rain,
You are staying at your homes, to raise your pork and grain;
Don't sell them at such a price, that their families cannot buy,
For you will bring distress upon them and make their children cry.

Remember what you told them, and what to them you said;
You promised that you would keep their families in daily meat and bread.
Stand firmly to your promise for they on you depend

It makes no odds how much you are pressed, or how much cramped you feel,
You must recollect the soldier that is fighting in the field,
For eleven dollars per month is all they get for pay,
While fighting for our rights in North America.

Your rights are equal with theirs, your interest is the same,
Be careful how you "Speculate," or you will bring yourselves to shame;
You will cause them to desert, in the field they will not stay.
While you are speculating on their families in North America.

If you do not like your condition, or the duties you must do,
Go join our noble army, and fight the battle through;
And ~~I think~~ before the war is ended I think that you will say,
It is a shame to "Speculate" in North America.

Come now my noble soldiers, come let your valor boast,
Don't let these "Speculators" drive you from your post,
And when the war is ended, and you are returning to your farms,
Your wife will fly to meet you, and clasp you in her arms.

Then she will begin to tell you, Oh! horrors to relate,
Of these mighty villains, and how they "Speculate."
She will tell you how she suffered while you were gone away.
A fighting for our rights in North America.

But keep your anger coolly, don't let them ever know
That they have brought distress upon you,
and your families down to woe;
And if you do not gain our freedom, I'm sure you are not
to blame,
But it is the "Speculators" that will bring us all to shame.

January 1863 A.H.B.

If asked who A.H.B. is, I shall be compelled to reply I do not know.

Whether male or female; of high or low rank. I am altogether uninformed.

But nothing is more evident than A.H.B. has a good understanding of the effects of Speculation on the masses of the people concerned in the war. At the date he wrote, speculation had risen into a terrific flame [*illegible*], and did not cease with the war. It has been one of the most potent agencies in defeating the Confederate cause—and is in a fair way to produce utter moral ruin, and, of course, financial, social and political ruin.

Observer A.H.B. is not one of the "cravenhearted," nor were may to be found at the date he wrote. About then I expressed sad feelings concerning our cause, on account of speculation as well as other things, but there was still a disposition not to give up the cause.

If speculation had been successfully combated, it is possible others evils might have been and a different result from that which ensued, might have been obtained.

The promises to care for the families of soldiers, alluded to by A.H.B., bring to recollection many cases that fell under my observation. I remember many that were ride [*illegible*] and falsified, but I can not now remember but one man who kept his promises to the soldiers. Not a few speculated upon the families they had solemnly promised to protect.

It is now 1879, and the impetus to speculation, received during the war, was so great that we are daily threatened with going down in the mighty vortex it has produced.

The next and last is "The Conscript Law," another agency highly destructive of the Confederacy. It seems our leading men were so confident, on account of our early successes, of a brief success, they ~~they~~ began too early to accomplish their aims. They must have thought if they did not take a firm hold on the reins of the government, that it would be too late when independence from the Federals was achieved. But it generally happens that when "well enough" is abandoned for better, all is lost. This is more apt to be true when illegitimate ends are sought.

By close inspection of the deeds of others we may discover the strand upon which they have wrecked, and by steering to a different point of the compass, may avoid a like catastrophe. Justice should ever be our polar star and if we strike upon reefs in the way though we may go down we will feel our consciences acquitted. Is it so with those who seek unjust aims! The answer ends here.

The Conscript Law

Composed by A.H. Bryson of Ellis County, Texas,
November, 1872.
Written by A. J. Willingham.

Attend young friends while I relate
What has happened here of late,
The vilest thing I ever saw,
Some folks call the Conscript Law.

It was bred and born in the Confederate States,
Where we poor souls have linked our fates.
We have joined the army and gone to fight
In a cause that we considered right.

Our gallant sons have volunteered
every time a call was heard;
They left their homes and parentage,
And joined the army of every age.

But our congress says this will never do,
We must have something else that is kinder news;
They stayed a while; at length they saw
The virtue in a Conscript Law.

They went to work and passed it through;
Our president thought that it would do.
From eighteen to thirty odd
Every man has felt the rod.

There were some ~~some~~ men above that age,
That wished a part on the public stage;
But for fear they might volunteer,
The Conscript Law again we hear.

They passed the law to forty-five,
And all our rights were then deprived.

It made no doubt how we were cramped
We had to march straight off to camp.

It made no odds how we were pressed,
Our families left without a dress;
We had to leave our families dear,
Without the right to volunteer.

They gave no time to sow our wheat,
Or to secure our families bread and meat;
They hurried us off at such a rate,
And trusted all to the future state.

It was in the camps the first I saw,
The misery of this despot law.
Yes, in camps near Tyler town,
All the misery may be found.

The lame and blind, there I saw
All subject to the Conscript Law.
They left their homes; were forced away,
And in the camps were bound to stay.

The Conscript Law—I fear its fate—
I hear it cussed from every State.
I hear them say in Arkansas,
The people run from the Conscript Law.

It is a question I wish to ask,
Why, in the name of God, this law was passed
When every time a call was heard
Our noble sons have volunteered.

Whether I am right or wrong, it seems to me
It will blot out our liberty;
For the Conscript was scarcely made,
Until another comes of a deeper shade.

The Exemption Law on record is found
To catch poor men and bind them down

While rich men are at home complete
With their stocks of cattle and [*illegible*]

The preachers too are exempt you see,
From fighting for our liberty
Mechanics too, they touched them light,
But make them swear with all their might.

The school teachers too, can stay at home,
All snugly seated in their room,
While we poor men are bound to go,
Exposed to rain and pelting snow.

Come Ladies, now a word to you,
What in the name of God will do you—
Your husbands gone, and bound to stay,
And you are left at home to work your way.

Yes! you are left at home without a friend,
Not any hopes you can depend,
With a heavy heart and aching head,
To toil and work for meat and bread.

To sweet-hearts too, I bid farewell,
My weeping tongue can never tell,
One half the trouble you have saw,
Occasioned by this Conscript Law.

And now before I leave this rhyme,
Another thought has struck my mind;
Where is the poor man—I ask, I say,
He is found in the camps, and bound to stay.

The enactment of the Conscript Law was accepted favorably, but as soon as its practical effects were experienced, it began to fall into disfavor. The wealthy found themselves bound to go into the ranks with the poor, or furnish substitutes—and that required money or good property. The poor found all the evils set forth in the preceding ballad, besides many others. For the poor there was no alternative into camp they must go. But the rich, for themselves and a few of such classes as they could not well dispense with, soon besought and obtained relief by Exemption Laws. They then became vigilant men, acting individually and in concert.

They would see to it that no other person staid at home unless he had good papers. Meeting a soldier just in from the army, they make especial inquiry concerning his business, how long he would be at home &c. Meeting him again before his time was half out, they manifest much surprise that he had not gone back to the army. Such arrogance, together with the bad treatment soldiers wives and children received during their absence, rendered a short stay at home unpleasant.

In this connection I will copy the writing of Alexander H. Stephens of Georgia, vice president of the Confederacy, on the Conscription law.

"But the measure upon which I differed most widely with the Administration were those which authorized the impressment of provisions at arbiting prices—the suspension of the Writ of *Habeas Corpus,* and the raising of the necessary military forces by Conscription. These last I considered not only radically wrong in principle, but as violation of the Constitution, and as exceedingly injurious to our Cause in their effects upon the people.

Major H__tes, Were you opposed to Conscription—I am surprised to hear you say that! I thought it was generally conceded that this principle and judicious measure was what actually saved Richmond in 1862, and sustained the cause as long as it was. Without it, I thought it was the general belief in the South, that the war, as the [*illegible*], would have [*illegible*] terms in proportion to population.

Conscription, therefore, was resorted from no *necessity* whatever as a means of raising troops. it was adopted as a policy, *mainly* with a view to securing a *different mode of officering,* those who were already voluntarily in the service, as well as those who might be called upon to enter it afterwards. Of this military view of the subject, it is not my purpose now to speak. A vast deal might be said upon it of both sides. All I mean now to say is, that, in my judgment, it plainly violated not only the spirit, but the letter of the Constitution; and moreover, had a most pernicious effect upon the public mind. The great mass of the people were perfectly willing to fight for their liberties, but they were utterly unwilling to be placed in a position, where it seemed they were required to do it by compulsion.

Moreover, if compulsion had been necessary at that time, or any time, to fill our armies, the war ought to have been immediately abandoned upon the disclosure of the fact; for no people are worthy of liberty or capable of preserving it, who have to be *compelled* to fight, either for its establishment, or its defence. Conscripts or men who are used by Rulers barely as machines in war, may overthrow liberty and prove efficient instruments in erecting Dynasties and Empires; but never have been, and never will be, the means of establishing free Institutions or maintaining them! This was my judgment then and will be ever! as for the Confederates, with half of their arms bearing people were virtually in for the war, before this demoralizing at was passed [*illegible*] the [*illegible*] their arms from the beginning to the and was achieved by this class of our soldiers. Very few of those who were brought in subsequently through the instrumentality all of the Conscription acts, affected any thing creditable to themselves of the country.

The desertions so much complained of were almost entirely from the latter class. I doubt if there were ten thousand conscripts, properly speaking, in all the armies together, at the time of final surrender. The Army of Virginia, which fought until it was literally "annihilated," was composed almost exclusively of the surviving remnants of the original voluntary enlistments. The same is true of the Army of Tennessee."

In this, as in many other views, I endorse Mr. Stephens, and think it will reward any student of the History of the late war, to read Mr. Stephens' *"The War Between The States,"* from which the preceding is copied, volume second, page 570.

Mr. Stephens is profoundly logical, is a wise statesman, and truly patriotic. Had our legislative halls, our executive and judicial departments, been filled by such men as Alexander H. Stephens, and Joseph C. Johnston, I sincerely believe we would have succeeded in wringing independence from the Federals. Of course this is but speculation, but it seems to me so evident that for those familiar with the circumstance, no argument is needed. But there are those who believe just the opposite. Men of things differently, and here as elsewhere we find great diversity. Some seem to think a thing must be so because they desire it to be so. The better way is, gather all the facts, pro and con, and let reason have full play [*illegible*] upon them before a decision is made. By thus proceeding, many errors will be obviated, and if committed, the consolation of having done the best we could know, affords relief.

The following poems are from more gifted pens than those I have already given.

My Maryland[3]
By *James R. Randall*

The despots' heel is on thy shore, Maryland!
His torch is at thy temple door, Maryland!
Avenge the patriotic gore
That flecked the streets of Baltimore,
And be the battle-guise of yore, Maryland! My Maryland.

Heark to an exiled son's appeal. Maryland!
My Mother-State, to thee I kneel, Maryland!
For life and death, for woe and weal,
Thy peerless [*illegible*] reveal,
And gird thy beauteous limbs with steel. Maryland!
My Maryland

Thou wilt not cower in the dust, Maryland
Thy beaming sword shall never rest, Maryland

Remember Carroll's sacred trust,
Remember Haward's [*illegible*] warlike thrust,
And all thy slumbers with the just, Maryland! My Maryland!

Come, 'tis the red dawn of day, Maryland!
Come, with thy panoplied array, Maryland!
With Ringgold's spirit for the fray,
With Watson's blood at Monterey,
With fearless love and dashing may, Maryland! My Maryland.

Come, for thy shield is bright and strong, Maryland!
Come, for thy dalliance does the wrong, Maryland!
Come, to thine own heroic throng,
Marching with Liberty along
And ring thy dauntless slogan-song, Maryland! My Maryland.

Dear Mother, burst the tyrant's chain, Maryland!
Virginia should not call in vain, Maryland!
She meets her sisters on the plain—
"Sic semper," 'tis the proud refrain
That baffles missions back amain, Maryland

Arise, in majesty again, Maryland! My Maryland!
I see the blush upon thy cheek, Maryland!
For th__ wasted bravely meek,
But lo! there [*illegible*] a shriek
From hill to hill, from cheek to cheek
Potomac calls to Chesapeake, Maryland! My Maryland!

Thou wilt not yield the vandal toll, Maryland!
Thou wilt not croak to his control, Maryland!
Better the fire upon thee roll,
Better the shot, the blade, the bowl,
From crucifixion of the soul, Maryland! My Maryland!

I hear the distant thunder hum, Maryland!
The Old Line bugle, fife and drum, Maryland!
She is not dead, nor deaf, nor dumb—
Huzza! she spurns the Northern scum!
She breathes—she burns! She'll come! She'll come! Maryland!
My Maryland!

But she did not come; the tyrant held too firm a grasp.

The following is quite in contrast with the one just written, and both, no doubt, emanated from earnest hearts.

A Prayer For Peace
(Written by S. Teakle Wallis of Baltimore, a Member of the Maryland Legislature while imprisoned during the Reign of Terror in 1861.)[4]

Peace! Peace! God of our fathers, grant us Peace.
Unto our cry of anguish and despair
give ear and pity [*illegible*] the lonely home
Where widowed beggar and orphan [*illegible*]
Fill their poor urns with tears; from trampled [*illegible*]
Where the bright harvest thou hast sent us, rots—
The blood of them who should have garnered it
Calling to Thee-from field of carnage, where
The foul-beaked vultures, sated, flap their wings.
O'er crowded corpses, that but yesterday
Bore hearts of brothers, beating high with love
And common hopes and pride, all blasted now,—
Father of Mercies! not alone from these
Our prayer and wail are lifted. Not alone
Upon the battle's scared and desolate track
Nor with the sword and flame, is it, O God,
That thou hast smitten us. Around our hearths
And in the crowded streets and busy marts,
Where echo whispers not the far off strife,
That slap over loved ones; —in the solemn hills
Of safe and quiet counsel—nay, beneath
The temple-roofs that we have reared to thee,
And mid their rising incense, —God of Peace.
The curse of war is on us. Greed and hate
Hungering for gold and blood: Ambition, bred
Of passionate vanity and sordid lusts,
Mad with the base desire of tyranous sway
Over men's souls and throught; have set their price
On human hecatombs, and sell and buy
Their sons and brothers for the shambles. Priests
With white, anointed, supplicating hands,
From Sabbath unto Sabbath clasped to Thee;
Burn, in their tingling pulses, to fling down
Thy censors and thy cross, to clutch the threats
Of kinsmen by whose cradles they were born

Or grasp the brand of Herod, and go forth
Till Rachel hath no children left to slay.
The very name of Jesus, writ upon [*illegible*]
Thy [*illegible*] beneath the spotless outstretched wings
Of Thing Almighty Dove is wrapt and hid
With blood of brother's flags and from the spires
That rise above them angry banners flood
blue skies to which they point, amid the day
[*illegible*] war songs tuned to mock Thy praise.

All things once prized and honored are forgot
The Freedom that we worshipped, next to Thee
The manhood that was Freedom's spear and shield;
The proud, true heart, the brave, outspoken word
Which might be stifled, but could never weaken
The guise, whate'er the profit, of a lie [*illegible*]
All these are gone, & in their stead, have come
These vices of the miser and the slave,—
Scorning no sh[*illegible*] that bringeth gold or power
Knowing no love, or faith, or reverence,
Or sympathy, or aim or hope,
Save as begun in self, and ending there.
With vipers like to these, O blessed God!
Scourge us no longer! Send us down, once more,
Some shining seraphim Thy glory clad,
To wake the midnight of our sorrowing
With tidings of Good Will. Peace to man
And if the start that through the darkness led
Earth's wisdom then, guide not our folly now
Oh, be the lightening Thine Evangelist,
With all its firey, forked tongues, to speak
The unanswerable message of Thy will.

Peace! Peace! God of our father, grant us Peace
Peace in our heart & at Thine altars; Peace.
In the red waters and their blighted shores;
Peace of the leaguered cities, & there it is too
That watch and bleed, around them & within,
Peace for the homeless & the fatherless;
Peace for the captive on his weary way,
And the mad crowds who jeer his helplessness
For them that suffer, them that do the wrong

Sinning and Sinned against—O God! for all—
For a distracted, torn and bleeding land—
Speed the glad tidings! Give us, give us Peace.

This poem is worth reading, and rereading, and most it is the prayer of all, this earth would know no more wars. They would cease if there would be none to espouse it. As the men of Nations are now developed, many ages will be required to work up humanity to that high moral excellence requisite to a hearty [*illegible*] to this profess. It is no less the duty, however, of each to do all in his power to hasten the end.

Extracts from a Pamphlet on the destruction of Columbia, S.C., published in 1865, and written by William Gilmore Simms, LL.L.[5]

The destruction of Atlanta, the pillaging & burning of the towns of Georgia, & the subsequent devastation along the march of the Federal Army through Georgia, gave sufficient [*illegible*]est of the treatment to be anticipated by S.C., should the same commander be permitted to make a like progress in our State. The Northern press furnished him the *cri de guerre* to be sounded when he should cross our borders. "*Vae victis!*"—woe to the conquered!—in the case of a people who had first raised the banner of Secession. "The howl of delight," (such was the language of the Northern press,) sent up by Sherman's legions, when they —looked across the Savannah to the shores of Caroline, was the sure fore-runner of the terrible hate which threatened our people should the soldiers be once let loose upon our lands. Our people felt all the danger. . . . .

The march of the Federals into our State was characterized by such scenes of license, plunder and general conflagration, as very soon showed that the threats of the Northern press, and of their soldiers, were not to be regarded as mere *bre*-[*illegible*]*ful* [*illegible*] Day by day brought to the people of Columbia tiding of atrocities committed and more intended [*illegible*] Daily did long trains of fugitives line the roads, with wives and children and horses and cattle, sicking [*illegible*] highways, half naked people cowered from the winter under bush tents in the thickets, under the eaves of houses, under the railroad sheds, and in old [*illegible*] left them along the route. All these repeated the same story of suffering, and poverty and nakedness. Habitation after habitation, village after village-one sending up its spiral flames to the other, presaging for it the same fate-lighted the evening and midnight sky with crimson horrors.

No language can describe nor can any catalogue furnish an adequate detail of the wide-spread destruction of homes and property. Granaries were emptied, and where the grain was not carried off, it was strewn to waste under the feet of the cavalry, or consigned to the fire which consumed the dwelling. The negroes were robbed equally with the whites of food and clothing. The roads were covered with butchered cattle, hogs, mules and the costliest furniture. Valuable cabinets, rich pianos, were not only hewn to pieces, but bottles of ink, turpentine, oil, whatever could efface or destroy, was employed to defile and ruin. Horses were ridden into the houses, people were forced from their beds, to permit the search of its hidden treasures.

The beautiful homesteads of the Parish country, with their wonderful tropical gardens, were ruined; ancient dwellings of black cypress, one hundred years old, which had been reared by the fathers of the Republic—men whose ancestors were famous in Revolutionary history—were given to the flames recklessly as were the rude hovels; choice pictures and works of art, from Europe, select and numerous libraries, objects of peace wholly, were all destroyed. The in black no less than white, were left to starve, compelled to feed only upon the garbage to be found in the abandoned camps of the soldiers. The corn scraped up from the spots where the horses fed, has been the only means of life left thousands but lately in affluence.

And thus plundering, and burning, the troops made their [*illegible*] portions of Beaufort, into Ba[*illegible*] the pursued, the same [*illegible*]. The villages of Beaufort of [*illegible*] Bemberg, Midway, were more or less destroyed; the inhabitants everywhere left homeless and without food. The horses and mules, all cattle, and hogs, whenever fit for service food, were carried off and the rest shot. Every implement of the workhorse and farmer, tools, plows, hoes, gins, looms, wagons, vehicles, were made to feed the flames.

From Barnwell to Orangeburg and Lexington was the next progress, marked everywhere by the same swiping destruction. Both of these Court towns were partially burned . . . .

Hardly had the troops reached the head of Main Street when the work of pillage was begun. Stores were broken open within the first hour after their arrival, and gold, silver, jewels and liquors, eagerly sought. The authorities, officers, soldiers, all, seemed to consider it a matter of course. And woe to him who carried a watch with gold chain pendant, or who wore a choice hat, or overcoat, or boots or shoes. He was stripped in the twinkling of an eye. It is computed that, from first to last, twelve hundred watches were transferred from the pockets of their owners to those of soldiers. Russed [*illegible*] saved the same fate; or was the Confederate currency repudiated. But of all these things hereafter in more detail.

At about 12 o'clock, the jail was discovered to be on fire from within. This building was immediately in rear of the Market, or City Hall, and in a densely built portion of the city. The supposition is that it was fired by some of the prisoners—all of whom were released and subsequently followed the army. The fire of the jail had been preceded by that of some cotton piled in the street. Both fires were soon subdued by the firemen. At about half-past one, A.A., that of the jail was rekindled and was again extinguished. Some of the prisoners who had been confined at the Asylum, had made their escape, in some instances, a few days before, and were secreted and protected by citizens.

No one felt safe in his own dwelling; and in the faith but General Sherman would respect the Convent, and [*illegible*] it properly provided, numbers of young ladies were confided to the care of Mother Superior and [*illegible*] and treasure was—[*illegible*] in full or [*illegible*] that they [*illegible*] in illusions; —[*illegible*] Irish Catholic [*illegible*] not brought [*illegible*] the city at all; we hoped [*illegible*]ide of the [*illegible*] But a few [*illegible*] among the corps which occupied the [*illegible*] of the conduct of these, a favorable account [*illegible*]. One of them rescued a silver goblet of [*illegible*] used as a drinking cup by a soldier, and returned it to the Rev. Dr. O'Connell. This priest, by t[*illegible*]was severely handled by the soldiers. Such, also was the fortune of the Rev. Mr. Shand, of Trinity (the [*illegible*] Church, who sought in vain to save a t[*illegible*] sacred vessels of his church. It was —[*illegible*] from his keeping, and his struggle to [*illegible*] provoked the [*illegible*] We are [*illegible*] on reaching Carnding [*illegible*] General Sherman restor[*illegible*] believed were these vessels to Bishop Davis had been discovered that the plate belonged to St. Peter's Church, in Charleston.

And here it may be well to mention, as suggested of many clues, an incident which presented a sad commentary on that confidence in the security of the Convent, which was entertained by the great portion of the people. This establishment, under the charge of the sister of the Right Rev. Bishop Lynch, was at once [*illegible*] Convent and an Academy of the highest class. [*Illegible*] were sent for education the daughters of Protestant [*illegible*] the most wealthy classes, throughout the State, These, with the nuns and those young ladies sent. [*Illegible*]on the emergency, probably exceeding one hundred the Lady Superior herself entertained the fullest confidence in the immunities of the establishment. But her confidence was clouded, after she had a conference with a certain Major of the Yankees; who described himself as an editor, from D [*illegible*] He visited her at an early hour in the day announced his friendly sympathies with Mother Superior and the sisterhood; professed hope for their safety; his promise to do all that he could to insure it—declared that he would was willing [*illegible*] she and [*illegible*] made such professions [*illegible*] and [*illegible*] disarm those suspicions his bad manners, inflated spe[*illegible*] a pompous [*illegible*] might otherwise have [*illegible*]. The [*illegible*] with such a charge in his hands, was naturally [*illegible*] to welcome all shows and prospects of [*illegible*] expressed her gratitude. He disappeared, and then after re-appeared bringing with him no less than eight or ten men none of them, as he admitted, orderlies. He had some specious argument to [*illegible*] perhaps, her guard had better be one of Protestant [*illegible*] This suggestion staggered the lady a little [*illegible*] seemed to convey a more potent, [*illegible*] he added, in a whisper. "For I [*illegible*] my sister, that Columbia is a [*illegible*] Terrible [*illegible*]. This officer, leaving his m[*illegible*] disappeared, to show himself no more [*illegible*] so left behind were finally among the mo[*illegible*] plunderers. The moment that the inmates, a [*illegible*] by the fire, were forced to abandon their house, [*illegible*] began to revel in its contents.

"Anis custodiat ipsas custodies"—who shall guard the guards—asks the proverb. In a number of cases, the guards provided for the citizens were among the most active plunderers, were quick to betray their trusts, abandon their posts, and bring their comrades in to [*illegible*] in the general pillage. The most dexterous [*illegible*] a [*illegible*] of these, it is the opinion of most persons, were chiefly Eastern men, or men of immediate Eastern or [*illegible*]. The Western men, including the Indiana, a portion of the Illinois & Iowa troops, were neither so dexterous nor unscrupulous—were frequently faithful & respectful and, perhaps it would be safe to assert that many of the [*illegible*] which escaped the sack and fire, owed their safe[*illegible*] the presence or the contiguity of these men. But we [*illegible*] trace our steps.

X X X X X X X X X X X X

The reign of terror did not fairly begin till night. In some instances, where parties complained of the morale, the guards said to [*illegible*] with a crusade. This [*illegible*] till morning [*illegible*] such [*illegible*] the work begun [*illegible*] and with hourly [*illegible*] gins and ho[*illegible*] were brought [*illegible*] were soon driven from [*illegible*] indeed idle against [*illegible*] pertinacious hostility of the [*illegible*] to pieces, & the [*illegible*] to themselves, left the field in the [*illegible*] the flames, spread from side to side [*illegible*] to rear, from street to street, & when [*illegible*] and inevitable progress was too slow [*illegible*] who had kindled them, they helped the [*illegible*] the application of fresh combustibles [*illegible*] agencies of conflagration. By midnight [*illegible*] from its Northern [*illegible*] Southern a solid wall of fire. By 12 o'clock, [*illegible*] black, which included the banking [*illegible*] treasury buildings, were consumed; [*illegible*] (Congarce) & Nickelson's Hotels; the m[*illegible*] manufactories of Evans & Cogswell—is [*illegible*] large block in the business portion [*illegible*] the old Capitol and all the adjacent buildings were in ruins. The range called the Granite was beginning to flame at 12, and might have been saved by ten vigorous men, resolutely [*illegible*].

At 10 o'clock, the hour was struck by the clock [*illegible*] Market Hall, which was even then illu[*illegible*] from within. It was it own last hour which it sounded, & its tongue was silenced forevermore. In less than five minutes after its spire went down with a crash, & by the time, almost all the buildings within the precinct were a mass of ruins.

[*pages missing*]

was [*illegible*] occupied mostly [*illegible*] same time, a body [*illegible*] the eastern out-[*illegible*] the dwellings of Mr. Se[*illegible*] Hampton, Dr. John [*illegible*] Mrs. [*illegible*] Mr. Latta, Mrs. [*illegible*] there were then some twenty fires [*illegible*] us. many different quarters, & wh[*illegible*] sounded from these quarters, a [*illegible*] was sent up almost simultaneously, [*illegible*] the Northernmost limit of the [*illegible*] Main street in its very center; [*illegible*] stores or houses. O [*illegible*] Bates, C.D. [*illegible*] & some others, in the heart of the m[*illegible*] portion of the town; thus envelop [*illegible*] almost every section of the de[*illegible*] period, thus early in the evening, th[*illegible*] of that drunkenness which preva[*illegible*] in the night, & only after all the [*illegible*] on Main Street had been rifled. T[*illegible*] engaged in this were well prepared with all [*illegible*] pliances essential to their work. They did not [*illegible*] torch. They carried with them, from house [*illegible*] pots vessels containing combustible [*illegible*] ended probably of phosphorous & other simi[*illegible*] turpentine, etc., & with balls of cotton so [*illegible*] in this liquid, with which they also [*illegible*] covered floors & walls, they conveyed the flames with wonderful rapidity from dwelling to dwelling. Each had his ready box of Lucifer matches [*illegible*] with a sc[*illegible*] upon the walls, the flames b[*illegible*] to rage. When houses were closely c[*illegible*] a brand from one was the means [*illegible*] destruction to the other. [*Illegible*] winds favored. They had been [*illegible*] day, & steadily prevailed from [*illegible*] and bore the flames so [*illegible*].

[*Illegible*] this is the view [*illegible*] to it, and that [*illegible*] believed by many. [*Illegible*] it is a very great mistake. Richmond was not saved by Conscription in 1862 or at any time. The great battles fought by the Army of Virginia, first under Johnston, then under Lee, which achieved such brilliant victories in saving Richmond at the period you speak of, were fought in May and June of that year. [*Illegible*] act of Conscription was passed [*illegible*] 16th of April before. That army was composed chiefly and almost entirely of volunteers already enlisted, and in the [*illegible*] for three years or the war.

[*Illegible*] is time a few Regiments whose term of service was for one year, and which had not expired when the act passed immediately organized under it for the future; but the term of voluntary service, in which they were enlisted, of most, if not all of these few, extended beyond the time in which the fate of Richmond on that occasion was determined. There may have been a very few Regiments whose term would have expired before that time, and composed of men who, without the passage of the act, might have quit the service. But the number of such regiments as those, must have been very small. Indeed, if any such did exist, (composed of men who would have quit the field at such an hour, without the res[*illegible*] of that act,) they were certainly not [*illegible*] of that [*illegible*] which can [*illegible*] of the scales of battles and conflicts.

The fact is, very [*illegible*] of them were there [*illegible*] of that act; not [*illegible*] brought there by [*illegible*] per cent at least of the fighting men of that Army who achieved these victories, were enrolled in Regiments already voluntarily enlisted for three years or the war, when the act of Conscription was passed.

The idea of belief that there was a necessity for that mode of filling our armies at the time, is altogether erroneous and unsustained by the facts of the case. I do not know the exact number, but I think I may venture to say that there [*illegible*] near four hundred thousand [*illegible*] voluntarily enlisted in the Con[*illegible*] armies for three years or the war [*illegible*] on every call the troops under the regular Constitutional militia system, the call had been responded to by the tender of more volunteers on those te[*illegible*] than the number asked for. Georgia alone had upwards of fifty Regiments, besides several Battalions, then in the field at Richmond, or elsewhere, *so enlisted.* In the last call before this act was passed, four more Regiments tendered their services on these terms, than were called for from this State. They were not received by the War Department upon the ground that their services were *not* needed. This was not more than two months before the passage of that act. The other Sta[*illegible*] in no degree be [*illegible*] Georgia [*illegible*] ness to respond with [*illegible*] of troops under [*illegible*] on the same [*William Henry King's diary ends abruptly here.*]

Appendix 3

Order to Colonel Randolph

HEADQUARTERS TRANS-MISSISSIPPI DEPARTMENT,1
Shreveport, La., September 24, 1863.

Col. G. P. RANDOLPH,
Collinsburg, La.:

COLONEL: The movements of the enemy in Louisiana will very soon render it necessary to call out the companies organizing for home defense. Under the provisions of the act, and for their greater efficiency, they will be organized into battalions and regiments.

The power of appointing field officers is with myself. No time should be lost in completing these organizations, and I desire that you will command the battalion or regiment that will be first formed in Northern Louisiana.

Col. J. L. Lewis, of Minden, has several companies under process of organization. B. Witherspoon, of Black Jack, De Soto Parish, Col. B. L. Hodge, cud W. S. Welch, of this place, have each been authorized to raise a company. There are other companies in process of formation, but a head is wanted to give life and organization to the whole. I inclose you your commission as colonel. The appointment of the other field officers will be made with your advice and on your recommendation.

Col. B. L. Hodge, from his energy, experience, and position, would be the best appointment that I can suggest for the lieutenant-colonelcy. I suggest this matter to your earnest consideration, and, if you take it in hand, will materially hasten the organization of a regiment.

Let me thank you for the prompt and patriotic zeal with which you have responded to every call made upon you by the authorities.

Very respectfully, your obedient servant,

E. KIRBY SMITH,
Lieutenant-General, Commanding.

Appendix 4

Henry King's Siblings and Children

The following information was derived from the King family Bible and from various communications with Shirley Hampton, the great-granddaughter of William Henry King.

William Henry King's Siblings

Charles Rufus King married Mary J. Lawrence (Lorance?) March 29, 1855. Charles R. King died April 26, 1860, and William Henry King served as tutor for their child Alice R. King. Mrs. Mary R. King remarried, to J. B. Cavett, February 9, 1862, only months before the men left Bossier for the Civil War. Mary R. King lived with her mother-in-law-to-be, Mrs. E. E. Cavett, at least two years before marrying her son.

Elizabeth Helen King was born July 15, 1830, in Madison County, Alabama. She married Marmaduke Dennison and moved to Lafayette County, Arkansas, where she died December 25, 1854.

Mary Merab King was born July 29, 1832, in Madison County, Alabama. She married Lysander Rathburn March 14, 1852. Mary Merab King Rathburn drowned in Dorcheat Bayou at the Marvel's "Murrel's" Bridge on April 12, 1860. Lysander Rathburn died circa 1863.

Penelope Caroline King was born October 5, 1834. She married Harvey Williamson June 24, 1854. They had two children, Thomas and Clara Williamson. Following Harvey Williamson's death she married Benjamin F. Keeth on February 24, 1876. She later divorced Keeth. She died April 1, 1908.

Lucretia Jane King was born October 29, 1836. She married James P. Strayhan (1829–1909). Lucretia Jane Strayhan died in 1870.

Julia Ann King was born February 27, 1839. She died July 5, 1849, in Madison County, Alabama, at age ten.

Stephen Corodan King was born May 9, 1841, in Madison County, Alabama. He married Lenora Virginia McLeish. He was murdered January 1888.

Thomas Whitfield King was born October 26, 1843, and died February 13, 1924. He apparently never married.

Gabriel Davy King never married. His death is recorded in William Henry King's diary.

William Henry King's Children (All Born to His Marriage with Balsona E. Kennard)

Mary A. King was born in 1856 in Rusk County, Texas. No other information is known.

James Alfred King was born November 30, 1857, in Rusk County, Texas. He married Elvira Matilda Singletary on April 18, 1883. He died January 15, 1935, in Morrison, Oklahoma.

Ella King was born in 1860 in Shelby County, Texas. She married Christopher Columbus Dill on January 29, 1880. No other information is known.

William Henry King Jr. was born November 11, 1862, in Shelby County, Texas. He was married to Sarah Catherine Fletcher. He lived near Cowden, Oklahoma, at the turn of the twentieth century. He died in 1974 in Eastland, Texas, and was buried in Sappington Chapel Cemetery near Cowden, Oklahoma.

Zachary King was born September 13, 1867, in Shelby County, Texas. He married Silah Wisdom in Forestburg, Texas, on July 10, 1887. He died January 5, 1901, in Prague, Oklahoma.

Marguerite Arabelle King was born May 9, 1870, in Shelby County, Texas. She was married to John Wesley Landers on May 29, 1887. She died in Forestburg, Montague County, Texas, on August 22, 1940. She was the grandmother of Shirley Hampton.

Molly King was born in 1872 in Shelby County, Texas. She was married to William Lewis and died prior to 1940.

Ada King was born in 1874 in Shelby County, Texas. She never married and died sometime after 1940.

Appendix 5

Confederate Vessels Operating on the Red River from March 1863 to June 1865

Information listed in this appendix was found in the following sources: (1) Frederick Way Jr., ed., *Way's Packet Directory, 1848–1994* (Athens, Ohio: Ohio Univ. Press, 1994); (2) William Henry King diary; (3) U.S. War Department, *War of the Rebellion: The Official Records of the Union and Confederate Armies* (*O.R.*), vol. 34, pt. 2; (4) *O.R.*, vol. 48, pt. 2; (5) David Dixon Porter, *Naval History of the Civil War* (Secaucus, N.J.: Castle Books, 1984); (6) Paul H. Silverstone, *Warships of the Civil War Navies* (Annapolis, Md.: Naval Institute Press, 1989); and (7) Mark K. Ragan, *Union and Confederate Submarine Warfare in the Civil War.* The numbers in parentheses below refer to these sources.

Combatant Vessels

CSS *Grand Duke,* tinclad—accidentally burned September 1863 at Shreveport (6)
CSS *Missouri,* ironclad—last Confederate naval vessel to surrender on inland waters (1, 2, 3, 6)
CSS *Cotton II* or *Mary T,* armed vessel tender (1, 2, 6)

CSS *Webb,* high speed ram—destroyed at Algiers, Louisiana, in 1865 while attempting to escape (6)

Five unnamed submarines were at Shreveport. They were the sisters of the CSS *Hunley* and were built at Shreveport. One was dismantled and taken to Houston; the other four remained at Shreveport and have yet to be found. (7)

Transports

Anna Perrett (2, 3)
Beauregard (possibly the *General Beauregard,* tinclad) (2, 3)
B.L. Hodge (1)
Blanchard (2)
Colonel Terry (3)
Countess (3,4)
Dixie (1,3)
Eva No. 7 (or another in the same line of *Evas*) (1, 2)
Frolic (1, 3)
General Quitman (1,4)
Indian No. 2 (1, 4)
Lafourche (1, 3)
Louis D'Or (1, 3)
Music (1)
New Falls City (1, 2, 3, 5, 6)
Osceola (1, 2)
Pauline (2, 3)
R. Blanton (2)
Starlight (1, 2)
T.D. Hine (1, 3)
Texas (1,2)
Trent (possibly the *Trenton*) (1, 2)
Trixie (2)
Twilight (1, 2)
Vigo (1, 3)
W. A. Andrew (1, 2)

Notes

Introduction

1. Alfred Jay Bollett, *Civil War Medicine: Challenges and Triumphs* (Tucson, Ariz.: Galen Press, 2002), 257.
2. King family Bible.
3. Personal communication with Shirley Hampton by Clifton Cardin, Feb. 27, 2003. Hampton is a great-granddaughter of William Henry King. Hereinafter cited as Hampton interview.
4. U.S. Dept. of Commerce, Seventh Decennial Census (1850), Madison County, Ala., unpublished tabulations in the National Archives and Records Administration, Washington, D.C.
5. Hampton interview.
6. Rusk County, Texas, marriage records, 1854.
7. King family Bible.
8. Ibid.
9. *Susan Chennault King v. William Henry King* suit filed in Bossier Parish District Court, Bossier Parish Records, 1862.
10. Ibid.

11. U.S. Dept. of Commerce, Eighth Decennial Census (1860), Shelby County, Tex., unpublished tabulations in the National Archives and Records Administration, Washington, D.C.
12. Hampton interview. Hampton agrees that King was not a medical doctor.
13. Ibid.
14. U.S. Dept. of Commerce, Ninth Decennial Census (1870), Shelby County, Tex., unpublished tabulations in the National Archives and Records Administration, Washington, D.C.
15. U.S. Dept. of Commerce, Eleventh Decennial Census (1890), Montague County, Tex., unpublished tabulations in the National Archives and Records Administration, Washington, D.C.; Hampton interview.
16. King family Bible.
17. Shelby County, Texas, marriage records, 1886.
18. Montague County, Texas, divorce records, 1899.
19. Hampton interview.
20. King family Bible.

1. Muster, Organization, and Training

1. Bellevue was the parish (county) seat of Bossier Parish, Louisiana.
2. Confederate Louisiana Gov. Thomas Overton Moore.
3. Proximo means in or of the next month after the present.
4. William Henry King and wife Balsona Elena Kennard King were residents of Shelby County, Texas. William chose to bring his wife to Bossier Parish to remain with Mrs. E. E. Cavett during the war. Almost all of King's family still lived in Bossier Parish and he had resided there in the early 1850s. The town of Collinsburgh was first called Pineville in 1847; its name was changed on June 28, 1856. The town was located at the intersection of the Old Benton–Plain Dealing Highway, Dutch John Road, and Collinsburgh Road, two miles west of Louisiana Highway 3. Most late-twentieth-century maps list the spelling as Collinsburg.
5. From the beginning to one end.
6. All interparish ferries were leased by the Bossier Parish Police Jury for one-year terms. Parish records list that in 1859 the Bodcau ferry was run by C. C. Nowell. By 1863 it was operated by John Lofton. See Bossier Parish Police Jury Record Books, 1859–63.
7. John W. Rabb, captain, Company B, 28th (Gray's) Louisiana Infantry Regiment Roll, May 11, 1862 (only roll on which borne), enlisted at Monroe, La., May 11, 1862. Andrew Booth, *Records of Louisiana Confederate Soldier and Louisiana Confederate Commands* (Baton Rouge: Commissioner, Louisiana Military Records, 1920), 3:230. All entries of personnel from Louisiana will be described from this three-volume set. The editors will follow the spelling and information order listed by General Booth, only deviating for clarity. John Wood Rabb began his military career as first sergeant in Bossier Volunteers in 1861. He had grey eyes, dark hair, light complexion, and stood six-foot-one. In the 1860 Census he was listed as a farmer and a resident of Rocky Mount, Louisiana. He married Maggie J. Herron on July 29, 1866. In 1886, when he visited the Confederate Reunions, he was known as Col.

J. W. Rabb. See U.S. Dept. of Commerce, Eighth Decennial Census (1860), Bossier Parish, Louisiana, unpublished tabulations in the National Archives and Records Administration, Washington, D.C. Additional information in the Cardin Collection and collections in the Bossier History Center, Bossier City, La.

8. Thomas W. Abney, first lieutenant, Company B, 28th (Gray's) Regiment, Louisiana Infantry; enlisted Monroe, La., May 11, 1862; on Rolls of Prisoners of War; paroled Shreveport, La., June 10, 1865, as captain; Booth, *Records of Louisiana,* 1:23. Thomas Walter Abney, was born June 21, 1831, in Fairfield District, South Carolina, the fourth son of Major Malchijah and Isabel Culbreth Abney. He came to Bossier Parish in 1845 and married Martha J. White of Lexington, Kentucky, on December 7, 1852. She died September 4, 1853. He married Mary E. Slack, December 28, 1860. Abney was principal of Red Land Academy, Cottage Grove Academy, and Bellevue Academy prior to joining the Marks Guards. He was paroled June 10, 1865, as a captain. Abney resided in Coushatta, Louisiana, in 1865. Following the "Coushatta Massacre" during Reconstruction, Abney was arrested by Federal soldiers and was carried to New Orleans and imprisoned. After returning to his home, impaired in health and with his business destroyed, Abney moved to Denton, Texas, where he lived until his death, November 6, 1902.
9. William M. Sentell, second lieutenant, Company B, 28th (Gray's) Louisiana Infantry Regiment; roll dated May 11, 1862 (only roll on which borne), enlisted Monroe, La., May 11, 1862; Booth, *Records of Louisiana,* 3:515.
10. John H. Marks Jr., second lieutenant, Company B, 28th (Gray's) Louisiana Infantry Regiment; roll dated May 11, 1862 (only roll on which borne), enlisted Monroe, La., May 11, 1862; Booth, *Records of Louisiana,* 2:877. John H. Marks Jr. was the son of Amous Nicholas and Rebecca L. Wright Marks. It was not uncommon to name a person "Junior," even though they were not a direct line descendent; for example, the individual could be named for an uncle.
11. Marks Guards became Company B of the 28th (Gray's) Louisiana Infantry Regiment. See Appendix 1 for a full account of the proceedings as carried in the *Bossier Banner,* May 6, 1862. The *Bossier Banner* was the principal newspaper in Bossier Parish at that time. It is the only newspaper in the region in which all of its prior copies exist.
12. This is Mrs. Callie N. Dickson. She was the widow of David Franklin Dickson, who died in August 1861. She was deceased by 1867 when probate was filed in Bossier courts. See Cardin Collection; Bossier Parish Records for 1867.
13. Miss Clara Dalrymple was the twenty-one-year-old daughter of Wilson and Margaret Wilson Dalrymple. Her brother John Dalrymple served in the army of Virginia. He died the next day, May 7, 1862. She was a first-generation American; both her parents and older brother were born in Ireland. She married 2nd Sgt. Joseph L. C. Graham on December 29, 1864. They both died soon after the war. See Cardin Collection.
14. This is Adelaide Amelia Abney (Oct. 22, 1847–Aug. 13, 1923), sister of aforementioned Thomas W. Abney. She married W. H. Scanland August 1, 1867. See Cardin Collection.
15. J. W. Hudson is John Wesley Hudson, a fifty-six-year-old planter from Georgia. By November 1862, J. W. Hudson paid Benjamin Walker to serve in his place for one year in the Minden Rangers under Capt. J. Y. Webb, paying in slaves. John Hudson

bought land in Bossier Parish in 1852 using military warrants, which would indicate he was a veteran of a previous war.

The Confederate engineers' map of Bossier Parish shows Hudson's location as the center of Section 17, Township 19 North, Range 10 West. See Confederate engineers' *Map of Bossier Parish, Louisiana,* on file at Records of the Office of the Chief of Engineers, Record Group 77, folio Z-33-9, U.S. National Archives and Records Administration, Washington, D.C. (hereinafter cited as C.S.A. Bossier Map).

16. Bayou Dorcheat. The C.S.A. Bossier Map refers to Dorcheat Bayou as Dauchitte Bayou.
17. Today Minden is the parish seat of Webster Parish, created during Reconstruction.
18. James W. McGuire, private, Company B, 28th (Gray's) Louisiana Infantry Regiment; enlisted Monroe, La., May 11, 1862; roll July and Aug. 1863, present; General Hospital, Shreveport, La., admitted Apr. 11, 1864, furloughed Apr. 20, 186[?]; Booth, *Records of Louisiana,* 2:1207.
19. Mount Lebanon in Bienville Parish.
20. Today Arcadia is the parish seat of Bienville Parish.
21. Monroe, on the Ouachita River, was the oldest European settlement in the interior of northeastern Louisiana. It dates back to Spanish colonial rule. The town was the headquarters of the Confederate subdistrict of North Louisiana and served as a training center for infantry.
22. Booth lists the soldier as R. B. Cavett (also Richard S. Cavett), private, Company B, 28th (Gray's) Louisiana Infantry Regiment; enlisted May 11, 1862, Monroe, La.; paroled at Shreveport, La., June 14, 1865; resident of Bossier Parish, La.; Booth, *Records of Louisiana,* 1:298. This is actually Richard Savanah Cavett, who was born circa 1829. He married Virginia J. Martin on May 26, 1853. Robert B. "Bruce" Cavett was another person, a minister, the husband of Isabella Herron. Both men served in this company.
23. King uses this word frequently. The editors translate this as immediately, as quickly as possible.
24. Vienna (pronounced "Vie-anna") is today in Lincoln Parish, created during Reconstruction. The Confederates had an infantry training base, Camp Jackson, just north of the village. However, since King does not mention it, the facility may have been inoperative during this time in 1862, or he was not aware of it as he passed near it.
25. Gum Springs is a small church community in Union Parish near its boundary with Lincoln Parish, located on Louisiana Highway 151.
26. Trenton is today's West Monroe, in Ouachita Parish. The town lies to the west of Monroe across the Ouachita River. During the Civil War, Trenton was the site of one of the infantry training camps.
27. The village of Douglas, in Lincoln Parish, was in 1862 part of Jackson Parish. It is located at the intersection of Louisiana highways 820 and 821, just north of the Town of Choudrant.
28. The Union navy arrived at New Orleans on April 25, 1862, and occupied the riverfront. Union army forces under Maj. Gen. Benjamin F. Butler formally occupied the city on May 1. The Confederate government of Louisiana, attempting to escape capture, fled up the Mississippi into the Red River. From there they entered the

Ouachita River and came to Monroe. Along with the governor and his entourage was the state treasury.

29. S. W. Odell, private, Companies F and G, 5th Louisiana Infantry Regiment; enlisted June 4, 1861, Camp Moore, La.; on Roll of Prisoners of War, detailed in Taylor General Hospital, Confederate States Army, paroled at Natchitoches, La., June 6, 1865; resident of New Orleans; Booth, *Records of Louisiana,* 3:13. As is often the case with Booth, only Odell's original and mustering out information is included. He obviously achieved some degree of authority by 1862.
30. Patrick O'Neil, private, Company B, 28th (Gray's) Louisiana Infantry Regiment; roll dated May 11, 1862 (only roll on file); enlisted May 11, 1862, Monroe, La.; Booth, *Records of Louisiana,* 3:36.
31. H. M. Matlock, private, Company K, Crescent Regiment, Louisiana Infantry; enlisted Bossier Parish, Sept. 14, 1862; roll Jan. and Feb. 1863, present, sick, in Camp Hospital. Also borne on Rolls of Company O, Consolidated Crescent Regiment, Louisiana Infantry, private. On Roll of Prisoners of War of furloughed and detailed men, C.S.A., paroled Shreveport, La., June 13, 1865. Resident of Bossier Parish, La. See Booth, *Records of Louisiana,* 2:914. Hartwell Marion Matlock was nineteen years old. According to his headstone at Boggs Cemetery in Bossier Parish, he was born November 18, 1842. See King's entry for May 22, 1862. Matlock, after his initial hesitation at joining military life, rejoined the Crescent Regiment and later served with distinction in Company B of the 6th Louisiana Cavalry Regiment as part of Harrison's Battalion in eastern Louisiana. See affidavit signed April 8, 1912, in Bossier Parish, by R. H. Allen, notary public, also a member of Company B, 6th Louisiana Cavalry Regiment.
32. David W. Herron, private, Company B, 28th (Gray's) Louisiana Infantry Regiment. Appears on roll dated May 11, 1862 (only roll on file). Enlisted May 11, 1862, Monroe, La. Absent or present not stated. Booth, *Records of Louisiana,* 2:288.
33. Israel Rodgers, private, Company B, 28th (Gray's) Louisiana Infantry Regiment. On Roll of Prisoners of War of furloughed and detailed men. C.S.A., paroled Shreveport, La., June 21, 1865. Resident of Bossier Parish, La. Booth, *Records of Louisiana,* 3:365. Israel Rodgers was born January 12, 1826. He was a master mechanic before the war. He died August 27, 1893, at his home in Ansel, Bossier Parish, Louisiana. See Cardin Collection.
34. J. A. Herron, private, Company B, 28th (Gray's) Louisiana Infantry Regiment. Enlisted May 11, 1862, Monroe, La. Rolls of Prisoners of War, Paroled Shreveport, La., June 14–15, 1865. Resident of Bossier Parish, La. Booth, *Records of Louisiana,* 2:288. James A. Herron was born circa 1821. He came to Bossier Parish in 1847. Herron died April 2, 1887, in Shreveport.
35. James L. Byrd, fourth corporal, Company B, 28th (Gray's) Louisiana Infantry Regiment; enlisted Monroe, La., May 11, 1862; Booth, *Records of Louisiana,* 1:209. James L. Byrd was born circa 1837 in Alabama. He married Sarah E. Lewis on December 25, 1859.
36. Benjamin F. Keith, private, Company B, 28th (Gray's) Louisiana Infantry Regiment; enlisted May 11, 1862, Monroe, La. On Register of Prisoners of War, dated Apr. 27, 1863; captured at Bayou Teche, La., Apr. 14, 1863. Sent to New Orleans to be exchanged. Paroled at Port Hudson, La., May 11, 1863. Roll for July and Aug. 1863,

prisoner. Paroled home. Booth, *Records of Louisiana,* 2:514. Benjamin F. Keith (also spelled Keeth by many descendents) was born February 8, 1830. He was the son of Jeremiah Keeth and Louiza Haney Doster. He married Nancy Bell and moved to Bossier Parish sometime in late 1860 or early 1861. After his first marriage ended, Keeth married Penelope King Williamson, William Henry King's sister, on February 24, 1867. He left her and moved to Texas. At that time she divorced him in 1883, claiming abandonment. He then married Faraby (sometimes written as Pheriba) Shivers in Texas. She died in Texas in 1907. He then moved back to Bossier and lived with his son. He died April 12, 1909, and is buried at Cottage Grove Cemetery, Bossier Parish, Louisiana. See Cardin Collection. Also listed as B. F. Koontz in Booth.

37. John Graves, private, Company C, 28th (Gray's) Louisiana Infantry Regiment. Enlisted June 28, 1863, Camp Jackson (Camp Vienna). Rolls of Prisoners of War, paroled Monroe, La., June 9, 1865. Resident of Jackson Parish, La. Booth, *Records of Louisiana,* 2:82.
38. James P. Strayhan, private, Company B, 28th (Gray's) Louisiana Infantry Regiment; enlisted Monroe, La., May 11, 1862; roll July and Aug. 1863, present. Roll of Prisoners of War of furloughed and detailed men, C.S.A., paroled Shreveport, La., June 17–21, 1865. Resident of Bossier Parish, La. Booth, *Records of Louisiana,* 3:720. James P. Strayhan was born August 17, 1829, in Alabama. He married Lucretia Jane King, younger sister of William Henry King, on July 10, 1853. She died July 11, 1870. The couple lived at Alden Bridge, Bossier Parish, after the war. He died in 1909. See Cardin Collection.
39. Pleasant H. Dudney, private, Company B, 28th (Gray's) Louisiana Infantry Regiment; enlisted Jan. 20, 1863, Bossier Parish, La. Federal Rolls of Prisoners of War show him captured at Bayou Teche, La., Apr. 13, 1863. Sent to New Orleans to be exchanged. Paroled below Port Hudson, La., May 11, 1863. Roll for July and Aug. 1863, prisoner, paroled. On Rolls of Prisoners of War, paroled at Shreveport, La., June 14, 1863. Resident of Bossier Parish, La. Booth, *Records of Louisiana,* 1:695. Pleasant Howard Dudney was born circa 1831 in Stewart County, Georgia. He married Harriett Ann Dixon on January 27, 1848. He came to Bossier Parish prior to the Civil War. Dudney lived in Plain Dealing after the war. He died in 1885 during a fever epidemic. See Cardin Collection.
40. Philip Cook Broom was elected third corporal in the Marks Guards. He was born in Fairfield District, South Carolina, circa 1833. Broom came to Bossier Parish in 1855 and engaged in farming until joining the Marks Guards in 1862. He served as an orderly sergeant. Broom lived in Rocky Mount, Louisiana, after the war and died June 8, 1893. See Cardin Collection.
41. Gabriel S. Davie, private, Company B, 28th (Gray's) Louisiana Infantry Regiment; enlisted May 11th, 1862, Monroe, La. Booth, *Records of Louisiana,* 1:548.
42. Calvin Tipton, private, Company B, 28th (Gray's) Louisiana Infantry Regiment; enlisted Monroe, La., May 11, 1862. Roll July and Aug. 1863, present. Roll of Prisoners of War, C.S.A., paroled Shreveport, La., June 14, 1865. Resident of Bossier Parish, La. Booth, *Records of Louisiana,* 3:838.
43. [?] Stroud, Surgeon Company, 30th Louisiana, Infantry Regiment. On Roster dated March [?], 1865, relieved; successor, W. W. Cross. Booth, *Records of Louisiana,* 3:728.

44. J. R. Cavett served as fourth sergeant in Company B. He was born in Alabama in 1835. Cavett moved to Bossier Parish in 1851. He married Martha Doles, January 1, 1861, and lived near Collinsburgh, Louisiana, after the war. He served as a member of the Bossier Parish Police Jury eight years and was a successful and progressive farmer. He died March 24, 1904. See Cardin Collection.
45. William H. King, private, Company B, 28th (Gray's) Louisiana Infantry Regiment; enlisted May 11, 1862 (King stated that he entered service Apr. 30, 1862), Monroe, La. Rolls of Prisoners of War show him captured at Bayou Teche, Louisiana, Apr. 14, 1863. Sent to New Orleans to be exchanged. Paroled below Port Hudson, May 11, 1863. Roll for July and Aug. 1863, prisoner, paroled home. Booth, *Records of Louisiana,* 2:571. This entry again proves that the Booth's list is, at times, woefully inadequate. King appears as a different soldier in Booth. He is also listed as W.H. King, sergeant, Company H, 4th Engineer Troops; Rolls of Prisoners of War, paroled Shreveport, La., June 13, 1865; resident of Bossier Parish, La. There is no mention in King's narrative that he was promoted above the rank of private. This promotion to sergeant probably occurred after January 9, 1865, the last entry in this diary that is known to exist.
46. Natchez, Mississippi.
47. Without advance preparation; more commonly *ad lib.*
48. J. S. West, Capt. A.Q.M. (Assistant Quarter Master), Company E, Field and Staff, 15th Louisiana Infantry Regiment. Roll May 27 to Sept. 1, 1861 (only roll on which borne), enlisted May 27, 1861, New Orleans. Roll states present. Record copied from Memorial Hall, New Orleans, by the War Dept., Washington, D.C., June 1903, appointed A.Q.M. Oct. 1, 1861, by the president. Transferred to Trans-Mississippi Dept. Booth, *Records of Louisiana,* 3:1044.
49. Natchez, Mississippi, was occupied by Federal forces on May 12, 1862.
50. Little Rock, Arkansas.
51. The geography King reports does not exist. The Ouachita River becomes the Black River at Jonesville and empties into the Red River northeast of Marksville. The Red empties into the Mississippi near Simmesport. He may be describing taking the Red River south to one of the northeast-to-southwest tributaries of the Ouachita—Beouf River, Tensas River, or Bayou Macon—ascending them as far as was navigable, and then continuing up the Mississippi River from Lake Providence or another landing. It is impossible to definitively clarify this passage.
52. William M. Sentell, second lieutenant, Company B, 28th (Gray's) Louisiana Infantry Regiment. Roll dated May 11, 1862 (only roll on which borne). Enlisted Monroe, La., May 11, 1862. Booth, *Records of Louisiana,* 3:515. William M. Sentell was born circa 1835 in Georgia. In 1860 he was a clerk in the Sentell store. He died during the war. See Cardin Collection.
53. H. [Henry] Gray, colonel, Field and Staff, 28th (Gray's) Louisiana Infantry Regiment. Roll for June 30 to Aug. 31, 1863 (only roll on file). Enlisted May 14, 1862, Camp Taylor. Booth, *Records of Louisiana,* 2:84. Henry Gray was promoted to brigadier general after the Battle of Mansfield and commanded the brigade.
54. Joseph L. C. Graham, first sergeant, first lieutenant, Company B, 28th (Gray's) Louisiana Infantry Regiment. Enlisted May 14, 1862, Monroe, La. Roll for July and Aug. 1863, present. Booth, *Records of Louisiana,* 2:75. Joseph L. C. Graham was

born circa 1829. He was a grocery store keeper prior to the war. He married Miss Clara Dalrymple December 29, 1864. He died in 1867. See Cardin Collection.

55. Corinth, Mississippi.
56. The side-wheel packet *W. A. Andrew* was built in Madison, Indiana, in 1857. The vessel weighed 229 tons, had a length of 132 feet, a width (beam) of 30 feet, and a depth below the waterline of 5.5 feet. It was owned by Capt. Robert Moody of New Orleans. In 1858 it ran the New Orleans–Grand Ecore route. It was sold in 1860 to Robert Means. The vessel entered the Confederate registry on March 29, 1862. It is listed as vessel number 5612 in *Way's Packet Directory.* See Fredrick Way Jr., *Way's Packet Directory, 1848–1994* (Athens: Ohio Univ. Press, 1994), 473.
57. Matlock's father is Charles L. Matlock of Bossier Parish. He had reported that his son was nineteen years old. See Cardin Collection.
58. Alford J. Spurlin, private, Company B, 28th (Gray's) Louisiana Infantry Regiment. Enlisted Monroe, La., May 11, 1862. Roll July and Aug. 1863, present. Roll of Prisoners of War, C.S.A., paroled Shreveport, La., June 14, 1865. Resident of Bossier Parish, La. Booth, *Records of Louisiana,* 3:668.
59. The side-wheel packet *Music* was built in Jeffersonville, Indiana, by Howard in 1857. It weighed 330 tons, with a length of 157 feet, a width (beam) of 32.3 feet, and had a draught of 6.2 feet. The vessel was owned by the New Orleans, Coast, and Lafourche Transportation Company. Her master was Captain Henry Streck. The vessel entered Confederate registry during the Civil War and was reported have been taken up the Red River for the duration of hostilities. It is listed as vessel number 4067 in Way, *Way's Packet Directory,* 334.
60. J. M. Blackburn, private, Company B, 28th (Gray's) Louisiana Infantry Regiment. Enlisted May 11, 1862, Monroe, La. Roll for July and Aug. 1863, detached service. Paroled at Shreveport, La., June 21, 1865. Resident of Bossier Parish, La. Booth, *Records of Louisiana,* 1:197.
61. The side-wheel packet *Twilight* was built by Howard in Jeffersonville, Indiana, in 1857. The vessel weighed 335 tons, had a length of 215 feet, a draught (beam) of 33 feet, and a depth below the waterline of 6 feet. In 1861 it was based in New Orleans and owned by William C. Buffington and captained by Thomas W. Scott. It was on the upper Red River during the Civil War. The vessel was sold on August 21, 1865, by the U.S. Marshal service and scrapped soon after. It is listed as vessel number 5471 in Way, *Way's Packet Directory,* 460.
62. Marcus O. Cheatham, captain, Company D, 28th (Gray's) Louisiana Infantry Regiment. Enlisted May 11, 1862, Monroe, La. Booth, *Records of Louisiana,* 1:321.
63. P. F. Miller, private, Company B, 28th (Gray's) Louisiana Infantry Regiment. On roll of Prisoners of War, C.S.A., paroled June [?], 1865. Resident of Caddo Parish, La. Booth, *Records of Louisiana,* 2:983. This could also possibly be Thomas F. Miller, private, Company B, 28th (Gray's) Louisiana Infantry Regiment. Enlisted Monroe, La., May 11, 1862. Roll July and Aug. 1863, present. See Booth, *Records of Louisiana,* 2:985.
64. Dr. Thomas S. Parham lived in Cotton Valley, now located in Webster Parish, then in Bossier Parish. He was born in Meriwether County, Georgia, in 1830. Dr. Parham was married in 1854 to Miss Susan J. McGowan, of DeSoto County, Mississippi, and in 1861, the family moved to Bossier Parish. In 1862 Dr. Parham enlisted in

the 28th Louisiana Regiment but was discharged due to a disability. He attended Louisville Medical College in Kentucky. Prior to the war, Parham was a Whig, but, like almost all Southerners following Reconstruction, he became a Democrat. See *Biographical and Historical Memoirs of Northwest Louisiana,* Chicago & Nashville, 1890.

65. Patrick V. O'Neill's sisters were Margaret B., Sarah Justina, Teresa H., Julianna H., Columbia A., and Isabella J. O'Neill. See Cardin Collection.
66. Ephraim M. S. Harper, private, Company B, 28th (Gray's) Louisiana Infantry Regiment. Appears on roll dated May 11, 1862 (only roll on file). Enlisted May 11, 1862, Monroe, La. Absent or present not stated. Booth, *Records of Louisiana,* 1:194. Ephraim Michael Seabrook Harper was born circa 1834 in Alabama, the son of David Harper. He married Malinda Carter July 10, 1860. See Cardin Collection.
67. Tonsillitis.
68. Unable to identify this soldier.
69. Thomas Keith, private, Company B, 28th (Gray's) Louisiana Infantry Regiment. Enlisted May 11, 1862, Monroe, La. Booth, *Records of Louisiana,* 1:514. Thomas E. Keith was born in South Carolina on August 21, 1828, the son of Littleton and Mary Coker Keith. He moved to Troy, Pike County, Alabama, where he married Mary Elizabeth Jane Oliver on November 1, 1845. He came to Bossier Parish in 1854 and settled near Rocky Mount, Louisiana. He was a farmer prior to the outbreak of the Civil War. He developed typhoid pneumonia and was sent home. He died August 30, 1863. See Cardin Collection.
70. Thomas M. Love, private, Company B, 28th (Gray's) Louisiana Infantry Regiment. Enlisted May 15, 1862, Monroe, La. Present on roll for July and Aug. 1863. Appears on Register of C.S.A. General Hospital, Shreveport, La. Admitted Oct. 1, 1864. Transferred to Greenwood, Oct. 5, 1864. On Rolls of Prisoners of War. Paroled Shreveport, La., June 14, 1865. Resident of Bossier Parish, La. Booth, *Records of Louisiana,* 2:800. Thomas M. Love was born July 15, 1835, the son of Fieldon and Cynthia Langley Love. He married Irena Barnett in 1855. She died in 1857. He came to Bossier Parish in 1857, following her death. He married Jacaideau (Jackey Odelia) Cochran on January 3, 1858. He lived at Loris, Louisiana, after the war. For a number of years he was a member of the Bossier Parish Police Jury. He died at his home, five miles west of Hughes Spur, Louisiana, of an acute attack of asthma, on January 23, 1905. His older sister, Mary Elizabeth Love, was married to Chesley Marion Burks, who also served in King's unit. See Cardin Collection.
71. King is describing the first reports of the Shenandoah Valley Campaign in Virginia beginning May 6, 1862. The Confederate leader was Maj. Gen. Thomas Jonathan "Stonewall" Jackson.
72. This is a reference to rumors in the aftermath of the disastrous Confederate defeat at the Battle of Pea Ridge (Elkhorn Tavern), Arkansas, on March 7 and 8, 1862.
73. Although the Virginia rumor is incorrect, the report from Corinth, Mississippi, was accurate. Confederate Gen. P.G.T. Beauregard evacuated Corinth on May 30, 1862.
74. This was the railroad bridge built just prior to the war for use as a trestle for the first transcontinental railroad, which was not completed. Today, a later bridge on the same site is used by the Kansas City Southern Railroad. At the time it was part of the Vicksburg, Shreveport and Texas Railroad. The roadbed for the railroad was

completed all across northern Louisiana prior to the Civil War; however, only the eighty-mile portion between Monroe and the Mississippi River opposite Vicksburg and a four-mile stretch between Shreveport and Greenwood were complete and serviced by trains. See Lawrence E. Estaville Jr., *Confederate Neckties: Louisiana Railroads in the Civil War* (Ruston, La.: McGinty Publications, 1989), 57–80.

75. Locomotive.
76. *Monroe Register,* June 3, 1862.
77. John J. Ellis, private, Company B, 28th (Gray's) Louisiana Infantry Regiment. Enlisted May 11, 1862, Monroe, La. Roll for July and Aug. 1863, prisoner. Paroled at Shreveport, La., June 17, 1865. Resident of Caddo Parish, La. Booth, *Records of Louisiana,* 1:770. John J. Ellis was born 1830 in Crawford County, Georgia. He was the fifth of eight children to John W. and Margaret Sanders Ellis. He married Adeline Tucker in 1854. Ellis moved to Caddo Parish in 1859. He was captured at Franklin, Louisiana, in 1864 and held prisoner twenty-one days then paroled home to Caddo Parish. See Cardin Collection.
78. Francis Wayland, *The Elements of Moral Science,* 6th ed. (Boston, 1855).
79. These were false rumors.

2. Home and Camp Jackson

1. William E. Dortch, 3rd corporal, Company B, 28th (Gray's) Louisiana Infantry. Enlisted May 11, 1862, Monroe, La. Present on roll for July and Aug. 1863. On roll of Prisoners of War. Paroled at Shreveport, La., June 14, 1865. Resident of Bossier Parish, La. Booth, *Records of Louisiana,* 1:662. William E. Dortch was elected fourth corporal upon formation of Marks Guards. He was born circa 1830 in Mississippi. Dortch married Mary A. Doyle July 23, 1856. He was overseer on the E. B. Suggs plantation prior to the war. He was listed as third corporal in Booth's. This may reflect a late-war promotion. See Cardin Collection.
2. Vigilantes.
3. Jonathan W. McGee, private, Company B, 28th (Gray's) Louisiana Infantry Regiment. Roll dated May 11, 1862 (only roll on which borne). Enlisted Monroe, La., May 11, 1862. Booth, *Records of Louisiana,* 2: 1192. Jonathan McGee was born circa 1844, the son of Mr. M. E. McGee. See Cardin Collection.
4. Lisbon, in Claiborne Parish.
5. John Randolph Griffin was born in Muscogee County, Georgia, on October 28, 1835. He graduated from the University of Alabama in July 1858, ranking second in his class. After studying law in Alabama, he moved to Bossier Parish in the fall of 1859. Griffin began the practice of law and was elected to the legislature in 1858. He served as chairman of the Committee on Military Affairs under Governor Allen's administration during the Civil War. In 1872 he was elected on the Fusion ticket as district attorney of the 18th Judicial District, but was counted out by the Lynch Returning Board. He died in San Antonio, Texas, on August 16, 1873. See Cardin Collection.
6. Ellerson's is the home of William Harrison Ellison. The Confederate engineers' map of Bossier Parish reveals that the plantation was located on both sides of the

road from Bellevue to Rocky Mount. The map defines the land as located in the southeast quarter of Section 31, and west half of Section 32 both in Township 21 North, Range 12 West, the northeast quarter of Section 6, and the northwest quarter of Section 5 both in Township 20 North, Range 12 West. William H. Ellison sold his plantation in 1865 for $12,000. See Bossier Parish Conveyance Records for 1865; C.S.A. Bossier Map; Cardin Collection.

7. King is describing the property of Dr. Anthony Childers and his wife, Epsy Ann Dixon Childers. But Childers did not die until 1865. The Confederate engineers map locates the property in the center of Section 15, Township 21 North, Range 13 West. See C.S.A. Bossier Map; Cardin Collection.
8. The tutorship that William Henry King held was that of executor for his father's estate. William Whitfield King died in 1857, and William Henry's older brother Charles Rufus King was made executor. Charles died in 1860. William Henry, being the next oldest child, was made executor. Unknown to William Henry, while he was away at war his mother, Susan Chennault King, sued to have him removed as executor to speed up the probate. This piece of evidence was crucial in the discovery of the positive identification of William Henry King by Clifton Cardin. See Bossier Parish Probate Records for 1862, recorded in book 6, pp. 188–91 (02123), Dec. 29, 1865.
9. Salem Baptist Church is located at Red Land, Bossier Parish, Louisiana. Reverend Leggett served there and at Rocky Mount Baptist Church before moving to Minden at the close of the war. See Cardin Collection.
10. Lee Carrier was a partner in the firm of Pickett and Carrier with John Pickett. See Cardin Collection.
11. Etcetera.
12. Collinsburgh in Bossier Parish.
13. George Washington Sentell was born in 1823, in Walton County, Georgia. He was reared and educated near Holly Springs, Marshall County, Mississippi. Sentell moved to Bossier Parish in 1847 and settled in Benton, where he ran a store. On December 19, 1853, he married Mildred A. Dickson. His wife and four of his nine children survived him. Four of his children were buried at Collinsburgh and one in Arkansas. George Washington Sentell moved to New Orleans in 1860, then back to Bossier in 1865, then again to New Orleans, where he built his fortune by starting the firm of Sentell & Prather, with John M. Prather. He maintained his connections with Bossier Parish through his company N. W. Sentell & Co. of Collinsburgh. He had several other plantations in Louisiana and Arkansas. In Arkansas, he was a partner in the firm J. B. Sentell and Bro., at Sentell's Landing in Lafayette County, Arkansas. G. W. Sentell died on October 16, 1885, in Shreveport. See Cardin Collection.
14. Jefferson A. Parker, private, Company B, 28th (Gray's) Louisiana Infantry Regiment. Roll dated May 11, 1862 (only roll on file). Enlisted May 11, 1862, Monroe, La. Booth, *Records of Louisiana,* 3:70. This may or may not be the soldier. This is the only soldier named Parker in Booth.
15. "Fagged down" meant to be utterly exhausted and incapable of continuing.
16. King heard the barrage from the U.S. navy's mortar scows in preparation for Adm. David G. Farragut's passage the following day.

17. John Gibson, private, Company B, 28th (Gray's) Louisiana Infantry Regiment. Roll dated May 11, 1862 (only roll on file). Enlisted May 11, 1862, Monroe, La. Booth, *Records of Louisiana,* 2:14.
18. This is the main channel of Bayou D'Arbonne. King's spelling is phonetically correct. His description also places Camp Jackson (or Camp Vienna) not in the town of Vienna, but slightly north of the village of Unionville, today on U.S. Highway 167 near the junction of Louisiana Highway 822.
19. This was a false rumor.
20. Winn Parish had a reputation for being against the popular convictions of the time. When Louisiana seceded from the Union, Winn Parish seceded from Louisiana, not from any sense of Unionism, but from not wanting to go along with politicians in Baton Rouge and New Orleans. When Louisiana joined the Confederacy, so did Winn Parish. It has always been a seat of populism, giving Louisiana three governors, including Huey P. Long and Earl K. Long.
21. Delhi (pronounced "Del-hie") is located in Richland Parish, east of Monroe.
22. An inflammation of the spleen. The blister was created by the application of mustard plaster.
23. Robert Hector Bradford, captain, Company F, 28th (Gray's) Louisiana Infantry Regiment. Elected captain May 6, 1862, Vernon, (Jackson Parish) Louisiana. Roll for Jan. and Feb. 1863, present. Commands detachment of companies F and G at Butte La Rose, La. Roll for July and Aug. 1863. Absent on business for the company, order of Colonel Gray. Official Rolls of Paroled Officers, captain, 28th (Gray's) Louisiana Infantry; Company F paroled at Meridian, Miss., May 10, 1865. Booth, *Records of Louisiana,* 1:82.
24. Tupelo, Mississippi.
25. King repeated the abbreviation in the original due to a barely legible word after making a correction in ink.
26. James E. Wood, sergeant, Company B, 28th (Gray's) Louisiana Infantry Regiment. Roll dated May 11, 1862 (only roll on which borne). Enlisted Monroe, La., May 11, 1862. Booth, *Records of Louisiana,* 3:1151.
27. The act of washing with saltwater. The surgeon would have broken the blister on King's back and injected salt water with a large syringe.
28. William Walker, lieutenant colonel, field and staff, 28th (Gray's) Louisiana Infantry Regiment. Roll June 30 to Aug. 31, 1863 (only roll on which borne). Enlisted [?]. Remarks: Present Appointed. Lt. Col., May 14, 1862. Booth, *Records of Louisiana,* 3:971.
29. Brig. Gen. John Selden Roane was born in Wilson County, Tennessee, in 1817. He was elected to the Arkansas legislature in 1844 and became Speaker of the House in that body in 1846. He served in the Mexican War and fought at Buena Vista. Roane served as governor of Arkansas from 1849 to 1852. Although an opponent of secession, he was appointed a Confederate brigadier on March 20, 1862. He fought at the Battle of Prairie Grove and for a brief period was the commander of the District of Arkansas. He then served in Arkansas, Texas, and Louisiana. He was paroled at Shreveport on June 11, 1865. See Ezra J. Warner, *Generals in Gray: Lives of the Confederate Commanders* (Baton Rouge: Louisiana State Univ. Press, 1993): 257–58.
30. Company.

31. Thomas M. Skinner, private, Company B, 28th (Gray's) Louisiana Infantry Regiment. Roll dated May 11, 1862 (only roll on which borne). Enlisted in Monroe, La., May 11, 1862. Booth, *Records of Louisiana,* 3:588. T. W. Skinner was born circa 1842 in Alabama. The 1860 Census lists him as living with R. Skinner. See Eighth Decennial Census for Bossier Parish.
32. No officer by this name is listed in Booth.
33. James Brice, captain, Company H, 28th (Gray's) Louisiana Infantry Regiment. Enlisted May 8, 1862, Monroe, La. Present July and Aug. 1863. Official Rolls of Paroled Officers, paroled at Meridian, Miss., May 22, 1865. Booth, *Records of Louisiana,* 1:112.
34. Eleanor Elizabeth Kennard Cavett, the aunt of William Henry King's wife, Balsona.
35. Charles Pinkney Thompson owned a farm in what was then eastern Bossier Parish, but is now western Webster Parish. The Confederate engineers' map of Bossier Parish shows its location at the center of Section 20, Township 19 North, Range 10 West. See C.S.A. Bossier Map.
36. Sometimes called remittent fever or bilious colic. Bilious pertains to an ailment of the bile or liver, resulting in headache and nausea. It was supposedly caused by an abnormal liver, probably gall bladder disease and, in some cases, may have been malarial in origin.
37. It is ironic that the very day that Benjamin Franklin Ratcliff came home from the Civil War, his oldest son, Frances E. Ratcliff, almost seven years old, died. Frances E. Ratcliff and his younger brother B. F. Ratcliff Jr. are buried on Dogwood Drive west of Plain Dealing, Louisiana.
38. James William Kennard was the brother of William Henry King's wife, Balsona. He was born December 20, 1834, in Lauderdale County, Alabama. He died in 1864. He was a member of the 17th Texas Cavalry Regiment. Personal communication with Shirley Hampton by Clifton Cardin, July 14, 2004 (hereinafter cited as Hampton communication); Eighth Decennial Census for Shelby County, Texas. Austin is located in Lonoke County, Arkansas.
39. This is a rumor regarding the so-called Laird Rams, to be built by the Laird shipyards in Liverpool, England. This is the yard that built the CSS *Alabama.* The British held up the order for the vessels on September 5, 1863. The individuals named by King were James Murray Mason, the Confederate commissioner to Britain, and John Slidell, the Confederate commissioner to France.
40. This is Confederate Brig. Gen. John Hunt Morgan and his raid into Kentucky during the summer of 1862.
41. Union Maj. Gen. (U.S. Volunteers) Don Carlos Buell, commanding the Army of the Ohio.
42. Washington is located in Hempstead County, Arkansas. The following year the town would become the provisional capital of Confederate Arkansas after Federal forces captured Little Rock.
43. Lewisville is the county seat of Lafayette County, Arkansas.
44. This is Confederate Brig. Gen. Horace Randal's 28th Texas Cavalry (Dismounted) regiment. Randal would become the commander of the Second Brigade of Walker's Texas Division during the Red River Campaign.

45. This is Stephen Corodan King, William's younger brother, who served in the Army of Northern Virginia.
46. This is Confederate Maj. Gen. John Cabell Breckinridge. He was engaged at Baton Rouge on August 5, 1862. The attack failed.
47. Lake Bistineau, in Bossier and Bienville parishes, was a major source of salt for the Trans-Mississippi Confederacy. Unlike the better-known saltworks at Avery Island in southern Louisiana, the Bistineau works were not a mine. The underground salt was close to the surface near the head of the lake, and a spring flowed through the formation. The brine water was placed in low flat trays to dry, then the salt was broken up and placed in either sacks or barrels.
48. The ironclad gunboat CSS *Arkansas.*
49. Mathias Liverman, private, Company B, 28th (Gray's) Louisiana Infantry Regiment. Enlisted May 11, 1862, Monroe, La. Present on roll for July and Aug. 1863. On register of C.S.A. Hospital, Shreveport, La., admitted March 20, 1864. Booth, *Records of Louisiana,* 3:773.
50. Penelope Whitfield King Bryan was to married Allen B. Bryan. She was the daughter of Stephen Allen King. Hampton communication, July 14, 2004.
51. Chalybeate Springs is located in northeastern Bossier Parish. Chalybeate Springs Baptist Church is located in Section 6, Township 23 North, Range 12 West.
52. Rev. Allen Winham was an early Bossier Baptist minister who established several churches, including Caney Creek Baptist Church and Chalybeate Springs Baptist Church. Reverend Winham is buried at Caney Creek Cemetery in Bossier Parish. See Cardin Collection.
53. M. King was the same person as Margaret King of Shelby County, Texas. D. E. King was Daniel Ellington King, the brother of Stephen Thomas King, both sons of Stephen Allen King. Hampton communication, July 14, 2004.
54. This refers to Confederate Brig. Gen. Albert Pike, whose conduct, perhaps misjudged by his contemporaries while leading Indian troops at the Battle of Pea Ridge, led to his arrest by Confederate Maj. Gen. Thomas Carmichael Hindman. He resigned his commission on July 12, 1862. The charges against him included that he was "insane or untrue to the South." See Warner, *Generals in Gray,* 240.
55. Confederate Maj. Gen. Thomas Carmichael Hindman. At this time he commanded the Trans-Mississippi Department.
56. Miliken's Bend in East Carroll Parish was located on the Mississippi River and above Vicksburg.
57. Cousin Thomas and brother Daniel were Stephen Thomas King and his brother Daniel Ellington King, the sons of Stephen Allen King and Sarah Ellington Deupree. Hampton communication, July 14, 2004.
58. Cottage Grove Cemetery is located in Bossier Parish, on Louisiana Highway 160, one and a half miles west of Louisiana Highway 3.
59. James Blair Gilmer, a very wealthy plantation owner, imported Dr. Walker from Ireland to keep his family and slaves healthy. See Cardin Collection.
60. This is the Confederate ironclad CSS *Arkansas,* which was scuttled on the Mississippi River above Baton Rouge.
61. E. G. Randolph, colonel, Louisiana. Confederate States Official Rolls Paroled Officers, C.S.A., Paroled Shreveport, La., June 8, 1865. Booth, *Records of Louisiana,* 3:244.

62. Confederate Maj. Gen. Richard Taylor, commander of the District of Western Louisiana.
63. Hindman.
64. Robert.
65. Washington, D.C.
66. Stephen Thomas King was the son of Stephen Allen King. Stephen Allen King, Eleanor King, and William Whitfield King (William Henry's father) were siblings. Hampton communication, July 14, 2004.
67. Murrell's Point on Lake Bistineau was an important ferry landing below Minden.
68. Lysander Rathburn was William Henry King's brother in law. Lysander married Mary Merab King, William's younger sister, on March 14, 1852. They had one son, Franklin Pierce Rathburn. Both parents were dead by 1863. See Cardin Collection.
69. A bone felon is a purulent infection under the fingernail.
70. To Monroe before the train for Vicksburg left the station.
71. King means Cheniere (pronounced "shinny") Creek.

3. Eastern Louisiana

1. A hogshead, abbreviated hhd, is a traditional unit of volume for liquids. Originally the hogshead varied with the contents, often being equal to forty-eight gallons of ale; fifty-four of beer; sixty of cider; sixty-three of oil, honey, or wine; or one hundred of molasses. It was often used to hold solid matter such as salt or sugar for transport. In the United States, a hogshead is defined to hold two barrels, or sixty-three gallons; this was the traditional British wine hogshead.
2. Camp Edwards was a training camp and cantonment (temporary living quarters specially built by the army for soldiers) in Richland Parish.
3. Tallulah, in Madison Parish, opposite Vicksburg.
4. Burdens.
5. Died.
6. This is the 11th Battalion of Louisiana Infantry commanded by Lt. Col. Jacob D. Shelley. See Arthur W. Bergeron Jr., *Guide to Louisiana Confederate Military Units, 1861–1865* (Baton Rouge: Louisiana State Univ. Press, 1989), 164.
7. Green false hellebore (*Veratrum virides*) was sometimes called Indian poke. All parts of the plant are poisonous. It was sometimes pounded and snuffed as a remedy for madness. Its use here is dubious.
8. Macajal J. Clark (also M. G. Clark), second junior lieutenant, third lieutenant, Company C, 28th (Gray's) Louisiana Infantry Regiment. Enlisted May 10, 1862, Monroe, La. Appears on a register of C.S.A. General Hospital, Shreveport, La., admitted Mar. 20, 1864. Died Mar. 21, 186[?]. Booth, *Records of Louisiana,* 1:345.
9. *Vicksburg Whig,* Oct. 11, 1862.
10. Albert Pike, who was very sympathetic to and enjoyed popularity with the pro-Confederate Indian tribes, had been the commander of Confederate forces in the Indian Territory of Oklahoma.
11. This is Confederate Gen. Braxton Bragg's invasion of Kentucky, which ended in his defeat at the Battle of Perryville. Among his subordinates was the future commander of the Trans-Mississippi Department, Edmund Kirby Smith.

12. Joseph H. Barr, private, Company B, 28th (Gray's) Louisiana Infantry Regiment. Enlisted May 15, 1862, Monroe, La. Booth, *Records of Louisiana,* 1:127.
13. Thomas M. Skinner, private, Company B, 28th (Gray's) Louisiana Infantry Regiment. Roll dated May 11, 1862 (only roll on which borne). Enlisted Monroe, La., May 11, 1862. Booth, *Records of Louisiana,* 3:588.
14. Either D. M. High, private, Company B, 28th (Gray's) Louisiana Infantry Regiment. Enlisted November 20, 1862, Bossier Parish, La. Federal Rolls of Prisoners of War. Captured Bayou Teche, La., Apr. 14, 1863. On Hospital Register. Admitted to Marine U.S.A. General Hospital, New Orleans, May 5, 1863. Discharged from hospital May 30, 1863. Took Oath of Allegiance June 6, 1863. Roll for July and Aug. 1863, prisoner, paroled home. Booth, *Records of Louisiana,* 2:302; or George W. High, private, Company B, 28th (Gray's) Louisiana Infantry Regiment. Appears on roll dated May 11, 1862 (only roll on file). Enlisted May 11, 1862, Monroe, La. Absent or present not stated, probably the latter. Booth, *Records of Louisiana,* 2:302.
15. *Memphis Appeal,* Oct. 9, 1862.
16. At the time, Richmond was the parish seat of Madison Parish. Today the parish seat is Tallulah.
17. The regimental quartermaster.
18. Albert Madden, private, Company H, 28th (Gray's) Louisiana Infantry Regiment. Enlisted Monroe, La., May 8, 186[?]. Federal Rolls of Prisoners of War, Captured Bayou Teche, La., Apr. 14, 1863, paroled below Port Hudson, La., May 11, 1863. Sent to New Orleans to be exchanged. Roll July and Aug. 1863, paroled. Roll to Aug. 31, 1863, acting brigade Q.M. On roll of Prisoners of War, C.S.A., paroled Monroe, La., June 16, 1865. Resident of Bienville Parish, La. Booth, *Records of Louisiana,* 2:831. Madden was apparently brevetted (field promotion) captain. There is insufficient information to determine how he rose in rank so quickly.
19. James C. Beard, private, Company B, 28th (Gray's) Louisiana Infantry Regiment. Enlisted May 11, 1862, Monroe, La. Booth, *Records of Louisiana,* 1:147.
20. Austin Miller, sergeant, Company B, 28th (Gray's) Louisiana Infantry Regiment. Roll dated May 11, 1862 (only roll on which borne). Enlisted Monroe, La., May 11, 1862. Booth, *Records of Louisiana,* 2:972. Austin Miller was third sergeant in Company B. He married Mary J. Steele, daughter of Lewis F. Steele, May 1, 1856. Miller had one daughter, S. E. Miller, born in November 1859. Miller was the District Court Recorder prior to the war. See Cardin Collection.
21. Abney.
22. Daniel H. Sheppard, first lieutenant, Company A, 28th (Gray's) Louisiana Infantry Regiment. Enlisted Monroe, La., May 8, 1862. Roll July and Aug. 1863, absent, on Col. Leave, since July 10, [?]. Official Rolls Paroled Officers, C.S.A., paroled Monroe, La., June 14, 1865, captain, 28th (Gray's) Louisiana Infantry Regiment as D. H. Sheppard. Booth, *Records of Louisiana,* 3:540.
23. Railroad.
24. A dray is a strong low cart, usually without side suports, or a carriage used for hauling heavy burdens.
25. Captain Madden.
26. John D. Beard, private, Company B, 28th (Gray's) Louisiana Infantry Regiment. Enlisted May 11, 1862, Monroe, La. Booth, *Records of Louisiana,* 1:148.

27. In medicine, nitric acid was used externally in a pure state as a caustic to destroy chancres, warts, and ulcers; diluted preparations were used to treat dyspepsia and other ailments. Poisoning by strong nitric acid produces a widespread gastroenteritis, burning pain in the esophagus and abdomen, and bloody diarrhea. There may also be blood in the urine. Death occurs from collapse or from secondary destructive changes in the intestinal canal. The antidotes are mild alkalis, together with the use of opium, to relieve pain. King was given very poor treatment.
28. Confederate Brig. Gen. Albert Gallatin Blanchard.
29. M. C. Cavett, third lieutenant, Company A, 19th Louisiana Infantry Regiment. Enlisted Dec. 11, 1861, Camp Moore, La. Present on roll to Dec. 31, 1861. Roll for May and June, 1862, dropped at the reorganization. Booth, *Records of Louisiana,* 1:298.
30. Bossier.
31. Ultimo (last month).
32. Francis M. Shaver, private, Company B, 28th (Gray's) Louisiana Infantry Regiment. Roll dated May 11, 1862 (only roll on which borne). Enlisted Monroe, La., May 11, 1862. Booth, *Records of Louisiana,* 1:529.
33. A combination of mercury and chalk delivered in the form of a blue pill.
34. Smith was apparently not formally enlisted into the regiment. There is no mention of him in Booth.
35. Harrisonburg, in Catahoula Parish, below which was Fort Beauregard at Trinity.
36. Avery Island in Iberia Parish.
37. Listlessness and dissatisfaction resulting from lack of interest; boredom.
38. Dr. Reuben Flannigan Gray, assistant surgeon of the 28th Louisiana Infantry Regiment was Col. Henry Gray's brother. He lived and practiced in Bienville Parish before and during the war. Following the conflict he moved to Lake Charles, Louisiana, where he practiced medicine until his death.
39. William O. Burns, sergeant, lieutenant, Company B, 28th (Gray's) Louisiana Infantry Regiment. Enlisted May 11, 1862, Monroe, La. Present July and Aug. 1863. Booth, *Records of Louisiana,* 1:197. William O. Burns was born circa 1837 in South Carolina. See Eighth Decennial Census for Bossier Parish.
40. Probably Dr. Benjamin Franklin Glover.
41. Dad-damned, a common curse word.
42. Columbia is the parish seat of Caldwell Parish.
43. Stephen F. Huey, private, Company I, 28th (Gray's) Louisiana Infantry Regiment. Enlisted May 14, 1862, Monroe, La. Appears on roll for July and Aug. 1862. Booth, *Records of Louisiana,* 2:378.
44. Rufus S. Richards, captain, Company I, 28th (Gray's) Louisiana Infantry Regiment. Roll dated May 11, 1862 (only roll on which borne), Enlisted Monroe, La., May 11, 1862. Booth, *Records of Louisiana,* 3:308.
45. James A. Boyd, captain, lieutenant colonel, Companies K, F, and S, 12th Louisiana Infantry Regiment. Enlisted Camp Moore, Louisiana, Aug. 13, 1861. Present on all rolls to Dec. 1862. Booth, *Records of Louisiana,* 1:74.
46. This is a severe gastroenteritis of typically unknown specific etiology; characterized by severe colic, vomiting, and diarrhea, sometimes colloquially known as "collywobbles." Also known as "stomach flu" or "intestinal flu," it is an inflammation of the stomach and intestines and can be caused by *Salmonella enteritidis.*

47. Probably Dr. D. H. H. Cummings.
48. William H. Sears, private, Company B, 28th (Gray's) Louisiana Infantry Regiment. Roll dated May 11, 1862 (only roll on which borne). Enlisted Monroe, La., May 11, 1862. Booth, *Records of Louisiana,* 3:502. W. H. Sears was born circa 1835 in Alabama. In the 1860 Census he was listed as living with John and Mary Sears. See Eighth Decennial Census.
49. John W. Martin, private, Company B, 28th (Gray's) Louisiana Infantry Regiment. Roll dated May 11, 1862 (only roll on which borne). Enlisted Monroe, La., May 11, 1862. Booth, *Records of Louisiana,* 2:893.
50. William H. Pinckard, private, Company B, 28th (Gray's) Louisiana Infantry Regiment. Enlisted May 11, 1862, Monroe, La. Roll July and Aug. 1863, present. Rolls of Prisoners of War, paroled Shreveport, La., June 14, 1865. Resident of Bossier Parish, La. Booth, *Records of Louisiana,* 3:149. William H. Pinckard was born circa 1834 in Louisiana. He married Henrietta D. Skinner July 19, 1854. See Cardin Collection.
51. Dr. Reuben F. Gray was born in Abbeville district, South Carolina, Aug. 12, 1811. He was a graduate of the University of Maryland, Baltimore, and at the medical college in Philadelphia. He was married in South Carolina, in 1839, to Miss F. C. Chiles. In 1857 he moved to Bienville Parish, Louisiana, where he remained until 1867. He then moved to St. Landry parish and two years later to Lake Charles, where he was at the time of his death. The biography does not mention that he was the brother to Brig. Gen. Henry Gray. See William Henry Perrin, *Southwest Louisiana Historical and Biographical,* published in 1891.
52. Dr. E. A. Shippley.
53. Loath.
54. This is probably J. D. Malone, private, Company B, 28th (Gray's) Louisiana Infantry Regiment. Enlisted Monroe, La., June 10, 186[?], present. On roll of Prisoners of War, C.S.A., paroled Shreveport, La., June 14, 1865. Resident of Bossier Parish, La. Booth, *Records of Louisiana,* 2:853. It may also be H. Malone, private, Company B, 28th (Gray's) Louisiana Infantry Regiment. Roll July and Aug. 1863 (only roll on which borne). Enlisted Monroe, La., June 10, 186[?], present. Booth, *Records of Louisiana,* 2:853.
55. Ex post facto, or after the fact.
56. *Shreveport South Western,* Dec. 24, 1862. The *South Western* was a major newspaper in Shreveport.
57. Joseph M. Bryan, private, Company B, 28th (Gray's) Louisiana Infantry Regiment. Enlisted May 11, 1862, Monroe, La. Booth, *Records of Louisiana,* 1:166.
58. Not of sound mind and hence not legally responsible; mentally incompetent.
59. After the Union army and navy captured New Orleans, the Confederate government of Louisiana settled upon Opelousas in Saint Landry Parish as the state capital. Events during the Teche Campaign forced them to move the capital again to Shreveport in the spring of 1863.
60. *Caddo Gazette,* Jan. 17, 1863. The *Caddo Gazette* was a prominent newspaper published in Shreveport.
61. Mary Doal Ciley Bennett Cane was the most prominent woman in Caddo and Bossier parishes in the nineteenth century. She was the widow of both Samuel

Bennett and James Huntington Cane. Mrs. Cane owned and operated the Elysian Groves Plantation across the Red River from Shreveport and is considered to be the mother of Shreveport, having opened the first store there in 1836, and the grandmother of Bossier City, since her grandchildren sold the first lots to that city in 1883. She, her first husband, and, upon his death, his partner and her second husband, were business partners of Henry Miller Shreve in the incorporation of Shreveport. She owned stores and warehouses on both sides of the river near the mouth of Cross Bayou. She was in Bossier when Shreve arrived in 1828 and died in 1902. She is buried in Oakland Cemetery in Shreveport.

62. King is describing the vicious fighting at Fredericksburg, Virginia, in December 1862. The battle was a huge victory of the Confederates.

4. Bayou Teche

1. The side-wheel packet *Texas* was built in Cincinnati, Ohio, in 1859. The vessel weighed 170 tons, had a length of 138 feet, a width (beam) of 30 feet, and a depth below waterline of 4.5 feet. It was owned by Capt. Charles W. Stinde of New Orleans. It ran the New Orleans–Red River to Shreveport and above route. Although it saw service in the Confederacy, the vessel retained its original ownership and survived the war. It was lost at Barbin's Landing, Louisiana, on March 8, 1867, when it hit a snag. It is listed as vessel number 5348 in Way, *Way's Packet Directory*, 449.
2. Edwin Cross, private, Company B, 28th (Gray's) Louisiana Infantry Regiment. Enlisted May 11, 1863, Monroe, La. Present on roll for July and Aug. 1863. Paroled at Shreveport, La., June 14, 1865. Resident of Bossier Parish, La. Booth, *Records of Louisiana*, 1:489.
3. The side-wheel packet *B. L. Hodge* was built in New Albany, Indiana, in 1857. The vessel weighed 289 tons, had a length of 176 feet, a width (beam) of 33 feet, and a depth below the waterline of 5.5 feet. It was named for B. L. Hodge, a prominent Shreveport attorney. The vessel's captain was Richard Sinott. It entered Confederate service in 1862. It was kept on upper Red River as a troop and supply transport. In 1865 Lt. Gen. Edmund Kirby Smith, commander of the Trans-Mississippi Department, chartered the *B. L. Hodge* for a trip from Shreveport to the mouth of Red River to return with U.S. commissioners to whom his forces surrendered on May 26, 1865. It is listed as vessel number 0419 in Way, *Way's Packet Directory*, 35.
4. Butte La Rose, in Saint Martin Parish occupied a strategic bend at the confluence of the Atchafalaya River and the Little Atchafalaya River. The site was a slight high rise in the middle of the great primordial Atchafalaya swamp. The Confederates built a fortification on the rise to prevent Union forces from gaining control of the region.
5. The side-wheel packet *Vigo* was built in Brownsville, Pennsylvania, in 1859. The vessel weighed 144 tons, had a length of 130 feet, a width (beam) of 26 feet, and a depth below the waterline of 4.6 feet. It was sold in 1860 to Capt. R. W. Doyle of New Orleans. The vessel worked at Mobile and New Orleans in 1861. Later that year it was sold to Capt. R. N. Doyle and ran the Red River route. After the war

it was taken to Louisville, Kentucky, and dismantled in 1868. It is listed as vessel number 5575 in Way, *Way's Packet Directory,* 469.

6. Fort DeRussy was the anchor of the Confederate defenses on the Red River. At the time King saw it, the fortification was incomplete and work had been halted. Lt. Gen. Edmund Kirby Smith, commander of the Confederate Department of the Trans-Mississippi from March 1863 to the end of the war, had it rebuilt and strengthened. He favored the fort and called it "Our Red River Gibraltar."
7. Old River was an ancient river channel that had, at different times, been part of the Mississippi, the Red, and the Atchafalaya rivers. The town of Simmesport was located on this four-mile-long channel.
8. Simmesport.
9. King means the *Louis D'Or,* a stern-wheeler packet built in Cincinnati, Ohio, in 1860. The vessel weighed 343 tons, had a length of 180 feet, a width (beam) of 32.6 feet, and a depth below the waterline of 7.2 feet. It was based in Franklin, Louisiana. Capt. Cheney Johnson operated the vessel on the New Orleans–Red River route. It is listed as vessel number 3576 in Way, *Way's Packet* Directory, 294.
10. King is referring to submerged trees or snags located in sharp bends or meanders in the Atchafalaya River. These sharp curves often took on the appearance of an inverted "U," thus appearing on a chart as an oxbow or ox harness. The fallen trees were often gathered by the stream's current into submerged piles called "rafts." These were deadly to wooden-hulled steamboats and accounted for the majority of steamboat losses.
11. Capt. David Hardy's Company G of the 28th Louisiana Infantry Regiment.
12. St. Martinsville is the parish seat of St. Martin Parish.
13. There is no vessel of this name or any similar name in *Ways Packet Directory.* It is listed as a transport vessel captured at Bayou Teche on April 14, 1863, in Paul H. Silverstone's *Warships of the Civil War Navies* (Annapolis, Md.: Naval Institute Press, 1989), 232.
14. New Iberia, originally called New Town, is now the parish seat of Iberia Parish.
15. Camp or Fort Bisland in St. Mary Parish, located near the village of Calumet between Morgan City (Brashear City during the Civil War) and Patterson (known as Pattersonville during the Civil War). Two other Confederate forts guarding the area were abandoned at the fall of New Orleans; these were forts Berwick and Chene. See Confederate engineers' *Map of St. Mary Parish, Louisiana,* on file at Records of the Office of the Chief of Engineers, Record Group 77, folio Z-33, U.S. National Archives and Records Administration, Washington, D.C.; *Houma Navigation Canal Deepening Project Terrebonne Parish, Louisiana: Cultural Resources Literature Search, Records Review and Research Design,* draft report prepared by Coastal Environments, Inc., for the U.S. Army Corps of Engineers, New Orleans District, Dec. 2003. Copy on file at Louisiana Division of Archaeology, Office of Cultural Development, Dept. of Culture, Recreation and Tourism, Baton Rouge.
16. The *Cotton* was a side-wheel gunboat originally known as the *Mary T.* The vessel was built in Jeffersonville, Indiana, in 1861. It had a length of 185 feet, a width (beam) of 34 feet, and a depth below the waterline of 8 feet. It saw service on the Red River and was based in Shreveport. It surrendered June 3, 1865, in Shreve-

port. It is listed as vessel numbers 1340 and 3841 in Way, *Way's Packet Directory,* 112, 314–15.

17. This was E. W. Fuller, captain, commanding the gunboat CSS *Cotton.* A Federal flotilla, including the USS *Calhoun, Kinsman, Estella,* and *Diane,* followed the lone Confederate gunboat in Berwick Bay fourteen miles up Bayou Teche in an effort to sink the troublesome CSS *Cotton.* The *Cotton* was burned by the Confederates to keep her from falling into Federal hands near the center of present-day Franklin.
18. William J. Cochran, private, Company B, 28th (Gray's) Louisiana Infantry Regiment. Enlisted May 11, 1862, Monroe, La. Present on roll for July and Aug. 1863. Paroled at Shreveport, La., June 14, 1865. Resident of Bossier Parish, La. Booth, *Records of Louisiana,* 2:367.
19. Timothy Oakley, private, sergeant, Company B, 28th (Gray's) Louisiana Infantry Regiment. Enlisted May 11, 1862, Monroe, La. Present on roll for July and Aug. 1863. On roll of Prisoners of War, paroled at Shreveport, La., June 14, 1865. Resident of Bossier Parish, La. Booth, *Records of Louisiana,* 2:1309.
20. William Carraway, private, Company B, 28th (Gray's) Louisiana Infantry Regiment. Enlisted May 11, 1862, Monroe, La. Roll for July and Aug. 1863, absent, sick furlough. Booth, *Records of Louisiana,* 1:264.
21. James Saulsburry, private, Company B, 28th (Gray's) Louisiana Infantry Regiment. Roll July and Aug. 1863 (only roll on which borne). Enlisted Camp Blanchard, Aug. 12, 1862. Remarks: Present. Booth, *Records of Louisiana,* 3:454.
22. Patterson in St. Mary Parish.
23. J. P. Vance (also on rolls as Joseph P. Vance), private, Company B, 28th (Gray's) Louisiana Infantry Regiment. Enlisted Bossier Parish, La., Jan. 20, 1863. Federal Rolls of Prisoners of War, captured Bayou Teche, La., Apr. 14, 1863. Paroled below Port Hudson, La., May 11, 1863. Sent to New Orleans to be exchanged. Roll July and Aug. 1863, prisoner, paroled home. Booth, *Records of Louisiana,* 3:906. Joseph P. Vance was born circa 1828 in South Carolina. He died in May of 1902 and was buried in Plain Dealing cemetery. He was brother to Dr. Thomas J. Vance of Minden, Louisiana. See Cardin Collection.
24. J. E. Robinson, corporal, Company B, 28th (Gray's) Louisiana Infantry Regiment. Enlisted Bossier Parish, Jan. 20, 1863. Roll July and Aug. 1863, present. On roll of Prisoners of War, C.S.A., paroled Shreveport, La., June 14, 1865. On roll of Prisoners of War of furloughed and detailed men, C.S.A., paroled Shreveport, La., June 17, 1865. Resident of Bossier Parish, La. Booth, *Records of Louisiana,* 3:135.
25. John W. Shaver, private, Company B, 28th (Gray's) Louisiana Infantry Regiment. Roll dated May 11, 1862 (only roll on which borne). Enlisted Monroe, La., May 11, 1862. Booth, *Records of Louisiana,* 3:529.
26. This is the brigade commanded by Confederate Brig. Gen. Henry Hopkins Sibley.
27. This was one of the armed reconnaissance probes conducted by the navy designed to test the veracity of the Confederate defenses along Berwick Bay and up the complex of streams that made up the Atchafalaya River basin.
28. This refers to actions prior to the fall of Fort Pulaski on April 11, 1863.
29. The attacks came in April. The *Shreveport Semi Weekly News* reported on May 4, 1863, that the waters of the Atchafalaya River were almost flooded to the level of

the guns. The paper also reported that there were only thirty-five men in the garrison and that the two 32-pdr cannons were only fired once or twice before the fort was overwhelmed.

30. The high-speed ram CSS *Webb* was an oceangoing side-wheeler originally called the *William H. Webb.* It was built in New York City in 1856. It weighed 655 tons and was approximately 200 feet in length. Before the war the vessel was used as an icebreaker. The *Webb* was instrumental in capturing the USS *Indianola* on February 24, 1863 (the incident King references). It participated in the Battle of Grand Lake (Atchafalaya River, Louisiana), in which the *Queen of the West* was lost. The ship made what was arguably the most famous vessel-to-vessel chase in the Civil War as it exited Shreveport and made a high-speed run down the Red and Mississippi rivers in April 1865 while being chased by several vessels of the Mississippi River Squadron. Capt. Lt. Charles Read beached and torched the vessel at Algiers to prevent its capture. It is listed as vessel number 5816 in Way, *Way's Packet Directory,* 488; Paul H. Silverstone, *Civil War Navies,* 231.
31. This was the capture of the Union ram USS *Indianola* on February 24, 1863.
32. Patrick H. Edwards, private, Company B, 28th (Gray's) Louisiana Infantry Regiment. Enlisted May 11, 1862, Monroe, La. Roll for July and Aug. 1863, present, detail. Booth, *Records of Louisiana,* 1:758. Patrick H. Edwards was born circa 1830. He married Julia A. Presnall on January 15, 1861. Bossier Parish marriage records, Book B, p. 401.
33. C. L. Vallandigham was the pro-Southern (Copperhead) governor of Ohio who was exiled to the South. In 1863 many of his speeches were collected in *The Record of Hon. C. L. Vallandigham on Abolition, the Union, and the Civil War*, published in Columbus, Ohio, by J. Walter & Co. The book was published through at least twelve editions by 1863.
34. Brashear City, today's Morgan City in St. Mary Parish.
35. USS *Indianola.*
36. The 18th Louisiana Infantry Regiment was Brig. Gen. J. J. A. Alfred Mouton's old regiment. At this point in the war, it was led by Col. Leopold L. Armant. The regiment would become part of the same brigade as the 28th Louisiana Infantry Regiment, along with the 24th Louisiana Infantry, or Crescent Regiment.
37. T. W. Pool, major field and staff, 28th (Grays) Louisiana Infantry Regiment. Roll June 30 to Aug. 31, 1863 (only roll on file), commissioned major, May 14, 1862, present. Official Rolls of Prisoners of War, C.S.A., paroled Monroe, La., June 14, 1865. Booth, *Records of Louisiana,* 3:171.
38. Francis Huergay, private, Company B, 28th (Gray's) Louisiana Infantry Regiment. Appears on roll for July and Aug. 1863 (only roll on file). Enlisted Nov. 1, 1862, Monroe, La., absent under arrest. Booth, *Records of Louisiana,* 2:377.
39. No soldier by this name is listed in Booth.
40. Calvin Tipton, private, Company B, 28th (Gray's) Louisiana Infantry Regiment. Enlisted Monroe, La., May 11, 1862. Roll July and Aug. 1863, present. Roll of Prisoners of War, C.S.A., paroled Shreveport, La., June 14, 1865. Resident of Bossier Parish, La. Booth, *Records of Louisiana,* 3:838. Calvin Tipton married Tibitha G. Martin, Aug. 23, 1859. The 1860 census records show his stepchildren as Curry. Bossier Parish marriage records, Book B, p. 460; Eighth Decennial Census.

41. Washington N. Kay, private, Company B, 28th (Thomas's) Louisiana Infantry Regiment. Enlisted May 15, 1862, Monroe, La., present on roll for July and Aug. 1863. On Rolls of Prisoners of War, paroled at Monroe, La., June 14, 1865. Resident of Bossier Parish, La. Booth, *Records of Louisiana,* 2:502. This Booth entry is in error. Kay was in Company of B of Gray's Louisiana Infantry Regiment, King's company. Washington M. Kay married Cerena C. Cochran June 9, 1858. Bossier Parish marriage records, Book B, p. 312.
42. James R. Pockrens, private, Company B, 28th (Gray's) Louisiana Infantry Regiment. Enlisted May 11, 1862, Monroe, La. On roll for July and Aug. 1863 (last on which borne). Booth, *Records of Louisiana,* 3:163. James R. Pockrus, listed as James R. Pockrens, married Almarinda Boggs January 26, 1859. Bossier Parish marriage records, Book B, 453.
43. David Hardy, captain, Company G, 28th (Gray's) Louisiana Infantry Regiment. Enlisted May 14, 1862, Monroe, La. Roll for Jan. and Feb. 1863, present. Appears on roll for July and Aug. 1862. Booth, *Records of Louisiana,* 1:186.
44. Robert Hector Bradford, captain, Company F, 28th (Gray's) Louisiana Infantry Regiment. Elected captain May 6, 1862, Vernon, La. Roll for Jan. and Feb. 1863, present. Commands detachment of Companies F and G at Butte La Rose, La. Roll for July and Aug. 1863. Absent on business for the commander, order of Colonel Gray. Official Rolls of Paroled Officers, Capt., 28th Louisiana Infantry Regiment, Company F, paroled at Meridian, Miss., May 10, 1865. Booth, *Records of Louisiana,* 1:82.
45. Truth.
46. The Confederate gunboat *Diana* was a side-wheel packet was built in Brownsville, Pennsylvania, in 1858 and weighed 239 tons. Its first home port was Galveston, Texas, where it was captured by U.S. forces on April 27, 1862. It was used as U.S. army transport until it was recaptured by the Rebels on March 28, 1863. The vessel was burned to prevent capture April 12, 1863, during the Teche Campaign. It is listed as vessel number 1540 in Way, *Way's Packet Directory,* 128. A superb account of the *Diana* is found in Morris Raphel, *A Gunboat Named Diana . . . and other exciting stories of Civil War battles which raged in the bayou country of Louisiana* (Detroit: Harlo Press, 1993).
47. This landing was a precursor to the battles of Bisland, fought April 12 and 13, and of Irish Bend, also known as the Battle of Franklin or the Battle of Nerson's Woods, on April 14.
48. King is describing the Battle of Bisland, fought on April 12 and 13. This was part of the Teche Campaign in which Union Maj. Gen. Nathaniel P. Banks and his XIX Corps tried to take Alexandria. Opposing this force were the Confederates of the Western District of Louisiana commanded by Maj. Gen. Richard Taylor. The American Battlefield Protection Program lists the battle summary as follows:

    > In April 1863, Maj. Gen. Nathaniel P. Banks launched an expedition up Bayou Teche in western Louisiana aimed at Alexandria. On April 9, two divisions crossed Berwick Bay from Brashear City to the west side at Berwick. On the 12th, a third division went up the Atchafalaya River to land in the rear of Franklin intending to intercept

a Rebel retreat from Fort Bisland or turn the enemy's position. Maj. Gen. Richard Taylor sent Col. Tom Green's regiment to the front to ascertain the enemy's strength and retard his advance. On the 11th, the Yankees began their advance in earnest. Late on the 12th, Union troops arrived outside the defenses in battle line. An artillery barrage ensued from both sides until dark when the Yankees, many of whom were hit by Rebel cannon fire, fell back and camped for the night. About 9:00 am on the 13th, the Union forces again advanced on Fort Bisland. Combat did not begin until after 11:00 am and continued until dusk. In addition to Rebel forces in the earthworks, the gunboat *Diana,* now in Confederate hands, shelled the Yankees. U.S. gunboats joined the fray in late afternoon. The fighting ceased after this. Later that night, Taylor learned that the Yankee division that went up the Atchafalaya and landed in his rear was now in a position to cut off a Confederate retreat. Taylor began evacuating supplies, men, and weapons, leaving a small force to retard any enemy movement. The next morning, the Yankees found the fort abandoned. Fort Bisland was the only fortification that could have impeded this Union offensive, and it had fallen. Casualties were 234 Union and 450 Confederate.

49. Pleasant H. Dudney, private, Company B, 28th (Gray's) Louisiana Infantry Regiment. Enlisted Jan. 20, 1863, Bossier Parish, La. Federal Rolls of Prisoners of War show him captured at Bayou Teche, La., Apr. 13, 1863. Sent to New Orleans to be exchanged. Paroled below Port Hudson, La., May 11, 1863. Roll for July and Aug. 1863, prisoner, paroled. On Rolls of Prisoners of War, paroled at Shreveport, La., June 14, 1863. Resident of Bossier Parish, La. Booth, *Records of Louisiana,* 1:695.
50. D. M. High, private, Company B, 28th Louisiana (Gray's) Infantry Regiment. Enlisted Nov. 20, 1862, Bossier Parish, La. Federal Rolls of Prisoners of War, captured Bayou Teche, La., Apr. 14, 1863. On Hospital Register, admitted to Marine U.S.A. General Hospital, New Orleans, May 5, 1863. Discharged from hospital, May 30, 1863. Took Oath of Allegiance, June 6, 1863. Roll for July and Aug. 1863, prisoner, paroled home. Booth, *Records of Louisiana,* 2:302.
51. Robert Goodwin, private, Company B, 28th (Gray's) Louisiana Infantry Regiment. Enlisted Jan. 20, 1863, Bossier Parish, La. Federal Rolls of Prisoners of War, captured Bayou Teche, La., Apr. 14, 1863. Sent to New Orleans to be exchanged. Admitted to Saint James U.S.A. General Hospital, New Orleans, Apr. 27, 1863. Died June 7, 1863. Remarks: Rebel prisoner. Report of deaths: Died June 8, 1863. Roll for July and Aug. 1863, prisoner. Paroled (so on roll). Booth, *Records of Louisiana,* 2:57.
52. The side-wheel packet *Laurel Hill* was built in Jeffersonville, Indiana, by Howard in 1859. It had a length of 199 feet, a width (beam) of 38.7 feet, and had a draught of 6.9 feet. It was captured by Union forces and used as a transport during the Red River Campaign. It is listed as vessel number 3386 in Way, *Way's Packet Directory,* 280.
53. Algiers is located on the west bank of the Mississippi River, opposite New Orleans. It was founded as a slave trading station by the French.

54. King was transported to Algiers aboard a train of the New Orleans, Opelousas and Great Western Railroad. Their line was completed from Brashear City to Algiers. See Estaville, *Confederate Neckties,* 39–56.
55. Wretches.
56. Belleville Foundry was located in Algiers.
57. *New Orleans Era,* Apr. 28, 1863.
58. This was one of a series of artillery emplacements guarding the Atchafalaya Basin. King's spelling makes it impossible to specifically identify which fortification this was.
59. Cajuns.
60. Port Hudson, the Confederate bastion above Baton Rouge.
61. Bayou Courtebleu, near Opelousas.
62. The side-wheel packet *Iberville* was built in New Albany, Indiana, in 1859. The vessel had a length of 179 feet, a width (beam) of 35 feet, and a depth below the waterline of 6.3 feet. It was built for the Bayou Sara Mail Company. It was used as a transport by the Confederates until captured. It was then used by the U.S. Army Quartermaster Corps as a transport. Under that service, it participated in the Red River Campaign in 1864. It is listed as vessel number 2700 in Way, *Way's Packet Directory,* 220.
63. The side-wheel packet *Morning Light* was built at Belle Vernon, Pennsylvania, in 1858. She weighed 198 tons, had a length of 144 feet, a width (beam) of 30 feet, and a depth below the waterline of 5 feet. She was owned and captained by William Dillon. He ran it on the New Orleans–Red River–Lake Bistineau route and the New Orleans–Tensas River–Bayou Macon–Black River route. The vessel was sold to C. Rodney in January 1863, and from there little is known of her fate. It is listed as vessel number 4035 in Way, *Way's Packet Directory,* 331.
64. Meridian, noon.
65. The USS *Richmond* was a screw sloop built at Washington, D.C., in 1858. It weighed 2,700 tons, had a length of 225 feet, a width (beam) of 42.5 feet, and a depth below the waterline of 17.5 feet. He had a crew of 260. During this period it carried an armament of twenty nine-inch smoothbore cannon, one 80-pdr rifle, and one 30-pdr rifle. See Silverstone, *Civil War Navies,* 38.
66. The USS *Essex* was an ironclad gunboat converted from a merchant snag boat by the great naval engineer James Buchanan Eads. It weighed 355 tons, had a length of 159 feet, a width (beam) of 47.5 feet, and a depth below the water line of 6.8 feet. During this period its armament consisted of one ten-inch smoothbore cannon, three nine-inch smoothbore cannon, one 32-pdr, one 12-pdr howitzer, and two 50-pdr rifles. It was famous for its fight with the CSS *Arkansas.* See Silverstone, *Civil War Navies,* 155–56.
67. The side-wheel packet *Starlight* was built in Jeffersonville, Indiana, in 1858. The vessel weighed 280 tons, had a length of 162 feet, a width (beam) of 31 feet, and a depth below the waterline of 6 feet. It ran the New Orleans to Shreveport route under Capt. Charles Hayes. It is listed as vessel number 5181 in Way, *Way's Packet Directory,* 432.
68. Jackson, in East Feliciana Parish.

69. Francis Monk, private, Company K, 28th (Gray's) Louisiana Infantry Regiment. Enlisted Monroe, La., May 17, 1862. Federal Rolls of Prisoners of War, captured at Bayou Teche, La., Apr. 14, 1863. Paroled below Port Hudson, La. Booth, *Records of Louisiana,* 2:1014.
70. This is a reference to Confederate Lt. Gen. John Clifford Pemberton, commander of the Department of Mississippi and Eastern Louisiana. His army was designated to defend Vicksburg at all costs. By the time King penned this passage, Pemberton's army had abandoned Jackson, fought and lost an engagement at Champion's Hill (to which King refers), and had fallen back to within the defenses of Fortress Vicksburg.
71. Dr. H. J. T. Harrington.
72. William Spencer, private, Company E, Crescent Regiment Louisiana Infantry. Enlisted Claiborne Parish, Jan. 17, 186[?]. Roll Jan. and Feb. 1863, present. Federal Rolls of Prisoners of War, captured Butte a la Rose, Apr. 20, 1863. Paroled below Port Hudson, La., May 11, 1863. Sent to New Orleans to be exchanged. Also borne on Rolls of Company C, Consolidated Crescent Regiment Louisiana Infantry, private. Federal Rolls of Prisoners of War, captured Fort De Russy, Mar. 14, 1864. On Hospital Register, admitted to C.S.A. General Hospital, Shreveport, La., July 24, 1864. Died July 24, 1864. On return dated Camp Buckner, near Alexandria, La., Dec. 31, 1864, of deceased soldiers. Died Shreveport, La., July 25, 1864. Booth, *Records of Louisiana,* 3:660–61.
73. Bayou Sara was the port village on the Mississippi River below St. Francisville in West Feliciana Parish, above Baton Rouge.
74. No soldier by this name is listed in Booth.
75. Woodville, in Wilkinson County, Mississippi, lies north of St. Francisville.
76. Natchez, Mississippi.
77. Trinity, near Jonesville in Catahoula Parish, lies at the confluence of the Ouachita and Tensas rivers.
78. Lake Concordia is an oxbow lake in Concordia Parish. Today, the town of Ferriday is located on it.
79. King had hoped to obtain a skiff to travel from Lake Concordia, via Cross Bayou, Caney Bayou, then Fish Lake to Tensas River, and from there to Trinity at the mouth of the Tensas. He was forced to take part of the land route on what is today U.S. Highway 84.
80. The stern-wheeler *S. H. Tucker* was built in Cincinnati, Ohio, in 1856. The vessel weighed 128 tons, had a length of 137 feet, a width (beam) of 25 feet, and a depth below the waterline of 4.5 feet. It operated on the Red and Ouachita rivers by Capt. Frank Smith. The *S. H. Tucker* was captured by the U.S. forces at Columbus, Kentucky, and taken to the U.S. naval at Cairo, Illinois. It is listed as vessel number 4896 in Way, *Way's Packet Directory,* 407.
81. Little is known of the *Pauline.* The vessel was obviously in Confederate service and was apparently captured by Federal forces later in 1863 or very early 1864. It was pressed into service in the U.S. Army Quartermaster Corps and served as a transport in the Red River campaign. It is not listed in *Ways Packet Directory.*
82. George W. Logan, lieutenant colonel, Chalmette Regiment, Louisiana Militia. Also on rolls of 2nd Battalion, Louisiana Heavy Artillery, lieutenant colonel, as

George William Logan. Official Rolls of Paroled Officers, paroled Shreveport, La., June 12, 1865. Booth, *Records of Louisiana,* 2:780.

83. Little River is a tributary of the Ouachita River, connecting it with Catahoula Lake. It empties into the Ouachita at Trinity, almost due west from the mouth of the Tensas River.
84. This route would take the vessel south from Trinity on the Black River (the lower portion of the Ouachita River) to its confluence with the Red River at the boundary of Concordia, Catahoula, and Avoyelles parishes. From there, the vessel would travel northwesterly on the Red River, past Alexandria, to Shreveport. King would have been across the river from his home if he traveled to Shreveport. It is unclear why he chose to travel to Monroe, unless he believed he would receive medical treatment faster by going to the Confederate hospital there and then proceeding home. He offers no explanation, and his course does not seem reasonable.
85. Columbia in Caldwell Parish.
86. Ouachita River.
87. Dr. T. M. Cavett was a Claiborne Parish doctor who settled in Minden, Louisiana, after the war. See Cardin Collection.
88. Toddy.
89. Col. Oran M. Roberts commanded the 11th Texas Infantry Regiment in Brigadier General Horace Randal's Second Brigade of Maj. Gen. John George Walker's First (Texas) Division of the Army of Western Louisiana.
90. "Mrs. Smiths" was the hotel in Bellevue that catered to the officials and workers of the courthouse. See Cardin Collection.
91. The Bossier Cavalry was led by Nathan A. Sentell. This was an independent company of cavalry originally under Capt. William Harrison. The company was sent to Mississippi in the spring of 1862 and served under various regiments from Mississippi, Tennessee, and Kentucky before being detached and transferred to the Trans-Mississippi Department in the spring of 1863. It became Company C of the 6th Louisiana Cavalry Regiment. Harrison became the regimental commander. See Bergeron, *Guide to Louisiana Units,* 49, 66, 175.
92. Confederate Lt. Gen. Edmund Kirby Smith, commander of the Department of the Trans-Mississippi.
93. Camp Pratt was a Confederate conscription, or boot camp, located at Spanish Lake in Iberia Parish.
94. This camp was located at the present-day site of the Louisiana State Fairgrounds. Numerous artifacts have been recovered from the site over the past decades. There has been no firm documentary evidence of this training area or its name other than a newspaper report in the May 25, 1863, *Shreveport Semi Weekly News* concerning the arrival of the 2nd Texas Brigade (Speight's) of the Department of the Indian Territory to the "Camp 4 Miles West of Shreveport, La. Monday May 18th 1863."
95. This is probably Dr. Solomon "Sol" Smith, chief surgeon of the Trans-Mississippi Department, a very close confidant of Kirby Smith, who, under much contention, succeeded Brig. Gen. William R. Boggs as chief of staff to Smith.
96. Benjamin F. Knight, private, Company B, 28th (Gray's) Louisiana Infantry Regiment. Enlisted May 11, 1862, Monroe, La. Booth, *Records of Louisiana,* 2:585. Benjamin F. Knight was born circa 1832 in Louisiana. See Eighth Decennial Census.

97. Randolph Slack, private, Company B, 28th (Gray's) Louisiana Infantry Regiment. Roll dated May 11, 1862 (only roll on which borne). Enlisted Monroe, La., May 14, 1862. Booth, *Records of Louisiana,* 3:589.
98. This refers to Confederate Lt. Gen. Theophilus Hunter Holmes, commander of the District of Arkansas. The unsuccessful attack on the Union stronghold of Helena, near the mouth of the Arkansas River, was on July 4, 1863.
99. This was the beginning of a concerted effort by the Trans-Mississippi Department to create defenses in the Red River Valley. The engineering was under the command of Brig. Gen. William R. Boggs. See Gary D. Joiner, *One Damn Blunder from Beginning to End: The Red River Campaign of 1864* (Wilmington, Del.: Scholarly Resources, 2003): 15–31.
100. The 10th instant (the previous day).
101. John Hunt Morgan and his raiders surrendered and were imprisoned in July following a brilliant raid in Kentucky, Ohio, and Indiana.
102. W. L. Yancy was a Unionist in Greenville County, South Carolina, who had been embroiled in the nullification crisis in 1832.

5. The Cattle Drive and Home

1. McAlpins was located near present-day Bradley, in Lafayette County, Arkansas.
2. Long Prairie may have been a village, but from King's later writing it appears to be literally a stretch of prairie adjoining Red River. The roads of the time are very similar to modern roads. This would place Long Prairie astride Arkansas Highway 160.
3. Spring Bank was a ford on Red River near the bridge on Arkansas Highway 160.
4. Bright Star is located near the village of Doddridge in Miller Country, Arkansas.
5. Daingerfield in Morris County, Texas.
6. Sulphur Springs in Hopkins County, Texas.
7. Black Jack Grove was near the boundary of Hopkins and Hunt counties on what is today U.S. Highway 67.
8. Herding.
9. White Oak was located near the present boundary between Franklin and Titus counties on today's U.S. Highway 67.
10. Wheatville in Morris County, Texas.
11. Unionville in Cass County, Texas.
12. Douglassville in Cass County, Texas.
13. Unclear meaning, perhaps *internecine.*
14. King is describing what he has heard about the actions surrounding the Battle of Chickamauga and the diversion of Lt. Gen. James Longstreet's Corps to Tennessee from Virginia to help stem the Union tide.
15. Confederate Maj. Gen. Joseph Wheeler.
16. This is Confederate Brig. Gen. Nathan Bedford Forrest. He would be promoted to major general in December 1863.
17. Union Maj. Gen. William Starke Rosecrans.
18. This was a second attempt by Union Maj. Gen. Nathaniel Prentiss Banks, commander of the Department of the Gulf, based in New Orleans, to invade Texas.

He sent the bulk of the XIX Corps overland across southern Louisiana to invade Texas. The force turned around in St. Landry Parish, near the town of Washington, accomplishing nothing.

19. This was a false rumor.
20. Brought in for interrogation in the belief he may have been a deserter or worse.
21. William Jones, private, Company B, 28th (Gray's) Louisiana Infantry Regiment. Enlisted May 11, 1863, Monroe, La. On Register of Prisoners of War. Captured at Franklin, La., Apr. 14, 1863. Paroled below Port Hudson, La., May 11, 1863. Forwarded to New Orleans to be exchanged. Roll for July and Aug. 1863, prisoner, paroled home. Booth, *Records of Louisiana,* 2:480.
22. Patrick H. Edwards, private, Company B, 28th (Gray's) Louisiana Infantry Regiment. Enlisted May 11, 1862, Monroe, La. Roll for July and Aug. 1863, present, detail. Booth, *Records of Louisiana,* 1:758.
23. Detained or arrested.
24. James W. Shields, private, Company B, 28th (Gray's) Louisiana Infantry Regiment. Enlisted Monroe, La., May 11, 1862. Roll July and Aug. 1863, detached service. Booth, *Records of Louisiana,* 3:548.
25. The ironclad CSS *Missouri* was built in Shreveport. The vessel weighed 183 tons, had a length of 183 feet, a width (beam) of 53.66 feet, and a depth below the waterline of 10.25 feet. Its armament consisted of one eleven-inch, one nine-inch, and two 32-pdr smoothbores. It was the last Confederate combat vessel to surrender on inland waters. Silverstone, *Civil War Navies,* 207.
26. Prattle.
27. Brownsville fell on November 6, 1863. This action was part of Union Maj. Gen. Nathaniel P. Banks's second attempt to invade Texas. The action received criticism from Washington since it did not achieve any strategic goal. The criticism led to a third attempt up the Red River the following spring.
28. An acute tick-borne illness caused by the bacteria *Rickettsia rickettsii.* The disease is characterized by a sudden onset of headache, chills and fever. It typically persists for two to three weeks and a rash appears on the extremities and trunk about the fourth day of illness.
29. King is referring to the building of a very sophisticated floating obstacle at Shreveport. The location was just north of today's intersection of Stoner Avenue and Clyde Fant Memorial Parkway. The obstacle was anchored on both banks of the Red River and had a removable, upstream-sliding plug that allowed vessels to enter and leave the Shreveport waterfront. The water pressure of the current made involuntary opening of the plug almost impossible. It was also held in place by iron bars. The raft was open below the water line and stabilized by ships' anchors. This served two purposes. First, the river flow would not be held back as with a dam. Second, and of equal importance, the Confederates secretly constructed five submarines at Shreveport that were sisters to the CSS *Hunley.* The vessels could foray south of the raft without being noticed. The depth of water below the base of the plug was at least twenty feet. The structure was guarded by the largest of the Confederate forts at Shreveport, Fort Turnbull, and by a smaller fort on the Bossier Parish side, Battery Ewell. The plans of the raft are in the Jerome Gilmer Papers in the Southern Historical Collection, Wilson Library, Univ. of North Carolina at Chapel Hill. The plans for the Shreveport defenses are in the same collection. The map of

the Shreveport defenses was created by the chief topographic engineer of the Trans-Mississippi Department, Maj. Richard M. Venable (hereinafter cited as Venable Map). For a discussion of the submarines, see Mark K. Ragan, *Union and Confederate Submarine Warfare in the Civil War* (Mason City, Iowa: Savas, 1999), 288 n.

30. Randolph was charged with building a home guard as a backup against a Union invasion. See U.S. War Dept., *War of the Rebellion: The Official Records of the Union and Confederate Armies* (Washington, D.C.: Government Printing Office, 1890–1901), vol. 26, pt. 2:351 (hereinafter cited as *O.R.* All references to the *O.R.* are to series 1 unless otherwise identified.) King would have a difficult time avoiding Randolph since he was based in Collinsburgh.
31. *Caddo Gazette,* Nov. 20, 1863.
32. President Jefferson Davis or Lt. Gen. Edmund Kirby Smith.
33. Confederate Maj. Gen. Sterling "Old Pap" Price formally assumed command of the District of Arkansas the following March 16. On September 10, 1863, Price evacuated Little Rock under strong pressure from Federal forces under Maj. Gen. Frederick Steele.

6. Shreveport

1. C. Wallace is Ceaser Wallace. He lived at Coates Bluff in Bossier Parish. There were two Coates Bluffs, one on either side of the Red River. Wallace's location was directly south of the present Bossier Parish Courthouse in Benton.
2. Lander Hamilton, private, Company B, 28th (Gray's) Louisiana Infantry Regiment. Enlisted May 11, 1862, Monroe, La. Federal Rolls of Prisoners of War, Captured Bayou Teche, La., Jan. 15, 1862, paroled Jan. 15, 1863. Roll for July and Aug. 1863, prisoner, paroled. Booth, *Records of Louisiana,* 1:167. Leander Hamilton married Mary A. Wallace January 19, 1856. His death in February 1880 created much notoriety. Hamilton was cutting down a tree and saw his pet pig was in danger of being crushed by the falling tree. He went to its rescue and was killed himself. See Bossier Parish marriage records for 1856; Cardin Collection.
3. This refers to Ceaser Wallace's home.
4. Venable Map.
5. Confederate Col. William Clarke Quantrill was the leader of the most notorious band of pro-Confederate partisan guerillas west of the Mississippi River. For a discussion of Quantrill's stay in Shreveport after the Lawrence, Kansas, raid, see Duane Schultz, *Quantrill's War: The Life and Times of William Clarke Quantrill* (New York: St. Martin's Press, 1996): 267–72.
6. This was the Reverend George Tucker, who was born in Tennessee on December 12, 1806, and died in Shreveport on December 31, 1882. Tucker was pastor of First Baptist Church (King's reference to "The Baptist Church") of Shreveport 1861–65. His wife was Abigail Hartsfield Tucker, who died in June 1890 at seventy-five. Both are buried in Oakland Cemetery in Shreveport. In 1861 Reverend Tucker organized a company of soldiers called the Caddo Confederates, which became Company I of the 27th Louisiana Infantry Regiment. See Bergeron, *Guide of Louisiana Units,* 137; *Shreveport Daily Times,* Jan. 23, 1881; archives of Erick J. Brock of Shreveport.

7. The county seat for Smith County is Tyler.
8. Supply.
9. Calmness.
10. King is probably referring to a military guarded gate at the intersection of McNeill Street and Texas Street. The arsenal and powder house were located on Cross Bayou at the end of McNeill Street. See Venable Map. The map does not show such a guard post.
11. Nat Lawrence, private, Company B, 28th (Gray's) Louisiana Infantry Regiment. Roll for July and Aug. 1863 (only roll on file). Enlisted Nov. 2, 1862, Bossier Parish, La. Reported absent with remarks: sick, furlough. Booth, *Records of Louisiana,* 2:681.
12. S. W. Self, Private, 28th Louisiana Volunteers, Company B (Gray's Louisiana Infantry Regiment). Federal Rolls Prisoners of War, captured Bayou Teche, La., May 11, 1863. On roll of Prisoners of War, C.S.A., paroled [?], June [?], 1865. Resident Caddo Parish, La., as S. M. Self. Booth, *Records of Louisiana,* 3:510.
13. Camp Ford Prisoner of War Camp at Tyler.
14. T. S. Crawford later became a judge, according to the 1870 Census for Caldwell Parish, Louisiana.
15. The Washington Road led from what is now Bossier City, through Benton, Plain Dealing, and on to Washington, Arkansas. It is now known as the Old Plain Dealing Highway.
16. *Caddo Gazette Extra,* Dec. 9, 1863. This refers to the Battle of Chattanooga, Tennessee, on November 23, 1863, and the Battle of Missionary Ridge on November 25.
17. The *Shreveport Semi-Weekly News,* Dec. 10, 1863.
18. This was Elliott's Ferry, located on the east bank of the Sabine River, eight miles northeast of Carthage, Texas, in Panola County. In the 1840s a small community grew around the ferry landing, which was located on the main road between Carthage and Shreveport. Frequent bouts of malaria and flooding forced most of the residents to River Hill on the bluff above the river, and the site was eventually abandoned. See Leila B. LaGrone, ed., *History of Panola County* (Carthage, Tex.: Panola County Historical Commission, 1979). Lawrence R. Sharp, "History of Panola County, Texas, to 1860" (Master's thesis, Univ. of Texas, 1940).
19. The Confederate command dispersed its resources in the event of a second Union incursion up the Red River or down from Little Rock, Arkansas.
20. *Caddo Gazette Extra,* Dec. 12, 1863.
21. These guns were most likely moved to the newly expanded fortifications at Grand Ecore. See *O.R.*, vol. 26, pt. 1, p. 322.
22. CSS *Missouri.*
23. *Caddo Gazette Extra,* Dec. 14, 1863.
24. Col. John Milton Sandidge was a Bossier resident who voted against succession but sold all his property and went to war when it became evident. Local oral tradition states that he had a conversation with President Lincoln and asked if Lincoln would invade the South if the South seceded. When Lincoln answered yes, he asked for a pass to go home and prepared for war. See Cardin Collection.
25. Morgan did escape on November 27, 1863.
26. *Caddo Gazette,* Dec. 18, 1863.
27. Kirby Smith's headquarters were located in a still-standing two-story building on the west side of the 500 block of Spring Street in Shreveport.

28. Oscar B. Sherwin, private, Company E, 13th Battalion Louisiana (Partisan Rangers). Enlisted Aug. 15, 1862, Monroe, La. Roll Nov. and Dec. 1862, absent, detailed to work in infirmary. Roll Jan. 1 to Apr. 30, 1863, absent, detached. Booth, *Records of Louisiana,* 3:545.
29. This is J. P. Vance.
30. Probably Robert Goodwin, private, Company B, 28th (Gray's) Louisiana Infantry Regiment. Enlisted Jan. 20, 1863, Bossier Parish, La. Federal Rolls of Prisoners of War, captured Bayou Teche, La., Apr. 14, 1863. Sent to New Orleans to be exchanged. Admitted to St. James U.S. Army General Hospital, New Orleans, Apr. 27, 1863. Died June 7, 1863. Remarks: Rebel prisoner. Report of deaths: Died June 8, 1863. Roll for July and Aug. 1863, prisoner. Paroled (so on roll). Booth, *Records of Louisiana,* 2:57. If Goodwin were not accounted for, the rumor of his desertion and treason would have been easily accepted.
31. *Caddo Gazette Extra,* Dec. 23, 1863.
32. Ibid.
33. Substitute.
34. CSS *Missouri.*
35. *Shreveport Semi-Weekly News Extra,* Dec. 25, 1863.
36. The camp was Camp Boggs, which was located on the northern end of the high hills south of Shreveport in what is today the Highland neighborhood. The southwest corner of the camp was located at the intersection of present-day Line Avenue and Jordan Street and extended to the present-day Hamilton Terrace School. See Edwin C. Bearss and William H. Tunnard, *A Southern Record: The Story of the 3rd Louisiana Infantry, C.S.A.* (Dayton, Ohio: Morningside Bookshop, 1988), 326, 328, 355, 339.
37. Niblitt's Bluff, near Vinton in Calcasieu Parish.
38. This confirmed that the camp was Camp Boggs. The spring in that camp was well known and sheltered. See Bearss and Tunnard, *A Southern Record,* 326, 328, 355, 339.
39. Cooke County Texas is located on the Red River, almost due north from present-day Fort Worth.
40. The December 18, 1863, *Shreveport Semi Weekly News* reported an Indian raid near Montague, Texas (where King would later live). The report stated that the Confederates guarding the border with the Indian Territory had only a company of soldiers to guard that area. The Indians severely wounded one man and stole their horses and pack mules.
41. This action was implemented as General Order No. 3 of 1864 and published in the *Shreveport Semi Weekly News* on January 15, 1864. Three surgeons, C. B. Nottingham, A. F. Clarke, and W. A. Hardy, were announced as the "members of the Board of Examining Surgeons for Conscripts in the Parishes of Louisiana, west of the Mississippi River."
42. See the Venable Map.
43. King is describing Fort Turnbull, the anchor fort on the Red River and the largest of the Shreveport inner fortifications.
44. King is only observing the guarding of the siege gun from an antitheft perspective. The object, of course, was to man the position and protect it from insurgents or an enemy attack.

45. King means that he is an "extra" in the guard service.
46. Bushwackers were usually rogue parties that marauded for themselves, paying only titular allegiance to either the Union or the Confederates. They were a constant problem in north central, northeast, and southwest Louisiana after the spring of 1864.
47. Confederate Lt. Gen. William Joseph Hardee commanded a corps at Chattanooga. Lt. Gen. Braxton Bragg turned over the Confederate Army of Tennessee that had just been defeated at Chattanooga to Hardee at Dalton, Georgia. The command was brief and Hardee was replaced by Gen. Joseph E. Johnston.
48. *Shreveport South Western,* Jan. 6, 1864. This was Maj. Gen. Mansfield Lovell, the commander of Confederate forces at New Orleans. He abandoned the city to Federal forces in April 1862. A court of inquiry exonerated him.
49. There were several buildings in Shreveport used as hospitals at various times during the Civil War. The most prominent, and the only two closely resembling King's description, were the Confederate Marine Hospital, located near the corner of Stoner Avenue and Centenary Boulevard, and the Commercial Hotel. Greenwood Cemetery occupies the area of the Marine Hospital and the adjacent grounds. The Commercial Hotel building was leased by J. S. Allen to the Confederate government for $250 per month for use as a hospital. It was located on Milam Street in lots 11 and 12, block 49, of the original plat of Shreveport. The *Shreveport Semi Weekly News* of February 2, 1864, reported that J. S. Allen's succession listed the property and that "by some slight improvement on the back building the rent will be largely increased." The back building might indicate a connect alley to which King refers.
50. Gaines Landing is located in Chicot County, Arkansas, in the southeast corner of the state.
51. Confederate Maj. Gen. Sterling Price, commander of the District of Arkansas.
52. Excessive flow of saliva.
53. George W. Riggins.
54. Paper money printed in Shreveport.
55. This was probably the parole camp south of Shreveport on a bluff above Bayou Pierre. Today, the location is near the southeast corner of the intersection of Flournoy Lucas Road and Ellerbe Road.
56. Andrew J. Groves, private, Company B, 28th (Gray's) Louisiana Infantry Regiment. Enlisted May 11, 1862, Monroe, La. Roll for July and Aug. 1863, detached service. Booth, *Records of Louisiana,* 2:116.
57. Lt. Col. William Harrison, commanding Harrison's Battalion of cavalry.
58. There was a skirmish at Spring Hill (also known as Spring Ridge), Arkansas, on February 9, 1864.
59. Instant, or the date just passed.
60. Coughing up blood from the respiratory tract; usually indicates a severe infection of the bronchi or lungs.
61. Pine Bluff is the county seat of Jefferson County, Arkansas. By early 1864 it was garrisoned by Union troops.
62. *Caddo Gazette,* Feb. 12, 1864.
63. S*hreveport Semi-Weekly News Extra,* Feb. 16, 1864.
64. This is Confederate Senator Louis Trezevant Wigfall of Texas. Although initially a supporter of Jefferson Davis, during the last two years of the Confederacy he

carried on public and conspiratorial campaigns to strip the Confederate president of power and prestige. He worked for military strength at the expense of state and individual rights. See Alvy L. King, *Louis T. Wigfall: Southern Fire-Eater* (Baton Rouge: Louisiana State Univ. Press, 1970).

65. This is Confederate Maj. Gen. Stephen Dill Lee.
66. *Washington (AR) Telegraph,* Feb. 20, 1864.
67. The corn sheds were located on the north side of Shreveport, below Cross Bayou. See Venable Map.
68. James W. Dunn, private, Company B, 28th (Gray's) Louisiana Infantry Regiment. Enlisted May 11, 1862, Monroe, La. Roll for July and Aug. 1863, absent, hospital at Shreveport, La. On Roll of Prisoners of War, paroled at Shreveport, La., June 14, 1865. Resident of Bossier Parish, La. Booth, *Records of Louisiana,* 1:717–18.
69. CSS *Missouri.*
70. The *Harrison Flag* newspaper of Marshall, Texas, covered a party on March 16, 1860, in which "Sam Williams, the Napoleon violinist, accidentally dropping in, was invited to the orchestra. On this subject we need not say more. Exercises in the poetry of motion followed as a matter of course."
71. Dr. John T. Catlett.
72. Brig. Gen. Tom Green led the Cavalry Corps of Texas troops. It would be almost a month before Green was allowed to cross over to Louisiana soil.
73. This is Confederate Maj. Gen. John George Walker's First (Texas) Division of the Army of Western Louisiana.

7. The Red River Campaign and Aftermath

1. This was an attempt to build a double-fortified obstruction, or raft. See Joiner, *One Damn Blunder,* 21–22; Gary D. Joiner and Charles E. Vetter, "Union Naval Expedition on the Red River," in *The Red River Campaign: Union and Confederate Leadership and the War in Louisiana,* ed. Theodore P. Savas, David A. Woodbury, and Gary D. Joiner (Shreveport, La.: Parabellum Press, 2003): 26–68.
2. Fort DeRussy fell on March 14 to Union forces led by Brig. Gen. Joseph A. Mower, commanding the 3rd Division, XVI Corps. See Joiner, *One Damn Blunder,* 45–51. This was the first action in the Red River Campaign of 1864.
3. Alexandria surrendered to the naval forces of Rear Adm. David Dixon Porter on March 16.
4. Shingles is an infection caused by the varicella-zoster virus, which is the virus that causes chickenpox. Shingles occurs in people who have had chickenpox and represents a reactivation of the dormant varicella-zoster virus. The disease generally affects the elderly, although it occasionally occurs in younger and/or immunodeficient individuals (as in the case of King.) Source: National Institute of Neurological Disorders and Stroke.
5. Epsomita or native sulphate of magnesia or Epsom salt.
6. Reckon.
7. No vessel by this name is listed in *Way's Packet Directory.*
8. Gov. Henry Watkins Allen.

9. David J. Elder Sr.
10. This conscription of slaves was part of a continuing plan to provide a workforce to build defensive fortifications to protect Shreveport. Later in 1864 the laborers were moved to a separate guarded compound southwest of Shreveport. This facility is labeled "Negro Camp" on the Venable Map. It was located near the current northern terminus of U.S. Interstate Highway 49 in what would later become the Mamie Jackson Housing Project.
11. As this passage was penned, Taylor was gathering his forces near Natchitoches. Porter brought his fleet to Alexandria on March 16. The force consisted of ninety vessels (including U.S. Army Quartermaster Corps transports).
12. On March 23, 1864, Kirby Smith issued Special Order No. 71, stating that "Shreveport and the adjoining country extending five miles beyond the fortifications, is declared an In-trenched Camp." This order closed all saloons and gambling halls and forbade gambling within the area. This was apparently in response to the activities of which King wrote on February 23. With the Red River Campaign well under way, it also effectively placed Shreveport under martial law. See *Shreveport Semi Weekly News,* Mar. 29, 1864.
13. This was a move to Camp Ford in Tyler, Texas.
14. To inosculate; to intercommunicate by anastomosis, as the arteries and veins. In this case, ripples from a pebble thrown into a pool of water intertwine.
15. King is referring to Saint Paul's Bottoms, which is today's Ledbetter Heights. This is the low area to the west of downtown Shreveport which was the first suburb of the town. It was an area of brothels and blue-collar dwellings.
16. Alexandria was occupied on March 16 without a struggle.
17. Brig. Gen. Tom Green was still in Texas as King wrote this passage. He would not cross over into Louisiana until April 6.
18. See Appendix 2.
19. The Verandah (or Veranda) Hotel was located at the northeast corner of Milam and Spring Streets in Shreveport. It was owned by brothers Henry (1815–79) and August (1829–78) Hassebrauck, natives of Germany. The Verandah burned down in June 1866. Information contained in the archives of Eric J. Brock of Shreveport.
20. The Union column reached Grand Ecore, four miles from Natchitoches, on April 3. See Joiner, *One Damn Blunder,* 75–91.
21. Rockport was located on the Ouachita River. It was the location of the ford the Union column used to cross that stream. No fighting took place there at that time. The first major engagement of the Camden Campaign (the northern portion of the Red River Campaign) would come at Poison Spring on April 18.
22. This is typical of rumors in the face of an advancing enemy. The Battle of Mansfield would be fought on April 8.
23. The home guard.
24. This is another false rumor. On April 7 the Union column advanced beyond Pleasant Hill in Desoto Parish and fought a sharp engagement with Tom Green's cavalry at Wilson's Farm. The head of the column then progressed ten miles north of Pleasant Hill and encamped at Carroll's Mill for the night.
25. Kirby Smith ordered Richard Taylor not to fight a battle on April 8 due to this proclamation. Taylor, realized that if the Union advanced into Mansfield he did

not have the resources to cover the three possible roads that ran from that town to Shreveport. He therefore decided to give battle three miles below Mansfield at the Moss Plantation. The result was a costly but decisive victory for the Confederates. Taylor used two divisions, the Louisiana Division, which included King's 28th Louisiana Infantry Regiment, and the Texas Division of Maj. Gen. John G. Walker.

26. This is a fairly accurate portrayal for early information from the battlefield. Captured wagons exceeded 260. There were at least twenty artillery pieces captured. The number of prisoners captured was significant, but the number is still debated. There were large numbers of missing and dead. Banks, the Union commander, left almost all of his dead and wounded on the battlefield.
27. King is describing the Battle of Pleasant Hill. He is referring to the additional forces of Brig. Gen. Mosby Parsons and Brig. Gen. Thomas Churchill. For an in-depth account of the battles of Mansfield and Pleasant Hill, see Richard Taylor, *Destruction and Reconstruction: Personal Experiences of the Civil War* (New York: Da Capo, 1995), 155–75; Joiner, *One Damn Blunder,* 93–122; Savas, Woodbury, and Joiner, *The Red River Campaign: Union and Confederate Leadership and War in Louisiana* (Shreveport, La.: Parabellum Press, 2003), 1–103; Ludwell Johnson, *The Red River Campaign: Politics and Cotton in the Civil War* (Kent, Ohio: Kent State Univ. Press, 1993). The fighting actually began at 4 P.M. and resulted in a tactical tie. Banks retreated toward Grand Ecore, thus changing the battle into a strategic victory for the Confederates.
28. Lt. Col. William Walker.
29. King is reporting rumors he heard in Shreveport. Kirby Smith decided to remove three divisions from Richard Taylor's command and take them to Arkansas to thwart the northern prong of the Union invasion. The three units were the Texas, Arkansas, and Missouri divisions. Taylor was bitterly opposed to this, believing that he could trap Banks and the entire Union force, including the naval vessels, if he retained these units.
30. Robert Goodwin, private, Company B, 28th (Gray's) Louisiana Infantry Regiment. Enlisted Jan. 20, 1863, Bossier Parish, La. Federal Rolls of Prisoners of War, Captured Bayou Teche, La., Apr. 14, 1863. Sent to New Orleans to be exchanged. Admitted to St. James U.S.A. General Hospital, New Orleans, Apr. 27, 1863. Died June 7, 1863. Remarks: Rebel prisoner. Report of deaths: Died June 8, 1863. Roll for July and Aug. 1863, prisoner. Paroled (so on roll). Booth, *Records of Louisiana,* 2:57.
31. Benjamin M. Richardson, private, Company B, 28th (Gray's) Louisiana Infantry Regiment. Enlisted Monroe, La., May 11, 1862. Roll July and Aug. 1863, present. Booth, *Records of Louisiana,* 3:309.
32. This was probably John A. D. Johnson, private, Company B, 28th (Gray's) Louisiana Infantry Regiment. Enlisted May 11, 1862, Monroe, La. Roll for July and Aug. 1863, present. Booth, *Records of Louisiana,* 2:453.
33. Pvt. James W. McGuire.
34. L. B. Hendricks, private, Company B, 28th (Gray's) Louisiana Infantry Regiment. Appears on roll for July and Aug. 1863 (only roll on file). Enlisted Jan. 20, 1863, Bossier Parish, present. Booth, *Records of Louisiana,* 1:267. Lucian Hendricks, called "Luke" was born circa 1832, in Louisiana, the son of William B. Hendricks. His father was a farmer who served as school director for the Bossier Parish school system. See Eighth Decennial Census; Cardin Collection.

35. This is remarkably quick reporting. Steele's column entered Camden on April 12 and 13. If King was reporting a rumor, it was, unlike most he heard, true. This may indicate that the telegraph line running from Shreveport through Minden and Homer, then north into Arkansas, was still in operation.
36. This is an odd statement. Brig. Gen. James Tappan's brigade fought at Pleasant Hill on April 9. On April 12 the brigade was below Shreveport. King may be referring to regimental components attempting to join the brigade, but his reference to a full brigade is incorrect. See Joiner, *One Damn Blunder,* 110.
37. Brig. Gen. Tom Green, commander of the Cavalry Corps. Green was killed at the Blair's Landing on April 12. He was arguably the best cavalry commander in the Trans-Mississippi on either side during the war. See Joiner, *One Damn Blunder,* 144–45.
38. King is describing the retreat of the Union gunboats under Rear Adm. David Dixon Porter. The term "hardly pressed" should be read as "hard pressed." The gunboats fought constant duels with Confederate artillery and snipers, as well as Confederate cavalry at Blair's Landing, since their retreat from below Tones Bayou in Caddo Parish. On April 13 the flotilla arrived a Grand Ecore at 1 A.M.
39. Maj. Gen. Frederick Steele, commander of the Department of Arkansas and the leader of the northern prong of the Union invasion.
40. King means Maj. Gen. John G. Walker's Texas Division.
41. The rumor of the dispatch was only partially correct. Taylor did not hold Grand Ecore or Natchitoches at that time, but the navy did suffer damage from constant action with snipers and artillery fire.
42. This is the movement of the three divisions from Taylor's command to Arkansas to halt Steele. The move was unnecessary, and in the case of Walker's command, devastating. The forces would have been used more successfully in Louisiana. See Joiner, *One Damn Blunder,* 107–22; Edwin C. Bearss, *Steele's Retreat from Camden and the Battle of Jenkins Ferry* (Little Rock: Eagle Press of Little Rock, 1990).
43. Robert Hector Bradford, captain, Company F, 28th (Gray's) Louisiana Infantry Regiment. Elected captain May 6, 1862, Vernon, La. Roll for Jan. and Feb. 1863, present. Commands detachment of Companies F and G at Butte La Rose, La. Roll for July and Aug. 1863, absent on business for the company, order of Colonel Gray. Official Rolls of Paroled Officers, captain, 28th Louisiana Infantry, Company F, paroled at Meridian, Miss., May 10, 1865. Booth, *Records of Louisiana,* 1:82.
44. Taylor was in desperate need of men. When Smith removed three divisions from him, the Louisiana forces consisted of the mangled Louisiana Division and the Texas Cavalry Corps, both without their original leaders.
45. This is another indication that the telegraph line was still running or there was some other means of rapid courier network in operation. Brig. Gen. John Marmaduke's forces destroyed Steele's supply column at Poison Spring on April 18.
46. This rumor was totally false.
47. This was the battle of Poison Spring mentioned above. King's information is very accurate.
48. Banks and his army were still at Grand Ecore and would not begin to move until April 21, and then south not east.
49. The news from Grand Ecore was accurate. The Confederates had taken control of both that port and the town of Natchitoches. The rumor about Camden was false.

50. The rear guard of Banks' column did burn the buildings at Grand Ecore. They were prevented from torching Natchitoches by the arrival of Confederate cavalry.
51. This was the rear guard action at Grand Ecore. The casualty figure was exaggerated.
52. Although the figures are somewhat exaggerated, the Battle of Mark's Mill, fought on April 25, was devastating to Steele. Upon receiving word of the disaster, he retreated from Camden on April 26.
53. The news King heard was probably from Kirby Smith's headquarters. Smith was enamored with Sterling Price and always praised him highly. Actually Price did very little to help the Confederate's cause in this campaign and created several tight predicaments for them. The most adept leader in the Arkansas portion of the campaign was Brig. Gen. John Marmaduke.
54. This is Capt. Joseph Lee Smith Kirby. He was Kirby Smith's first cousin, the son of his mother Frances's brother, Reynold Marvin Kirby. Kirby Smith brought three first cousins into the Confederacy with him. See Joseph Howard Parks, *General Edmund Kirby Smith, C.S.A.* (Baton Rouge: Louisiana State Univ. Press, 1954), 19, 108, 123.
55. Pontooneers were troops that handled wagon-born portable pontoon bridges for river crossings.
56. Dover's Powders were an anodyne diaphoretic. The compound was created by a Dr. Dover, an English physician. The powder contained ipecac and opium, compounded, in the United States, with sugar of milk, but in England (as formerly in the United States) with sulphate of potash, and in France (as in Dr. Dover's original prescription) with nitrate and sulphate of potash and licorice. During the 1860s the compound could be any of the above, depending on the medical education of the person prescribing and formulating it.
57. King may be referring to the Battle of Jenkins Ferry on April 29. Steele did retreat from the Saline River, but Confederate losses due to an ill-conceived battle plan by Kirby Smith were very high. The Texas Division lost two of its three brigade commanders.
58. King is describing movements by the Army of Northern Virginia prior to the battles of the Wilderness and Spotsylvania.
59. This refers to the Battle of Jenkins Ferry.
60. This was incorrect. The pontoon bridges that Kirby Smith needed were in Shreveport in King's unit. Smith was unable to pursue Steele past the Saline River. Realizing that further operations were futile, Smith released the three divisions he had commandeered back to Taylor on May 3. They were not able to reach Taylor's command in time to trap Banks's army.
61. Confederate casualties were listed as 800 to 1,000 killed, wounded, or missing. Union casualties were approximately 700 killed, wounded, or missing. See *O.R.*, vol. 34, pt. 1, pp. 557, 758. See also Joiner, *One Damn Blunder*, 131–35.
62. Brig. Gen. William Scurry and Brig. Gen. Horace Randal were brigade commanders in Walker's Texas Division.
63. The prisoners were routed through Shreveport on the way to Camp Ford in Tyler, Texas.

64. No vessel by this name is listed in *Way's Packet Directory.*
65. Campti is located in Natchitoches Parish. The train was a supply train of wagons, not a railroad train.
66. *Caddo Gazette Extra,* May 10, 1864.
67. The Confederates launched an unsuccessful attack to retake New Bern, North Carolina, on May 5.
68. Loggy Bayou is an outflow of Lake Bistineau and serves as the southern boundary of Bossier Parish.
69. The side-wheel packet *New Falls City* was built in Paducah, Kentucky, in 1860. It had a length of 301.3 feet, a width (beam) of 39.7 feet, and had a draught of 7.6 feet. It weighed 880 tons. In 1862 the vessel was owned by Captains Henry Switzer, James B. Woods, William J. Lewis, and Archie Woods. It was part of the Confederate defense fleet and anchored in the mouth of Coushatta Chute (Bayou Coushatta). On March 18, 1864, Kirby Smith ordered it to be brought to the foot of Scopini Cut-off and sunk to halt the progress of the Union fleet. See Joiner, *One Damn Blunder,* 22–26; *O.R.,* vol. 34, pt. 2, pp. 1056–57. It is listed as vessel number 4166 in Way, *Way's Packet Directory,* 344.
70. The side-wheel packet *Osceola* was built in Louisville, Kentucky, in 1858. It weighed fifty-eight tons. Dimensions are unknown. The vessel entered Confederate registry in 1861 and operated on the New Orleans to Jefferson, Texas, and upper Red River route. F. L. Woodridge reported that the vessel was sent to Mobile after the war. This may be in error, or the vessel may have been raised and repaired after King saw it. It is listed as vessel number 4340 in Way, *Way's Packet Directory,* 358.
71. The side-wheel packet *Countess* was built in Cincinnati, Ohio, in 1860. It had a length of 150 feet, a width (beam) of 30 feet, and a draught of 4.8 feet. The vessel was owned by Capt. William C. Harrison and captained by a man named Wilson. The vessel operated in Confederate service, probably under contract during the Civil War. *Way's Packet Directory* incorrectly states that it was lost on the falls at Alexandria while fleeing Porter's fleet in April 1864. Besides King's spotting of the boat, it is mentioned after April 1864 in *O.R.,* vol. 48, pt. 1, p. 402 (being in Shreveport in April 1865) and again in *O.R.,* ser. 2, vol. 8, pt. 1, p. 59 (as the flag-of-truce bearing vessel in January 1865). It is listed as vessel number 1348 in Way, *Way's Packet Directory,* 113.
72. Campti was torched on April 4 during the navy's movement toward Shreveport from Grand Ecore.
73. The guard of the boat was the walkway around portions of the upper hull. If the vessel were a transport, the guards could be extended several feet to create more deck space. The case of the *R. Blanton,* a stern-wheeler, the guards would extend almost the length of each side of the vessel.
74. Campti.
75. This vessel is not listed in *Way's Packet Directory.*
76. The first of Banks's troops left Alexandria at 7 A.M., May 13.
77. This was incorrect.
78. This was another incorrect rumor. Banks was reinforced in Alexandria, but they were not attacked.

79. King is referring to the sinking of the transport *Emma* at David's Ferry (near Echo in Rapides Parish) on May 1; the sinking of the transport *City Belle,* also at David's Ferry, on May 4; and the sinking of the gunboats *John Warner, Signal,* and *Covington* at Dunn's Bayou on May 5.
80. This was a Kouns Line steamer, although it is difficult to prove that it was, in fact, the *Era No. 7.* There were at least fourteen side- and stern-wheelers named *Era* in the Kouns Line. *Era No. 7* supposedly sank on February 24, 1863, twenty miles below Warrenton, Mississippi. The vessel did run the New Orleans to Red River route and the Ouachita River to Camden, Arkansas, route. Civil War–era steamboat records, particularly west of the Mississippi River, are difficult to reconstruct at best. If this was the *Era No. 7,* it was built in Freedom, Pennsylvania, in 1859. It is listed as vessel number 1891 in Way, *Way's Packet Directory,* 154.
81. Federal troops torched large portions of Alexandria on May 13.
82. Union troops burned Grand Ecore on April 21.
83. These were the survivors of the *John Warner, Signal,* and *Covington* being moved to Camp Ford.
84. This was the same action from May 1, 4, and 5.
85. St. Maurice in Natchitoches Parish.
86. King is describing Cane River Creoles. See Gary B. Mills, *The Forgotten People: Cane River's Creoles of Color* (Baton Rouge: Louisiana State Univ. Press, 1977).
87. King wrote that Union forces reached Simmesport near the mouth of the Red River. The column was plagued by high water from the Atchafalaya River and did not exit until May 19–20.
88. There is no vessel by this name in *Way's Packet Directory.* It is also unclear whether or not King is referring to the *R. Blanton.*
89. Walker's Division was ordered to the mouth of the Red River to support Taylor when the Confederates believed the high water would assist them in trapping the Union troops. Walker did not reach Simmesport in time.
90. Although not a certainty, this vessel may be the side-wheeler *Trenton,* built in Monongahela, Pennsylvania, in 1851. It had a length of 122.3 feet, a width (beam) of 24 feet, and had a draught of 5.3 feet. The vessel ran the New Orleans to Ouachita River route. Although the vessel was off the lists by 1857, it is the only vessel that closely matches King's mention. It is listed as vessel number 5445 in Way, *Way's Packet Directory,* 459.
91. *Dum vivimus, vivamus* (While we live, let us live).
92. The Scopini cut-off played a major role in the Confederate defenses protecting Shreveport. It was a narrow channel cut in 1859 across the base of a large meander in the Red River. The Confederates built a dam at the western end of the bend of the former riverbed. An ancient crossover shunt called Tone's Bayou connected the former channel with Bayou Pierre, another ancient bed of the Red River. The Confederates planted black powder in the dam when the Union gunboats were at Alexandria and destroyed the structure, thus sending about 75 percent of the river's flow into Bayou Pierre. The maneuver almost trapped the Union flotilla. The fact that King wrote this passage on May 24 illustrates how quickly the Rebels repaired the dam and restored navigation on the river by their own vessels. The Tone's

Bayou works were defended by two forts that were all but impossible to see from the river. The Confederates took great care to keep their engineering feat a secret. King apparently did not see any of this and made no comment. The cut-off through which the *Blanchard* navigated was quite narrow and the current through it was treacherous.

93. King is describing what he has heard of the Battle of Hanover Junction and the North Anna River.
94. The Battle of Yellow Bayou, the last engagement of the Red River Campaign, was fought on May 18.
95. Confederate losses were 608 men killed, wounded, and missing. For a description of the Battle of Yellow Bayou see *O.R.*, vol. 34, pt. 1, pp. 304, 320, 329, 337, 347–48, 357, 364, 367, 370, 467, 594, 624, 631; Taylor, *Destruction and Reconstruction,* 191; Joiner, *One Damn Blunder,* 171–72.
96. *Caddo Gazette Extra,* May 30, 1864.
97. King means *desideratum,* or something desired as a necessity.
98. Taylor was removed from command on June 10, 1864, after a series of harsh communications with Kirby Smith. See *O.R.*, vol. 34, pt. 1, pp. 538–48. Also on June 10, the Confederate Congress passed a joint resolution of thanks to Taylor citing his "brilliant successes" at the twin battles of Mansfield and Pleasant Hill. See *O.R.*, vol. 34, pt. 1, p. 597. On August 15, Taylor was promoted to the rank of lieutenant general and ordered to take command of the Department of Alabama, Mississippi, and East Louisiana. See *O.R.*, vol. 39, pt. 2, p. 777. The District of Western Louisiana included all of the state except that portion lying east of the Mississippi River and north of Lake Pontchartrain. That area, called the Florida Parishes, formed part of the Department of Alabama, Mississippi, and East Louisiana. King's view is very much in the minority among both participants in the Red River Campaign and historians who have studied it. For another minority view on Taylor, see *O.R.*, vol. 34, pp. 550–60. This is a letter from Lt. Edward Cunningham, aide-de-camp to Lt. Gen. Edmund Kirby Smith and chief of artillery at Shreveport to his uncle Richard Cunningham in Virginia.
99. *Caddo Gazette Extra,* June 22, 1864.
100. John Morgan and his raiders were operating in Kentucky and were harassing the towns of Mt. Sterling, Lexington, Georgetown, and Frankfort during June.
101. *Caddo Gazette Extra,* June 23, 1864. This is unclear, but King may be describing the initial investment of Petersburg, Virginia.
102. The Union forces were at Tupelo, but no action had occurred there at that time.
103. These were false rumors.
104. Both generals died in combat, leading their brigades from the front at the Battle of Jenkins' Ferry.
105. Consolidated Crescent Infantry Regiment.
106. Excessive discharge of liquid from a cavity or organ, as in watery diarrhea.
107. Calomel is mercurous oxide, a white tasteless compound used as a fungicide and occasionally in medicine as a purgative.
108. As U.S. Grant's campaign against Robert E. Lee progressed, the rumors in the Trans-Mississippi became more fantastic. Although he reported what he heard,

King began to exhibit a note of healthy skepticism. No further mention will be made regarding the truth of rumors unless the statements were corroborated or the rumors affected King.

109. Wild Indigo (*Baptisia tinctoria*) is an herbaceous perennial principally used for its antiseptic qualities.
110. As with most, this is a false rumor.
111. *Caddo Gazette Extra*, July 26, 1864.
112. This is Confederate Lt. Gen. John Bell Hood.
113. This is the Battle of Ezra Church.
114. It is unclear to what King is referring. It may be a composite of remnants of the 24th and 25th Texas cavalry regiments that were formed into Kirby Smith's bodyguard. This body was actually a large company. Personal communication with Steve Bounds, site manager of Mansfield State Historic Site, Mansfield, La., July 1, 2004.
115. Fort Morgan was captured by Union forces on August 23, 1864.
116. Confederate Maj. Gen. Nathan Bedford Forrest briefly seized Memphis on August 21, 1864.
117. General Order, Aug. 4, 1864. See *O.R.*, vol. 41, pt. 2, p. 1039.
118. Brig. Gen. William R. Boggs, chief of staff.
119. This refers to Clement Larid Vallandigham and Gov. Horatio Seymour, both of New York and harsh critics of Abraham Lincoln. The rumor was false.
120. King means George Brinton McClellan of Pennsylvania as the presidential candidate and George Hunt Pendleton of Ohio as the vice presidential candidate on the Democratic Party ticket in the 1864 elections.
121. Former Maj. Gen. George B. McClellan, the democratic nominee for the Union presidency.
122. The Confederates evacuated Atlanta on September 1 and Federal troops entered the city on September 1 and 2.

8. Arkansas

1. Noon.
2. This route is necessary because, as King reported on June 28, "Red River was rising yesterday." The rising of the Red River actually flooded the Red Chute Flats east of the current Bossier City. This made passage due east impossible. His unit took the next best route, which was longer but not flooded.
3. This is the wagon supply train containing the unit's pontoon bridge components, engineering equipment, food, blankets, and everything needed for the march.
4. Bayou Dorcheat.
5. Monticello is the county seat of Drew County, Arkansas.
6. Longview in Ashley County, Arkansas.
7. Warren is the county seat for Bradley County, Arkansas.
8. This is Confederate Maj. Gen. John Horace Forney, who succeeded Maj. Gen. John G. Walker and was commander of the Texas Division. Forney had been peri-

odically under Kirby Smith's command since the first Battle of Manassas. Smith appears to have fostered Forney's career.

9. Prairie De Ann (or D'Ane) in Nevada County, Arkansas.
10. County seat.
11. There was a Federal expedition aimed at Monticello, Arkansas, beginning September 9, 1864.
12. King probably means the Bradley Ferry over the Ouachita River, just outside Camden.
13. Petersburg did not fall until the following April.
14. This was the execution of Capt. John Guynes of Company F, 22nd Texas Infantry Regiment, on October 12, 1864. Maj. Gen. John B. Magruder ordered all four of his divisions commanded by Polignac, Parsons, Churchill, and Forney (Walker's division) to witness the execution. The offense was mutiny when attempting to cross the Mississippi River. See J. P. Blessington, *The Campaigns of Walker's Texas Division* (Austin: State House Press, 1994), 279; Arthur Bergeron, *The Civil War Reminiscences of Major Silas T. Grisamore, C.S.A.* (Baton Rouge: Louisiana State Univ. Press, 1993), 173; Richard Lowe, *Walker's Texas Division, C.S.A.: Greyhounds of the Trans-Mississippi* (Baton Rouge: Louisiana State Univ. Press, 2004), 245.
15. This refers to Confederate Maj. Gen. Sterling Price's ill-fated Missouri expedition. Price was near Jefferson City on October 9 but did not take the city.
16. Dalton, Georgia, surrendered to the Confederates on October 13.
17. An artificer is an enlisted man responsible for the upkeep of small arms.
18. Gabriel Davy King.
19. This was a false rumor.
20. Confederate Brig. Gen. William Lewis Cabell was captured on Price's raid into Missouri in October. He was not killed or wounded. After the war Cabell served as mayor of Dallas, Texas, for four terms. Brig. Gen. John Sappington Marmaduke was captured at Mine Creek in Kansas as part of Price's Missouri raid. He was not wounded in this action. After the war Marmaduke was elected governor of Missouri in 1884.
21. Cane Hill in Washington County, Arkansas.
22. Maj. Gen. James Fleming Fagan.
23. Tulip in Dallas County, Arkansas.
24. Boggy Depot was located in south central Oklahoma in southeastern Atoka County.
25. *Washington Telegraph,* Nov. 26, 1864.
26. City Point, Virginia, was a huge depot for the Union. It was located at the confluence of the James and Appomattox rivers.
27. This is a term for people who simply hoped for an end to the fighting in the Civil War.
20. This is a reference to Union Maj. Gen. Phillip Sheridan's campaign of utter destruction in the Shenandoah Valley in late 1864. Many of the units in his army were from the XIX Corps that fought in the Red River Campaign in the previous months.
29. Beaufort is the county seat of Beaufort County, South Carolina.
30. Augusta is the county seat of Columbia County, Georgia.

31. Marshall is the county seat of Harrison County, Texas. It is located about forty miles west of Shreveport and hosts a number of war-related industries.
32. Union Maj. Gen. William T. Sherman occupied Savannah, Georgia, on December 21, 1864.
33. The Battle of Nashville was fought December 15–16, 1864.

Epilogue

1. W. H. King, sergeant, Company H, 4th Engineer Troops. Rolls of Prisoners of War, paroled Shreveport, La., June 13, 1865. Resident of Bossier Parish, La. See Booth, *Records of Louisiana,* 2:571; Compiled Service Records of Confederate Soldiers Who Served in Organizations from the State of Louisiana, Microscopy No. 320, Reel 349, National Archives and Records Administration, Washington, D.C.
2. *Supplement to the Official Records of the Union and Confederate Armies, Part II—Record of Events,* vol. 73, serial no. 85 (Wilmington, N.C.: Broadfoot Publishing Co., 1998), 614–19.
3. Ibid., 615.
4. Ibid., 618–19.
5. Ibid., 618.
6. This is Capt. Joseph Lee Smith Kirby. He was Kirby Smith's first cousin, the son of his mother, Frances's brother, Reynold Marvin Kirby. Kirby Smith brought three first cousins into the Confederacy with him. See Parks, *General Edmund Kirby Smith, C.S.A.,* 19, 108, 123.
7. *O.R.,* vol. 34, pt. 4, p. 664.
8. Richard Lowe, *Walker's Texas Division C.S.A.: Greyhounds of the Trans-Mississippi* (Baton Rouge: Louisiana State Univ. Press, 2004), 235–42.
9. Ibid., 248–49.
10. Ibid., 253–56.
11. Winters, *Civil War in Louisiana* (Baton Rouge: Louisiana State Univ. Press, 1963), 422–23. Bearss and Tunnard, *A Southern Record,* 335–37.
12. *O.R.,* vol. 48, pt. 1, 193–94; Winters, *Civil War in Louisiana,* 425.
13. Winters, *Civil War in Louisiana,* 426.
14. Ibid., 427.
15. Parole dates of many Confederate soldiers are contained in the *Confederate Research Sources* database, accessible through the Web site Ancestry.com.

Appendix 2

1. See the King diary entry for April 1, 1864.
2. This song is based on the tune "Wait for the Wagon," a popular song of the 1850s that was composed by R. Bishop Buckley, a member of a minstrel group. The melody was used for this and other songs during the Civil War.
3. "Maryland, My Maryland" was written by American journalist and poet James Ryder Randall. He was born in Baltimore in 1839 and attended Georgetown

University. He was teaching in Pointe Coupee, Louisiana, in 1861 when he heard that Federal troops had been fired on in his hometown of Baltimore and that a close friend had been killed in the fighting. His anger led him to write "Maryland, My Maryland." The poem was first published in the *New Orleans Sunday Delta.* In Maryland it was set to the music of a familiar German Christmas carol, "O Tannenbaum," and it became popular in that state and throughout the South. It was adopted as Maryland's state song in 1939. A bill was introduced in the Maryland House of Delegates in 2001 to replace it as the state's song, but the bill received an unfavorable report in committee.

4. Severn Teakle Wallis (1831–91) was a political reformer and member of the Maryland legislature. An influential lawyer in Baltimore, Wallis was a member of the Royal Academy of History of Madrid, Spain, and a fellow in the Royal Society of Northern Antiquities of Copenhagen, Denmark. He was involved in active protest against the passage of Civil War troops through the city of Baltimore, an action that brought about his arrest and fourteen months imprisonment. He was a cofounder of the Maryland Historical Society in 1844 as well as a charter member of the Board of Trustees of the Peabody Institute in 1980. He served as president of each of these organizations.
5. William Gilmore Simms (1806–70) was born in Charleston, South Carolina. Although he had planned to become a doctor and ultimately studied law, he chose the path of writer. He was editor and part owner of the *Charleston City Gazette,* where his writing opposed the doctrines of nullification. The newspaper failed. He then became an outstanding Southern novelist.

Appendix 3

1. *O.R.,* vol. 26, pt. 2, p. 251.

Selected Bibliography

Manuscript Collections

Allen, N. S., Papers. Archives and Special Collections, Noel Memorial Library, Louisiana State Univ., Shreveport.

Brock, Eric. "A Necropolis of Graves at Oakland Cemetery." Eric Brock Papers. Archives and Special Collections, Noel Memorial Library, Louisiana State Univ., Shreveport.

Cardin Collection. Bossier History Center, Bossier City, La.

Carter, Jonathan H. "Correspondence Book." MS, National Archives and Records Administration, Washington, D.C.

Dearman, Scott. "Order of Battle of the Confederate Army at the Battle of Mansfield, Louisiana. Major General Richard Taylor, April 8, 1864." Compiled by Park Historian Scott Dearman, Mansfield State Historic Site, Mansfield, La., n.d.

Fowler, W. S. "Medical Register, 1863–1865." Archives, Univ. of Texas, Austin.

Fullilove, Mrs. [Elizabeth] Thomas Pope. Journal, 1915. Copy in the private collection of Bill Stephenson, Shreveport, La.

Fullilove, Tom. Confederate diary, 1862–65. In the private collection of William Lane Stephenson, Shreveport, La.

King Family Bible. In the private collection of Shirley Hampton, Fort Worth, Tex.
King, William Henry. Diary. Texas State Archives, Austin.
Knapp, Julius L. Diary, Company I, 116th New York Volunteer Infantry Regiment, January to December 1864. In the private collection of Jim Sandefur, Shreveport, La.
Knox, R. A. Letter, 2nd Texas Cavalry, 1864. In the private collection of Jim Sandefur, Shreveport, La.
Leonard, Albert Harris. "Memoirs." MS, Archives of Eugene P. Watson Memorial Library, Northwestern State Univ., Natchitoches, La.
Louisiana Division of Archaeology. Submissions for the National Register of Historic Places for Forts Randolph and Buhlow. Archives of the Division of Archaeology, State of Louisiana, Baton Rouge.
Marston, James. Family diary. In the private collection of James Marston, Shreveport, La.
McClung, R. L. "Three Years in the C.S. Army (P.A.C.S.)." TS, Mansfield State Historic Site, Mansfield, La.
Shackelford, Ellen. Papers. Southern Historical Collection, Univ. of North Carolina, Chapel Hill.
Spyker, Leonidas Polk. Diary. Archives and Special Collections, Noel Memorial Library, Louisiana State Univ., Shreveport.

Government Documents

National Archives and Records Administration. Navy Yard documents, Shreveport, Confederate Navy Subject File, RG 45, Washington, D.C.
State of Louisiana. Bossier Parish Conveyance Records, 1865.
———. Bossier Parish Marriage Records, 1859.
———. Bossier Parish Police Jury Records, 1859–63.
———. Bossier Parish Probate Records, 1862, 1867.
———. Caddo Parish Assessor's Office Records, block 45, lots 11, 12.
———. *Official Report to the Conduct of Federal Troops in Western Louisiana, during the Invasions of 1863 and 1864, Compiled from Sworn Testimony under Direction of Governor Henry Watkins Allen.* Shreveport: Confederate State of Louisiana, 1865.
State of Texas. Montague County Divorce Records, 1899.
———. Rusk County Marriage Records, 1854.
———. Shelby County Marriage Records, 1886.
U.S. Congress. *Report on the Joint Committee on the Conduct of the War, 1863–1866.* Vol. 2, *Red River Expedition.* Millwood, N.Y.: Krauss Reprint, 1977.
U.S. Dept. of Commerce. 7th Decennial Census (1850). Caddo Parish and Bossier Parish, La. Unpublished tabulations in the National Archives and Records Administration, Washington, D.C.
———. 7th Decennial Census (1850). Madison County, Ala. Unpublished tabulations in the National Archives and Records Administration, Washington, D.C.
———. 8th Decennial Census (1860). Caddo Parish and Bossier Parish, La. Unpublished tabulations in the National Archives and Records Administration, Washington, D.C.
———. 8th Decennial Census (1860). Madison County, Ala. Unpublished tabulations in the National Archives and Records Administration, Washington, D.C.

———. 8th Decennial Census (1860). Shelby County, Tex. Unpublished tabulations in the National Archives and Records Administration, Washington, D.C.
———.9th Decennial Census (1870). Shelby County, Tex. Unpublished tabulations in the National Archives and Records Administration, Washington, D.C.
———. 11th Decennial Census (1890). Montague County, Tex. Unpublished tabulations in the National Archives and Records Administration, Washington, D.C.
U.S. War Dept. *Atlas to Accompany the Official Records of the Union and Confederate Armies.* Washington, D.C.: Government Printing Office, 1891–95.
———. *Official Records of the Union and Confederate Navies in the War of the Rebellion.* 31 vols. Washington, D.C.: Government Printing Office, 1895–1929.
———. *War of the Rebellion: The Official Records of the Union and Confederate Armies.* 128 vols. Washington, D.C.: Government Printing Office, 1890–1901.

Maps

Bossier Parish, Louisiana, map. RG 77, folio Z-33-9, Records of the Office of the Chief of Engineers, U.S. National Archives and Records Administration, Washington, D.C.
Clark, John. Map No. 8 of the Red River Campaign. John Clark Collection, Cayuga County Museum, Auburn, N.Y.
———. Map of Fort DeRussy. John Clark Collection, Cayuga County Museum, Auburn, N.Y.
Hunter Collection. Watson Library Research Center, Northwestern State Univ., Natchitoches.
LaTourette Map (c. 1850). RG 77, folio M72, National Archives and Records Administration, Washington, D.C.
Lavender Soil Map (1906). Archives and Special Collections, Noel Memorial Library, Louisiana State Univ., Shreveport.
Morse, George. Survey Map (1842). Louisiana Dept. of State Lands, Baton Rouge.
St. Mary Parish, Louisiana, map. RG 77, folio Z-33, Records of the Office of the Chief of Engineers, U.S. National Archives and Records Administration, Washington, D.C.
U.S. Army Corps of Engineers. *Red River Index, ARK.–TEX, to Mississippi River, Index of 1990 Mosaics.* Vicksburg, Miss.: U.S. Army Engineer District, 1990.
U.S. Army Topographic Engineers. RG 77, folio M103-1 and M103-2, National Archives and Records Administration, Washington, D.C.
Venable, Maj. Richard, C.S.A. "Shreveport and Environs," 1864. Jerome Gilmer Papers, Southern Historical Collection, Univ. of North Carolina, Chapel Hill.

Contemporary Newspapers and Periodicals

Bossier Banner, May 6, 1862
Caddo Gazette, January 17, 1863
Caddo Gazette, November 20, 1863
Caddo Gazette, December 18, 1863
Caddo Gazette, February 12, 1864

Caddo Gazette Extra, December 9, 1863
Caddo Gazette Extra, December 12, 1863
Caddo Gazette Extra, December 14, 1863
Caddo Gazette Extra, December 23, 1863
Caddo Gazette Extra, May 10, 1864
Caddo Gazette Extra, May 30, 1864
Caddo Gazette Extra, June 23, 1864
Caddo Gazette Extra, June 24, 1864
Caddo Gazette Extra, July 26, 1864
Harrison Flag (Marshall, Texas), March 16, 1860
Memphis Appeal, October 9, 1862
Monroe Register (Monroe, Louisiana), June 3, 1826
Shreveport Semi Weekly News, May 4, 1863
Shreveport Semi Weekly News, May 25, 1863
Shreveport Semi Weekly News, December 18, 1863
Shreveport Semi Weekly News, December 25, 1863
Shreveport Semi Weekly News, January 15, 1864
Shreveport Semi Weekly News, February 2, 1864
Shreveport Semi Weekly News, February 16, 1864
Shreveport Semi Weekly News, March 29, 1864
Shreveport South Western, December 10, 1863
Shreveport South Western, January 6, 1864
The Era (New Orleans), April 28, 1863
Vicksburg Whig, October 11, 1862
Washington Telegraph (Washington, Arkansas), February 20, 1864
Washington Telegraph, November 26, 1864

Books and Articles

Alexander, William Lee. "An Appraisal of the 1862 New Mexico Campaign: A Confederate Officer's Letter to Nacogdoches." Ed. Martin Hardwick Hall. *New Mexico Historical Review* 52 (Oct. 1976): 329–35.

Ambrose, Stephen E. *Halleck: Lincoln's Chief of Staff.* Baton Rouge: Louisiana State Univ. Press, 1962.

Anders, Curt. *Disaster in Damp Sand: The Red River Expedition.* Carmel, Ind.: Guild Press of Indiana, 1997.

Anderson, Charles G. *Confederate General William R. "Dirty Neck Bill" Scurry, 1821–1864.* Snyder, Tex.: Snyder Publishing Co., 1999.

Anderson, John Q., ed. *Campaigning with Parsons' Texas Brigade, CSA: The War Journals and Letters of the Four Orr Brothers, 12th Texas Cavalry Regiment.* Hillsboro, Tex.: Hill Junior College Press, 1967.

Andrews, J. Cutler. *The North Reports the Civil War.* Pittsburgh: Univ. of Pittsburgh Press, 1983.

Arceneaux, William. *Acadian General: Alfred Mouton and the Civil War.* Lafayette: Center for Louisiana Studies, Univ. of Southwestern Louisiana, 1981.

Arkansas Adjutant General's Office. *Report of the Adjutant General of Arkansas for the Period of the Late Rebellion, and to November 1, 1866.* Washington, D.C.: Government Printing Office, 1867.

Bacon, Edward. *Among the Cotton Thieves.* Detroit: Free Press Steam Book and Job Printing House, 1867. Reprint, Bossier City, La.: Everett Companies, 1989.

Bailey, Anne J. *Between the Enemy and Texas: Parson's Texas Cavalry in the Civil War.* Fort Worth: Texas Christian Univ. Press, 1989.

———. "Chasing Banks Out of Louisiana: Parsons' Texas Cavalry in the Red River Campaign." *Civil War Regiments* 3, no.1 (1993): 212–35.

———. *Texans in the Confederate Cavalry.* Fort Worth: Ryan Place Publications, 1995.

Bankston, Mary L. B. *Camp-Fire Stories of the Mississippi Valley Campaign.* New Orleans: L. Graham Co. Publishers, 1914.

Bartlett, Napier. *Military Record of Louisiana: Including Biographical and Historical Papers Relating to the Military Organization of the State.* New Orleans: L. Graham and Co., 1875.

Bearss, Edwin C. *Steele's Retreat from Camden and the Battle of Jenkins Ferry.* Little Rock: Eagle Press of Little Rock, 1990.

Bearss, Edwin C., and William Tunnard. *A Southern Record: The Story of the 3rd Louisiana Infantry, C.S.A.* Dayton, Ohio: Morningside Bookshop, 1988.

Bearss, Edwin C., and William H. Tunnard. *A Southern Record: The Story of the 3rd Louisiana Infantry, C.S.A.* Dayton, Ohio: Morningside Press, 1988.

Bergeron, Arthur W., Jr. *The Civil War Reminiscences of Major Silas T. Grisamore, C.S.A.* Baton Rouge: Louisiana State Univ. Press, 1993.

———. "A Colonel Gains His Wreath: Henry Gray's Louisiana Brigade at the Battle of Mansfield, April 8, 1864." *Civil War Regiments* 4, no. 2 (1994): 1–25.

———. "General Richard Taylor as a Military Commander." *Louisiana History* 23 (Winter 1982): 35–47.

———. *A Guide to Confederate Military Units, 1861–1865.* Baton Rouge: Louisiana State Univ. Press, 1989.

Biographical and Historical Memoirs of Northwest Louisiana. Chicago: Southern Co., 1890.

Blanton, DeAnne, and Lauren M. Cook. *They Fought Like Demons: Women Soldiers in the American Civil War.* Baton Rouge: Louisiana State Univ. Press, 2002.

Blessington, J. P. *The Campaigns of Walker's Texas Division.* Austin: State House Press, 1994.

Boggs, William R. *Military Reminiscences of Gen. Wm. R. Boggs, C.S.A.* Durham, N.C.: Seeman Printery, 1913.

Booth, Andrew, ed. *Records of Louisiana Confederate Soldier and Louisiana Confederate Commands.* 3 vols. Baton Rouge: Commissioner, Louisiana Military Records, 1920.

Bounds, Steve, and Curtis Milbourn. "The Battle of Mansfield." *North and South* 6, no. 2 (Feb. 2003): 26–40.

Boyd, D. F. "General Richard Taylor, C.S.A." *Confederate Veteran* Vol. 36 (Dec. 1928), 412–13.

Bridges, Joyce Shannon Bridges, ed. *Biographical and Historical Memoirs of Northwest Louisiana.* Nashville: Southern Printing Co., 1890.

Britton, Wiley. *The Civil War on the Border: A Narrative of Operations in Missouri, Kansas, Arkansas and the Indian Territory during the Years 1861–62.* 2 vols. New York: Putnam's, 1890–99.

———. "Resume of Military Operations in Missouri and Arkansas, 1864–65." In *Battles and Leaders of the Civil War.* Vol. 4. New York: Yoseloff, 1956. 374–75.

———. "Union and Confederate Indians in the Civil War." In *Battles and Leaders of the Civil War.* Vol. 1. New York: Yoseloff, 1956. 335–38.

———. *The Union Indian Brigade in the Civil War.* Kansas City, Mo.: Franklin Hudson, 1922.

Brock, Eric, and Gary D. Joiner. *Red River Steamboats.* Charleston: Arcadia, 1999.

Brooksher, William Riley. *War along the Bayous: The 1864 Red River Campaign in Louisiana.* Washington: Brassey's, 1998.

Burgess, Lauren Cook. *An Uncommon Soldier: The Civil War Letters of Sarah Rosetta Wakeman, Alias Pvt. Lyons Wakeman, 153rd Regiment, New York State Volunteers, 1862–1864.* Pasadena, Md.: Minerva Center, 1994.

Cade, Edward W. *A Texas Surgeon in the C.S.A.* Ed. John Q. Anderson. Tuscaloosa, Ala.: Confederate Publishing Co., 1957.

Cardin, Clifton D. *Bossier Parish History: The First 150 Years, 1843–1993.* Shreveport, La.: Aero Press, 1993.

Casdorph, Paul D. *Prince John Magruder: His Life and Campaigns.* New York: John Wiley & Sons, 1996.

Castell, Albert. *General Sterling Price and the Civil War in the Wes*t. Baton Rouge: Louisiana State Univ. Press, 1968.

Christ, Mark K., ed. *Rugged and Sublime: The Civil War in Arkansas.* Fayetteville: Univ. of Arkansas Press, 1994.

Coastal Environments. *Houma Navigation Canal Deepening Project Terrebonne Parish, Louisiana: Cultural Resources Literature Search, Records Review and Research Design.* Draft Report prepared by Coastal Environments, Inc., for the U.S. Army Corps of Engineers, New Orleans District, Dec. 2003.

Craig, William J. *West of the Mississippi with Waller's 13th Texas Cavalry Battalion, CSA.* Comp. and ed. Charles Spurlin. Hillsboro, Tex.: Hill Junior College Press, 1971.

Crute, Joseph H., Jr. *Units of the Confederate States Army.* Midlothian, Va.: Derwent Books, 1987.

Debray, Xavier Blanchard. "A Sketch of Debray's Twenty-Sixth Regiment of Texas Cavalry." *Southern Historical Society Papers* 13 (1885): 153–65.

———. *A Sketch of the History of Debray's (26th) Regiment of Texas Cavalry.* Austin: Eugene von Boeckmann, 1884. Reprint, Waco: Village Press, 1961.

DeSoto Parish History: Sesquicentennial Edition, 1843–1993. Mansfield, La.: DeSoto Parish Historical Society, 1995.

Dimitry, John. *Louisiana.* Vol. 10 of *Confederate Military History,* ed. Clement A. Evans. Atlanta: n.p., 1899.

Division of Engineers. *Red River and Tributaries, Louisiana, Arkansas, Oklahoma, Texas. Interim Review of Reports with Respect to Improvement of Navigation (1945).* Vicksburg District, U.S. Army Corps of Engineers, Vicksburg, Miss.

Dollar, Susan E. "The Red River Campaign, Natchitoches Parish, Louisiana: A Case of Equal Opportunity Destruction." *Louisiana History* 43, no. 4 (2002): 411–32.

Dorsey, Sarah H. *Recollections of Henry Watkins Allen, Brigadier General Confederate State Army, Ex-Governor of Louisiana.* New York: M. Doolady, 1866.

Dunnavent, R. Blake. *Brown Water Warfare: The U.S. Navy in Riverine Warfare and the Emergence of a Tactical Doctrine, 1775–1970.* Gainesville: Univ. of Florida Press, 2003.

Dyer, Frederick H. *A Compendium of the War of the Rebellion.* 3 vols. Dayton, Ohio: Morningside, 1979.

Edmonds, David C. *The Conduct of Federal Troops in Louisiana during the Invasions of 1863 and 1864: Official Report compiled from Sworn Testimony under the Direction of Governor Henry W. Allen, Shreveport, April, 1865.* Lafayette: Acadiana Press, 1988.

Edwards, John N. *Shelby and His Men; or, The War in the West.* Cincinnati: Miami Printing and Publishing Co., 1867.

Estaville, Lawrence E., Jr. *Confederate Neckties: Louisiana Railroads in the Civil War.* Ruston, La.: McGinty Publications, 1989.

Evans, Clement A., ed. *Confederate Military History.* Extended ed. Vols. 12 (Missouri), 13 (Louisiana), 14 (Arkansas), 15 (Texas). Wilmington, N.C.: Broadfoot, 1989.

Fearn, Francis, ed. *Diary of a Refugee.* New York: n.p., 1910.

Fitzhugh, Lester N. *Texas Batteries, Battalions, Regiments, Commanders and Field Officers, Confederate States Army, 1861–1865.* Midlothian, Tex.: Mirror Press, 1959.

———. "Texas Forces in the Red River Campaign." *Texas Military History* 3 (Spring 1963): 15–22.

Foote, Shelby. *The Civil War: A Narrative.* Vol. 1, *Fort Sumter to Perryville.* New York: Random House, 1958.

Fordyce, Benjamin A. *Dr. Benjamin A. Fordyce Echoes: From the Letters of A Civil War Surgeon.* Ed. Lydia P. Hecht. Houston: Bayou Publishing, 1996.

Fordyce, Benjamin A. *Echoes from the Letters of a Civil War Surgeon.* Longboat Key, Fla.: Bayou Publishing, 1994.

Frankignoul, Daniel. *Prince Camille de Polignac Major General, C.S.A. "The Lafayette of the South."* Brussels, Belgium: Confederate Historical Association of Belgium, 1999.

Freeman, Douglas Southall. *R. E. Lee: A Biography.* 4 vols. New York: Charles Scribner's Sons, 1934–35.

Freemantle, Arthur Lyon. *The Fremantle Diary: Being the Journal of Lieutenant Colonel James Arthur Lyon Fremantle, Coldstream Guards, on His Three Months in the Southern States.* Ed. Walter Lord. Boston: Little, Brown and Co., 1954.

Gallaway, B. P. *The Ragged Rebel: A Common Soldier in W. H. Parsons' Texas Cavalry, 186l–1865.* Austin: Univ. of Texas Press, 1988.

Grabeau, Warren E. *Ninety-Eight Days: A Geographer's View of the Vicksburg Campaign.* Knoxville: Univ. of Tennessee Press, 2000.

Grant, U.S. *Personal Memoirs of U.S. Grant.* New York: Da Capo, 1982.

Griggs, George W. *Opening of the Mississippi; or, Two Years' Campaigning in the South-West.* Madison, Wis.: William J. Park and Co., 1864.

Grisamore, Silas. *Reminiscences of Uncle Silas: A History of the Eighteenth Louisiana Infantry Regiment.* Ed. Arthur W. Bergeron Jr. Baton Rouge: *Le Comite des Archives de la Louisiane,* 1981. Reprint ed. titled *The Civil War Reminiscences of Major Silas T. Grisamore, CSA* (Baton Rouge: Louisiana State Univ. Press, 1993).

Guernsey, Alfred H., and Henry M. Alden, eds. *Harper's Pictorial History of the Civil War.* Vol. 2. Chicago: Puritan Press, 1866.

Gunby, A. A. *Life and Services of David French Boyd.* Baton Rouge: Louisiana State Univ. Press, 1904.

Gute, Fredricka Doll, and Katherine Brash Jeter. *Historical Profile of Shreveport: 1850.* Shreveport: Shreveport Committee of the National Society of the Colonial Dames of America in the State of Louisiana, 1982.

Harrell, J. M. *Arkansas.* Vol. 10, *Confederate Military History.* 12 vols. Atlanta: Confederate Publishing Co., 1899.

Heartsill, W. W. *Fourteen Hundred and 91 Days in the Confederate Army: A Journal Kept by W.W. Heartsill for Four Years, One Month, and One Day or, Camp Life; Day by Day, of the W. P. Lane Rangers from April 19th, 1861 to May 20th, 1865.* Ed. Bell Irvin Wiley. Wilmington, N.C.: Broadfoot Publishing Co., 1992.

Hewitt, Lawrence Lee. *Port Hudson: Confederate Bastion on the Mississippi.* Baton Rouge: Louisiana State Univ. Press, 1987.

Hollandsworth, James G., Jr. *The Louisiana Native Guards: The Black Military Experience during the Civil War.* Baton Rouge: Louisiana State Univ. Press, 1995.

———. *Pretense of Glory: The Life of General Nathaniel P. Banks.* Baton Rouge: Louisiana State Univ. Press, 1998.

Huffstodt, Jim. *Hard Dying Men: The Story of General W.H.L. Wallace, General T.E.G. Ransom, and Their "Old Eleventh" Illinois Infantry in the American Civil War (1861–1865).* Bowie, Md.: Heritage Books, 1991.

Irwin, Richard B. *History of the Nineteenth Army Corps.* Baton Rouge: Elliott's Book Shop Press, 1985.

Jarratt, J. A. *Reminiscences of a Great Struggle Told by Heroes of the Confederacy.* Mansfield, La.: J. A. Jarratt, 1907.

Jeter, Katherine Brash, ed. *A Man and His Boat: The Civil War Career and Correspondence of Lt. Jonathan H. Carter, CSN.* Lafayette, La.: Univ. of Southwestern Louisiana, 1996.

Johansson, Jane Harris, and David H. Johansson. "Two Lost Battle Reports: Horace Randal's and Joseph L. Brent's Reports of the Battles of Mansfield and Pleasant Hill, 8 and 9 April 1864." *Military History of the Southwest* 23, no. 2 (Fall 1993): 149–67.

Johnson, Ludwell H. *Red River Campaign: Politics and Cotton in the Civil War.* Kent, Ohio: Kent State Univ. Press, 1993.

Johnson, Robert U., and Clarence C. Buel, eds. *Battles and Leaders of the Civil War.* 4 vols. Secaucus, New Jersey: Castle, 1986.

Johnston, Joseph E. *Narrative of Military Operations during the Civil War.* New York: D. Appleton and Co., 1874.

Joiner, Gary D. *40 Archaeological Sites in the Red River Campaign.* Archives of the Division of Archaeology, State of Louisiana, Baton Rouge.

———. "I Will Fight Banks If He Has a Million Men." *DeSoto Plume* 37, no. 3 (Spring 2002): 2–10.

———. *One Damn Blunder from Beginning to End: The Red River Campaign of 1864.* Wilmington, Del.: Scholarly Resources, 2003.

———. "The Red River Campaign." *Hallowed Ground* 3, no. 4 (Winter 2002): 18–21.

———. "The Red River Campaign: The Battle of Mansfield—Last Decisive Confederate Victory, Largest Action West of the Mississippi River." *Confederate Veteran* 51, no. 6 (Nov./Dec. 2003): 52–55.

———. "Up the Red River and Down to Defeat." *America's Civil War* (Mar. 2004): 22–29. This was also published in *Pivotal Battles and Campaigns of a Decisive Year—1864: Grinding, Relentless War* (Leesburg, Va.: Primedia Publishing, 2004), 11–17.

Joiner, Gary D., and Charles E. Vetter. "The Union Naval Expedition on the Red River, March 12–May 22, 1864." *Civil War Regiments* 4, no. 2 (1994): 26–67. Also published in *The Red River Campaign: Union and Confederate Leadership and the War in Louisiana.*

Ed. Theodore P. Savas, David A. Woodbury, and Gary D. Joiner. Shreveport, La.: Parabellum Press, 2003.

Joiner, Gary D., and Stephen R. James. *Phase I Cultural Resources Investigation: Harrah's Entertainment Project, City of Shreveport, Caddo Parish, Louisiana.* Archives of the Division of Archaeology, State of Louisiana, Baton Rouge.

Jones, Terry L. *Historical Dictionary of the Civil War.* 2 vols. Lantham, Md.: Scarecrow Press, 2002.

Kerby, Robert L. *Kirby Smith's Confederacy: The Trans-Mississippi South, 1863–1865.* Tuscaloosa: Univ. of Alabama Press, 1972.

Kinard, Jeff. *Lafayette of the South: Prince Camille de Polignac and the American Civil War.* College State: Texas A & M Univ. Press, 2001.

King, Alvy L. *Louis T. Wigfall: Southern Fire-Eater.* Baton Rouge: Louisiana State Univ. Press, 1970.

King, Wilburn H. *With the 18th Texas Infantry: The Autobiography of Wilburn Hill King.* Ed. L. David Norris. Hillsboro, Tex.: Hill Junior College Press, 1996.

LaGrone, Leila B., ed. *History of Panola County.* Carthage, Tex.: Panola County Historical Commission, 1979.

Lane, Walter P. *The Adventures and Recollections of General Walter P. Lane, a San Jacinto Veteran.* Marshall, Tex.: Jenkins Publishing Co., 1970.

Louisiana: Comprising Sketches of Parishes, Towns, Events, Institutions, and Persons, Arranged in Cyclopedic Form. Vol. 3. N.p.: Century Historical Association, 1914.

Lowe, Richard. *Walker's Texas Division, C.S.A.: Greyhounds of the Trans-Mississippi.* Baton Rouge: Louisiana State Univ. Press, 2004.

Lubbock, Francis R. *Six Decades in Texas* . . . Austin, Tex.: Ben C. Jones and Co., 1900.

Mahan, D. H. *A Treatise on Field Fortifications Containing Instructions on the Methods of Laying Out, Constructing, Defending, and Attacking Intrenchments, with the General Outline Also of the Arrangement, the Attack, and Defense of Permanent Fortifications.* New York: John Wiley, 1863.

Manakee, Harold R. *Maryland in the Civil War.* Baltimore: Maryland Historical Society, 1961.

Martin, David. "The Red River Campaign: The Ill-Fated Western Expedition of Nathaniel P. Banks, 7 March to 20 May, 1864." *Strategy and Tactics,* no. 106 (1986): 11–20.

Maury, D. H. "Sketch of General Richard Taylor." *Southern Historical Society Papers* 7 (1879): 343–45.

McClellan, George B. *McClellan's Own Story.* New York: C. L. Webster and Co., 1887.

McCormick, Andrew W. "Battles and Campaigns in Arkansas." In *Sketches of War History.* Vol. 6, MOLLUS Ohio. Cincinnati: Monfort, 1908.

McElfresh, Earl B. *Maps and Mapmakers of the Civil War.* New York: Harry N. Abrams, 1999.

McGowen, Stanley Sidney. "Augustus Buchel: A Forgotten Texas Patriot." *Military History of the West* 25, no. 1 (Spring 1995): 1–21.

———. *Horse Sweat and Powder Smoke: The First Texas Cavalry in the Civil War.* College Station: Texas A & M Univ. Press, 1999.

McWhiney, Grady. *Cracker Culture: Celtic Ways in the Old South.* Tuscaloosa: Univ. of Alabama Press, 1988.

———. "The South's Celtic Heritage." *North Louisiana Historical Journal* 24, no. 4 (Fall 1993): 135–43.

Military Analysis of the Civil War: An Anthology by the Editors of Military Affairs. Millwood, N.Y.: KTO Press, 1977.

Miller, Francis T., ed. *The Photographic History of the Civil War.* 10 vols. New York: Review of Reviews, 1911.

Mills, Gary B. *The Forgotten People: Cane River's Creoles of Color.* Baton Rouge: Louisiana State Univ. Press, 1977.

———. *Of Men and Rivers: The Story of the Vicksburg District* (1978). Vicksburg District, U.S. Army Corps of Engineers, Vicksburg, Miss.

Moat, Louis S., ed. *Frank Leslie's Illustrated History of the Civil War.* New York: Fairfax Press, 1977.

Moore, Frank, ed. *The Rebellion Record: A Diary of American Events.* New York: Putnam (vols. 1–6) and Van Nostrand (vols. 7–12), 1868.

Nicolay, John G., and John Hay. *Abraham Lincoln: A History.* New York: Century Co., 1909.

Noll, Arthur Howard. *General Kirby-Smith.* Sewanee, Tenn.: Univ. of the South, 1907.

Oakes, James. *The Ruling Class: A History of American Slaveholders.* New York: W. W. Norton, 1998.

Oates, Stephen B. *Confederate Cavalry West of the River.* Austin: Univ. of Texas Press, 1961.

Official Report to the Conduct of Federal Troops in Western Louisiana, during the Invasions of 1863 and 1864, Compiled from Sworn Testimony under Direction of Governor Henry Watkins Allen. Shreveport: State of Louisiana (C.S.A.), 1865.

O'Flaherty, Daniel. *General Jo Shelby: Undefeated Rebel.* Chapel Hill: Univ. of North Carolina Press, 1954.

O'Pry, Maude Hearn. *Chronicles of Shreveport and Caddo Parish.* Shreveport, La.: Times Publishing Co., 1928.

Paris, Compte de [Louis Philippe Albert d'Orléans]. *History of the Civil War in America.* 4 vols. Philadelphia: Porter and Coates, 1875–88.

Parks, Joseph Howard. *General Edmund Kirby Smith, C.S.A.* Baton Rouge: Louisiana State Univ. Press, 1954.

Parrish, T. Michael. *Richard Taylor: Soldier Prince of Dixie.* Chapel Hill: Univ. of North Carolina Press, 1992.

Pearson, Charles. *Historical Survey and Assessment of Waterborne Commerce and Transportation and an Inventory of Underwater Cultural Resources on the Red River* (1995). Archives of the Division of Archaeology, State of Louisiana, Baton Rouge.

Pellet, Elias P. *History of the 114th Regiment, New York State Volunteers.* Norwich, N.Y.: Telegraph and Chronicle Press Print, 1866.

Perrin, William Henry. *Southwest Louisiana Historical and Biographical.* N.p., 1891.

Petty, A.W.M. *A History of the Third Missouri Cavalry: From Its Organization at Palmyra, Missouri, 1861 Up to November Sixth, 1864: With an Appendix and Recapitulation.* Albany, Mo.: Century Reprints, 1997.

Petty, Elijah Parsons. *Journey to Pleasant Hill: The Civil War Letters of Captain Elijah P. Petty, Walker's Division, C.S.A.* Ed. Norman D. Brown. San Antonio: Univ. of Texas Institute of Culture, 1982.

Pierson, Marshall Samuel. "The Diary and Memoirs of Marshall Samuel Pierson, Company C, 17th Reg., Texas Cavalry, 1862–1865." Ed. Norman C. Delaney. *Military History of Texas and the Southwest* 13, no. 3 (1976): 28–38.

Plummer, Alonzo. *Confederate Victory at Mansfield Including Federal Advance and Retreat to Natchitoches.* Shreveport, La.: Kate Beard Chapter No. 397, United Daughters of the Confederacy, 1964.

Porter, John C. *Texans in Gray: A Regimental History of the 18th Texas Infantry, Walker's Texas Division in the Civil War.* Edited by James Henry Davis. Hughes Springs, Tex.: Heritage Oak Press, 1993.

Ragan, Mark K. *Union and Confederate Submarine Warfare in the Civil War.* Mason City, Iowa: Savas, 1999.

Raphael, Morris. *A Gunboat Named Diana . . . and other exciting stories of Civil War battles which raged in the bayou country of Louisiana.* Detroit: Harlo Press, 1993.

Reed, Rowena. *Combined Operations in the Civil War.* Lincoln: Univ. of Nebraska Press, 1978.

Savas, Theodore P. "A Death at Mansfield: Col. James Hamilton Beard and the Consolidated Crescent Regiment." *Civil War Regiments* 4, no. 2 (1994): 68–103.

Schultz, Duane. *Quantrill's War: The Life and Times of William Clarke Quantrill.* New York: St. Martin's Press, 1996.

Seale, Richard. "Pine Hills and Plantations: Some Social and Economic Views of the Civil War in Natchitoches Parish." *North Louisiana Historical Association Journal* 25, no. 4 (Fall 1994): 107–32.

Shannon, George W., Jr. "Cultural Resources Survey of the Port of Shreveport-Bossier, Caddo and Bossier Parishes, Louisiana: Unpublished Report for the Caddo/Bossier Port Commission." Archives of the Division of Archaeology, State of Louisiana, Baton Rouge.

Sifakis, Stewart. *Compendium of the Confederacy: Florida and Arkansas.* New York: Facts on File, 1992.

———. *Compendium of the Confederate Armies: Kentucky, Maryland, Missouri, the Confederate Units and the Indian Units.* New York: Facts on File, 1995.

———. *Compendium of the Confederate Armies: Louisiana.* New York: Facts on File, 1995.

———. *Compendium of the Confederate Armies: Texas.* New York: Facts on File, 1995.

———. *Who Was Who in the Confederacy.* New York: Facts on File, 1988.

———. *Who Was Who in the Union.* New York: Facts on File, 1988.

Silverstone, Paul H. *Warships of the Civil War Navies.* Annapolis, Md.: Naval Institute Press, 1989.

Simon, John Y. *Grant and Halleck: Contrasts in Command.* Milwaukee, Wis.: Marquette Univ. Press, 1996.

Simson, Jay W. *Naval Strategies of the Civil War: Confederate Innovations and Federal Opportunism.* Nashville, Tenn.: Cumberland House, 2001.

Smith, Steven D., and George J. Castille III. *Bailey's Dam.* Anthropological Study No. 8. Baton Rouge: Dept. of Culture, Recreation and Tourism, Louisiana Archaeological Survey and Antiquities Commission, 1986.

Snell, Mark A. *From First to Last: The Life of Major General William B. Franklin.* New York: Fordham Univ. Press, 2002.

Spencer, John. *Terrell's Texas Cavalry.* Burnet, Tex.: Eakin Press, 1982.

Stephens, Robert W. *August Buchel, Texas Soldier of Fortune.* Dallas: n.p., 1970.

Stoker, William Elisha. "The War Letters of a Texas Conscript in Arkansas." Robert W. Glove, ed. *Arkansas Historical Quarterly* 20 (Winter 1961): 355–87.

Sutton, Aaron T. *Prisoner of the Rebels in Texas: The Civil War Narrative of Aaron T. Sutton, Corporal, 83rd Ohio Volunteer Infantry.* Ed. David G. Maclean. Decatur, Ind.: American Books, 1978.

Taylor, Richard. *Destruction and Reconstruction: Personal Experiences in the Civil War.* New York: Da Capo, 1995.

U.S. Navy Dept. *Civil War Naval Chronology 1861–1865.* Washington, D.C.: Government Printing Office, 1971.

U.S. Navy Dept. *Dictionary of American Fighting Ships.* Vol. 2. Washington, D.C.: Government Printing Office, 1963.

Vallandigham, C. L. *The Record of Hon. C. L. Vallandigham on Abolition, the Union, and the Civil War.* 12th ed. Columbus, Ohio: J. Walter & Co., 1863.

Vandiver, Frank E. *Ploughshares into Swords: Josiah Gorgas and Confederate Ordnance.* College Station: Texas A & M Univ. Press, 2002.

Vetter, Charles Edmund. *Sherman: Merchant of Terror, Advocate of Peace.* Gretna, La.: Pelican, 1992.

Warner, Ezra J. *Generals in Blue: Lives of the Union Commanders.* Baton Rouge: Louisiana State Univ. Press, 1993.

———. *Generals in Gray: Lives of the Confederate Commanders.* Baton Rouge: Louisiana State Univ. Press, 1993.

Way, Frederick, Jr., ed. *Way's Packet Directory, 1848–1994.* Athens: Ohio Univ. Press, 1994.

Wayland, Francis. *The Elements of Moral Science.* 6th ed. Boston: Gould and Lincoln, 1855.

Weddle, Robert S. *Plow-Horse Cavalry: The Caney Creek Boys of the Thirty-Fourth Texas.* Austin, Tex.: Madrona Press, 1974.

Wells, Carol. ed. *Civil War, Reconstruction and Redemption on Red River: The Memoirs of Dosia Williams Moore.* Ruston, La.: McGinty Publications, 1990.

Wiley, Bell Irvin, ed. *Fourteen Hundred and 91 Days in the Confederate Army: A Journal Kept by W.W. Heartsill for Four Years, One Month and One Day or Camplife; Day-by-Day, of the W.P. Lane Rangers from April 19th, 1861 to May 20th, 1865.* Wilmington, N.C.: Broadfoot Publishing, 1992.

Wiley, William. *The Civil War Diary of a Common Soldier: William Wiley of the 77th Illinois Infantry.* Ed. Terrence J. Winschel. Baton Rouge: Louisiana State Univ. Press, 2001.

Williams, T. Harry. *Lincoln and the Radicals.* Madison: Univ. of Wisconsin Press, 1941.

Winschel, Terrence J. "To Rescue Gibraltar: John G. Walker's Texas Division and the Relief of Fortress Vicksburg." *Civil War Regiments* 3, no. 3 (1993): 33–58.

Winters, John D. *The Civil War in Louisiana.* Baton Rouge: Louisiana State Univ. Press, 1963.

Wright, Marcus J. *Arkansas in the War, 1861–1865.* Batesville, Ark.: Independence County Historical Society, 1963.

———, comp. *Texas in the War, 1861–1865.* Ed. Harold B. Simpson. Hillsboro, Tex.: Hill Junior College Press, 1965.

Theses and Dissertations

Bailey, Georgianne. "Between the Enemy and Texas: Parson's Texas Cavalry in the Civil War." Master's thesis, Texas Christian Univ., 1987.

Bergeron, Arthur W., Jr. "General Richard Taylor: A Study in Command." Master's thesis, Louisiana State Univ., 1972.

Johansson, M. Jane Harris. "Peculiar Honor: A History of the 28th Texas Cavalry (Dismounted), Walker's Texas Division, 1862–1865." Ph.D. diss., Univ. of North Texas, 1993.

Kinard, Jeff Sowers. "Lafayette of the South: Prince Camille de Polignac and the American Civil War." Ph.D. diss., Texas Christian Univ., 1997.

McGowen, Stanley Sidney. "The Lineage and History of the 1st Regiment of Texas Cavalry in the Civil War." Master's thesis, Tarleton State Univ., 1993.

———. "Horse Sweat and Powdersmoke: The 1st Texas Cavalry in the Civil War." Ph.D. diss., Texas Christian Univ., 1997.

Miller, Robert E. "Missouri Secessionist General Mosby M. Parsons." Master's thesis, Univ. of Missouri in Saint Louis, 1982.

Morris, Curtis Brooks. "The Life of Edward Clark: A War-Time Governor of Texas." Master's thesis, Stephen F. Austin State Univ., 1954.

Prushankin, Jeffery Scott. "A Crisis in Command: Richard Taylor and Edmund Kirby Smith in Confederate Louisiana during the Red River Campaign." Master's thesis, Villanova Univ., 1996.

Sharp, Lawrence R. "History of Panola County, Texas, to 1860." Master's thesis, Univ. of Texas, 1940.

Snyder, Perry Anderson. "Shreveport, Louisiana, during the Civil War and Reconstruction." Ph.D. diss., Florida State Univ., Tallahassee 1979.

Index

Page numbers in **boldface** refer to illustrations.

www.ingramcontent.com/pod-product-compliance
Lightning Source LLC
Chambersburg PA
CBHW030540161225
36838CB00038B/514

* 9 7 9 8 8 9 5 2 7 0 8 3 7 *